TOOLS
OF THE
WRITER'S
TRADE

TOOLS
OF THE
WRITER'S
TRADE

.

WRITERS TELL
ALL ABOUT THE
EQUIPMENT
AND
SERVICES
THEY FIND THE
BEST

THE AMERICAN SOCIETY
OF JOURNALISTS
AND AUTHORS

EDITED BY DODI SCHULTZ

HarperCollins*Publishers*

FIRST EDITION

Designed by Barbara M. Marks

Library of Congress Cataloging-in-Publication Data

Tools of the writer's trade : writers tell all about
　　the equipment and services they find the best /
　　American Society of Journalists and Authors :
　　edited by Dodi Schultz—1st ed.
　　　　　p.　　　cm.
　　Includes index.
ISBN 0-06-016363-1
　　1. Authorship.　2. Journalism—Authorship.　I.
Schultz, Dodi.　II. American Society of
Journalists and Authors.
　　PN151.T65　1990
808'.02—dc20　　　　　　　　　89-46514

---

90 91 92 93 94 CC/RRD 10 9 8 7 6 5 4 3 2 1

CONTENTS

.

INTRODUCTION

·

Going on sixscore years ago, a writer named Sam Clemens ("Mark Twain")—already a celebrated journalist, humorist, and lecturer, without benefit of mechanical devices—became the first author to produce a book-length manuscript with the aid of a recent invention known as "the Type-Writer." That book, *The Adventures of Tom Sawyer,* was published in 1876.

Clemens was pleased to let the public know how much he liked the gadget. In fact, another work he turned out on it was a signed testimonial for what he termed "this curiosity-breeding little joker." The promotional copy declared that he'd abandoned its use, since every letter he'd written on it had produced a return-mail request for more information.

Some of Clemens's fellow scribes doubtless rushed to embrace the new technology, while others surely shuddered at the thought of invoking the literary muse while perched before a piece of machinery. (Would Bulwer-Lytton, had he lived a few years longer, have written that the *typewriter* is mightier than the sword? The image lacks a certain something.)

Time passed. Typewriters became one word. Some became portable, others electric; still others claimed, not altogether convincingly, to be both electric *and* portable. The keys that operated on a piano principle, along with the sliding carriage, were superseded in some machines by the spinning, shifting ball element.

But those were not earthshaking changes. The first harbinger of what was soon to quicken writers' heartbeats, whether in ecstasy or in panic, came in the late 1970s, not long after *Tom Sawyer*'s centennial. We began to hear words and phrases like "memory," "disk," and "word processor." And strange mouthfuls like "kilobyte." Plus peculiar terms like "software" and "hardware," which denoted not nonchafing diapers and workshop tools but something completely different.

A few years before, the American Society of Journalists and Authors membership newsletter had begun to include a column, called "BUY-line," in which we exchanged information about a variety of goods and services. In that column, reference books were recommended, discoveries of finer-pointed felt pens shared, and the merits of various typewriters and tape recorders argued. Suddenly we found a new subject was taking over—so much so that, before long, we gave it a column of its own. That move triggered a tongue-in-cheek counterpoint column mounting a stout defense of the status quo.

The dust has settled now. The writers who rushed to spend anywhere from $6000 to $10,000 a decade ago for electronic writing systems primitive by today's standards have modernized for far less than half those sums. Most of the writers who resisted finally realized that (a) removing the retyping tedium (not to mention erasing, cutting, and pasting) was a highly desirable end and (b) one did not need a technical grasp of the means. It took a while, but it finally dawned upon us that we could dial a phone or drive a car without being intimately familiar with its innards.

The ASJA newsletter's "Computer Corner" column has long since gone, as has its "P's and Q's" (for parchments and quills) counterpart. (The computer column was written by the late Marvin Grosswirth, "P's and Q's" by one of this book's contributors, Evelyn Kaye, who today happily uses a computer along with lower-tech devices.) But the "BUY-line" column continues, still a forum for members to share experiences, recommendations, and advice about hardware, software, information sources, selling aids, problem solvers, and just about anything else we find helpful.

This book is an outgrowth of that column—more accurately, of that concept. A few of the items in it have previously appeared in the Society's newsletter. Most of them are new, written expressly for this book by ASJA members across the country, working writers all, in response to an open invitation to join in sharing with writers everywhere the kind of practical information we usually exchange just among ourselves. Many, in the selfless spirit of sacrifice so common among writers, actually postponed work on pressing assignments in order to provide multiple contributions to this book. (There is no cure for writer's block, but there is alternative medicine.)

Writers, even members of a single organization, are hardly a monolithic lot. You can expect some conflicting advice. You can expect writers who agree on a particular preference to disagree about the reasons.

You can expect some strong opinions. And you can expect some surprises. But you can surely expect to find, here, **many** hints that will help you, as a writer, to perform more creatively, faster, more effectively, more efficiently, with less effort, with more pleasure and less pain.

DODI SCHULTZ
EDITOR

1

THE
PROGRAMS
THAT
PROCESS
WORDS

It took a while, and there was—still is, in some quarters—a lot of resistance, but most ASJA members are now using computers, along with packages of electronic commands called "programs." Such packages are known as "software." In fact, they are completely intangible. The tangibles—printers, computers themselves, and so on—are known as "hardware."

Those who acquire this equipment that has wrought a revolutionary change in the writer's trade speak of "using computers," as we just did, or becoming "computerized." What we really *use*, though, are the tools the *programs* give us. The intrepid souls who rushed to embrace the new technology in the early days learned a vital lesson and, happily, passed it on to those of us who hung back, fearful and not a little bewildered: Select your software first; then find a suitable machine to run it. (The machines, discussed in Chapter 3, are at this writing grouped in two major "families," to which you'll find a few references here.)

That advice is still valid—and invaluable—and so that is where we begin.

The chief programs—in many cases, the only programs—we use are known as "word-processing" programs. Are we now "word processors"? No, that's another term for the programs; we're still writers. But we're no longer cutters, pasters, erasers, and retypers; the software takes care of that.

The programs mentioned by contributors are in alphabetical order, interspersed with pointers on choosing and using these ubiquitous, and now virtually indispensable, tools.

SOME SOFTWARE BASICS

You need to know not only what a particular software package will do, but how easy it will be to use. This is a brief lesson in software "interfaces"—the encounters that allow you, the writer, to tell the software what to do. Writing itself is simply a matter of typing on the keyboard, exactly as you would on a typewriter. But as soon as you decide you want to move a paragraph, boldface a heading, or mark a word to be included in your index, you need to get the software's attention, using some sort of interface, to activate these functions. Common interfaces:

Function keys. These extra keys are at one side, or across the top, of computer keyboards and are numbered F1, F2, F3, etc. Hitting each key gets you a different "service"; these might include a "help" screen, a change in print format, or beginning and ending commands blocking off a piece of text. In some programs, such as *WordPerfect,* the function-key system may include holding down another key ("Ctrl," "Shift," or "Alt") at the same time as the function key, giving access to a wide array of commands. Function-key-controlled software comes with a "template," a cutout chart that fits around your function keys to help you remember which combinations do what.

Control keys. By hitting a control key simultaneously with particular alphabetic keys, you activate certain commands. In *WordStar,* for example, you request cursor movement, print-format commands, blocking, cut-and-paste, and many other functions with control keys, never moving your hands away from the main part of the keyboard. Touch typists may find that control-key-driven software is preferable, since once the control-key functions are memorized, they become automatic and permit you to write very rapidly, editing as you go.

Menus. A software menu, as in the ordinary meaning of the word, is a list from which you make a choice by pressing a particular key.

Usually, it is displayed at the top or bottom of your screen (i.e., above or below your text, which also remains on the screen), and you temporarily use your keyboard to give commands according to the menu's instructions rather than for writing. There are often several layers of choice in a menu; a first choice such as "file," for example, may produce a second-level list such as "open a new file," "change file name," "save file," and so on.

Command lines. A few word-processing programs are controlled mainly by commands you type in after hitting a particular key to enter "command mode."

"Hot keys." Some small accessory programs used in conjunction with word-processing software [see Chapter 2] are "RAM-resident." That is, they are placed, for use, in the effervescent short-term memory that expires when you turn off the computer.[1] Such a program is summoned to the screen with a "hot key" which acts like a toggle switch—once for "on," again for "off." The key to be used for this purpose is usually determined when the program is installed in residence.

—LEE JOLLIFFE

Bank Street Writer Plus

What does a word processor do that a typewriter won't? It will move blocks of text around; copy text from one place to another; find and replace a word or words throughout a manuscript; delete a word or line at a keystroke; insert a word or several words anyplace in the text; save what you've written in a "file" on a disk, which can be recalled at any time for further editing; and, when you are satisfied with what you have written, issue appropriate instructions to your printer for putting it on paper.

Bank Street Writer Plus—the latest version of an inexpensive, easy-to-use program that has been around for a long time—will do all those things very nicely. The program also now includes a 60,000-word spelling corrector and a thesaurus. (In my opinion, no word processor is worth its salt if it doesn't have a spelling checker. No matter how often I proofread a manuscript, I'll overlook typos and misspellings a spelling checker will catch. It's not infallible, however: If you type "right" when you meant to type "write," or "there" instead of "their" or "to" for

---

[1]RAM is an acronym for "random access memory," a description that is evidently meaningful to computer programmers. The French phrase, *mémoire vive* ("live memory"), seems a more accurate description.

"too," the spelling checker won't catch your goof, because what's there is a legitimate word.)

Some of the other things *Bank Street Writer Plus* will do: give bold-face and underline commands to your printer, center a line or lines, put a "header" (such as a short version of your article title) at a top corner of each page. You can also program the function keys to perform certain commands or type a word or phrase for you.

Bank Street Writer Plus will not perform some of the more complex operations of the big, powerful (and more expensive) word processors, such as indexing, generating tables of contents, snaking columns, importing graphics, etc. The question, of course, is whether or not you need the more complex functions. If not, this program may do all the word processing you'll ever need.

Bank Street Writer Plus is published by Broderbund Software, Inc., 17 Paul Drive, San Rafael CA 94903; (415) 492-3500 or (800) 521-6263. It's available for both Apple and IBM/compatibles and lists for $79.95.

—CHARLES BOECKMAN

HOW I WROTE A "PHONE BOOK" WITH MY WORD PROCESSOR

My phone book—personal and professional—is a file, titled "Contacts," I've created with my word processor. It also contains my professional diary (meetings attended, people met, etc.) and a "Things to Do" list. I put the diary and the list in the same file because when I consult them I'm likely to need an address or phone number, too. Having all of this information in the same file saves time and energy.

An example: While preparing an article on, say, skydivers, I enter the names of five skydivers in their proper alphabetical positions in my phone directory. Following each name, I enter the word "skydiver." A year later, if I want to phone one of them but have forgotten his or her name, I simply use the "Quick Find" command to locate each of my "skydiver" entries until I come to the right one.[2]

Alternatively, I'll sometimes make entries for subjects (skydiving, for instance) rather than using the names of individuals. For people and subjects that I write about frequently, I cross-file under both names and subjects. It takes time, but it pays off in the end.

A diary entry will usually contain a date, the type of event, people

[2]"Quick Find," a command used to locate a particular word or phrase in *WordStar*, may be known by other names in other programs, but the same principle applies.

encountered, and other relevant data. Again, to retrieve information, I use "Quick Find"; usually, I'll remember at least one salient feature that will respond to the command. If all else fails, I browse around the relevant chronological area until I find the correct entry.

I've rapidly amassed hundreds of entries in my phone book, and the entire "Contacts" file now runs to scores of pages. To expedite searches, I've separated entries, using "-a-," "-b-," etc. To speed to the "T" entries, for example, I instruct the program to go first to "-t-." Voila!

I also carry a hard copy [on paper] in my appointment book, reprinting it regularly so that it's always up to date.

—ROBERT L LIEBMAN

■ ■ ■

I keep all my addresses and phone numbers, personal *and* business, in a single long file. Periodically, I revise it, give it a new date at the top so I know how current it is, and print out several copies, so I can keep a copy of my "address book" upstairs, downstairs, in the bag I carry downtown for an appointment, and in the glove compartment of my car. Because I often forget names, I include cross-references; I thus have entries such as "Accountant: See Penney" and "Lawyers: See Case & Case."

—PAT McNEES

ETG Plus

We hear a lot about the big powerhouse word processors such as *Word-Perfect, WordStar,* and *Microsoft Word.* There are other programs that merit consideration. One I particularly enjoy using is *ETG Plus.* If there is such a thing as a word processor that is fun to use, this is it.

ETG stands for "Easy Text and Graphics" and, as the name implies, it's a word processor that supports graphics (and requires a computer with graphics capabilities). It has a "paint" program in which you can do your own artwork; clip art can also be brought into the program, and you can then do interesting things with it—rotate it, flip it, make it larger or smaller, alter its shape. Several font choices are available for text within the paint program.

There are symbols or "tools" at the side of the screen for drawing squares, circles, lines, etc.; anyone who has worked with an art program is familiar with that kind of thing. But in every other paint program I've seen, one has to memorize what the various icons stand for or look them up in the manual. *ETG* makes it easy: As one highlights the various tools, a line across the bottom of the screen explains what the tool does. When completed, artwork can be transported to the text part of the program.

The *ETG* word processor has all the usual facilities: headers, footers, search and replace, block manipulation, etc. A pop-up menu at the bottom of the screen instantly gives you all the information you need to operate it. It doesn't do indexes or tables of contents, and it doesn't do columns. But it does import graphics well, allowing you to place them where you wish, resize them, and then adjust the text around the graphics.

There are several useful extra features. Punch the F8 key and a digital clock appears on your screen showing the date and time; you also have the option of setting a timer and an alarm. The F9 key gives you a calendar of the current month, which can be changed to view other months. F10 produces a calculator that looks and acts much like a real calculator.

To my way of thinking, the feature that really gives a unique touch to this program is its filing system. Normally, when you name a piece of text (a file)—which you must do before you can save it on a disk— you're restricted to eight characters plus a three-character suffix. If you were saving the text of an article titled, say, "The Sex Life of the Female Hippopotamus," you'd come up with something like "FEMHIPLF.-SEX." Try to figure out what *that* means when you look it up six months later! *ETG Plus* lets you create file names with up to twenty characters.

The filing system itself also has a unique graphic approach: You see a stack of binders or volumes on the right side of the screen. If you type "Hippopotamus" in a particular area, it is instantly filed alphabetically and appears as the title of one of the stacked binders. Highlight it, and a hand appears, pulling the volume out part way. Then, a row of file folders appears; type the subheading "Hippo Sex Life" and it, too, is immediately sorted alphabetically and applied to the tab of a file folder. To pull out the file you want to work with, you highlight it, a paper clip appears on the file, and the text and graphics you had stored there appear on the screen.

The manual for *ETG Plus* is quite clear, written at high-school level, which is about my speed; too many programs have instructions that only a computer programmer could understand. It prints foreign-language characters, including Spanish, French, German, Scandinavian, and Greek, as well as math and other symbols. Another nice feature is that it is a WYSIWYG program, meaning "What You See Is What You Get." This means that if you want italics, you will actually see *italics* on the screen; the same is true of underlining, **boldface,** ^{super}script, and _{sub}script. There is also an excellent, fast spelling checker with a 100,000-word lexicon, as well as a thesaurus with 220,000 synonyms.

ETG Plus lists for $89.95 plus $3.50 shipping and handling from the Savtek Corporation, P.O. Box 1077, Waltham MA 02254; (800) 548-7173.

—CHARLES BOECKMAN

FullWrite

After bringing out one very good program, *dBASE,* Ashton-Tate has been neglecting its publicity for years. The company never told us about *FullWrite,* which is for the Macintosh. A reader of our column did. A novelist, she swore it was fantastic. After a thorough review, we agree: It's a sleeping star! No word-processing program can do what it can do.

It's got everything you need for powerful word processing—speller, thesaurus, outliner, indexer, notater, contents-page tabulator, and bibliography keeper. In addition, it's a full-fledged "desktop publishing" layout and design program. It can kern almost like a commercial linotype machine (squeezing skinny letters like "f" and "l" closer to the letters next to them, so as not to leave spaces). It can draw so well it can even make fancy Bezier curves. In addition, it imports files from other Mac programs and sticks them wherever you need them in your manuscript.

FullWrite can also vary its line spacing infinitely to give a good page fit for copy. It can avail itself of whatever fonts and type sizes your printer can produce. It can print at a 50 percent reduction. It can print the trim-size registration marks that show printers where to trim a printed page. It even prints two-page spreads for printers that can handle oversize paper.

The program can't move or delete tabular columns. It protects orphans but not widows.[3] It doesn't double-underline or do math. It won't support a multibin sheet feeder or queue printing. But *FullWrite*'s only serious disadvantage is its memory demand: it requires 1MB [one megabyte, or 1000 kilobytes] and needs 1.5MB to 2MB to do a really seamless job.

---

[3] An orphan is the last line of a paragraph, often not a full line of type, falling at the top of a new page; a widow is the first line of a paragraph falling at the bottom of a page. "Protection" will keep the last two lines, and/or the first two lines, of a paragraph together.

FullWrite's list price is $395. Ashton-Tate may be reached at (800) 437-4329.

—JUDI K-TURKEL and FRANKLYNN PETERSON

SAVE MONEY: SHOP BY MAIL

I'm a great fan of mail-order software, which is one-third to one-half cheaper than when purchased in a computer store. (Mail-order prices are, however, competitive with those of the larger discount chains.)

To shop for mail-order software, buy copies of the major computer magazines and study the software ads, which are always in minute print and consist mostly of listings of products and prices. If a specific program isn't mentioned, the company may still stock it, so if other prices in the ad look good, call and inquire.[4]

When I was looking for a top-of-the-line word-processing program, I telephoned two or three mail-order houses to double-check their prices, make sure they had the latest versions, and see if they had the product in stock and ready to ship. Most did. I also called the software companies to ask whether they would support programs bought at discount. Some would, some wouldn't, and this was, of course, a factor in my ultimate decision.

—MARIAN FAUX

Microsoft Word

One of the most useful features of my word-processing program, *Microsoft Word*, is its capacity for multiple "windows." I can split the monitor screen into up to eight distinct sections (although I usually need only two or three at a time). I can look at all of them at the same time—which is sometimes useful, even though each window doesn't display much type—or I can "zoom" any window so it fills the screen, keeping the other windows on tap; I can then toggle to another full-screen window or back to showing all of them. I can also copy and/or move text back and forth from one window to another.

How do I use multiple windows? Typically, I'll have interview notes in one window, my manuscript draft in another, an outline for the manuscript in a third, perhaps a related document such as a piece of correspondence in a fourth, and my original article proposal in a fifth.

---

[4]Also see appendix for a full list of order-by-mail-or-phone office-supply sources, which includes sources of software and other computer supplies.

And if I want to see two (or more) sections of a manuscript, I can divide the screen in half (or thirds) and view different sections at the same time, scrolling them up and down independently. It's terrific.

—JOAN SCOBEY

■ ■ ■

In word processors, the two leaders in terms of features important to writers are *Microsoft Word* and *WordPerfect*. We have worked intensively with both to write and edit articles, books, and newsletters.

In our opinion, *Word* is by far the quicker program to learn, because it has on-screen menus (they can be turned off once you're familiar with them) and mnemonic commands. We've put office interns who had never used a computer before to work using it and, within an hour, they were typing letters and drafts of articles. *Word*'s letter commands—such as "i" for italics, "f" for format, "p" for print—are also great for touch typists; you rarely have to move off the regular keyboard to perform a task.

While *Wordperfect* 5.0 [the version released in 1988] is better than *Word* 4.0 [the latest version available at this writing] for desktop publishing and handles graphics more elegantly, *Word* 5.0, which we are currently testing and which will be available by the time you read this, does practically as well. [See page 17 for an explanation of version numbers.]

If you do a lot of editing, *Word* is preferable to *WordPerfect*. Everything is easier and faster to find and use, because of the mnemonic command structure. Second, an "undo" command restores your document to its condition before your last command, whatever that may have been. And third, you needn't search for hidden codes, so you'll never inadvertently delete important print and format commands along with block deletions.

—JUDI K-TURKEL and FRANKLYNN PETERSON

Microsoft Works

I believe this is the only program most professional writers would ever need. *Microsoft Works* not only includes a state-of-the-art word processor; it also will do virtually all of an author's accounting, including keeping tax records, and filing. And it incorporates database, spreadsheet, and graphics functions, as well as communications. All of these parts work smoothly together and, while they are not as powerful as the most powerful stand-alone programs you can buy, they are full-featured.

While some writers I know prefer to use the most recent version of *Microsoft Word* for word processing and use *Works* only for other applications, I haven't found anything I want the *Works* word processor to do that it can't.

There is available a dynamite spelling checker, *WorksPlus Spell* (published by Lundeen & Associates of Oakland, California) that is one of the biggest and best available for any word processor—and one of the fastest, at about two double-spaced pages a second. And it accurately counts the number of words after checking the spelling. (If your word processor doesn't count words, a rule of thumb is to take the number of kilobytes, subtract two, and multiply by 170.)

When I bought *Works,* the program cost about $300. I've upgraded as time has passed (Microsoft is great about providing upgrades for very little money), so I don't know what the full program costs now. The spelling checker cost me $95 and is worth a million dollars as far as I'm concerned (now, if they could only teach it syntax).

The tutorial that comes with *Works* is pretty good, although, like most instruction manuals written by programmers, it assumes too much knowledge on the reader's part and leaves things out. *Using Microsoft Works* (Que Corporation, $18.95) is a godsend.

—JEFF MORGAN

TAKE A TIMESAVING SHORTCUT

You can speed your typing, when using a word-processing program, by coining abbreviations for long words that will be repeated frequently in your manuscript. (Example: For a piece on skiing in France, I typed "vel" for Courchevel and "aum" instead of Aiguille du Midi.) Then, when you're through, use your word processor's search-and-replace function to replace the abbreviations with the real terms throughout. This is a handy timesaver for lengthy foreign place names, as well as long, hard-to-spell technical terms.

—LUANNE PFEIFER

Multimate

If you do, or plan to do, a lot of writing for corporations, you might consider using the *Multimate* word-processing program. Why *Multi-*

mate? Because, in my experience, it's the word processor most corporations use.

I have actually landed some corporate assignments because I have *Multimate* and can simply present my clients with disks they can run on their computers. Although there are "translation" programs that convert documents from one word-processing format to another, many corporations don't have such a translator. Thus, knowing *Multimate* may give you the edge in getting a corporate assignment.

I've found *Multimate* a very easy system to master and an excellent program with which to write articles and books, as well; I use it for all my work.

—DAVID W. KENNEDY

LOGGING OPERATION

Using my word-processing program (*Displaywriter III,* which I run on an IBM PC), I log all my calls on phone files so that I can properly bill magazines for them. While few magazines will pay your air fare from the Midwest to Honolulu or Miami, they will usually repay you the few dollars' cost of calling there. Those dollars could really add up by the end of the year if you paid them yourself.

I set up such a file for each magazine, using such names as "PHONE.-BOY" (for *Boys' Life*), "PHONE.AH" *(American Health),* and "PHONE.RD" *(Reader's Digest).* Each is a document with five columns. The first four are for the date, name of person called, phone number, and article for which the call was made; the fifth is for the cost of each call, entered when the phone bill arrives. Depending on the volume of calls, I bill the magazine monthly or when the total approaches $100.

Obviously, this system is particularly applicable for magazines with which you have a continuing relationship and for which you write frequently. But for any assignment where you anticipate a high volume of calls in doing your research, you should establish a procedure for keeping track. Keeping the log with your computer makes it easy to make multiple copies for the magazine (it can also be helpful to the fact-checker) and for your own files. And later, such a log becomes a directory of sources and numbers related to a particular subject.

—HAL HIGDON

Sprint

This program is nothing less than great. It's a word processor that lets the user choose the style of interface. Thus, if you're used to *WordStar,* a second writer works with *WordPerfect,* and a third is familiar with *Multimate,* you can all work on the same manuscript with *Sprint,* each using his or her own style of interface. It also means that you can hire someone to type for you no matter what word-processing software the typist has been taught.

Sprint is produced by Borland, 4585 Scotts Valley Drive, Scotts Valley CA 95066; (800) 255-8008. It is also available through the CompuAdd catalog [see appendix].

—LEE JOLLIFFE

■ ■ ■

Borland's *Sprint* is one of the newest of the big, powerful word processors on the market. It has a number of features that make it different—most notably, the ability to "act like" your choice of other programs such as *WordPerfect, WordStar, Multimate,* or *Microsoft Word.* If you're used to one of these, you can set up *Sprint* to mimic the program you already know. (It also has conversion capability and can convert files to and from those and other programs—although I haven't actually tried this feature, so I don't know how well it performs.)

A feature of *Sprint* that writers will appreciate is its habit of automatically saving and backing up everything you write every three seconds. That keeps your disk drive humming, which is a trifle disconcerting—but it can give you a feeling of security to know that you're not going to lose your copy if the electricity conks out.

Otherwise, *Sprint* does all the things today's top word-processing programs are supposed to do, such as handling columns and doing indexes and tables of contents. It can open up to 24 files at once and display up to six windows simultaneously. The makers claim it can accomplish a number of tasks, including paging to the end of a document and search-and-replace, faster than some other leading word processors. *Sprint* is limited in its handling of graphics: It allows you to draw simple boxes and lines and can print graphics, but it can't show graphics on the screen or flow text around them. It works with some 350 printers.

The list price is relatively low for a major word-processing program, $199.95. Most of the big ones list at near $500, although of course they can be had for discount prices from many mail-order firms.

—CHARLES BOECKMAN

ARTICLES WITH ALIASES

My articles go through several file names before they're completed. The procedure may sound complicated, but in practice it's easy and helpful, especially when doing several versions of the same story.

To start, I put everything—interview transcripts, notes, names and phone numbers of contacts, early drafts—into one file. With everything in one place, I can quickly move bits of information around, and it's easier than moving between separate files.

At some point, I get the How many words have I written? itch. I scratch by moving the article itself into a separate file to do a word count, which can't be done while it's still in the larger file, because the counter will count everything. Usually, at this point, the article is near completion, and I finish it in its own file. If the assignment gods have been kind, I will be doing several versions of the piece, and I will soon have, say, "Freud-1," "Freud-2," "Freud-3," etc., files.

When the final piece is winging its way to the editor, I move all the versions into one file—"Freud"—and do an annotated contents list at the top: "I: 'Freud-1,' 800 words, to *Freud Magazine,* published 1/89; II: 'Freud-2," 500 words, to *Schizoids Monthly,* editor undecided whether to use; III: 'Freud-3,' same as 'Freud-2' but with British spelling for possible U.K. publication." Making it one file means the directory of files won't get cluttered; the contents section also has the virtue of providing more information than standard, brief file names, and that's especially helpful if some time has elapsed and I want to resuscitate an article.

—ROBERT L LIEBMAN

Wordbench

This program, written by the Bank Street School of Education, is available for Apple II computers (list, $150) as well as for IBMs and compatibles ($190); we recently reviewed it in our syndicated column. In addition to a word processor per se, it has an outliner, a notecard file, and a file for research references and bibliographies. The four parts are integrated so they can be used together and information may be moved between them.

Let's say you want to create a manuscript. You begin by designating a "folder" to hold your notes and drafts. Using the outliner, you outline the project. Using the notecard component, you type in your notes. Using the reference tool, you enter your sources. (The notes and references may be linked, now or later, to each other and to parts of the outline.) After that, writing is easy: You move notes into the outline, move them both into the word processor, and flesh it all out into full-scale text. You can expand or condense what's seen on the screen to include the entire document or just the outline and the section you're working on at the moment.

Wordbench includes a cute little multifunction "Brainstormer." One of its parts forces you to sum up, in a few words, whom you're writing for and what you're writing about. Another menu selection permits you to type away, choosing either to see what you're writing or to hide it until you're ready to look at it, but you can't change anything until you're done.

The word processor isn't as powerful as some others, but it does have a spelling checker, a thesaurus, and a word counter; it keeps track of footnote numbering; and it indents long quotations correctly. It also lets you write your own "shortcut" keystroke combinations (called "macros" by most other programs) for frequent tasks such as typing your name and address. The menus are easy to understand, as are the instructions. We strongly recommend the program for Apple owners; others should compare it with fuller-featured programs that include outliners.

Wordbench is published by Addison-Wesley, 1 Jacob Way, Reading MA 01867; (800) 447-2226, except in Massachusetts, (800) 446-3399.

—JUDI K-TURKEL and FRANKLYNN PETERSON

■ ■ ■

If you have school-age children, you may have heard of *Bank Street Writer,* a widely hailed beginners' word-processing program for kids. *Wordbench* comes from the same software-writing team and gives adults the kind of creative support kids get from *Bank Street Writer.* Most word processors treat typists, managers, and writers as if their needs were alike; this one doesn't. Nor does it make a pretense of being a combination word processor and desktop publisher. It's strictly a program for writing. It includes a linked outliner and note-taker and, after combining material from them, one proceeds to actual writing.

The software has a great segment called the "Brainstormer," which makes use of several creative-writing techniques. "Freewriting" encourages you to write quickly and freely, without pondering, and prompts you to "keep writing" if you slow down or pause for too long. "Invisible writing" helps you write a first draft without stopping to polish it by showing nothing but asterisks on the screen until you're ready to begin to edit. "Nutshelling" offers you eight lines of 63 characters each and insists that you state your purpose in one or two concise sentences, while "goal setting" asks for your subject, point of view, audience, and purpose to help you focus your work.

There are typical word-processing functions, as well, including a spelling checker and a thesaurus. You can also view one file while working in another. *Wordbench* can create a table of contents, but it lacks indexing capability. Otherwise, wow!

—LEE JOLLIFFE

EVEN FOR SPELLING-BEE WINNERS

When I bought my *WordPerfect* word-processing program, the last parts of it I planned to use were the spelling checker and the thesaurus. I was sure I didn't need the former and positive I'd prefer the feel of a real book in my hand to a digital *Roget's*.

To my surprise, I found that within two weeks of first using them I couldn't live without either one. Turns out my brain cells had been disintegrating at a slightly faster rate than I had realized, and I'm no longer the spelling whiz I was at age eleven, when I was the local spelling-bee star.

I don't think there's anything magic about *WordPerfect*'s speller or thesaurus. All the top word-processing programs have them, and there are also lots of on-disk spelling checkers and thesauruses that can be purchased separately.

You may as well get as much bang as you can for your buck. That means buying a program with at least 90,000—preferably 150,000—words, as well as one that will let you add words to its list.[5] I can't imagine any seasoned pro not wanting this handy tool quite literally at his or her fingertips.

—MARIAN FAUX

WordPerfect

Before I acquired a computer, I wrote first drafts in longhand. Because I am a terrible typist, I employed a secretary, one with enough patience to tirelessly retype. Unfortunately, I am a five- to six-draft writer.

Now, I write directly on my computer, an IBM-PC, with *WordPer-*

---

[5]Otherwise, the spelling checker will repeatedly balk at proper names, including yours, as well as slang, coined words, and esoteric technical terms you may need to use frequently.

fect. I still write draft after draft after draft, but it's a lot easier now. The speller is a marvelous aid, too.

—HELEN WORTH

■ ■ ■

I use the Mac version of *WordPerfect* on my Macintosh computer. It's one of the better word-processing programs in both this version and the one for IBMs and compatibles.

—STEPHEN MORRILL

■ ■ ■

My word processor is *WordPerfect.* I like the cut-and-paste facility, and I use the split screen a lot. It's an incredible advantage. When I'm transcribing tapes for one article, for example, and I realize there are quotes that I'll want to use for another article, I use the double screen, making copies of those sections; I then have the start of a query for a second story.

—CHARLENE SOLOMON

■ ■ ■

There are many, many word-processing programs on the market, and the top sellers are all effective. How to select one? Choose either (a) the same one a helpful, computer-smart friend uses, so he or she can guide you in getting going, or (b) *WordPerfect.* Why *WordPerfect?* Two reasons: (1) It has enough pleased customers to make it the number one selling word-processing program in the world. (2) It has a toll-free customer assistance service that—well, words just can't describe how wonderful it is.

The latest model of *WordPerfect,* at this writing, is version 5.0. Like just about every other major program, it works most satisfactorily if your computer has a hard disk drive. However, by jiggling the program around a tiny bit, it can be made easily usable on a computer with just two floppy drives. If you're a registered *WordPerfect* 5.0 owner, I'll be happy to share this information with you; contact me through ASJA.

—WENDY MURPHY

■ ■ ■

I use *WordPerfect;* I have the 4.2 version and am upgrading to the 5.0 release, which offers desktop publishing capabilities. I love it. It is simple to learn and use and provides just about everything a writer needs. I have never lost or scrambled data, as can happen with some programs.

I have a Tandon computer in my office, plus an NEC laptop for travel, and *WordPerfect* runs on both of them. The two machines use different-size disks, but I can transfer files between them with a program called *The Brooklyn Bridge,* which was easy to install internally and thus doesn't need to be loaded every time I wish to make a transfer.

—ROSEMARY ELLEN GUILEY

■ ■ ■

An excellent book to help you get the most from your *WordPerfect* software is *Using WordPerfect,* by Beacham and Walton (Que Corporation, 1987); I paid $17.95 for my copy.

—NANCY WHITELAW

■ ■ ■

WordPerfect has been, in all its recent versions, especially famed for its macro capabilities. The macro technique lets you boil down a frequently used series of keystrokes of any length and combination of functions to just two keystrokes; it can be applied to text you'll use frequently (e.g., Sincerely [space], Your Name, or a character in a novel or play), resetting of margins or line spacing (e.g., going from single-spaced draft to double-spaced manuscript), changing to another of your printer's typefaces, whatever.

Other features that *WordPerfect* users have found particularly attractive are its virtually blank screen, except for a page-and-line statement at the very bottom; the speed of learning it; the many personalization possibilities (you can set your own standards for page length and many other matters); a very "user-friendly" manual, as well as an on-disk tutorial (plus the aforementioned free customer back-up advice); and its superb handling of such tasks as pagination, footnotes, and merges.

As to books on *WordPerfect,* or *any* program: They can be quite helpful, incorporating tips that aren't necessarily found in your manual, but be sure before you buy that they apply to the release, or version, you're using. A new version, comparable to a new edition of a book, usually adds new features, corrects problems, and generally improves the program.

Software publishers assign a number to each new release (the very first version is usually considered 1.0), the extent of departure from the old one typically denoting the degree of change. Thus, *WordPerfect* 4.2, released in late 1986, was not radically different from version 4.1, while version 5.0, which appeared in mid-1988, incorporated major modifications. (The book recommended above clearly applies to version 4.2.) *The WordPerfect Encyclopedia,* by Leo J. Scanlon (Bantam, 1988), a concise, well-organized reference, covers all three of these versions.

WordPerfect is published by WordPerfect Corporation, 1555 North Technology Way, Orem UT 84057; (800) 321-4566, except in Utah, (801) 225-5000. —D.S.

KEEP COSTS DOWN: UPGRADE

Bear in mind that every time a software developer improves a program such as *WordPerfect* or *WordStar,* registered owners have the option of acquiring the improvements at a reduced rate. *WordStar* 5.5, for example, recently succeeded version 5.0. If you already have version 5.0, the upgrade fee is $89; for a version 4.0 (or earlier) owner, the fee is $119. Version 5.5 brand new lists for $449 at this writing, so the upgrade savings are dramatic.

—DAVE KAISER

WordStar

I've tried a number of word-processing programs over the years, and *WordStar* remains my favorite. Its primary virtue is that it is control-key driven. Once you get past the learning curve, the control keys come automatically, and you fly, fly, fly on the keyboard, with nothing to slow your thoughts. The program also provides all the text functions I need as a writer, including indexing, marking for table of contents, and importing and exporting text from other software such as spreadsheet programs; there are many print commands, spell-checking, mail-merging, and so on.

Getting started is relatively easy, since it's a WYSIWYG (What You See Is What You Get) program: text displayed on the screen will appear the same when you print it. Thus, you can get going quickly and learn the shortcuts and extra functions gradually.

I am using *WordStar* 4.0 at this writing. Earlier versions are fine as well, but I advise steering clear of both *WordStar* 5.0 and something called *WordStar 2000.* The latter isn't like *WordStar* at all, and *WordStar* 5.0 is very bug-ridden. One hopes the revision of version 5.0 will be "cleaner."

—LEE JOLLIFFE

■ ■ ■

Just before the deadline on this book, I received the latest *WordStar* version, 5.5. It offers some very impressive additions.

WordStar was a pioneer among word-processing programs for personal computers. The first version came out in 1979, and it quickly became the world's most popular, because it was by far the most powerful. It has its own unique approach to control keys; the typist has access to all of *WordStar*'s commands without lifting his or her hands from the home row. (By contrast, many other popular word processors make heavy use of the function keys, which can slow down a fast touch typist.)

But while *WordStar*'s command-key design speeds touch typing, earlier versions turned some writers (including me) off because of the difficulty in memorizing the commands. That changed with the 5.0 version, when "pull-down" menus were added; the menus are easily accessible with a touch of the "Alt" key plus another key corresponding to a line at the top of the screen. Nothing could be quicker or easier, and eventually one can learn the "classic" commands familiar to users of prior versions.

With version 5.5, *WordStar* has taken a big step into the desktop publishing area, allowing you to capture a graphic image on screen, store it, and insert it in a document. You can also get a preview of how your page will look with "Page Preview," one of the powerful new features introduced with the 5.0 version. With it, you see a miniature version of the pages you've typed, and a "zoom" command enlarges portions of a page for a closer look. In version 5.5, the feature has been enhanced to integrate text and graphics in its display. There are also additional type fonts, which can be scaled to virtually any size.

WordStar 5.5 has simplified column setup; you enter the between-columns space and number of columns, and the program calculates and sets up the format. Document formatting has been speeded up and given better control, and several preformatted style sheets are included. An interesting "typewriter mode" has been added, in which your printer responds directly, as if you were using a typewriter (useful in addressing envelopes or typing quick notes). "Star Exchange" is a newly added converting system that translates files from other popular word processors, including *WordPerfect* and *Microsoft Word,* to *WordStar* format. The program also includes such modules as "TelMerge" (for easy access to telecommunications services) and "MailMerge" (to merge data from such other programs as spreadsheets and to create customized mass mailings).

There was a time when "user friendly" was not a term applied to *WordStar,* but that has changed. While it is as powerful as any of the big high-tech word processors on the market today, I find it the easiest to use.

WordStar is published by MicroPro International Corp., 33 San Pablo Avenue, San Rafael CA 94903; (800) 227-5609.

—CHARLES BOECKMAN

NEATNESS COUNTS, BUT JUSTIFICATION DOESN'T

When you graduate from a typewriter to using a word-processing program on a computer, don't be led astray. Because something *can* now be done, it doesn't necessarily follow that it *should* be done. The justified right margin is a good example.

Most of us tried to keep our typed manuscripts neat and nice-looking. Now, with this wonder of the electronic age, a simple formatting command can create an absolutely, perfectly even right margin. The pages suddenly look super-neat!

That's deceptive. Only a very good word-processing program combined with a very good printer will space the lines out well. In many cases, all the extra spaces needed to make the end-of-the-line letters line up are inserted between the words. If you aren't using short words, there will be rather few breaks between words in each line. Hence, those breaks will become unnaturally big, ugly gaps—holes. Such copy is not easy to read, and the pristine evenness of the right margin is not likely to elate your editor.

Even a better system, with tiny fragments of extra space also dropped in between characters, may give editors problems. Magazine editors—I've been one—often look at copy, estimate average characters per line, and use an in-house formula to get a rough idea of how much printed space a piece requires and how much cutting might be needed. Right-justified copy throws those calculations off.

—ED NELSON

XyWrite

It took some arguing, but about a year ago a friend persuaded me to abandon *WordStar* for *XyWrite,* a powerful word-processing program that does everything a writer could ask and more. It operates ten times as fast as the latest *WordStar* version I've tried. It counts words in an entire document or in a passage, backward or forward; its commands are mnemonically logical and easy to learn. It even seems to run my printer better. Many publishers are now using this program.

—VICKY HAY

■ ■ ■

If you grew up at newspapers or magazines, chances are you used an Atex terminal. Well, two of the guys from Atex founded their own company, called XyQuest, and invented *XyWrite*. Many of the commands of *XyWrite* are identical or similar to Atex commands. Because I'd used an Atex terminal for six years, I found *XyWrite* very easy to learn. In fact, I've never read the manual, except to look up how to do something new.

All of *XyWrite*'s commands make beautiful, mnemonic sense—e.g., "CA" for "call up a file," "SA" for "save to disk," "DIR" for "directory." What could be simpler? Not only is it elegantly logical, it's fast and powerful. Because it's command-driven, you don't have to wait for menus to scroll on screen all the time, although you can have them by asking for "help."

XyWrite does everything a writer could possibly want to do, including margins, pagination, footnoting, sub- and superscripting, boldfacing, chapter headings, envelopes and labels, and so on. My current favorite is mail merge. The other day, I watched gleefully as my printer produced 26 cover letters in a row, matched to a list of editors in another file; I had to type the letter only once.

And *XyWrite* also does "windows"—nine, to be precise. This is useful if, say, you have to interview a number of people for one story, and you want to create separate files for them to keep them straight. The windows let you have nine files accessible with a keystroke, instead of wasting time calling them up one at a time to search for that essential quote.

—PATRICIA MANDELL

■ ■ ■

XyWrite (pronounced as if the initial letter were "Z") is a big, powerful word-processing program that will do everything and do it fast. It was originally designed to make a personal computer work like the word-processing component of the Atex typesetting system. Because *Xy-Write* files are saved in ASCII format [see the following section], it reduces conversion problems for copy that will be used in professional typesetting. Consequently, *XyWrite* is popular with many newspapers and magazines.

The heart of the program's operating system is the command line at the top of the screen. Striking the F5 function key places the cursor on that line. Most commands are quite logical: "LM" for "left margin," "RM" for "right margin," "SA" for "save," "CA" to call up a file, "QU" for "quit." As a reviewer for the magazine *Personal Computing* put it, "There is a certain sparse elegance in the way the program has been designed." As with any word-processing program, with continual use, you eventually memorize most of the commands you'll need.

XyWrite has a 100,000-word spelling checker and a 220,000-word thesaurus. Nine files can be opened simultaneously in nine windows. It provides footnote and index facilities, automatic hyphenation, columns that can be edited and formatted independently as well as "snaking" for newspaper or newsletter applications. The program also allows the user all kinds of customizing options; you can get into some rather complex procedures that way, but the company has user support readily available.

This is not the simplest program to learn, but it's no harder than most of the other major powerful word processors and, at least in my experience, is easier to use than some. The average user can probably master the fundamental commands reasonably fast, but it takes some time to learn the vast number of procedures of which such a powerful word processor is capable.

XyWrite lists for $445 but can probably be found at discounted prices in some software stores or mail-order catalogs. The publisher is Xy-Quest, 44 Manning Road, Billeria MA 01821; (508) 671-0888.

—CHARLES BOECKMAN

■   ## WILL IT SUFFER IN TRANSLATION?   ■

If you're using your word-processing program simply to produce a manuscript, on paper, to be read by human eyes, fine. But under some circumstances, you may need to provide that manuscript on a disk (or via modem) to be read by somebody else's computer and worked on by somebody else's (an editor's, a coauthor's) word-processing program, which may not be the same one as yours. Or someone may be providing material that way to you. A manuscript retrieved from a disk into an alien word-processing environment will, as often as not, come up gibberish rather than words. This is because of the differing codes embedded in the text by the various programs. There are, essentially, three answers to this problem.

One is a built-in translator. Some word-processing programs include conversion features for certain other programs. As mentioned earlier, *Sprint* can convert to and from *Microsoft Word, Multimate, WordPerfect,* and *WordStar,* while *WordStar* can convert from *Microsoft Word, WordPerfect,* and others. *WordPerfect* includes a "Convert" mini-program that can translate text between itself and *Multimate* or *WordStar,* as well as some more obscure systems. Other word processors may also include such features (sometimes unknown to their owners, who haven't read the entire manual).

A second method is relaying only bare-bones text:

STRIP TO THE ESSENTIALS

One method for interchanging text files between various word-processing programs is little known. It's producing a "stripped" file, also called a "straight ASCII" file, a "DOS" file, or a "text" file—a document without the control codes various word processors use to produce such results as underlining or boldface.[6] The way to do this differs depending on the program you're using; check your manual.

—SHARI STEINER

■ ■ ■

There's a little program called *Textcon,* available on electronic bulletin boards around the country and also sometimes advertised in computer magazines. It's a godsend for writers submitting articles to publications in electronic form, whether by modem or on disk.

Textcon converts files created with various word-processing programs to a common format by stripping the internal command codes that make it difficult or even impossible for a file in one format to be read by another word processor. The result is a clean file that a publisher's system can read and edit.

One of *Textcon*'s most attractive features is that it is in the category of software called "shareware."[7] This means it's available to try out for

[6]ASCII—pronounced "ASKy"—stands for American Standard Code for Information Interchange.

[7]"Shareware" doesn't denote programs freely shared with others, nor are such programs in the public domain; their authors own the rights, including copyright. Rather, shareware is software sold on what might be termed an honor system. It is not "bought" at the time of ordering or receipt; the initial charge simply covers the cost of disk(s) and ship-

free. Only if users like it are they expected to send Chris Wolf, the man who wrote it, a modest registration fee (it's in the $10 to $20 range).

—THOMAS A. LANKARD

A third translation alternative is one of the following programs expressly designed for handling the task (there are others in addition to those cited):

R-Doc/X

I use *WordPerfect;* many of my publishers use *XyWrite* and want manuscripts submitted on disk as well as on paper. No problem. When a manuscript is ready to mail out, I feed its *WordPerfect* files into one end of the translation program and out the other end comes a *XyWrite*-formatted text. I use a translation program called *R-Doc/X;* another one I've heard good things about is *Software Bridge.* Important: Make sure the one you select can handle both your word-processing program and the one you'll be translating text into and/or from.

—WENDY MURPHY

Software Bridge

A conversion program that translates word-processing files from one format to another can save the day if you're sharing documents with a collaborator who uses a different word processor, or you're sending copy to an editor who does so, or you yourself decide to switch word-processing programs and you need to convert all your files.

I've been using a very useful conversion program called *Software Bridge,* picked as "editors' choice" for 1989 by *PC Magazine.* It easily translates between a number of popular and lesser-known word processors, including *DisplayWrite, Microsoft Word, Multimate, Samna, Sprint, Volkswriter, Wang, WordPerfect, WordStar,* and *WordStar 2000.* The instructions are clear and concise.

Software Bridge is marketed by Systems Compatibility Corporation,

---

ping. If you decide to use the program, you register with the author, for a fee which may vary but is usually relatively low. You will then be entitled to receive whatever the particular author offers by way of support, which may include a manual, notices of (or free) upgrades, telephone backup, et al.

401 North Wabash Avenue, Suite 600, Chicago IL 60611; (800) 333-1395, except in Illinois, (312) 329-0700.

—CHARLES BOECKMAN

Word For Word

Another translator I've seen that seems to work well is *Word For Word.* The formats to and from which it can convert files include many of the popular word processors such as *DisplayWrite, IBM Writing Assistant, Microsoft Word, Multimate, PFS:Write, WordPerfect,* and *WordStar.* This program also offers a special conversion called "Smart ASCII," which has the ability to preserve full-page formatting instructions that may otherwise be removed.

Word For Word is by Design Software, Inc., 1275 West Roosevelt Road, West Chicago IL 60185. It comes in two versions—a full-scale "professional" package and a "limited" one that works with fewer formats.

—CHARLES BOECKMAN

2

UTILITIES
AND
OTHER
USEFUL
SOFTWARE

Mostly, writers who use computers use word-processing programs that perform the functions traditionally handled by typewriters (plus scissors, paste, and other classic necessities). Many writers, though, make use of additional software—sometimes, communications programs to run devices for electronic copy-filing (see Chapter 11), often, as described here, accessories to their word-processing programs, or the little office-housekeeping aids known as "utilities." As in Chapter 1, the programs our contributors chose to cite are presented in alphabetical order.

ARC

No matter how large the capacity of a disk, even a hard disk, there will come a day when it's too full for comfort. And for those without hard disks, no matter how many floppy disks we buy, we're always buying more. One way to save money and storage space is with a utility called *ARC*. The letters stand for "archive."

Archives are stored files you want to keep but to which you need access only infrequently—text of a published book (you may want to do a later edition), magazine articles too old for recycling but containing possibly useful material, that unfinished novel you'll return to "someday." *ARC* reduces the space required to store files by an average of over 50 percent.

My own practice is to periodically back up all the newly created files on my hard disk by one copy on a 5¼-inch floppy disk and a compressed or *ARC*'d copy on a 3½-inch high-density floppy. (If I need to use the first backup copy, it's faster to read it in the uncompressed state.) I keep the two in different parts of the house, for safety's sake.

The program can also be used to compress rarely used applications programs, such as an income tax preparation program you use only once a year. The latest version of *ARC* will unpack and execute compressed programs with a single command.

ARC is "shareware" and is available from System Enhancement Associates, Inc., 21 New Street, Wayne NJ 07470.[1]

—MARVIN J. WOLF

Battery Watch

Laptop computers are becoming increasingly popular with writers. These portable, battery-operated computers (they can also be plugged in) have a lot of great features, and a few that can be disconcerting— such as the battery's suddenly going dead when there's no electrical outlet within reach. But there's a program called *Battery Watch,* designed to monitor the battery.

Battery Watch stays "in residence" in your computer while you're working with other programs on your screen. When you first install it, a screen appears listing popular makes of laptops, and you indicate your model. The program knows approximately how long a fully charged battery for your make and model should operate, based on the drain of various components.

As you work, *Battery Watch* keeps an eye on how much energy your floppy drive, hard disk, display, etc., are consuming. Every two and a half seconds, it updates the information and recalculates how much longer your battery will operate at the current rate of power consump-

---

[1]See appendix for a full list of order-by-mail-or-phone office-supply sources, which includes sources of software and other computer supplies. For an explanation of the term "shareware," see the footnote on p. 23.

tion. When you want to check on your battery, you press a designated set of keys and a "window" pops up in the middle of your screen with a gauge giving the time left before your battery needs a new charge.

This works quite well if you pack up your trusty laptop and, say, start off on a plane trip or settle down to taking notes at the library. If, in the course of a day's work, you rely part of the time on the battery and part of the time on electricity from a wall socket, there is a problem: *Battery Watch* keeps basing its calculation on the power being used. As the manual points out, you have to do some estimating of how much charge the battery has gained while you're plugged in.

I found the program's estimates a little on the generous side with my Tandy 1400. After running the program a few times, you can be a better judge of its accuracy in your computer (depending, in part, on the age and efficiency of your battery); you may have to add or subtract a bit.

Battery Watch also has another useful feature, called "Deep Discharge." Most laptops are powered by NiCad batteries, which have a nasty quirk: They learn to "remember" how long they've been charged. If you always recharge your battery after it's been used for 90 minutes, for example, after a while, it will refuse to hold more than a 90-minute charge. The remedy is to occasionally fully discharge, and fully recharge, the battery (which can take up to twelve or fifteen hours with some units). The "Deep Discharge" feature automatically turns components on and off to drain the battery more quickly.

At this writing, the cost of *Battery Watch* is $39.95. It's sold by Traveling Software, North Creek Corporate Center, 18702 North Creek Parkway, Bothell WA 98011; (800) 343-8080.

—CHARLES BOECKMAN

Calendar Creator Plus

I looked for a long time before I found an appointment calendar program that met my needs. It's *Calendar Creator Plus,* one of the easiest-to-use computer programs I've ever seen, with help right on the screen if you need it; you'll be comfortable with it in about fifteen minutes.

With this extremely versatile program, you can enter all your deadlines, appointments, travel plans, whatever, and print out daily, weekly, monthly, or yearly calendars, as well as two-day, three-month, and six-week schedules. The best part is that you can keep as many different kinds of calendars as you want and print them in any combination, creating overlays for different needs and combining them or using them separately.

I keep calendars with deadlines for different clients and types of work, and the printouts tell me instantly what's due a particular week. I print out a monthly calendar and post it on the refrigerator, so my family knows when I'm not going to be home; a weekly calendar for my desk, with more details about appointments and deadlines; and a weekly "administrative" calendar for my bulletin board that lists regular chores like paying bills.

Calendar Creator Plus will also handle "floating" events—e.g., something that occurs on the second Tuesday, or the fifteenth, of each month. And events can carry over from year to year, such as birthdays (it will even calculate age!) or be repeated on a certain schedule.

Calendar Creator Plus costs $49.95 and is published by, and available from, Power Up! Software Corporation [see appendix].

—CHARLES AUSTIN

CompareRite

This software was originated by a Massachusetts company marketing to attorneys (it was recently purchased by MicroPro, publisher of the *WordStar* word-processing program), and its function is "redlining," comparing one draft of a document to another.

Its usefulness in our field is primarily for free-lance editing of documents created by others, especially people in corporations. Many provide their text on disks rather than on paper, and you edit the document on screen. But they want to "see" the changes you've made.

I make a copy of the client's disk and freely edit it. I then generate a *CompareRite* file. The program provides a printout showing the text I removed with slashes striking it out and the text I've added printed in boldface. The person who wrote the original retains a sense of control, because the review copy is available, yet I don't have to muck up my file trying to indicate all my revisions.

CompareRite is available packaged with *WordStar,* or separately for about $140, from MicroPro International Corporation, 33 San Pablo Avenue, San Rafael CA 94903; (800) 227-5609.

—LEE JOLLIFFE

EZScreens

An interesting utility program, developed by Elyse Sommer, an ASJA member, is called *EZScreens.* It's designed for those who use *WordPerfect* on IBMs or compatibles (while parts of the program can be used in systems with two floppy disks, you need a hard disk to realize maximum benefits). It offers 60 macros, a dozen batch commands, and many other nice things. Since the author is a writer, the instructions are in English and do not require a technical dictionary. *EZScreens* sells for $70.

—GEORGE DELUCENAY LEON

ForComment

This software [developed by ASJA member James A. Levine] is useful on large writing projects with multiple authors or reviewers; up to 15 people can review and comment on the same document. It's easy to learn—but everyone involved does have to learn it, which is its main drawback.

ForComment annotates a document, collates all the comments, and identifies the reviewer who made each one. It allows single-keystroke insertion of suggested changes the author decides to adopt, but it doesn't let reviewers change the original. It can import files from many word-processing programs and other software.

ForComment is published by Broderbund Software, Inc., 17 Paul Drive, San Rafael CA 94903; (415) 492-3500 or (800) 521-6263.

—LEE JOLLIFFE

■ ■ ■

IBM or compatible owners who use teamwork to prepare books, articles, or reports will appreciate *ForComment* from Broderbund, which sells for about $300. If you move any file (or a copy) into its system, it lets up to 16 people comment and suggest revisions, preserving the entire trail of comments and changes from first to final draft. And it keeps your original words intact while other people fool with them, since reviewers can't actually change them but can only propose changes.

The program dates, initials, and collates all suggestions. It then splits your screen so you can read your unchanged copy and, line by line, anything your reviewers say about it. You can tell at a glance whose comments are whose, and you can try out any revisions you like. You can even print out the document (or any part of it) with page numbers, headers or footers, and all suggestions shown as footnotes or endnotes. Incorporation of suggestions is quick and easy.

The program even has three "security levels" restricting the extent to which reviewers can change their input. "High" security prevents deletion of anything, even a reviewer's own notes. "Medium" allows changes only during that reviewing session and only by the person who wrote the comment or suggestion. "Low" security lets a comment or suggestion be changed at any time, but only by the person who wrote it in the first place.

ForComment comes with an author disk and manual plus several reviewer disks and brief reviewer manuals; you can send for more reviewer materials if you need them. The version we saw recognized only documents created by *Multimate, WordPerfect,* and *WordStar,* in addition to unformatted ASCII text [see p. 23 for explanation]. We hope future versions will correct this minor flaw.

—JUDI K-TURKEL and FRANKLYNN PETERSON

Grammatik III
This program by Reference Software is grammar-checking software that picks up your errors and lapses of usage and suggests ways of fixing them; it catches split infinitives, passive voice, awkward constructions, and punctuation mistakes. It's available from CompuAdd [see appendix].

—LEE JOLLIFFE

Headliner
I've run across an unusual program that can be a useful tool for writers in creating titles, slogans, headlines, or jingles, or in thinking of catchy phrases when the old creative well runs dry. Called *Headliner,* it is a data bank of over 33,000 expressions culled from books, songs, TV shows, movies, ads, proverbs, idioms, and quotations.

You key in a word or phrase, and the program searches for expressions that have a similar sound-alike word or phrase, or that rhyme or form acronyms or alliterations. It even checks for profanity or off-color meaning in four languages! Obviously, you can't use verbatim the words from the data bank; they are intended to be modified or to provide a creative springboard for your own thinking. The program is easy to use, the instructions clear and understandable.

Headliner is $99 (there is a 30-day money-back guarantee, less a $20 restocking charge) from the Salinon Corporation, 7430 Greenville Avenue, P.O. Box 31047, Dallas TX 75231; (214) 692-9091.

—CHARLES BOECKMAN

Hot Line

A program I'm wild about is a phone dialer called *Hot Line*. It comes with 10,000 names, addresses, and telephone numbers of organizations all around the country. It also gives you the ability to create a private directory—actually, five different private directories—and alphabetizes by the first word automatically. I have all sorts of categories in *Hot Line*, from window washers to research resources to single men!

—SHIRLEY CAMPER SOMAN

■ ■ ■

Every writer has his or her favorite computer utilities. One of mine is a neat little program called *Hot Line Two*. It's a phone dialer, logger, and directory maker that comes complete with two national directories—a huge 10,000-item compendium, and a smaller 5000-item one for those who are running short of disk space.

I've used *Hot Line Two* to make a general-purpose directory which contains the names of friends, relatives, and sources and other business contacts with whom I deal on a regular basis. I also use it to make separate directories of sources for every project I'm working on.

For example, right now I'm working on a story on competitive intelligence. I've created a directory, named "CI," of all my sources for just that story. I also created a CI log file. When I need to talk to one of those sources, I call the directory to my screen, highlight the name, and press a key. The computer does the dialing for me and keeps track of the length of the call. When I've finished talking, the name of the person, the phone number, and the connection time are recorded in the CI log. When the project is complete, I can simply print out the directory and send it along with my manuscript to my editor as a source list. When my phone bill arrives, I can print the log and send it to the magazine for reimbursement with no questions asked; the log and the source list tally. In addition, I don't lose money by forgetting to bill for some calls—or beat my head against the wall wondering, six weeks later, why the hell I ran up a $6.50 bill for a call to Arizona.

Hot Line Two is published by General Information Inc., 401 Parkplace, Kirkland WA 98033; (800) 722-3244. It is available for approximately $50 through the discount houses.

—KEN ENGLADE

Lap-Link Plus

This very useful tool is actually a hardware–software package that connects a laptop computer to an IBM/compatible desktop via a cable (included). It will also link up two desktops, or two laptops, for that matter. The software is extremely easy to use. Once hooked up, the two linked computers can exchange files and programs at lightning speed.

Most laptops use 3½-inch disks, while many of the desktops use the larger 5¼-inch disks. But with *Lap-Link Plus,* it's a snap to put a program from your desktop on your laptop, or to transfer text you've written on your laptop onto the hard drive or floppy disk in your desktop. The program, by the way, comes on both size disks.

The way it works: Once the computers are connected and the program is up and running, you'll see a split screen on each computer. They list directories on computer "A" and computer "B" side by side. You have all kinds of options in controlling transfers. You can transfer all the contents of one disk to another, or you can "tag" several files for transfer, or you can transfer just a single file. After your instructions are carried out, the program does a validity check and lets you know if the transfer was accomplished successfully.

There is also a *Lap-Link Mac* version of the program that may be used to transfer files from an IBM/compatible computer to any Apple Macintosh machine. I've found *Lap-Link Plus* to be user-friendly; I use it a lot, and I love it.

The current price of *Lap-Link Plus* is $139.95. It's available from Traveling Software, North Creek Corporate Center, 18702 North Creek Parkway, Bothell WA 98011; (800) 343-8080.

—CHARLES BOECKMAN

Maxthink

I've grown addicted to a program called *Maxthink,* which is an outline-processor. To explain why, let me tell you how I used to work in the pre-*Maxthink* days. If your methods have anything in common with mine, you'll find this program a boon.

Everything I write is long and detailed. Interviews I conduct are wide-ranging conversations that often run for up to two hours and produce ten pages of single-spaced notes. When it comes time to write, I find myself with a volume of information that needs to be boiled down and organized.

I used to get a few packs of filing cards and a red marking pen. I would take the transcript of each interview and reread it, underlining quotes I planned to use. Each underlined item had a file card that went along with it. On the main part of the file card, I jotted a summary of the item; in the upper left-hand corner, I wrote the name of the interviewee and the page of the transcript ("Jones, 2"); in the upper right-hand corner, I wrote the general category or aspect of the story I thought the item would fit into ("competitors' comments").

The cards were put in piles according to category. By the time the process was over, I'd have one pile called, say, "competitors' comments," with cards from five different interviews telling me on what pages of those five transcripts I could find snappy quotes. Each category then became part of a bare-bones master outline that guided me in writing the piece ("competitors turn apoplectic when talking about Joe Subject's rapid rise").

With *Maxthink*, I've computerized the process. The cards are gone.

Maxthink, first of all, allows you to make a new topic or subtopic by hitting one key, and it offers a variety of outline formats, from a plain numbered list to the standard (I., A., 1., a.) to the military (1.1, 1.2). I now transcribe all interviews in *Maxthink* instead of my word-processing program. Each time an interviewee expresses a new thought, I hit the topic button. By the time I've finished typing the transcript, I have a page and reference number for every idea expressed in the interview.

Maxthink includes a feature called "Binsort" which comes into play at this point. At the top of the interview, I set up a list of categories and hit a couple of keys. The categories become "bins" into which I "drop" each idea (by hitting one key) as I review the transcript. The "Binsort" step takes me about fifteen minutes and puts the interview into outline form. Then, before writing the piece, I read through all the interviews while composing a master outline which includes citations ("Competitors' Comments: Jones 2:24, Smith 7:87, Roberts 15:102").

The *Maxthink* method saves time and effort, compared with the filing cards, and still gets me thinking in an ordered way. The program allows you to move blocks of information all over the place, just by hitting a few keys. You can try out several trains of thought until you find the one that feels just right.

What's not to like about *Maxthink?* The manual is irritating, unless you are very—well, West Coast. The designer of *Maxthink*, a man named Neil Larson, tells you things about himself that you don't need to know and expends considerable energy tooting his program's horn. In his exuberance, he forgets to be perfectly clear in explaining how things work. The misspelled names of great writers (e.g., "E.M. For-rester") also grate.

Hang in there. Mr. Larson, sitting out there in his Birkenstocks, is as nice and empathetic a vendor as you could hope to deal with. He himself is the technical support department, and he'll talk you through any problem on his toll-free number.

Maxthink costs only $89 and has been well reviewed in computer publications in comparison with other outline processors. It runs on IBM and compatible machines and is available from Maxthink, 44 Rin-con Road, Kensington CA 94707; (800) 227-1590.

—KATHARINE DAVIS FISHMAN

MemoryMate

This program is a memory-resident free-form filing system and data manager that accepts random information. You can enter notes, memos, lists, thoughts, and ideas any way you wish, and an entry can be retrieved by searching for any word in it. The data are infinitely cross-referenced, and you don't need special file names or key words to recall your information.

MemoryMate has a "view" command that allows you to toggle back and forth between it and the display screen of another program you're using. You can copy text from *MemoryMate* to another program, and vice versa.

The program also has a useful "reminder" feature, which allows you to schedule your records to appear automatically on your screen on any date you designate. The result, for example, might be that as you are writing away one day, a notation will suddenly appear on your screen to remind you that a payment is due on your computer.

Another nice feature of *MemoryMate* is that its files don't take up memory space. The data remain on disk, so that the files are limited only by the amount of available disk space. The program can also run as a stand-alone program, if you don't want it to be memory-resident.

MemoryMate is produced by Broderbund Software, Inc., 17 Paul Drive, San Rafael CA 94903; (415) 492-3500 or (800) 521-6263.

—CHARLES BOECKMAN

MoneyMate

Sit a writer in front of a computer and the writer will immediately think "word processing" and other functions related to writing per se. There are, however, other useful functions a computer can perform, such as keeping financial records.

A professional writer is, in a sense, a small independent business. As such, he or she needs to keep a simple set of books, a record of expenses and income. Too often, when tax time rolls around, there ensues a frantic scramble through drawers crammed with receipts and check stubs. If you own a computer, there is a better way.

There are a number of appropriate personal-finance programs which will help keep your checkbook straight and, at the punch of a key, deliver a printed summary at the end of the year. I investigated a number of them. One I like is *MoneyMate*. It's simple to learn and easy to use; I had it up and running the first day, with just an occasional glance at the easily understood manual.

First, you set up a list of categories, each defined as either "inflow" or "outflow." What could be easier? What you pay for items such as printer ribbons, pencils, and paper—your outflow—is listed under a category such as "office expenses." Money you receive for an article is, of course, inflow. You are permitted up to 200 categories, and the program can handle up to ten different bank accounts.

A series of menus make it easy to follow the program's various functions. I like the way you enter expenses paid by check. A picture of a check appears on the screen, and you fill it out as you did the original check, including the date and check number. From there, you go to a screen that allows you to enter the category. Say it's "office expenses." You don't even have to type the entire word. Type a few beginning letters, "offi," hit a key, and the program calls up the rest of the phrase for you. (I think it's good practice to pay with a check whenever possible, since the canceled check is an additional receipt. Of course the program keeps track of cash expenditures, as well.)

MoneyMate is published by Practical Software, Inc., 131 North Garden Avenue, Clearwater FL 34615-9855; it lists for $69.95.

—CHARLES BOECKMAN

Norton Utilities

Have you ever pressed the wrong key on your computer and lost an entire file? Or did you ever delete one on purpose only to change your mind later and wish you had kept it? Novices will be delighted to learn that such files can often be retrieved from both hard and floppy disks, even though you thought they had vanished.

When you tell your word-processing program to delete a file, it does drop that file from the "active list" and does consider that space on the disk available for use by another file. But it doesn't actually erase the memory of that portion of the disk. Until a new file is placed in that space, the old one still resides there—nameless, yet perfectly retrievable.

But how to get it back? Most word-processing programs can't help you. If you can afford additional software, however, there are several programs that *can* help. One of the most popular is called *Norton Utilities,* a package of computer tools that includes a routine called "Quick UnErase," which can restore dropped files if the space hasn't been filled.

Norton Utilities provides other useful features as well, including "Wipefile," which completely obliterates a file when you really want to get rid of it forever. There are also routines for recovering removed directories, testing disks, and recovering hard disks which you reformatted by accident. Overall, this is a very handy bit of software.

—CHARLES A. SALTER

PC Outline

This is my most important writing tool. It has all the versatility you wish you could get from other outliners like *ThinkTank* or the outliner in *WordPerfect.* For instance, you can write multiline entries, so once your thoughts start to flow, the outliner doesn't restrict you. You can move text around easily, as well as changing its position in your hierarchy. You can open several outlines at once and easily pull material from one to another (I use this feature when writing several articles on similar topics).

Another important feature is that *PC Outline* doesn't use up much of your computer's memory. You can install it to run alongside your word-processing program and open outlines in "windows" above the text you're drafting. You can easily move back and forth from outline to draft, with both visible at once.

And it's extremely easy to learn; the computer-proficient may not even need the manual. I wrote my Ph.D. dissertation using this software, and every writer I've told about it loves it. I can't recommend it highly enough.

At this writing, *PC Outline* is available as shareware [see footnote on p. 23] from Brown Bag Software, File #41719, Box 60000, San Francisco CA 94160-1719; (408) 559-4545. The firm asks $29.95 for the software alone (after you've tried it); for a manual and free technical support for a year, the cost is $49.95 plus $5 shipping. For disks, manual, and support, send $89.95 plus $5 shipping.

An updated version of the program, to be called *PC Outline Plus*, is currently being planned. It will have a spelling checker, as well as optional command emulation of *Microsoft Word, WordPerfect, WordStar,* and *XyWrite*. It will not be available on a shareware basis.

—LEE JOLLIFFE

PopUps

A memory-resident helpmate like *Sidekick* [described later in this chapter], *PopUps* also has a calendar and a calculator. Instead of the other *Sidekick* features, however, it has a dandy utilities program and a cute and helpful alarm clock.

The alarm clock allows you to set a time for it to pop up on screen, announced by a couple of beeps, and remind you it's time to call your mother (or an interviewee), pick up your kid at school, or check the turkey in the oven. It can also be set to flash the time on your screen at preselected intervals. The utilities can be used to copy a file from one disk to another (useful for making backup copies of the document you're working on), delete files from a disk (or directory or subdirectory), view the contents of a file, rename a file, check a disk for available space, and read a directory or subdirectory.

And it can turn your computer/printer into a nifty electronic typewriter, printing out what you've written before or what you're working on now. This feature also permits you to control your printer: On a dot-matrix printer, you can instantly cause it to print bold, double-width, or half-height characters—very useful for writing oneself a note or printing just a portion of a large file.

PopUps is available at most software stores for under $100.

—MARVIN J. WOLF

Prufread

This is a program that should interest any writer who uses the mail-merging facilities of a word processor to send multiple submissions of material, for instance in marketing second rights. *Prufread* cleans up secondary merge files by removing duplicate names from mailing lists.

I've found it more than a little useful. There seems to be a gremlin sitting on my shoulder when I'm preparing a mailing list, and when I print out the results, duplicate lines appear. The program flags them, prints them, and deletes them if you desire. It also finds instances where you have failed to follow the very specific rules of mailing-list setup.

As far as I know, *Prufread* is the only program of its kind. I think it is well worth the price of $69.95. It runs on IBMs and compatibles and is available from Jan Ewing Custom Computer Services, 409 West 24 Street, Suite 14G, New York NY 10011; (212) 675-1974.

—GEORGE DELUCENAY LEON

Reflex

This data-management program, from the publisher of the *Sprint* word processor, is ideally suited to the writer's needs. Unlike software with more sophisticated capabilities, *Reflex* is easy to learn and use.

The beauty of this little program is that it not only offers a practical way to keep records; it also allows the information to be sorted and retrieved in many different ways. Records of article submissions and queries, for example, can be instantly sorted according to publication, or subject, or fee paid, or date of submission—whatever data you've included.

If you have a query that's been in the mail more than a few times, it's easy and helpful to call up a list of the places it's been sent. Or, if you're wondering how many article fees you received in September and October of last year, you can retrieve that information handily.

The program is also useful for maintaining and sorting virtually any other kind of record—address files, expenses, recipes, quotations, etc. Your records can be viewed on your screen in a variety of formats; they can then be printed out as viewed or in easily designed report formats. *Reflex* can also present figures—for tracking expenses or sales, for example—in pie-chart or graph form.

All in all, *Reflex* makes formerly tedious record-keeping a breeze, if not a pleasure. It is available at most computer stores or from Borland, 4585 Scotts Valley Drive, Scotts Valley CA 95066; (800) 255-8008.

—MICHELE McCORMICK

RightWriter

This program flags grammar, style, spelling, and usage errors, including overuse of jargon and the passive voice. It also calculates reading level, which can be very useful in helping to convince corporate clients that their writing really does need your fine touch; offers a "strength" analysis; makes sentence-structure recommendations; and suggests replacements for words it deems less than desirable.

RightWriter is compatible with most leading word processors. The latest (3.1) version lists for $95. It is published by RightSoft, Inc., 4545 Samuel Street, Sarasota FL 34233; (800) 992-0244. It is also available from CompuAdd [see appendix].

—LEE JOLLIFFE

Sardine

Ultra-small laptop computers—notably, the Tandy 100, 102, and 200 and the NEC 8200 and 8300—have remained popular with writers despite the proliferation of more sophisticated (and heavier) portables. Some of them are limited in performance, but there are various enhancements on the market that can increase the capabilities of these compacts. One is *Sardine,* a spelling checker. It comes in two forms, a chip called a ROM chip or a 3½-inch disk (priced the same either way).

There is good news and bad news. The chip version includes the "T-word" feature found in *Ultimate ROM II* [described later in this chapter], which provides many word-processing features, such as search and replace, word count, boldface, underlining, and others. The 30,000-word speller is said to be lightning fast, handling over 13,000 words per minute. I tried the chip version, and I agree that it is extremely fast. Corrections can be inserted automatically.

The bad news is that the one text-processing enhancement not included with *Sardine*'s "T-word" features is "ROM-View 80." This increases the display from 40 columns [characters] to 60 without scrolling or up to 80 columns [the normal display on a desktop screen] with scrolling (except on the Tandy 200). So you're stuck with a 40-column display.

There is a way around the problem: You can purchase *Ultimate ROM II,* which does include the enhanced display, and buy *Sardine* in the disk version, which is slower than the chip. It is also more difficult to install, and the instructions are not the easiest to follow, but once these hurdles are overcome, it works well.

—CHARLES BOECKMAN

Sidekick

Writers who spend most of the working day at the computer can benefit from a number of "memory-resident" utility programs which are switched on at the beginning of each session. Once activated, they are invisible until invoked, usually with one or two key strokes. Among the most useful is *Sidekick,* which includes a "notepad," a calendar, a calculator, an automatic telephone dialer, and a communications program.

The calculator is just that—an electronic calculator that pops up on your screen, permits all sorts of calculations, and disappears with a key stroke. The communications program is a full-featured one, allowing you to interrupt your word processing temporarily to call an electronic mail service, send or receive a fax message, transmit or receive a file.

Using the dialer requires an internal or external modem to be connected to a telephone line, with phone directories created as ordinary text files. The dialer allows you to search for any number stored in any number of directories and to automatically dial it. You hear the number dialed over the computer's speaker; you then pick up the handset and touch the space bar on your keyboard to turn off the speaker.

The calendar can be used as an appointment scheduler. It can also scroll backward or forward, decades or centuries into the past or future. (If you want to know what day of the week it was on August 14, 1945, this is a painless way to find out.) You can also print out a calendar for any month or year. One need never buy another calendar.

The "notepad" is actually a stripped-down version of *WordStar,* and it can be used to view or create a second word-processing file without having to leave the first. It's useful for writing notes to oneself, tacking new information onto an existing file, scanning one file while working on another, transferring data between files, and dozens of other applications.

Sidekick is published by Borland, 4585 Scotts Valley Drive, Scotts Valley CA 95066; (800) 255-8008.

—MARVIN J. WOLF

SmartNotes

Electronic Post-It Notes—that's *SmartNotes.* While several software packages have some note-making function, *SmartNotes* rides in your computer's current memory and can be used almost anywhere; a good instance is on file names, where the permitted eight characters may not be enough to describe a document. The program is "hot key" operated. A drawback is that your notes are saved in separate files from the documents you put them on, so you can't print a "marked-up" or annotated version of a document.

SmartNotes sells for about $80 and is published by Personics Corporation, 2352 Main Street, Building Two, Concord MA 01742; (617) 897-1575.

—LEE JOLLIFFE

SuperFile

This is a data-filing program, with which I've generated my own "Reader's Guide to Home & Workshop Literature." In my home-workshop field, I've found the published reader's guides useless, since they list only a sampling—perhaps 25 percent of what's actually published, selected seemingly at random. Thanks to *SuperFile,* I now have my own index, listing almost everything that appears in national magazines (a few really bad articles are omitted). With this program, entries are made in random order, along with key "sorting" words assigned by me.

How does it work? Let's say I want to approach *Popular Science* about an article on tool techniques. Has this magazine done such a piece lately? What has been published recently in other magazines along these lines?

First, I do a search of my index using the key words "tools" and "techniques"; this will sort out all article entries coded with both those words. I get a printout showing magazine, issue, page, subject, and a coded opinion of the piece recorded when the information was entered. I then do another quick search using "tools" in combination with "PS" (for *Popular Science*); this will reveal what that magazine has published on tools, and when, over the past several years. And then, if hand drills and routers look promising as tool-technique topics, I can do further searches using those terms as key words.

Where do I find the actual articles, if I need to do so? The magazines are in boxes up in the attic.

—THOMAS H. JONES

SuperKey

An elegant and inexpensive program, *SuperKey* allows you to "reprogram" the keys of your keyboard. You call *SuperKey* to your screen with a "hot key," then just follow its instructions. You first hit the key you want to redesignate, then hit the key or string of keys you want that key to represent, then save the new designation, known as a "macro."

Since I'm a *WordStar* fan, I have a set of *SuperKey* commands that emulate the *WordStar* cursor movement commands (I call that file "WS.FIX"). I use them whenever I'm working in another program, such as *PC Outline;* the advantage is that I don't have to relearn cursor movement commands in each program.

Another way to use *SuperKey* when you're writing is to write single-key macros for words you're using often. For instance, in this text, I might have set up *SuperKey* macros to type the word "program" or, for that matter, *"SuperKey"* itself. Then I could put each in with a single keystroke—say, the digits "1" and "2." It's especially useful when you're writing or typing something nightmarish, like a reference list; in writing my Ph.D. dissertation, I used *SuperKey* to type such oft-repeated references as *Journalism Quarterly.*

SuperKey is published by Borland, 4585 Scotts Valley Drive, Scotts Valley CA 95066; (800) 255-8008.

—LEE JOLLIFFE

Text Collector

Text you type into your computer can sometimes go the way of a single sock in the laundry. That's when a text retrieval program can come to the rescue.

The one I like best (after testing several others) is called *Text Collector.* It's extremely flexible, powerful, easy to use, and easy on the pocketbook. It can search a whole disk or directory of files like a speed demon, gathering bits of information into one place (without changing the original files). And unlike conventional database programs, which require you to type information within a specified format, using that program's editing commands, *Text Collector* searches through text entered with your regular word-processing program.

You can, however, use it like a conventional database, if you wish. For example, you could tag certain information with symbols like "+" or "[" and then tell *Text Collector* to search for text starting or ending with those symbols. I did this to pull out names of authors and source information for an index and bibliography for a reference project and saved many hours of time.

The clear and simple manual is hardly needed, since on-screen help is always available.

Text Collector, for IBMs and compatibles, is $69 plus $3 for shipping from O'Neill Software, 440 Davis Court, Suite 2822, San Francisco CA 94222; (415) 398-2255. A version for CP/M computers [an earlier operating system], called *Electra Find,* is also available ($49 plus $3 shipping).

—ELYSE SOMMER

Tornado

I once made notes on little pieces of paper, on 3- by-5-inch file cards, on the backs of envelopes, and in my pocket appointment book. I lost or misplaced many notes. An inventive bit of software called *Tornado* has gone a long way in organizing my life and the things I used to write notes about.

Tornado is a program that provides random access to the stored information. It's like having a pile of file cards that you can either stack neatly and riffle through, or spread out and scan. I use it to keep lists of books to read, reminders of music I want to buy, addresses, notes for articles, short quotes, and other pieces of information.

Entry of information is completely free-form, and you recall stored data with simple designations; a typical command I might issue is "G F-14," meaning, "Get me all references to the Grumman F-14 Tomcat fighter"—and there they are, on screen, ready to be scanned or printed. You can also print, save, or discard your material with single-key commands.

Tornado is $99.95 from Micro Logic Corp, P.O. Box 174, Hackensack NJ 07602; (201) 342-6518.

—DAVID A. ANDERTON

■ ■ ■

I've been using a data-filing tool that stores random pieces of information in a way that is excellent for writers. The usual data bank is set up with rigid "fields," a fine system for storing addresses or inventory lists. A writer needs a way to toss scraps of information into a pile, like a stack of papers on a desk, and an efficient method of quickly fishing out what is needed. *Tornado,* a "random information processor" by Micro Logic Corp, is exactly that kind of program.

Tornado is a fairly easy program to learn. It is "resident"; that is, the information you've stored is waiting behind the scenes while you use your favorite word processor. Suppose you've reached a point in your article where you need some vital information. You hit a "hot key" combination—it might be "Alt-J"—and presto, your information is on the screen.

Tornado files information in a way that resembles stacking notes (the developers of the program say it mimics thinking methods). You recall data by content rather than by file names or "fields," and *Tornado* connects information, just as your mind retrieves facts by association. The result is a very fast search-and-display operation.

A fiction writer would find this software helpful in referring to the cast of characters. In a lengthy novel, it is sometimes troublesome to recall all the characters' names. With the touch of a "hot key," the list of characters can be brought to the screen; if further information is needed about a particular character, a related file can be made available instantly.

The program accepts 25,000 "windows" of free-form random facts, and each can handle anything from a single word up to 32,000 characters. You can actually use the program for simple text-processing tasks such as brief reports or correspondence.

—CHARLES BOECKMAN

Ultimate ROM II

Mobile writers who find compact laptop computers great might like to know about an enhancement that can expand the capabilities of these little machines. Such a program is *Ultimate ROM II,* which is designed to work with the Radio Shack 100, 102, and 200 and the NEC 8201.

This software has a number of excellent applications. For one, it improves the editing capabilities and printer commands of these small computers to the point that they can do almost everything a desk computer can do in word processing: You can tell your printer to double-space, underline, boldface, etc., and you have the usual word-processing conveniences such as moving blocks of copy around. You are no longer limited to a 40-column [character] display; you can have a 60-column display, without scrolling, that will surprise you with its clarity and legibility, as well as an 80-column display with scrolling.

Ultimate ROM II also has a sophisticated database that lets you store data in one file and switch it to others. In addition, you can set up formulas that perform calculations based on data you feed in. And that's not all. There is an outlining-and-brainstorming feature, called "Idea," which lets you crunch notes and ideas into a format that outlines your thoughts; it's useful both in plotting fiction and in organizing article information in a coherent framework.

If you have a portable disk drive, the "T-Word" application gives you greater control over disk operations such as selecting files, merging files, and printing files from disks.

The nice thing is that you get all these features without sacrificing any free memory to speak of, since the program is in ROM ["Read Only Memory"]; according to the maker, it would otherwise take up as much as 32K of memory. It's contained in a chip that you simply snap into the proper port; anybody can do it.

Ultimate ROM II is available from Traveling Software, Inc., North Creek Corporate Center, 18702 North Creek Parkway, Bothel WA 98011; (800) 343-8080. It is priced, at this writing, at $99.95 and is sold with a 30-day money-back guarantee.

—CHARLES BOECKMAN

Undelete, a/k/a *Unerase*

Writers who have experienced that sinking feeling in the pit of the stomach after touching the wrong key on a computer keyboard and watching in horror as an entire article or book chapter evaporates into the ether need worry no more. There's a splendid little program that dispels the dread of sending text to an untimely death.

Fittingly, the two names by which the program is known are *Undelete* and *Unerase.* It is worth a thousand times the space it fills on a disk. It is "shareware" [see the footnote on p. 23] and is available on electronic bulletin boards all around the country. You'll also find it advertised in some computer magazines by public domain/shareware software vendors.

—THOMAS A. LANKARD

UniForm

This is an excellent program for computer users who want to be able to send disks to publishers, or other writers, who use different kinds of computer equipment—i.e., equipment that's usually not compatible. This software enables you to reformat a disk to virtually any format, including the IBM/compatibles' DOS and CP/M, and then copy material you've already written from its disk onto the new-format disk.

UniForm is available for about $68, including shipping, from MicroSolutions Computer Products, 132 West Lincoln Highway, DeKalb IL 60115.

—MITCH FINLEY

WordPerfect Library

The best working calendar I have ever found is in *WordPerfect Library* (which also contains other tools such as a calculator and a macro editor). It allows you to make notes of things to do, record appointments, and jog your memory. I use it to remind me of deadlines and to keep track of manuscripts.

For example, if I put a manuscript into the mail today, I place a note on the calendar for two weeks later to check for a reply and another note, four weeks later, to check for payment. If there is a delay in acceptance or payment, I can enter additional notes about phone calls or letters.

The calendar also has a time-clock feature: It issues a sound signal at a time you specify, so you don't lose track of time while working. I set it for two-hour intervals, for exercise breaks.

Another great feature is that the calendar is active for decades, into the next century. I use it to keep track of due dates on bonds and other investment securities that may mature many years from now; it's a lot easier than running down to the bank to look these things up.

—M. LAWRENCE PODOLSKY

XTree

An excellent tool I use for systematizing the files stored on a hard disk is known as *XTree*. Once installed, it comes on without my needing to touch the keyboard. It tells me the drive I'm currently in; the space remaining; directories, subdirectories, and files; and commands for a number of chores that can be done without going into a special program, such as moving, deleting, or printing a file. These are not its only features, but they are the ones I use most often and find particularly helpful.

—KAY CASSILL

▪ DESKTOP PUBLISHING ▪

Many have been misled, or at least mystified, by this phrase that, at first glance, seems to suggest that a lone operator at a single desk is somehow capable of assuming all the functions of, say, HarperCollins. Not exactly. Essentially, "desktop publishing" denotes a system combining software (mostly) and hardware (prominently, a printer capable of turning out type that looks more like typeset—as, book or magazine—type than typewriter type). The software involves programs that not only compose text (or work with programs that do) but can also fulfill design and layout functions and incorporate graphics. Desktop publishing capability is probably not a pressing need for the average writer, but it may be quite useful for some kinds of assignments. Here are comments from two contributors.

NEWSLETTERS, FLYERS, MAYBE A BOOK

Desktop publishing has become the hottest item in the world of personal computing since word processing, and programmers have leapt on the bandwagon with a large array of software. But what use is desktop publishing to a writer? With a computer and one of the new laser or ink-jet printers, a writer can create materials that come very close to print-shop quality—newsletters, brochures, catalogs, flyers, educational and technical material, reports. One could conceivably even publish one's own book.

Some of today's more powerful word processors, such as *WordPerfect* 5.0 and *WordStar* 5.5, have built-in capabilities for doing some desktop publishing; they can use graphics, lay out text, and instruct a printer to produce a variety of fonts. Programs specifically designed for this purpose offer even more features.

One such program, relatively inexpensive (list, $130), is *PFS: First Publisher;* it requires neither a hard drive nor a mouse [a separate cursor-control device], but both are preferable. It permits doing your own drawing, as well as altering (resizing, flipping, rotating) "clip" art. The program comes with a library of templates for newsletters, letterheads, menus, et al.; you can also set up your own forms.

Byline, published by Ashton-Tate, is another excellent program, which works quite well with two floppy disk drives and lists for $295. It can import text from *WordStar, WordPerfect,* and *XyWrite,* as well as text in ASCII form from other programs, and it also has its own word-processing system; clip art from a wide array of sources can be utilized and edited. *Byline* is a relatively easy program to learn, its instructions are easy to understand, and its two-page-spread screen format makes it ideal for producing booklets and pamphlets.

A budget-priced program is *Publish-It Lite,* by Timeworks (444 Lake Cook Road, Deerfield IL 60015), a younger sibling of the maker's *Publish-It,* a medium-priced desktop publishing program that has received warm reviews. The *Lite* version, which lists for only $59.95, is an effective, easy-to-use program. It will accept text from the major word processors only in ASCII format, but text can also be typed directly. It does a nice, attractive job on short newsletters and brochures, but documents are limited to four pages and automatic headers, footers, and page numbers aren't provided.

—CHARLES BOECKMAN

GOOD FOR GRAPHS, CHARTS, AND TABLES

Using the 5.0 version of *WordPerfect* and the Hewlett-Packard LaserJet Series II printer, I've done simple, text-oriented desktop publishing without too much trouble or expense. This system is less versatile than, for instance, the *Ventura Publisher* program, which handles complicated graphics, but it's easier to use, faster, and more appropriate for text-oriented projects. I use it to create sales training programs, monographs, business plans, and other materials that include tables, charts, and graphs; I've also printed letterheads.

The LaserJet II comes with two resident fonts, but, for greater versatility, I use software called *BitStream Fontware* to generate proportionally spaced fonts in three different typefaces and in sizes from 6 to 72 points. At this writing, registered users of *WordPerfect* can obtain a free copy of this software, and other typefaces can be purchased. A hand scanner with software (the *Complete Hand Scanner*) allows you to embellish copy by adding and editing existing graphics such as charts and line drawings and to incorporate (but not edit) existing text.

—BARBARA GOODHEART

3

THE
HARDWARE
DEPARTMENT

The core tools of the modern writer's trade are word-processing programs, or word processors, and the adjunctive programs that help them process— write, edit, file—their words more effectively. These packages of electronic instructions, known collectively as software, are covered in the first two chapters. Here, we look at choosing and using the hardware, the equipment operated by those electronic instructions. It consists, basically, of computers (whose monitor screens and keyboards may or may not be buyable separately) and printers, plus some pieces of accessory equipment. (*Note:* Modems, which are devices designed for direct communication between computers, are discussed in Chapter 11.)

• DESKTOP COMPUTERS AND ACCESSORIES •

There are, basically, two major "galaxies" in the current computer universe—the IBM-and-compatibles cluster, and the Apple-Macintoshes. The first group, often referred to simply as PCs, which use an operating system called PC-DOS or MS-DOS [it's made by Microsoft]— also known as just plain DOS—have generally been considered the strongest at working with text materials, the Apple-Macintosh group superior at graphics and design. That has been changing to a degree, and many writers (though a minority) process their words on Macs, while there are an increasing number of PC programs that produce fine visuals as well as text.

Still, the "feel" of working with each of these basic types is different enough from the other that, if you're about to acquire this kind of equipment for the first time, you ought to try both before committing yourself; different strokes for different folks, y'know. The operative word here is "committing": The two kinds of systems (but not various machines within the systems) are essentially incompatible. Once you've spent your money on one, you won't easily be able to deal with material produced by the other system on your equipment, or to use software created for it.

—WENDY MURPHY

■ ■ ■

In the view of most observers, there are not major differences among brands within the IBM/compatibles group (the kind more widely employed by writers). One computer may offer greater internal memory, or floppy-disk-drive capacity, than another, so that the specified requirements of the software you'll use and the likely sizes of documents you'll be creating may be deciding factors (many computers' capabilities may be expanded at a later date). As some contributors note, there may also be variations in such personal preferences as keyboard touch and monitor quality. Beyond these factors, price—as with any purchase—is a consideration, and you may want, mainly, to be sure the machine's made by a reputable company. When I bought my own (IBM-compatible) computer, for example, I chose a brand produced by a firm whose hardware, I'd heard from other writers, featured remarkably sturdy construction and was unlikely to need repairs. —D.S.

SHOP AROUND FOR BARGAINS
Watch for bargains in new and used computers. Newer models can cause prices to drop on slightly older machines that are perfectly fine for your purposes. For example: The IBM PC-XT is based on a chip, the microprocessor, known as the 8088. Newer PC-AT models use a chip

known as the 80286; still newer ones use the 80386. These newer machines have made the XT "outdated" for many purposes, because they are three or four times as fast in running complex accounting and other highly sophisticated programs.

This means a bonanza for writers: XT prices, at this writing, have dropped dramatically. When they first came out, they sold for more than $1000; they are now available for half that, and the price promises to keep going down. The same thing is currently happening to the AT, which cost close to $2000 and is now available for about $1000.

—DAVE KAISER

■ ■ ■

I envy writers shopping for a computer system these days. The price of computers has fallen dramatically since the early 1980s. I think it was around 1981 when my wife (who is also a writer) and I paid over $6000 for two Radio Shack model III computers with a mere 48K memory and a printer. Even at that price, they paid for themselves many times over. Together, we wrote some 25 books on them. But these days, one can purchase an IBM clone with 640K memory and a hard disk for less than $1500.

For a beginning writer on a limited budget, there are some terrific buys out there in used computers. When IBM-compatible MS-DOS machines became the "standard" in modern computing, a lot of earlier, perfectly good computers were shoved into closets. You'll find early Apple, Radio Shack, and others in garage sales, pawnshops, and classified ads at almost giveaway prices. They have their limitations, but don't sell them short; they can still do a very respectable job of word processing.

Of course, as in shopping for a used car, let the buyer beware. Find out the history of the used computer you're considering. If it had rough treatment, such as in a school, you could be buying a lot of trouble. On the other hand, if the owner of a small business used the machine very little before deciding to buy something more advanced, fine. (If you're a computer neophyte, you might have a knowledgeable friend help check out the machine.)

Another advantage of buying a used computer is that the seller frequently throws in several packages of software with the deal. They might include a word-processing program. That can amount to a big extra saving. The cost of several new software packages could almost equal that of the computer itself.

—CHARLES BOECKMAN

NO LONGER A LUXURY

As we all remember, the first pocket calculators cost about a hundred dollars and did basic arithmetic. Today, solar-powered calculators that will handle higher mathematics are given away in cereal boxes.

In 1981, Jinx and I decided that our volume of work demanded computerizing. There weren't many options. Apple was just moving out of the suburban garage where the *wunderkinder* had conceived it. IBM was denying that it would even consider making a personal computer. That pretty much left Radio Shack and the company that was still called Commodore Business Machines and had not yet become a glorified toy company. We bought two Commodore computers, a dual disk drive, a daisy-wheel printer, cables, and two copies of a word-processing program; the price for this system—the heart of which was a computer with only 32K (32,000 bytes) of memory—was $12,000.

We have bought other computers since. To underscore the changes in prices: We just bought a Macintosh SE with two 800K drives, a 20-megabyte hard disk, and a megabyte (1,000,000 bytes) of working memory. The cost (U.S. Virgin Islands): $2000.

If you own any Macintosh computer, you simply must have *The Macintosh Bible* (Publishers Group West) on your bookshelf. Our 1987 edition cost $21.

—JEFF MORGAN

THANKFUL FOR MEMORY

After years of using CP/M [an older operating system] and MS-DOS computers and laughing at the Apple Macintosh "toys," I nevertheless looked at a Macintosh when I needed a new machine. Despite the fact that I'm an old IBM man, I have to say that the Macintosh is, to my mind, the finest personal computer on the market today.

Unfortunately, it is also the most expensive personal computer on the market. But I've seen how some writers cripple themselves with inadequate machines, and I've always been willing to pay the price for equipment that exceeds my needs, rather than vice versa.

Memorize this word: *memory.* Today's computer programs are far superior to those of just a few years ago. But they're also huge. Any writer buying a computer today should definitely buy a hard disk, and it should be at least a 40MB [megabyte] hard disk. Ditto for RAM: I made a big mistake and bought only 2MB; I should have gotten at least 5MB.[1]

The reason: Only with such generous amounts of memory can you take full advantage of the "multitasking" features of the newer equipment. These features permit you to have several documents, even several programs, running at once—but only if you have the memory.

—STEPHEN MORRILL

WATCH THE MONITOR

I've written about ergonomics [the study of working conditions], and I'd like to comment on monitor type and position. There are some computer work-station units on the market that have upper shelves for monitors. They may look efficient in terms of saving space, but they are not ergonomically designed.

Such units require the user to look up at the monitor, which causes muscle fatigue and eyestrain. A monitor should be placed so that the user looks ever so slightly down at the screen. It's important to buy a monitor that swivels and tilts to allow for comfortable adjustment.

As to the color of the screen characters: I've used both green and amber, and I find the amber much easier on the eyes. The cheap white-on-black monitors should be avoided.

—ROSEMARY ELLEN GUILEY

JUNIOR BACKUP

My office computer is a bargain-basement IBM PC-Junior, which is surprisingly powerful. I bought it for about $1200, which was no great bargain—but today, used Juniors can be snapped up cheap, and they're really worth snapping up as an extra, backup, or special-use machine.

One warning: Juniors overheat. When mine does, it suddenly loses its cursor and starts to display fascinating designs, point by agonizing

---

[1] RAM is "random access memory," the "working" memory that remains alive while the computer's on.

point, all over its delightful color monitor. This is no minor problem, as you can imagine.

—TONI L. GOLDFARB

BUYING BY MAIL: WHO'LL FIX THE GLITCHES?

A friend who knows computers tells me you can save a lot of money using mail order. It's true that the laptop I bought for nearly $1000 can be had for $100 less by mail. Fine, but getting service by mail is a little harder.

When I made the switch to computer several years ago, I hired as a consultant a friend who taught computer use at a local university. He helped design my system (using those catalogs to obtain the best prices). When I became confounded by computerese, he translated it into English. When I needed repairs, he made them at a reasonable price.

Alas, my friend moved out of town. Fortunately, I located another consultant, who runs a one-man business selling and servicing computers, and I found he's a person I can trust. (I recently purchased a laptop computer from him for use on the road.)

Since I don't know how to distinguish a bit from a byte, having such an advisor allows me to stay more current than I would if I were dependent on my own minimal expertise. And I hate thumbing through catalogs. Sure, I sometimes pay a little more—but when a glitch develops in my machines, I can get help from him, either by phone or with a service visit.

A key question to ask when you seek to purchase any electronic or mechanical tools of the writer's trade: Who will service it when it breaks?

—HAL HIGDON

■ ■ ■

Too many people shy away from mail-order computers, when they could be saving hundreds, if not thousands, of dollars by buying through the mails. I'll admit I was nervous when my husband, a computer junkie, suggested that my best bet for a new computer would be a Dell System 200, sold only through mail order. What, no support? No local dealer's shoulder to cry on when I got into trouble?

But I couldn't be happier, and the fact that it was mail order has proved to be absolutely no problem. If anything, Dell seems to try harder because it's mail order. The company provides excellent support, which I rarely need and, since they maintain a toll-free 800 number, there's no difference between calling them and calling a local dealer.

Dell computers, which are IBM-compatible, are highly rated by most computer magazines. The company offers a 30-day, no-questions-asked return policy and a one-year limited warranty on its machines; the latter includes on-site service. If a product requires replacement, it's sent by overnight air express; two days later, the item being replaced is picked up. The customer is never without a computer and doesn't even have to leave home to make the exchange.

This is not the only mail-order computer company, but it is one of the more established and highly rated ones. To shop around, study the ads in computer magazines.

Dell Computer Corporation is at 9505 Arboretum Road, Austin TX 78759; (800) 426-5150.

—MARIAN FAUX

■ ■ ■

If you have a computer-wise dear friend of infinite patience when you're buying your first computer—a friend who'll help get you going and keep you going—save money and buy from a reliable mail-order supplier; ask the friend to name a good one (there are lots of them) and help you make your selection.

But if you're on your own, ask computer-owning acquaintances for the names of generously helpful local dealers, and then buy from one of them. It will cost you more up front, but the assistance they'll give will make it worthwhile. By the second time you buy a computer, you may have enough self-confidence in your stand-alone abilities to feel relaxed about buying via mail order.

—WENDY MURPHY

KEY CONSIDERATION

Many writers don't have the financial wherewithal to afford the full-featured personal computer system they want when they take that initial step into the electronic age. But the weakest link in the almost-no-name entry-level system that most first-time buyers ultimately find themselves saddled with isn't the additional memory or hard disk drive a salesperson tried in vain to sell them. It isn't a battery-powered clock, either, or the bare-bones word-processing software that came bundled with the system.

What's most important is the physical link between a writer and the words on the screen—the keyboard. A $50 keyboard with poorly arranged, mushy keys and cheaply soldered connections that start coming adrift after the first year of regular, everyday use is no bargain.

The fix isn't expensive. There's no need to spring for a megabuck Keytronic, IBM, or other expensively promoted unit. The Omni Key/ 102, from Northgate Computer Systems of Plymouth, Minnesota, has the "clicky" touch of an IBM Selectric (the all-time standard), a comfortable and logical layout, some thoughtful additions to the numeric keypad, and a price of only about $100. And it comes with a three-year warranty.

—THOMAS A. LANKARD

■ ■ ■

When I decided to get a computer and word-processing software a few years ago, my son, who is a physician, recommended that I buy an AT&T because its keyboard is so sensitive that it responds to minimal pressure. This feature has proved to be worth its weight in gold.

I have not only completed two full-length book manuscripts since then, but I have done so without the severe pain in my wrist and elbow which used to occur after typing just a few pages on my electric typewriter. Along with following the doctor's advice, I highly recommend trying the soft touch of the AT&T keyboard to anyone who suffers from the sort of repetitive strain injuries that some experts have linked to computer work.

—CELIA G. SCULLY

PREVENTIVE MEDICINE

If you occasionally feel numbness in your fingers, hand(s), or wrist(s) after a long stint at the keyboard, you may be encountering the first symptoms of a condition called carpal tunnel syndrome (CTS). It's usually caused by repeated wrist movement that eventually damages a particular nerve running through the wrist (known anatomically as the carpus). CTS can eventually lead to partial paralysis and muscle atrophy. Surgery is the ultimate cure.

Prevention is better. "Warm up" before starting work by doing wrist circles and stretching your fingers. Give your hands a two- or three-minute break every half hour or so. And invest in a "wrist rest" to go with your keyboard. Resembling a heavily padded picture frame, the device fits around the keyboard and keeps your wrists parallel to your desktop, greatly reducing stress and strain on the nerve. Wrist rests are sold under a number of brand names and are available at office-supply stores for about $35.

—ANDREA WARREN

TRAVELING MAC

The Macintosh SE computer is ideal for the writer living or working regularly in several countries. It fits under an airplane seat in a padded bag with a wide strap. (If its companion Imagewriter II printer is also needed, it can be packed in luggage padded with styrofoam, socks, and underwear.)

Also important, the Mac SE accepts a variable voltage supply, adapting to anything from 100 to 240 volts. It thus accommodates the U.S. and Canadian standard of 110 volts, Japan's 100, France's and Italy's 220, and England's 240. It also works well in countries like Mexico, with a variable voltage of anywhere from 110 to 125 volts. All you need are small adaptor plugs to fit different wall sockets; they're available at Radio Shack stores for a few dollars.

The Mac SE is bulkier and heavier than a laptop, but the full screen and Macintosh software compensate. Also, it comes with two 800K internal disk drives or one plus a built-in 20MB hard disk. If I'm away on a brief assignment taking notes or writing for a day or two, I might take a laptop. Anything longer, I prefer the comforts of home—the SE.

—ERICH HOYT

TANDON TAKES A POUNDING

For several years, I used an Apple computer (both the II and the IIe). The Apple, however, isn't the best computer for professional writers, in my opinion. It is limited in terms of software, compatibility with other systems, and keyboard functions.

Since 1986, I've used a Tandon PCX, a Japanese brand which is comparable to the IBM PC-XT; it has a 10MB hard disk and 640K random access memory. I bought it at the Computer Factory in White Plains, New York. I also looked at the Leading Edge, which was comparable in price and features, but decided against that brand because of service: Tandons may be serviced by the Computer Factory, while Leading Edge machines must be shipped to Massachusetts. Tandon also offered a one-year warranty, versus 90 days for IBM (I can't remember what Leading Edge's was).

I've pounded the heck out of this machine and have had only one minor problem with it: After about eight months, the hard disk drive developed an annoying whine. It was simple to fix—I had the machine back the same day—and cost nothing, because the warranty was still in force.

I would recommend that any writer contemplating a computer purchase buy a machine with a hard disk. I can store in excess of 300,000 words on mine. While I always back up material on a floppy disk, having everything in internal storage makes work faster and easier. And I consider 640K RAM a minimum requirement. I would also recommend having two built-in floppy disk drives; my Tandon has only one, which makes copying files from one floppy to another a little cumbersome.

—ROSEMARY ELLEN GUILEY

TWO COMPATIBLE COMPUTERS

I use a Kaypro IBM-compatible computer; that compatibility is important to me, since I use IBM computers at my major client's office. It has a 30MB hard disk and two floppy disk drives, one 5¼-inch and one 3½-inch. The two different drives are vital, since the 3½-inch drive can accept disks from my Toshiba laptop computer (I use the same word-processing software, *WordStar,* in both).

Having these compatible computers is marvelous, since I take my laptop all over the U.S., as well as to Japan; I can write anywhere, bring the disk back, and simply slip it into my main computer for editing and/or rewriting.

—ELYSE M. ROGERS

HAVE A COMPATIBLE FRIEND (OR TWO)

For those days when the equipment's down and it's deadline time, have the name of a friendly fellow writer—or two (one may be on vacation)—with a compatible computer (and printer), so you can produce a manuscript in time to save the day and the deadline.

—ELAINE FANTLE SHIMBERG

LOVE AT FIRST BYTE

I approached computerization most reluctantly, with a bad case of high-tech paranoia. Now, I am fully overcome with admiration for the mystical powers of the box in front of me. It was the user-friendliness of my computer that made the transition possible, even easy. And it was the low price of the machine that pushed me over the brink.

I bought an Amstrad PCW8256 from Sears (they don't sell Amstrads anymore in this region, although they continue to offer service). The computer came with word-manipulating software that was easy to master, and within a few hours I was entering data.

The sole drawback to an Amstrad commitment is that the disks are not interchangeable with any other machine. That's a problem when editors want disks as well as hard copy—a problem I've solved, somewhat, with a modem and friends' IBMs or Macs. Other than that, my relationship with my Amstrad was love at first byte (sorry, couldn't resist).

—BILL LONDON

CP/M STILL AVAILABLE

Although I'm often green with envy when I see fellow writers' computers that seem to turn cartwheels, I'm still using the trusty Kaypro 4 dinosaur I bought in 1984. It has never broken down or required replacement. It does exactly what I want it to do. So why switch? (It occurs to me that there must be many owners of early—CP/M—Kaypros who *are* upgrading and will unload one of these great little "VWs of the computer world," plus the programs that came with it, dirt cheap. If you're a writer on a budget who desperately needs a computer, it's worth considering.)

Another beauty of the machine was that it came bundled with lots of free software. Besides *WordStar,* it came with a spelling checker (which will also count words); I added a thesaurus and a macro creator *(SmartKey).* A year ago, I bought a NEC PC-8401A laptop portable for about $300; it is compatible with the Kaypro 4 and transfers copy back to it for storage (it also came with *WordStar* built in). I bought the portable by mail from Damark International, 6707 Shingle Creek Parkway, Minneapolis MN 55430.

As any dinosaur owner can attest, CP/M programs are not readily available, but Central Computer Products does have a catalog of such programs and offers fast service by mail or phone.[2]

For those in the New York City area: Kaypro CP/M computers are

[2]See appendix for a full list of order-by-mail-or-phone office-supply sources, which includes sources of software and other computer supplies.

sold and repaired by Tech-Mate Computers, 321 Fifth Avenue, New York NY 10016; (212) 686-3630.

—CAROL TONSING

■ ■ ■

If you just want to do basic word processing [and compatibility with other current systems isn't a consideration], and you see an old Kaypro 2 offered for sale with bundled software, buy it. This is the Volkswagen of computers—solid, gray, slow, and virtually indestructible. The CP/M operating system is dated, but this shouldn't worry the average writer. The screen is smallish but very clear, and the machine uses standard 5¼-inch disks.

—DAVID BOUCHIER

IF YOU DO SWITCH SYSTEMS

When my old CP/M-operated Kaypro 2 expired, I really panicked, because I had disks full of important data to which I needed access. Oliver Office Equipment came to my rescue. The firm's computer expert had me back in business in 24 hours. I purchased a Kaypro PC (the new, IBM-compatible generation), and a quick and easy program that even a computer illiterate like me could handle converted all my CP/M files to DOS.

Oliver Office Equipment is at 5 North Village Avenue, Rockville Centre NY 11570; (516) 766-6191.

—MARY-ELLEN SIEGEL

■ ■ ■

For permanent manuscript filing, I prefer keeping hard [paper] copies instead of disks; otherwise, you can have a problem when you change computers. I've used three different computers, and in no case could the old disks be used on the new system.

When I switched from my Kaypro 4 to a Zenith, which meant changing from a CP/M to an MS-DOS system, I *had* to get three disks changed, so I could continue work on a book then in progress. If you're faced with this problem, you can either shop around for software to adapt the disk contents to work on the new equipment or seek out a specialist to take on the task. I chose the latter course.

The job was done expertly, at a cost of $40 per disk, by International

Systems Solutions, 1463 Burney Lane, Cincinnati OH 45230; (513) 232-2854.

—GEORGE LAYCOCK

DO YOU NEED A SERVICE CONTRACT?

As someone who considers herself a relatively well-informed consumer, I'm always chagrined to learn that a friend has been talked—or, if you ask me, suckered—into laying out hard-earned cash for a service contract. I almost always oppose them as expensive and impractical for free-lance writers—or anyone else, for that matter.

The logic of my opposition is as follows. Most products either break down right away, in which case they're lemons and should be replaced, or after several years' use, in which case they're entitled to. Few repairs cost more than $500 (the average price, for example, of replacing a hard disk in your computer), and most average between $100 and $200; but while you're waiting for this breakdown, you're spending upward of $1000, over time, on the service contract.

If you're worried about having the cash to lay out for major repairs, as many free-lancers are, then start your own rainy-day "service contract savings account," socking away a small amount every month. At least you'll be earning interest on your money, instead of just giving it away. And if your equipment doesn't need repairs (and it probably won't), you can use the money that has accumulated over several years to go to the Bahamas instead.

—MARIAN FAUX

■ ■ ■

I've never purchased a service agreement; I think they're a waste of money. It *is* important to buy equipment—especially computers and printers—from reputable dealers who also have their own service departments and who have good return policies. I usually stay away from the rock-bottom-price outfits, because their customer service is terrible and their return policies very limited.

—ROSEMARY ELLEN GUILEY

INSURING YOUR COMPUTER

It's possible to include computer coverage in your homeowner's policy, but it's wiser to obtain a specialized policy. Computer insurance is available at a reasonable price from at least three or four companies specializing in it; such firms advertise in the leading computer magazines. Premiums start at about $40 for $2000 worth of insurance, and most policies have a $50 deductible. Some policies specifically state that a machine is covered only while it is in the home or office, not if it is being transported; read the fine print.

—DAVE KAISER

...

Most homeowners' insurance policies have limited coverage, if any, for computers used in a home office. The Safeware Insurance Agency, an independent agency in Columbus, Ohio, offers broad coverage of computers and related equipment at reasonable rates.

The standard policy—which covers hardware and software purchased in the U.S., Puerto Rico, or Canada—protects against the usual perils, such as fire and theft, and against loss due to accidental damage or power surges, as well. Equipment is also covered in transit, essential for a laptop computer used for working on the road (but not when left in an unattended vehicle). Coverage is for the cost of repair or replacement, with a $50 deductible and no depreciation. The premium is based on full valuation; at this writing, $2000 coverage costs $39, up to $5000 costs $69, up to $8000 costs $89, and higher amounts are also available.

Safeware claims to have more than $1 billion worth of equipment insured and, with these generous provisions, it's not surprising. The policy, written by Central National Insurance of Omaha, is available in all states except Kansas and Texas, where somewhat different provisions apply. Safeware may be reached toll-free at (800) 848-3469.

—RUTH DUSKIN FELDMAN

IT MAY NOT BE YOUR FAULT

When beginning to use a computer, do yourself a big favor and learn from my experience. Don't assume that problems you have are necessarily your fault, no matter how technologically inept you might be.

After a frustrating period of many weeks, I eventually discovered that the problems I was having were due to defects in the system—not, as I had assumed, to my ignorance. Eventually, every part except the monitor had to be replaced or repaired. I could have kept "learning" forever and never actually learned.

I've discovered that this is not all that unusual an occurrence. It is also not unusual to run into the kind of putdown I experienced at my computer store. At one point, after refusing to acknowledge that a problem I was having could possibly be the fault of his equipment, the dealer said, "Bonnie, you can't buy a car and expect them to teach you to drive!" Only years of consumer and journalistic aggressiveness kept me from (a) killing him or (b) crumbling. And only by insisting that the system be tested and retested was I able to get him to repair or replace the defective parts.

—BONNIE REMSBERG

WRITE YOUR OWN INSTRUCTIONS

A wonderful guy, the late ASJA member Bern Hurwood, gave me an invaluable tip when I got my first computer. Bern said to get a small notebook and write down how to do things with the computer once you figure them out. Referring to the notebook is faster than wading through the manual, and your how-to-do-it description is probably clearer. He was right. The book is especially handy for things you do only once in a while. Start a new page for each item.

I have a second notebook for my second (laptop) computer. This computer came with a built-in modem, so I started the notebook right side up for the regular computer notes, then flipped it over to make notes on its telecommunications operation working in the other direction.

—JANICE HOPKINS TANNE

HAPPY HINT(z)(s)

After revising a company history seven times on an electric typewriter as the manuscript struggled up the corporate ladder, I figured that was about it. Enough cut and paste! Three upgraded systems later, I am now happily pounding on a Compaq Deskpro 286. Not that I'll ever be able to use all the technical intricacies—after two years, I'm still learning the wonders of the machinery—but it has made life much more pleasant for me and the bank.

A few hints, from my experience:

(1) Never put a drink close to the equipment. Always have the coffee, tea, or soda an arm's length away, in case of spills.

(2) Be sure your workroom is well-lighted, without a glare on your screen; an added glare guard is helpful.

(3) A thesaurus package on the computer is handy, but it will never beat out the variety of possibilities available from a good book.

(4) Don't let the kids play games on your gear.

(5) Write like hell to pay for the damn thing.

—MARTIN HINTZ

PLEAS/EASE FOR KEYS

Computer keyboards can take the abuse of your pounding fingers for years and years; ordinarily, that's not what does them in. Spilled liquids are the biggest keyboard killers, with coffee leading the list of drippy offenders. *Never* put your coffee cup (or teacup, or soft drink) near the keyboard.

Another slower, slyer keyboard danger is plain old airborne gunk—dust, hair, whatever's in the air where you live. The stuff falls down between the keys, gets onto the electronic surface below them, and in time causes the keys to start reacting erratically or not at all. Prevent this by covering the keyboard when you're not using it. You can buy keyboard covers, but even a simple sheet of paper or cardboard will help. And, periodically, pass a vacuum-cleaner hose across the keys.

—WENDY MURPHY

■ ■ ■

Even if you're very careful, and you never keep a liquid on your desk where it can spill onto your keyboard, you may find that after hundreds of hours of use, some of the keys on your keyboard begin to stick or fail to make contact. There's a remedy for this problem.

Electronics and TV stores sell a product called Contact, which is sprayed on the keys (with the computer off) while tapping them; the liquid removes the oxides that build up on the keys and prevent them from making proper contact. (This and similar products sold under other brand names are also used on remote controls for TV sets and VCRs.)

—GEORGE DELUCENAY LEON

UNIVERSAL COVER-UP

For those who use an IBM-compatible type computer whose manufacturer may not have provided a dust cover—or a well-designed dust cover—a universal, transparent vinyl dust cover sold by the Radio Shack stores for $9.95 will do the trick. It fits all computers set up in the typical way—monitor sitting on top of central processing unit, with keyboard sitting in front of the CPU. It's even large enough to accommodate a swivel stand underneath the monitor.

—MARK L. FUERST

DON'T BLOCK THOSE SLOTS

My cat would like to sleep on top of my computer monitor, because it's nice and warm there. Alas, the reason it's nice and warm is that the heat-exhaust vents are there; having a fat cat blocking those slots could prove injurious to my computer—and to my wallet. So I put something up there that is (a) small enough in cross-section that it doesn't interfere with the vents itself, (b) pointy/lumpy enough to be uncomfortable to lie upon, and (c) too heavy to knock off. In my case, I chose Figment, a pewter horned dragon acquired in a Disney World gift shop. My cat now sleeps in the window.

—STEPHEN MORRILL

WATCH OUT! BACK UP!

Hard disk drives are a tremendous convenience, well worth the money at today's prices. Many moderately priced desktop computers now come with them, as do laptops. Common hard-disk storage, which you can get at quickly, is 20 megabytes (MB, or "megs")—20 million characters, or about three million words. That's the capacity of 55 [360K] floppy disks, even if you could fill each one of them up (you can't fill floppies with long documents much past halfway without getting "disk full" messages).

But there's a terrorist lurking in every hard disk—the danger of a hard-drive "crash" that leaves you with no way to get at your three million hard-sweated words. Most commonly, such crashes result from a sudden power failure (it can happen if someone accidentally kicks your computer's power cord). The read-write head can drop onto the area where your directories are stored, wiping them out before you can say, "Please, God, don't let it crash." (To avoid this during a normal shutdown, your computer should be programmed to SIT—Seek Internal Track—when you quit for the day.)

The solution is simple, inexpensive, and easy if you make it part of your routine: Back up the material on your hard drive with floppy disks. Special backup devices and software are available, but at this writing, they're expensive—and unnecessary. Just save all your work on the hard drive for convenience *and* on a floppy disk for safety. It takes only a moment. There's no need to periodically and laboriously copy the complete contents of your hard drive onto a crate of floppies.

I also suggest one other protective step. Instead of using the same floppy disk day after day, use at least three, and rotate them, so you'll always have more than one version of what you're working on. Some writers, in a variation of this system, have found that using seven back-up disks—one for each day of the week—is quick, easy, and offers maximum protection.

—WARREN JAMISON

■ ■ ■

Hard-disk users are divided into those who religiously back up their hard-disk material on floppy disks and those who are going to be very, very unhappy. How to be one of the first group? You can buy fancy backup programs that will do it for you automatically. Or, you can use my simple system:

Format and label a disk for each category of material you wish to save. Get a disk tray (or plastic box, or whatever) to hold your disks and place it at one side of your computer. Each time you call up, from your hard disk, Chapter 5 of your book, or an article you're working on for magazine X, or your checkbook spreadsheet, pull out the appropriate backup disk and place it on the desk at the other side of your computer. Then, at the end of the day, or your working session, copy onto those disks all additions and changes you've made and return them to their tray.

Do this routinely, and you'll never worry about losing precious data.

—STEPHEN MORRILL

■ ■ ■

Even if you don't have a hard-drive system, it's a good idea to have a backup copy of the precious words you've put on disk, just in case. I always make such a backup disk at the end of my work period; often, when I've produced a sizable amount of material, I stop even earlier and make a copy, just to be sure I have it.

My working disk is kept handy in a disk rack on my desk. The backup copy goes into a steel file cabinet for safekeeping. For a long project, such as a book, the backup disks go into my safe-deposit box; after all, what more precious material is there than disks that represent many months of hard labor?

—BERNICE CURLER

BANISH THAT STATIC

We hear much about power drops and spikes that can menace our computer systems. Often overlooked: the danger of static electricity. Walking across a nylon rug on a cold, dry day can generate several thousand volts of static electricity—which merely gives you a minor tingle when you touch something metallic but is an entirely different story for your computer. The chips that handle computer operation and memory are very sensitive to such charges; if you touch the computer or its keyboard when you're carrying a static charge, you can end up with several hundred dollars' worth of repairs.

A simple precaution: Buy an antistatic mat that fits under the keyboard; they're carried by most computer stores, as well as by the mail-order firms that sell computer accessories. Touch the mat before you put your fingers to the keys, and you can be reasonably certain that those chips will continue doing their jobs.

Since the danger is greatest on cold, dry days, another safeguard is to run a humidifier. Maintaining a higher level of humidity reduces the chances of static buildup. It's also good for the sinuses.

—GEORGE DELUCENAY LEON

EYE-LEVEL REFERENCE

For taking notes, or copying a quote, from another source while using your computer, nothing beats a goose-neck secretarial paper holder for positioning your material conveniently near your screen. These jointed-spring contraptions, available in business-supply stores, clamp onto the edge of your desk, pivot and stretch over a wide arc, and can be adjusted to just about any angle or height. A ledge at the bottom can support any book short of an unabridged dictionary. The cost is about $25.

—JAMES P. JOHNSON

■ ■ ■

An adjustable arm, called the Curtis Clip, is fastened to your computer monitor with a strip of Velcro and swings out to hold the page you're working from. Since the page is then at the same level as the screen, you needn't keep turning your head back and forth or cope with eyestrain from continual focal-distance adjustment.

—GEORGE DELUCENAY LEON

■ ■ ■

The Curtis Clip is one of the few efficient ways to hold pages in a convenient position while you're working from them. It's a simple Velcro-attached right-angled device with an arm that swings out to position copy just to the left of my computer. (It could as easily have been attached to the right side or, for twice the price of $6.95, both sides.) It holds anything from a single sheet to approximately twenty pages. Made by Curtis Manufacturing, a subsidiary of Rolodex, the Clip is available at computer and office-supply stores.

—DAVID A. ANDERTON

FOR FIX-IT-YOURSELFERS

Curtis Manufacturing Co., Inc. makes a very handy Computer Tool Kit with everything you need for simple computer fixes and upgrade installations strapped into an easy-to-carry padded, zippered case. The tools include two flat screwdrivers, two Phillips screwdrivers, a Torx screwdriver (for Compaqs), two nutdrivers, a chip inserter, a parts retriever, and a tweezer.

The manufacturer is at 30 Fitzgerald Drive, Jaffey NH 03452; (603) 532-4123. The kit lists for $29.95, but I got mine for $21 at an office-supply discount store. I've had it for over a year, and every time I need a tool, it just seems to be there.

—BARBARA SCHWARTZ

SPECIAL INPUT: THE SCANNER

How would you like a secretary who types more than 200 words a minute, knows your word-processing program, and doesn't complain about working at midnight or 5 A.M.?

As this is written, I'm updating my first book. I didn't have a computer twenty years ago, when *Poisons in Your Food* was published, so the original manuscript did not exist on disk. I didn't want to have to sit down and key the entire text into my computer. Solution: a scanner.

I purchased a Dest scanner, with programs called *Text Pac* and *Publishing Pac,* for $1400; this was a bargain deal, since Dest was about to upgrade the scanner and software. I was interested only in text reading.

The scanner doesn't read the book's text perfectly, but the mistakes it makes can be quickly remedied with the spelling checker in my *WordPerfect* program. The device does read computer- or typewriter-generated material perfectly and automatically transfers it into *WordPerfect* so I can go right to work on it.

There are OCR (for Optical Character Recognition) packages that do read typeset material without any errors, and I'll probably buy one in the future—but for now, the Dest fits my needs quite well.

—RUTH WINTER

■ ■ ■

The Handscan allows you to scan typewritten text from paper right into your computer for editing. I bought it for a couple of large government jobs, and it was well worth the $600 investment. It does not scan typeset text—books, magazines, etc.—but by the time you read this, there will probably be a model that does. (A friend of mine has a scanner, bought for under $200, that scans pictures. It's impressive, but I think personally it's too much of a toy for a writer; if I had one, I'd have too much fun playing with it and get nothing else done.) The Handscan is made by Saba Technologies, 9300 South West Gemini Drive, Beaverton OR 97005.

—MARTA VOGEL

SUPPORT GROUP FOR COMPUTER USERS

FOG is a nonprofit computer users' group based in the San Francisco area; I've found it most helpful when I've needed help in resolving computer problems. Granted, you'll have to find a way to get around the problem while awaiting an answer to your letter. But if you're in the middle of a critical paragraph and your machinery locks up, you can contact FOG by phone.

And the group's publications may well have given you enough wise guidance ahead of time that the problem doesn't arise. Those publications are *FOGhorn,* which focuses on the computers with the CP/M operating system, and *FOGlight,* oriented to the newer MS-DOS system (IBM and compatible computers). Membership, which is $30 a year at this writing, includes a subscription (to the publication of your choice), as well as access to the organization's library of public-domain software (cost, about $4 per disk) and to about 50 electronic bulletin boards across the country (excellent communications software is also available at throwaway cost).

For further information, write Executive Director Gale Rhoades at P.O. Box 3474, Daly City CA 94015-0474.

—ED NELSON

■ ■ ■

Computers have brought writers many advantages—speed, ease of editing, spelling checkers, etc. There are also headaches and frustrations in coping with increasingly sophisticated equipment and software. To the rescue comes FOG, a national organization of personal computer users.

For dues of $30 a year, a member receives an informative monthly newsletter (either *FOGhorn* or *FOGlight*), has access to a large public-domain software library, and can get expert help five days a week. There are 10,000-plus files in the FOG library; they can be ordered on disk or downloaded from the group's on-line bulletin board. In moments of despair, a member can call the FOG office Monday through Friday for help from a live, user-friendly "guru." And a member can also be put in touch with over 2000 local computer users' groups worldwide.

—CHARLES BOECKMAN

▪ THE TRAVELING COMPUTER ▪

We've all seen publicity pictures of authors, feet on desk, keyboard on lap, writing away on a computer, a looming presence on the desk next to the sneakered or sandaled feet. Such a computer has come to be known as a "desktop" computer (as opposed, one surmises, to a computer stationed *under* the desk). A much smaller sort of machine, newly attached to its keyboard (well, yes, like a typewriter) and sufficiently lightweight not to pose a threat to the average person's thighbones, is now termed a "laptop" computer (as opposed to . . .). It operates on batteries, and it travels.

TINY TOTEABLE

There was only one way I could manage a four-week media tour combined with the start-up of a three-times-a-week newspaper column in the summer of 1987—a laptop computer. After considerable research, I settled on less power and more comfort and convenience in the form of a Tandy 102 from Radio Shack.

Its biggest plus: it is a modest three pounds in weight, meaning that I can put it in my briefcase along with all my research materials and not be burdened by an extra bag or a sagging shoulder. "Portables" that weigh in at ten or eleven pounds are just not portable enough for me. And when airlines are limiting carry-on baggage, it could be a real problem boarding a plane with a briefcase, a suitcase, *and* a computer bag.

The disadvantages of this model are its relative slowness (it's possible to outtype it and get gibberish), its small screen, and its limited capacity. An advantage, aside from its light weight, is that it's simple and very easy to get up and running. It has a plug, which is useful for hotel rooms, but its batteries are more than adequate for a cross-country flight.

What really makes it work, though, is an add-on chip called *T-Word*, from Traveling Software. *T-Word* does a number of amazing things; it provides both enhanced word-processing capabilities (search and replace, merge, et al.) and formatting and printing capabilities (without it, the 102 won't double-space text), and it enhances storage capacity by letting the user link up with a portable disk drive.

I've used the portable disk drive for temporary storage, and I will eventually take the time to learn how to dump data into my regular office computer. For now, I find that the Tandy holds several columns, each about 750 words long (I wouldn't care to write a very long piece on it, although I could) and, via a cable linkup to a printer, I can print what's in it.

This one gets three stars, in my book. It would deserve four if only it were a bit faster.

—GRACE W. WEINSTEIN

■ ■ ■

I have a Tandy 102, a little jewel with 32K capacity; it can also store information on a portable disk drive. The screen is small, but traveling with so little extra weight, 4½ pounds, is great. Not only can I input into it while waiting for a delayed plane at an airport but, with the built-in modem, I can send an article by telephone from Europe to my main computer in Los Angeles. Graphics are also available if you need charts and the like.

A lot of schools use this computer because of its small size and low price—$599 at this writing, with sale prices even lower.

—FREDA GREENE

BOOST IN A BRIEFCASE

My NEC Multispeed laptop weighs about seven pounds, fits in a briefcase, and travels both out of town and to local libraries; I feel it has boosted my productivity enormously. After examining a number of models, I concluded that the NEC had the best keyboard touch and the clearest LCD screen (a gas panel display is optional).

The machine has 720K random access memory and two drives that use 3½-inch disks. It runs either on external electricity or on its own internal battery, which lasts for about eight hours and is recharged by simply plugging the computer into an outlet overnight.

—ROSEMARY ELLEN GUILEY

FULLY COMPATIBLE

My laptop computer, the 6.4-pound Toshiba 1000, was list-priced at $1199 when I bought it in 1988, but available for much less if one shopped around. Although it is small (a little over twelve inches wide and two inches high) and light (it comes in its own carrying case), it is a full-featured IBM-compatible machine. Its rechargeable NiCad battery offers up to five hours of cordless use. It has a 720K 3½-inch disk drive and 512K of RAM.

The T1000 operates with MS-DOS 2.11 in ROM and boots up automatically from ROM, leaving the diskette drive free for loading application programs. The 180-degree-adjustable screen has 80-by-25-line "supertwist" liquid crystal display. There is Color Graphics Adaptor (CGA) compatibility. I use *WordPerfect* for writing while traveling. When I return, I just pop the disk into my office computer and work on it some more before printing.

As to airports, I've had no problem when traveling in the States; I remove the disks and ask to have the T1000 hand-inspected. This did not work on a trip to Switzerland, where officials insisted on sending the computer through the security machine (they did permit me to remove the disks). I held my breath, hoping that their equipment wouldn't wipe out anything. It didn't, but it was a nervous moment!

—JUNE ROTH

SPECIAL SCREENING

If you decide to buy a laptop computer, be sure to get a *back-lit* screen. I bought a Toshiba T1100-plus just as this screen technology was coming onto the market. The Toshiba has a double-twist liquid crystal display (LCD) screen; a Zenith model I looked at had back-lighting, but it was much more expensive. I now wish I'd made the extra investment. An LCD screen can be difficult to read in dim light, on planes, at twilight, or even when you're very tired.

—VICKY HAY

BEST INVESTMENT

Being a traveling writer (as opposed to a travel writer) can create problems. Thankfully, technology is offering a variety of solutions, not all of them inexpensive but still real bargains considering the drudgery they save.

Early in 1988, I signed a book contract that required me to spend considerable time in a city 900 miles from home. Packing up my desktop computer system and carting it along with me was not a viable option. I invested some $1700 in a Zenith 183 laptop. A lot of reviewers have raved about the Zenith's back-lit screen; personally, I'm not that crazy about it, but considering the other advantages, the Zenith was a terrific buy, one of the best investments I've ever made.

I chose the Zenith because the price was right, because I liked the feel of the keyboard, and because it had a feature I felt I absolutely could not do without—a 10-megabyte hard disk. The hard disk—a 20MB would have been even better, but at the time, they were prohibitively expensive—gave me plenty of room to load *WordPerfect* and the handful of utility programs to which I have become addicted.

I didn't bother packing a printer, because I didn't plan on needing any hard copy until I returned. I did make room for a modem, however; if I suddenly found I needed on-paper copy, I could always send my material to a colleague back home and get him to print it for me. This turned out to be a wise decision. I planned on spending six weeks away, but it stretched to fourteen, and I did indeed need some material printed before I could get home. Also, having the modem allowed me to send my colleague backup copies of my files as a safety measure.

Because I had the operational equivalent of my desktop in my laptop, by the time my research was completed, I not only had an electronic file cabinet full of notes, I also had a good outline of my book, as well as rough drafts of several chapters. This proved invaluable when I got home and began writing in earnest. I shudder to think what it would have been like to come back with a suitcase full of handwritten notes and start from scratch.

Incidentally, another wise investment was to buy a different-size drive for my desktop computer. Originally, it came with two 5¼-inch drives and a hard disk. When I bought the laptop, which uses 3½-inch disks, I swapped one of the desktop drives for a 3½-inch drive. Now, I can transfer material directly from the laptop to the desktop, and vice versa, without worrying about extra cables or auxiliary software. The new drive cost less than $250, including installation.

—KEN ENGLADE

LAPTOP–DESKTOP CONNECTION

If you buy an IBM-compatible laptop computer that uses 3½-inch disks and own an IBM-compatible desktop that uses 5¼-inch disks, you can hook the two together with a device called *The Brooklyn Bridge*, which costs about $100. The connection allows you to copy your word-processing (or other) software, as well as text files, from the larger to the smaller disks (or vice versa).

—VICKY HAY

TOP QUALITY

My laptop computer is the Zenith Supersport 286. It offers a crisp and readable back-lit display, the 20-megabyte hard drive provides plenty of storage, and the keyboard is as easy to use as that of a full-size computer. It uses 3½-inch diskettes, but an optional external drive (approximately $200) makes it possible to transfer data to any IBM-compatible machine that uses 5¼-inch diskettes. It doesn't come cheap; I paid $2700 at discount. But the quality is superb, and having a packable computer makes it possible to keep up your productivity without being tied to your desk.

—JUDITH KELMAN

THE TOUCH FANTASTIC

I sometimes suspect that the guardian angel of writers inspired the invention of the laptop computer. As far as I'm concerned, it is the ultimate tool of our trade. The laptop frees the writer to move around— to write on an airplane, on the patio, in bed. No longer are we chained to a desk.

And now, we've entered the age of lightweight, IBM-compatible portables that pack all the technology of big desk computers. Right now, I am comfortably situated on my favorite window seat, typing away on a Radio Shack (Tandy) 1400LT. It has a back-lit "supertwist" screen that is as clear and easy on the eyes as any desktop monitor, in any light or even no light at all. It comes with 768K RAM. There are two 3½-inch disk drives with 720K of memory each; if I wish, I can install a 20-megabyte hard disk in place of one of them. The removable battery pack operates for approximately three hours between charges, and an AC adapter will power it if you are near an outlet.

The keyboard touch is fantastic, which is probably why I fell in love with the 1400LT the first time I turned it on and typed a few words.

I'm very picky about keyboard feel. I've been a fast touch typist since I was in high school. If a keyboard doesn't respond properly, it gets in the way of my thinking; with the right feel, I'm hardly aware that I'm typing. A typewriter or computer might be the best buy in the world and have every feature in the book, but unless it has a keyboard touch that I can live with, I'll turn thumbs down on it.

The 1400LT keyboard doesn't have a numeric keypad. But for word processing, which is what most writers are going to use the computer for, a numeric keypad isn't all that essential, and leaving it off does make for a more compact keyboard. If a user plans to crunch a lot of numbers, there's a simple solution: a full-size keyboard can be plugged into the machine.

The prices of laptops have been considerably higher than those of desktops, but they are coming down. At this writing, the 1400LT lists for $1799. It has been on sale for $1299, however, and by the time this is published, the price may be still lower—or there may be a newer model.

—CHARLES BOECKMAN

■ ■ ■

My office computer is an IBM PC-XT "clone" with 640K of RAM, a hard disk, a modem, and all the bells and whistles I need to write books and articles and communicate electronically. But it's too big and heavy to pack up on my frequent trips. So I bought a Tandy 1400LT, a laptop portable. Now, I wish I'd bought it first. I never would have sunk money into the desktop.

The 1400 has a back-lit "supertwist" screen, blue and shades of red on glowing white. It's so bright that it could serve as a night light, except that as an energy-conservation measure, the machine automatically shuts off the screen if no key has been pressed for some preselected time.

The two 720K 3½-inch drives and 768K of RAM, and the compact keyboard, add up to more than enough to do anything a writer needs to do with a computer. The absence of a hard disk means small waiting periods while the machine accesses the drives—but compared to the slowness of old-style 5¼-inch floppy drives, this is a fast machine. At around sixteen pounds (including rechargeable batteries), it's still light enough to tote easily in its soft case—in which there's room for extra disks, an instruction manual, a modem, and odds and ends. (There is an optional internal modem for around $200, but I preferred the Migent Pocket Modem, about $150, which can be used with any computer.)

My desktop computer has both 5¼- and 3½-inch drives, so I can interchange disks with my laptop and use the same software. If the 1400 were my only machine, I would have bought a monochrome monitor like the one my desktop uses (a plug receptacle is provided), the same keyboard my desktop uses (another receptacle), and an external hard disk (still another). Then I could use it at home with the plug-ins and use the built-ins while traveling.

I've used the laptop for about everything my desktop does and, except for the lack of a hard drive, there's nothing the laptop won't handle equally well. I take advantage of airport layovers to send and receive electronic mail. I transcribe tapes at 37,000 feet. I write or rewrite copy in my hotel room. A laptop turns formerly wasted travel time to productive use.

At this writing, Radio Shack sells the 1400LT for around $1800. I found it at National Computer Supply, a Radio Shack franchise dealer (1200 Highway 377, Granbury TX 76048) for about 20 percent less; they accept phone and major credit-card orders.

—MARVIN J. WOLF

BUCKLE UP FOR SAFETY

If you're toting your laptop on an auto trip, protect it with a lapbelt; any one in your car will serve. Just thread the belt through the carrying-case handle and tighten it so that it fits snugly.

—BARBARA SCHWARTZ

CURE FOR CABIN FEVER

In 1988, I bought a Spark laptop computer by Datavue. It is truly wonderful. It has two 720K 3½-inch disk drives, weighs just under ten pounds, and is very portable.

I had lusted after a laptop for years. But I was finally able to justify the expense (it listed for $1500; I bought it at 47th Street Photo in New York for $1200) when I co-authored a book with a psychologist who lived half an hour from my home. I would type on the laptop as we worked together, then transfer the material later to my regular office computer.

A laptop is psychologically freeing: you're set loose from the geographically restrictive mother ship and hence less likely to succumb to a bad case of Cabin Fever. When I feel CF coming on, I take my laptop and trek off to a hotel lobby or a small cafe. I like the hubbub of voices around me, and most places are pleased to have a writer in "residence." I'm good for about four hours, and if I ever get that solar cell hooked up to the laptop, I'll be truly independent.

I don't think laptops are that much of a luxury anymore. Any machine that a writer depends on so much should have a backup; the laptop provides that. I don't go into a wild panic, as I used to, if my desktop computer goes on the blink. I tell the repairman to take his time; I have another computer. And I don't feel out of sorts if we have a blackout or I have a long wait at an airport.

The flip side is that you never have an excuse not to work.

—MARTA VOGEL

MY ONE AND ONLY

I was one of the first ASJA members to convert to word processing, back in the early '80s. My first computer was a clunky thing that took up my whole desk, and I never felt really comfortable with it. Somehow, I always had the feeling I was typing into a television set.

In 1988, I bought a Zenith laptop (the model number doesn't matter, because it's no longer made). What a difference! Instead of a flickering TV screen, it offered a flicker-free back-lit display that doesn't hurt my eyes and also doesn't make me feel as if Johnny Carson will appear any minute. It is also small—when folded up, about the size of a large loose-leaf notebook.

I don't use it to travel, because I seldom travel. It is, instead, now my office computer, and I dearly love it. I'd recommend a laptop to anyone who feels even slightly uncomfortable with computers. Somehow, it doesn't feel like a computer; it's more like an especially easy-to-use typewriter. Laptops also use 3½-inch disks, which hold more data than the 5¼-inch disks, take up much less space, and are considerably less fragile.

Before buying, go to a computer store and try various models. Check, especially, the feel of the keyboard (most, like my Zenith, have a slightly smaller-than-standard keyboard) and the screen display.

—KATHRYN LANCE

LAPTOP—OR DESKTOP?

Writers tend to ramble where the current assignment takes them. Without a machine to write on, they produce little during travel time except scribbled notes. The laptop has changed all that. I recently helped a friend pick one out, a Zenith SuperSport with a 20-megabyte hard disk. No bigger than an old-fashioned portable typewriter, that little machine does everything my AT&T 6300+ megamonster does, weighs a fifth as much, and has the footprint of a ballet dancer.[3] The market offers a number of other fine brands, as well—Datavue, Tandy, Sharp, NEC, etc.

Granted, most of these smallies are not true laptops; at twelve to fourteen pounds, they are really too bulky to use in an airplane seat. But they are certainly portable from one desk or table to another. If you're considering buying a personal computer, you might give the so-called laptops consideration. Laptops they are not, but powerhouses in miniature they are. Even if they are never taken off the desk, they will fill all of a writer's needs in a fraction of the desk space used by conventional machines.

One caution. Despite advertising claims, a "supertwist" LCD screen is not good enough. Be sure the screen is back-lit. And test its readability with your own eyes.

—BERN KEATING

OUT IN THE COLD

While I was on assignment at the World Alpine Ski Championships in Vail, Colorado in February 1989, the temperature plunged to minus 25 degrees. Early one morning, after I walked over to the press center with my laptop computer, I found, to my horror, that the text on the screen was locked; I could neither clear the screen to type another story nor return to the main menu to send my story by modem.

I was about to panic when I remembered something from college chemistry class: batteries are often affected by cold weather. I set my laptop in a sunny window. In ten minutes I was back in business writing on what I like best—the wild, wonderful world of winter snow.

—LUANNE PFEIFER

▪ PRINTERS ▪

In the beginning were two kinds of printers for use with personal computers: the letter-quality printer, using a type element such as a daisy wheel or a thimble and producing, relatively slowly, the sort

---

[3]"Footprint" is often used, when speaking of a computer or related equipment, to suggest the desk space occupied by the device. The origin of the term is obscure; it had not previously been applied to typewriters, telephones, or other items likely to take desktop stances.

of nice type turned out by an excellent office typewriter such as an IBM Selectric; the dot-matrix printer, whose racing printhead formed characters with dots spaced widely apart, characters sometimes even lacking ascenders and descenders (the parts projecting above and below lower-case height, as in such letters as "d," "h," "p," and "q"). Dot-matrix text was often quite illegible, and manuscripts produced by those printers were universally deemed unacceptable.

Now, dot-matrix printing has been vastly improved. The number of pins used to form characters has been increased in most of the newer models. The dot-matrix "look," while much superior to the early version, is reserved for fast "draft mode," while the printer can also produce (somewhat more slowly) very near letter-quality type quite acceptable for manuscripts and correspondence. But because the type is produced, as on a typewriter, by metal striking a ribbon riding past paper on a platen, dot-matrix printers are still noisy.

Enter the newest kind of printer—or, rather, kinds. Both are mercifully quiet. Ink-jet printers create characters by spraying little drops of ink in a matrix, with very nice, high-quality results; they are more expensive than dot-matrix printers. Laser printers use lasers and electrically charged toner to produce an on-paper image (the technology is closely related to that used by copiers); their output is beautiful, they are generally faster than ink-jet printers, and they are most expensive of all.

Aside from these basics (speed, decibels, type appearance), your choice may also hinge on what you're planning to print on (ordinary paper, letterheads, envelopes, labels) and the ease of changing back and forth from continuous (tractor) feed to individual pieces of paper or other materials.

SEE FOR YOURSELF

A hint to heed when you're shopping for a printer: Have the salesperson run off a sample, on ordinary paper, in front of you (almost every printer has a "self-test" feature that prints a full-page display of all the characters the printer can produce). Don't depend on preprinted literature that purports to show what the printer can do; such samples may have been photographed, are sometimes reduced in size, are often reproduced on special glossy paper, and are not always true representations of the printer's performance.

—GEORGE DELUCENAY LEON

LASER LOVERS

I'm in love with my LaserJet. Every time it prints out a beautiful, letter-quality page on my stationery, I thank my lucky stars I bought it.

When I went looking for a letter-quality printer, I found that the top models sold for about $600 to $700. I bought my LaserJet used, from the Boston Computer Exchange, for only $900, in 1988, and I think the difference was well worth the price. Even though it was then a year old, it's still going strong and looks as if it will last for many more years to come.

I never have paper jams or mechanical problems. I can print envelopes and address labels. Best of all, the cartridges seem to last forever: I'm currently on my seventh ream of paper on the same cartridge; that's 3500 copies. (By contrast, my copier cartridges punk out at two reams, but I suppose that's because I'm always copying clippings with photos, which uses a lot of ink.) And whenever I've had questions about how to do something, I've found the Hewlett-Packard hotline folks to be very sharp and helpful.

You can find used laser printers at several other places in the U.S., including Interstate Computer Brokers (d/b/a Computer Bank) in Mountain View, California.

—PATRICIA MANDELL

■ ■ ■

Although it might seem a luxury to have a Hewlett-Packard LaserJet printer, I've found it a big improvement. And since I managed to find it on sale (newer models were coming out) at a retail outlet near a large university, I bit the bullet and had it installed. Cost: just under $1000.

The only time I was sorry was when I had to have it checked and have a small repair made. Since I hadn't had the foresight to buy a maintenance contract, I found it expensive to have it picked up by a local company and shipped to the manufacturer (it weighs too much for me to tote myself). As soon as I got it back, I did get a maintenance contract and, although it seems expensive, I now feel more confident about future repairs.

—KAY CASSILL

FAST, QUIET, AND ELEGANT

The Hewlett-Packard DeskJet printer produces elegant documents that look as if they were done on a laser machine. Actually, it's an ink-jet printer and can be had at discount for about $675. It's fast and quiet.

If it matters, you can buy cartridges with additional type fonts.

One small warning: The DeskJet is designed to take U.S. letter-size paper (8½ by 11 inches), legal-size paper (8½ by 14 inches), something called "A4" or "European" paper, and number ten envelopes. If you want to use smaller notepaper in it, patient efforts may be required to persuade it to print straight, and it accepts smaller envelopes only grudgingly. Since the DeskJet is a great printer, I'd say it's worth giving up the notepaper.

—KATHARINE DAVIS FISHMAN

REASONABLE AND RELIABLE

I wanted a dot-matrix printer that was reasonably fast and reasonably inexpensive. My Panasonic 1081i is both. I paid $199 for it at Computer Factory in late 1987, and it has been operating reliably since then, with no problems. Its output is near letter quality; no client or correspondent has ever complained about the print. The manual is, of course, gibberish—but with luck, you may not need it.

—DAVID A. ANDERTON

TWO PRINTERS, AND A TYPEWRITER ON THE SIDE

I find near letter quality still not as good as letter quality. I have two printers—the NEC 3550, which is a letter-quality printer, and the Panasonic 1091i, a near letter-quality dot-matrix printer. The Panasonic is much faster, and I use it for drafts, but I run off all finished manuscripts on the NEC, for which I have a tractor feed (essential if one wishes to print long documents on continuous form without one's personal attendance). I have never had a single problem with either printer.

For short notes, envelopes, etc., I use an IBM Correcting Selectric, which I've had since 1981. It was my primary writing tool before I got my first computer.

—ROSEMARY ELLEN GUILEY

DAISY WHEELS: DEPENDABLE AND DISCOUNTED

Most of the advantages of dot-matrix printers over daisy wheels aren't really significant to writers. Dot-matrixes are much faster—but we do the great bulk of our editing and revising on the screen anyway, so that when you print out your text, you should be able to feel it's the final draft, or darn close to it. Therefore, you can start it through the printer and excuse yourself from the scene. If the printing takes 25 minutes instead of seven, so what?

None can dispute that formed-character printers—"daisy wheels" or "thimbles"—present clearer, more handsome letters. Besides, they've been coming down in price lately (and as more exotic technology, such as laser printing, comes into wider use, they may come down further). Juki and Citizen are a couple of low-cost brands that do reasonably well, even if they do it slowly. I particularly like my old Epson DX-10; though it produces only about sixteen characters a second, that's far faster than I'll ever be able to type.

—ED NELSON

■ ■ ■

My printer is a daisy-wheel letter-quality Brother DX-15XL (also sold under the brand names Fortis and Comrex), and it is top-notch. I bought it after reading a very enthusiastic review in the *New York Times* computer column. It was a bargain then, and it still is. Today's newer-model printers operate faster, but I don't find my printer agonizingly slow; it's easy to use, and it produces beautiful, neat, clean copy.

—TONI L. GOLDFARB

■ ■ ■

Although laser printers are now "in," most are very expensive, and many are overrated. But the laser-printer revolution has had one very good effect for free-lance writers: Prices for high-quality daisy-wheel printers have dropped dramatically. When *they* were in, a good Epson or Diablo sold in the neighborhood of $1200 to $1600; now, the same models are available for under $500 and sometimes as low as $200 on a dealer sellout.

Daisy-wheel printers provide letter quality that most $3000 laser printers can't duplicate. Daisy-wheel printers like the Diablo 620 are being sold new, at this writing, in the $200 price range. Its big brother, which has in-board memory and is slightly faster, is selling for around $350. These printers, which used to sell for over $1000, are steals. They are also dependable workhorses. I've been through several computer systems, and the old faithful daisy-wheel printer has been perking along without fail.

A publication called *Computer Shopper,* which can be found on newsstands, is a good source for such bargains.

—DAVE KAISER

FEEDING A PRINTER A BITE AT A TIME

I prefer a printer that is hand fed. In a typical work day, I'll probably feed my printer a couple of letterheads, some letters that run more than one page, several envelopes, some nonstandard-size paper for photo captions, and some material for which I want to include carbon copies (I have a copier, but carbons are quick, cheap, and often suitable for the purpose).

When I want to use automatic-feed computer paper to print a manuscript, my printer handles it very well, as long as I check every so often to make sure it's running straight. For now, I don't feel a tractor feed would be worth the cost.

—JANET GROENE

■ ■ ■

I'm now on my second computer and printer. My first printer (the Radio Shack Daisy Wheel II, no longer made) used a tractor feed. My current one, the Epson LQ-800, is near letter-quality (near enough that editors accept it) and uses a sheet feeder.

Having tried both, I think I prefer sheet feed; I find it more convenient. You can use the backs of old drafts for new ones, and there's no ripping off the tractor-feed paper edges. I have to add, though, that the sheet feed is slower and is more likely to get the paper misaligned; the tractor feed could print for hours without much supervision, while the sheet feed needs constant attention, something like a small child.

—KATHRYN LANCE

PROBLEMS AND SOLUTIONS

I have a Toshiba 351 [dot-matrix] printer of which I am very fond, except for two things: (1) The paper-end switch almost drove me crazy when I tried to print on short pieces of paper; (2) the lever that sets the distance of the printhead from the platen is not readily accessible.

I solved problem number one by carting the printer into the shop and having the technician disable the paper-end switch by cutting the wires. That sucker now *never* refuses to operate because it thinks it's out of paper. Of course, I have to make sure it *is* never out of paper.

I haven't been able to solve the other problem, only to work around it. The printer's design is such that one must lift the cover and move a lever all the way forward to get maximum distance between printhead and platen when printing envelopes (or thick paper), then open the cover and move it back again for normal printing. What I've learned to do is print in shifts—all sheet material in one load, all envelopes (separated by forced page breaks in *WordPerfect*) in another; it's not ideal, but it works.

—KEN ENGLADE

A BUTLER OF A PRINTER

Even the easiest tractor-feed arrangement for a printer is a pain if you have to take out the paper and line it up again several times in a work session. Say, for instance, that you print an article and then want to print an envelope, or a letter on your stationery. Having a good printer that will accept the single sheet or envelope without asking you to empty its tractor feed is a blessing.

Mine is the NEC 5300. Turn the "select" button off, pull the baler handle forward, and in two seconds, the tractor-fed paper backs out of the way and I can insert an envelope or a letterhead. Turn off the button and pull the lever forward again, and up comes the tractor paper. The 5300 also helps when you want to tear off a just-printed tractor sheet: Simply pull the baler handle forward, and the paper rises just enough to line up the perforations with the sharp edge of the plastic covering the platen; tear off the sheet, and, in a few seconds, the tractor paper reverses and realigns the top of the paper with the printhead.

This is a smart, polite machine, a butler of a printer.

—WALLACE KAUFMAN

HOLDING AREA

A peripheral worth looking into, especially if you write books or other many-paged manuscripts, is a spooler, also called a buffer or dump; it acts as a temporary way-station between computer and printer. Computers put out information at a much faster rate than printers can handle it; consequently, the computer has to wait, just as you do, while the printer prints. A spooler holds material and patiently feeds it to the printer, allowing you to use your computer for something else while the printer's working.

I found a spooler that has 64K of memory, meaning it will hold enough text to fill about 35 double-spaced manuscript pages (assuming about 250 words per page); it came from Central Computer Products [see appendix] and cost (in 1987) $69 (including cables) plus shipping and handling. Several other sources offer similar units, and some have much larger memories and more features; their prices are also greater.

—GEORGE DELUCENAY LEON

A PLACE TO STAND

I've used a number of printer stands, but most of them were pretty shaky and did nothing to stop my printer's lamentable habit of routing the printout back into the "in" slot, causing truly monumental jams. Finally, I found a good one, sturdily built of extremely thick chromed wire, in a configuration that keeps incoming paper separate from outgoing. I can now set the printer up for long, long runs without watching over it like a mother hen. Bliss!

The stand slopes, holding the printer at an angle so that you can easily read the printout. The printer sits above a tray that holds up to 1000 sheets of paper. A hook-on basket attaches at the back to refold the printout. Once it's set up, the whole thing can be moved as a unit.

I bought my stand from UARCO Computer Supplies in Illinois.[4] It cost $32.90, and there is a discount if four or more are ordered at once.

—BARBARA SCHWARTZ

■ ■ ■

When you're using continuous (tractor-feed) paper, you need some device to hold the printer off the desk to make room for the stack of fresh paper below and the printout behind the printer. Take a look at a device called Curtis Universal Printer Legs, which lists at this writing for $12.95 at computer stores. It's not exactly universal: the structure of my particular printer prevents proper refolding of the printout, so I just let it pile up on the desk. It looks sloppy but otherwise, the support works fine, and the "legs" position the printer at a good angle for work.

—DAVID A. ANDERTON

■   GOOD CONNECTIONS   ■

Finally, some notes on your supply of electricity as well as the crucial links between items of hardware.

---

[4]Again, see the appendix. Similar desktop stands, as well as free-standing models, are available from a number of mail-order sources.

CABLES

Your computer and your printer must be connected in order for you to get your words out of RAM and onto paper. That function is filled by a cable.

Cable comes in two types. The toughest is round, shielded cable. It's the more expensive type, but you'll only have to buy it once. Flat ribbon cable is cheaper and is good for use under carpeting, but it has a tendency to wear out if people walk on the carpet it's under; it also creeps and kinks (don't ask me how). The main advantage of ribbon cable is that you can order more than you need, roll up the rest neatly, and keep it for future use.

You may have heard that the cable between computer and printer must be as short as possible in order to avoid data dropout. That is nonsense. I've used cables 30 feet long, my computer store uses some in excess of 50 feet, and my local school system uses cables as long as 100 feet. The average writer, of course, will not need to go to that length.

Another warning you may hear is not to run printer cables across telephone or electrical cords. I have two computers, three printers, and a rat's nest of phone, computer, printer, and power cords. I've never had the slightest problem.

—STEPHEN MORRILL

■ ■ ■

Cables are of utmost importance, since they transmit information from one machine to another. They must fit the equipment perfectly to avoid incorrect data transmission.

A company called Cables & Chips is an excellent source. They have most cables in stock and will custom-meet unusual needs. You tell them the precise pieces of equipment you want to connect and how long a cable you require, and they will provide one, at surprisingly low cost. And their cables are hand-soldered instead of merely crimped, insuring more solid connections and, usually, longer life (crimping can allow the wires to slip out if tension is exerted on the cable).

Cables & Chips is at 2323 Front Street, New York NY 10038; (212) 619-3132. The firm will ship its cables (and chips) anywhere in the country.

—GEORGE DELUCENAY LEON

PURGE THE SURGE

A surge is a sudden jump in the amount of electricity coming in through your power lines. Big, heavy equipment turned on somewhere in your area can cause it; so can power-feed switching by the electric company. Ordinary electrical devices can often ignore surges—but they can knock the socks off the delicate electronic components in your computer and printer.

You need a surge protector (also known as a surge suppressor). You plug it into an outlet, plug the equipment you want to protect into it, and that's all there is to it. Prices run from around $10 for a one-outlet protector up to $30 to $50 for multioutlet units; mine, which cost $35, has six outlets.

Important: Get a *surge* protector, *not* an inexpensive—and, for most situations, relatively useless—*spike* protector.

—WENDY MURPHY

∎ ∎ ∎

After coming close to losing my mind worrying about how to keep from losing material in case of a power surge, I got a MasterPiece Plus. It fits neatly under the monitor of my computer and has controls for the computer, monitor, printer, and two auxiliary ports. Now, when I'm ready to start work, all I do is turn on the master switch and everything starts; when I'm ready to stop, I have only one button to push to turn things off. And I can rest easy, knowing that my work is protected.

—KAY CASSILL

∎ ∎ ∎

One *must* buy a surge protector! It costs only a few dollars and protects your equipment from unexpected fluctuations in the electrical current. I learned this lesson the hard way, when my husband used my old computer as a summer storm was beginning and blew out the card; it cost $150 to repair. Even though I have a surge protector now, I shut down at the first rumble of thunder, just to be on the safe side.

—ROSEMARY ELLEN GUILEY

SPARE POWER

If you live any place where power outages occur, even rarely, consider spending about $200 for a Datashield PC-200, a surge-suppressor-plus made by PTI Industries of Scotts Valley, California. Not only does it serve as a surge and spike suppressor, but it also stores 200 watts of power—more than enough to run your computer for up to half an hour after the power goes off, so you can save your data and shut down in an orderly fashion.

—JEFF MORGAN

ELECTRIC CHECKUP

If you tend to look warily at each socket into which you plug a piece of expensive electronic equipment, the $5.95 Grounded AC Outlet Analyzer from Radio Shack can give you some peace of mind. Plug it into any three-wire outlet, and it tells you whether or not that outlet is wired correctly. It won't tell you anything about the quality of the current, though; you'll still need a surge protector.

—BARBARA SCHWARTZ

PROCESSING WORDS IN THE WOODS

For writers who find themselves in difficult power situations—electrical outages or no electricity at all—I can recommend a marvelous antidote: the Coleman Powermate generator. It's a compact device (roughly 10 inches in any direction, weight about 10 pounds) with a carrying handle, and it puts out 110 volts AC and 12 DC (it's the former that keeps my computer running).

It starts up with the simple pull of a cord and runs for a couple of hours on a pint or so of regular gasoline, at which point it's time to refuel and break for lunch. I take it along to a rustic island in Maine and place it a distance away at the end of a long heavy-duty outdoor-use extension cord so I don't have to listen to the putt-putt. It has never disappointed, which is more than I can say for most utility companies. The cost was a couple of hundred dollars.

—WENDY MURPHY

4

THE
OTHER
WRITING
MACHINES

In the first three chapters, you'll find comments on computers and the programs, word-processing and other, that writers run on them. Most ASJA members are using computers for their writing now. Still, there are a significant number of holdouts. Some are sticking with ordinary typewriters, the machines that turn out words the old-fashioned way—directly on paper—and can't remember anything at all. Others have moved on to minimal-memory electronic typewriters. Quite a few have opted for a kind of hybrid, one of the "dedicated" word processors that offer generous text displays and even many features found in computer-run word-processing programs.

About the latter: Writers who find the computer decidedly off-putting may conclude that one of these machines—essentially, a single-minded computer with software permanently installed—is ideal. The dedicated word processor does, as Vance Packard points out, bear a reassuring resemblance to a typewriter.

If all you'll ever want to do with electronic writing equipment is write; if what you write won't be of very great length; and if you intend to spin out your words only in hard-copy form (on paper)—then this may be precisely the kind of machine that will ease your work without your springing for a clutch of alien gizmos. And this kind of word processor has indeed become far more sophisticated and versatile in recent years, while retaining relative "user friendliness" and ease of learning.

Be aware of the limitations, though. The machines can run no other software, either the word-processing programs described in Chapter 1 or the variety of adjuncts—note-takers, outliners, layout and graphic programs, other handy extras—of Chapter 2. Even as pure writing tools, the built-ins can't truly equal the best of the word-processing software made for wider-use computers. The amount of text that can be stored on disk is notably smaller. Perhaps most important, there is no compatibility, in software communication or in disk size or readability, between these machines and either family of computers. Publishers use computers, as do businesses, organizations, and most working writers. Writers who wish to—or are asked to—submit manuscripts in electronic form (on a disk or via modem), or co-author or co-edit material in that form, must start with text created on (or retyped into) a conventional computer.

Of course, even if you've gone the computer route, your treasured typewriter—and to many a writer, a typewriter that has put one's words on paper over the years is no mere tool but a cherished companion—needn't necessarily be abandoned when a more advanced writing device is acquired. And probably *shouldn't* be.

THE TYPEWRITER, NOW AND FOREVER . . .

Yes, the majority of writers today are hooked on the word processor and computer, presumed lifelines to success. But there remain a few of us who have stayed with the machine that puts print on paper right in front of us, period. True, you cannot move paragraphs around and instantly delete whole words and even pages. Many readers will doubtless roar with laughter at anyone so old-fashioned in this computer age. But for me, it will always be the typewriter. Tradition and habit are hard to break.

—BLYTHE FOOTE FINKE

. . . AND ONE FOR THE ROAD

There's nothing like a good, solid IBM typewriter, and even though I have a computer, I've held onto my Selectric 71 for years and years. It still works great and, when it doesn't, IBM sends a repair person out to make it work great again (for a fee, of course).

I've also got an extra typewriter that I take on the road—a portable electric Smith Corona, the kind that takes a cartridge ribbon. It's fairly heavy, not really an easy carry, but it works very well and has some neat features, including a half-space to let you squeeze another letter into a word or line and an "extra" key on which you can put a special character or punctuation mark (which can be ordered from SCM).

—TONI L. GOLDFARB

AN ELECTRONIC WONDER

The best typewriter I've ever had is my Silver Reed EX34, an electronic wonder that is truly simple to use and has not been supplanted by my computer. It has about two pages' worth of memory (which I usually use in little bits rather than in a single lump), automatic correction, and a host of other features that make me very happy. An added bonus is that it can be hooked up, if you wish, as a daisy-wheel printer. I recommend it highly.

—BONNIE REMSBERG

AFTER UNEASY RELATIONSHIPS, A LOVE AFFAIR

Personally, I have always had an uneasy relationship with typewriters. They sometimes seem to have a mind of their own which is often at odds with mine. But I finally found a machine with which it's been a love affair from the beginning: the Brother Word-Processing Typewriter AX-28.

For those of us who have fought the computer age tooth and nail (or byte by byte), this word processor/typewriter with 16K memory is a great transition machine.[1] It has a built-in 70,000-word spelling dictionary. It offers layout functions, editing, changing formats, block transfer, and printing your text in terrific-looking type. In addition, you can

[1]K, for kilobyte, is a unit of electronic memory or storage space. It denotes precisely 1024—that is, approximately 1000—bytes, or characters, and is equivalent to about 130 to 170 words; call it 150, on the average. Memory of 16K is thus more than adequate for a 2000-word story.

use it as a regular typewriter, getting a line-by-line display. Its keys are comfortable to use. It's light in weight, under ten pounds, for true portability.

Because this machine performs as a standard portable electric typewriter, you can learn at your own speed how to use its word-processing functions. And there is a convenient 800 number for you to call when you get bogged down with a problem that the user-friendly 65-page manual isn't solving for you.

The cost of this gem in a discount store is about $300.

—ABBY STITT

FAST ADJUSTMENT, VAST IMPROVEMENT

I've always doubted that I had the particular sort of brain required to cope with a computer as a writing tool. However, I've coped with a word processor just fine and find it a vast improvement over a typewriter.

My transition to a word processor, in fact, was easy, because I'd been using an Olivetti typewriter, and I simply switched to an Olivetti ETV 240 word processor. It had the same basic keyboard as the typewriter, and it looked pretty much like the typewriter, which to me was important in erasing my fear of the thing and helping me make a fast finger adjustment.

—VANCE PACKARD

GOOD FOR MEETING MODEST NEEDS

Anyone looking for a low-cost word-processing unit complete with printer might want to consider the Magnavox Videowriter 250, sold in the U.S. by Philips of Holland. It takes one 3½-inch disk, which can hold 54 items; any one item can be as long as 75 pages. The text screen shows orange letters on a black background, and the instructions, which are very clear, are on a smaller orange screen, in black letters. (There is also a concise, equally clear instruction booklet.) A split-screen feature permits moving text back and forth between documents. There is a dictionary, as well as a "help" feature to assist when mysteries arise.

Printing is somewhat slow—about a minute and 25 seconds per page—but of high quality. A style key switches the print from normal to wide, subscript, bold, and underlined. The processor and printer are in one unit, 14 by 14 by 7 inches, with an excellent keyboard attached by a coiled cord.

If there is a disadvantage, it is the smallish text screen, about 6 by 3 inches. Another, for some users, may be the lack of provision for continuous paper feed (there is a plug in the back of the unit, though, which I am told is for an automatic feeder). But the price is great: I paid only $529 at 47th Street Photo in New York. Ribbons for the printer may be had for $10 each.

This machine would not be ideal for heavy, continuous use on large projects like books, but it seems quite suitable for modest needs.

—JUDSON GOODING

A PIECE OF CAKE

$649—that's not much more than you might pay for a good piece of word-processing software. But it's what I paid for an entire system, word processing and all. The PWP 12 by Smith Corona came complete with a 21-line monitor, processor, key pad, and typewriter (XE 6000), with a 35,000-word spelling dictionary, called Spell Right, thrown in. It suits my needs very well.

It does all the things a word processor is supposed to do—deletions, corrections, searching, searching/replacing, block deletes, block moves, etc. Internal memory stores more than 30 pages, and external storage on "micro-disks" is unlimited. The user manual is better than average and, since the system doesn't include a lot of crap you can live without, you can pick it up in a hurry (for trouble-shooting, Smith Corona has an 800 number).

The $649 was a sale price; "list" is in the $800 to $900 range. Smith Corona makes a variety of typewriters that hook up to the system, and the prices vary, but most of them, I think, are under $1000.

I've had some exposure to the IBM PC and similar equipment, plus a couple of computer-run word-processing programs, since I bought my system. Compared to them, the PWP 12 is a snap to learn in a hurry and a piece of cake to work with. I recommend it.

—RAY DREYFACK

FAREWELL, OLD FRIENDS

In 1947, I sat at a wobbly table on the screened porch of a Butler hut on Guam and began typing out my first daily column for the *Guam News*. A typhoon was predicted. Armed Forces Radio said the Army was in Condition One, the Navy was in Condition Two, and the Air Force was in No Condition As Yet. But I had a typewriter and a deadline, and my story came first. Never mind that the typewriter's keys were all upper case, the ribbon was hopelessly worn, and I had to flick the key back into place manually after I struck each letter. (In that place, in those days, if you wanted a real typewriter, you married an admiral.) "Farewell, old friend," I said when the time came to hand it back to the navy requisition officer.

When I returned to the States, I first worked with a forlorn little manual machine. Eventually, I found a big Navy-surplus Underwood for the grand price of $15, which I considered really upscale (or would have, if that term had been in use in the '50s). On it, I turned out tales for the confession markets, real articles, and two books.

Then, in 1961, I graduated to a Smith Corona electric typewriter. The transition was terrible. By now, the Underwood was my best friend, and I felt I had heartlessly abandoned it—so I kept it, sitting beside the intruder. With the latter, I produced four more books. When two of those went from hardcover into paperback, I reluctantly delegated the Underwood to my eldest daughter. A couple of her friends knocked it over and smashed it to smithereens. Farewell, old friend.

I continued with the Smith Corona. One brief stint of 9-to-5 work set me to lusting for an IBM Selectric; when I had that machine for my own, the world had better stand back. Still, the Smith Corona continued to serve me well. Then, my son presented me with an IBM Selectric. I relegated the Smith Corona to a guest room.

The moment of modern truth came when I read an item in our ASJA membership newsletter: electronic-phobia folks, nitwits who are terrified of new gadgets, it said, this is the one for you. "This" was the Smith Corona Personal Word Processor System 14. I clipped the piece, hurried to my dealer, and bought the system. I can truthfully say that this little fellow is an angel, about as friendly as anything I have ever used. I love it. I recommend it wholeheartedly.

Have I bade farewell to my IBM? Hell, no. But then I'm not absolutely sure the world is really round, either.

—ELOISE ENGLE

IT'S A MIRACLE

I did *not* want to move into the twentieth century. They could keep their computers, word processors, bytes, and other arcane language to themselves. I was doing just fine, thank you. My trusty IBM Selectric and I were turning out more books and articles than anyone else I knew.

Then, my daughter got married—to a twentieth-century machine freak, my luck, and he couldn't stand my stubbornness. He actually bought me, without asking, a Smith Corona Personal Word Processing System 14 with XE 6200 typewriter. I said thank you but was quietly anguished, terrified. It sat in its box for months.

One day, I got curious.

The thing is terrific. My life has changed. You do not have to be an MIT graduate to work it. It does everything I need. I can move stuff around on the page. I can delete. And I adore the "Insert" button. It's like a regular typewriter, except that the words come out on a science-fiction-type screen and it respectfully beeps if you misspell a word. And when you press the "Print" button, gorgeous printed pages come out of the place where you insert paper in a regular typewriter.

It's a miracle!

—SHERRY SUIB COHEN

NOT EXACTLY, BUT IT'S A REAL GREAT FLY SWATTER

For years, I longed for a computer, but big prices and complex instruction manuals intimidated me. And from my timid talks with salespeople or computer experts, it seemed to me that if I bought a fancy machine with loads of filing capacity and almost endless methods of communication and printing, I would really be buying an elephant gun when a fly swatter would be more appropriate. I make a good living at writing, and I do it 50 hours a week, but I don't churn out stuff at such a rate that a few moments saved on a computer would mean my salvation.

I found my solution in an easy-to-use, inexpensive dedicated word processor, the Smith Corona Personal Word Processing System 14. It consists of a simple screen that sits atop a box containing a single disk drive, and it has a large "mouse" [control device] that offers the following functions: menu, search, correct, insert, page end, stop code, and cursor control. There is also a button that instantly converts the attached XE 6000 printer (with a Spell Right dictionary) into a typewriter. In fact, the printer *looks* like a typewriter, and it functions as such when commanded to do so; at another command, it rolls out what has just appeared on the screen.

The screen meets my needs: It's easy to read, big enough to see well. And this is a WYSIWYG system (What You See Is What You Get). The machine handles simple formatting, all the functions listed above, and can do underlining and a few other tricks to make a manuscript look nice for an editor.

Best of all, the PWP is easy to use—*very* easy. It took about five minutes to scan the directions and get started. In the beginning, it had a nasty habit of "freezing" and refusing to accept commands. (I lost some pages and went nuts, as one normally does under such circumstances.) But my friendly around-the-corner PWP dealer hustled over and fixed things. If you don't have a friendly dealer, you can still get the machine fixed easily at the place where you bought it; compared to big computers, this baby is a cinch to transport and to tinker with.

The price is more good news: It cost me $500 for the screen and $300 for the printer/typewriter. At that rate, I could—and did—buy a set for my teenagers and an extra typewriter for myself.

Of course, there are times when I wish I had an elephant gun, and times when the printer's relatively slow pace is infuriating. At some later date, I may indeed switch to a computer. But I've resisted so far, letting ease and convenience keep me away from complications and expense. This little fly swatter of a word processor is working well for me, thank you.

—MAXINE ROCK

CONFESSION OF A TECHNOPHOBE

Until recently, all my writing was done on a "truck"—a heavyweight Olympia manual typewriter—or, when on the go, on a lightweight Underwood portable. All the enthusiastic words of encouragement from fellow writers about the advantages of word processing could not assuage my technophobia, a dread of computers and electronic devices that threatened my control of my writing instrument. I felt comfortable only when using a machine that felt like a typewriter and fed out paper I could hold in my hand to make revisions.

For other writers who feel that way, let me recommend the Smith Corona 100 personal word processor. It is not a computer but a dedicated system, complete unto itself, that works like a typewriter, prints like a typewriter, and enables you to make unlimited corrections while you store your golden words on a disk like a real computer.

It actually makes writing fun: You can fool around with ideas; check them out on a page-size screen that hooks up with the typewriter keyboard; and, if you don't like what you've written, erase them and try something else. *You remain in control.* It's a snap to learn to use the system, and there's an 800 number you can call for instant help if you need it.

In just a few months, I've used this system to write a book, two major articles, and dozens of letters. The thing even corrects my spelling errors, something of an affront to my professional image but nevertheless a welcome editing tool. And it can store an entire book on a disk.

Its suggested retail price, at this writing, is $899, but it can be had for well under that at stores everywhere.

—ARTHUR HENLEY

MORE THAN SATISFACTORY, DESPITE DRAWBACKS

In June 1987, we bought a Smith Corona Personal Word Processing System 14 (with the XE 6100 electronic typewriter) from 47th Street Photo in New York; we paid $600 plus shipping charges. Except for one suspenseful mishap, the rig has proved more than satisfactory.

In late October of that year, our attempts to retrieve text filed on disks began to fail. Of course, the 90-day warranty had by then expired. A local dealer diagnosed the problem as a failed shield and reported that it was a malady the store had found in roughly half the PWPs it had sold.

We were referred by the people at Smith Corona's toll-free number to the nearest factory-authorized service center. We left the machine there and were told there'd be a minimum $59.95 charge. Before we departed on a scheduled three-week trip, we wrote to Smith Corona pointing out that, despite the expired warranty, the problem had been caused by a design defect and we felt the firm ought to do the reasonable thing and absorb the cost of the repair. We picked up the repaired machine when we returned from our trip; there was no charge. The gear has worked indefatigably ever since.

SCM no longer makes the PWP 14 (it may be available on the secondhand market), but the firm states that it will support this model with spare parts and service indefinitely.

Two drawbacks should be mentioned.

Many computer owners now carry laptop (as opposed to desktop) versions of their machines on trips; information is easily transferred from them to their stay-at-home counterparts. We thought of getting a more portable PWP to use when we travel. Alas, the portable PWP 6 doesn't use the same disks as the sedentary PWP 14, so it would be idle to take along the manuscripts we've got cooking, except as printouts. Too bad, that incompatibility. But we might still get the compact one for in-transit and far-away work.

And some editors now want manuscripts delivered electronically—i.e., on a disk that works on an IBM PC or compatible computer. One such editor agreed to accept our hard (paper) copy, planning to use an

OCR (Optical Character Recognition) scanner to digitalize our prose, but our fee for the assignment was lower than it might otherwise have been. Another approached us with an assignment but withdrew the offer after learning that we could not deliver the text on a PC-compatible disk.

—HENRY and ELIZABETH URROWS

SOME OF US GREW UP SPEAKING TYPEWRITER

Have you noticed that many business letters arrive, these days, addressed *by hand?* The reason is that some small businesses (and some fellow writers) have converted to computer-run word processing cold turkey, chucking the trusty typewriter out along with the correction fluid and carbon paper.

As a full-time writer who has had both a computer and a typewriter for seven years, my advice is to hang on to that typewriter. The most obvious reason is those envelopes and mailing labels; it's difficult and inconvenient to address one or two envelopes or labels on most computer printers, so many of us just don't bother. But I've been told by a friend who works part time at the post office that envelopes with typed addresses generally get delivered a day or two faster than handwritten ones. They also look more professional—a plus for any freelance writer.

The typewriter can also come in handy when you need to type something short—a note, a recipe—and don't want to bother booting up [starting] the computer, turning on the printer, inserting disks. I use my typewriter, too, for some first and intermediate drafts of particularly difficult work; perhaps it's because I grew up speaking typewriter as my second language, but it still works better for me for some tasks than any electronic marvel.

My favorite typewriter is the factory-reconditioned IBM Correcting Selectric II I bought twelve years ago (for $1200). I am a very good typist, and of the dozens of typewriters I have used, this is the best. It has a keyboard that is still the standard for all keyboards. The correcting feature is simple to use and makes nearly as light work of typos as a word processor. The machine stands up to the heaviest use; mine has typed three to five drafts of ten books, plus innumerable articles, letters, and journal entries. When I was using it exclusively, I used to have it cleaned and serviced about once a year; now, I get it checked out every two or three years. It is so well made that hardly anything ever goes wrong.

Unfortunately, the Selectric II hasn't been made for years (electronic typewriters, which are not nearly so good, seem to be all one can buy these days). Nevertheless, I understand that reconditioned Selectrics are still to be found. Mine still has, and will continue to have, an honored place in my office.

—KATHRYN LANCE

IF ALL ELSE FAILS

I strongly recommend keeping a manual typewriter up on a closet shelf, for those times when something absolutely, positively must be done by tomorrow and your electric typewriter or your computer has died or your area has suffered a blackout (yes, it happened to me). You will forgive all the months and years it sat there, taking up precious space, when it comes through for you in a magic monent.

—DIANA BENZAIA

■ ■ ■

My computer is on the Formica-topped counter I call a desk. My IBM Correcting Selectric II is immediately behind me, perched on two two-drawer file cabinets, and is used for, yes, envelopes, labels, and notes on my 4¼- by 5½-inch memo sheets. In its case (it is called "portable," although it is the weight of a small sixth-grader) beneath a table is the latter's predecessor, a lethargic but serviceable Adler Satellite 2001. (The Selectric could falter.) And because a blackout has happened to me, too, in a dark corner under the far end of the counter, clothed in a dust cover, is an ancient Royal no-electricity-needed standard office manual. A couple of working flashlights and a supply of candles couldn't hurt, either.   —D.S.

REFLECTIONS:
QUESTIONS
OF
TIME

The times, of course, do change. Writers, like others, must adapt. Some do so with alacrity, others with anxiety, still others with a little bit of both. Here, two writers reflect on their craft and on the tools they choose to employ. And, in different ways, on the tyranny of time.

THE MARQUAND WAY

William Faulkner wrote with fine pens in tiny letters. Hemingway stood at a high desk and wrote with pencils on a yellow legal tablet. Malcolm Lowry also wrote standing up, leaning on his left hand so that, over the years, it actually became deformed (he never wrote anything good after *Under the Volcano,* anyway). John P. Marquand stood up, too, but in his own patrician way; pacing in his handsome office, he dictated those marvelous upper-crust novels to a Bostonian lady sitting at a typewriter.

These writing habits presuppose having great blocks of time. Lee Smith, author of several delightful novels, once remarked on the particular people who could write only on yellow pads with number two pencils and commented that she had written most of her prose while waiting for her kids at swimming meets or soccer games.

Many other successful women writers have told of getting started between household chores. An anthropological explanation of women's superiority in using time may be that, over the years, they have often been called upon to attend to a multiplicity of tasks while men were out on single-minded forays. Before *You'll Love My Mother* made her rich and famous, Naomi Hintze said, "I used to write on the kitchen table between diaper changes, like everybody else."

The ability to write in small snatches of time is not exclusive to women, of course. Bob Considine, the well-known sports writer and author, used to write his books between innings. James D. Horan commuted for many years between his home in New Jersey and a job in New York; he wrote some forty books on the Hoboken Ferry. The prolific Richard Gehman always carried his typewriter with him; Dick once wrote an entire article (and finished off an entire bottle of whiskey) on a drive from Los Angeles to Las Vegas (the Society's first president, Maurice Zolotow, was at the wheel).

I am inclined to Marquand's approach, with modern improvements. I dictate into a microphone, sitting down, as I look out the window at the trees and the birds. A nice young person, not necessarily Bostonian, types it or word-processes it for me. I review and edit it, again sitting down, with my headphones bringing me Mozart.

—BOOTON HERNDON

THE ELECTRONIC COTTAGE

When I bought my first computer in 1980, I stepped rather cautiously into the world of technology, wondering whether it would be a boon or an expensive bust. It didn't take me long to discover just how incredibly advantageous technology can be.

Today, my home office is a veritable "electronic cottage" (the term was coined by another ASJA member, futurist Alvin Toffler), filled with all kinds of gear that takes the drudgery out of writing and enables me to communicate instantly with sources and clients anywhere in the world. I now spend an average of $3000 a year to keep up to date technologically.

At this writing, my equipment includes an IBM-compatible Tandy 1000 SX personal computer, which I've owned for two years and plan to replace soon; *Microsoft Word* 4.0 word-processing software; a daisy-wheel printer which will, in the near future, be succeeded by a faster and quieter Hewlett-Packard laser printer; a Canon PC-10 copier (it's wonderful to be able to make copies right here in my office, rather than trekking four blocks to the nearest copy shop); a Panafax UF-150 fax machine, which I use to send copies of text, back-up materials, and other documents to clients, as well as to receive materials from them (this instantaneous communication has greatly reduced my reliance on messengers and the mails); a phone-answering machine; a second, separate phone line, connected to my fax machine and also used for computer transmissions; a television and VCR to view videos of speeches and other resource materials.

Why am I so hooked on technology? One reason is increased productivity. Using this equipment, I can write faster and earn more money. Moreover, by making the process of writing less laborious, technology has freed my creativity and, I'm convinced, made me a better writer.

But another reason, not so obvious though equally important, is that technology helps me win key assignments and charge higher fees. Many of my writing assignments are for corporations—executive speeches, marketing materials, annual reports, and so on. In this area, it's critical to keep pace. I can charge clients more not only because of my writing skill but also because my equipment is technologically compatible with theirs and I can, therefore, better serve their needs.

Through this combination of more assignments and higher fees, technology has increased my annual income by perhaps 50 percent, paying for itself many times over. Here's a recent example:

A company in the Midwest, several hundred miles from my office in New York, was trying to fend off a hostile takeover. The company president wanted to send a letter to employees assuring them that their jobs were safe, and he wanted to distribute the letter that very day. I received a telephone call at 8 A.M. asking me to take on the assignment.

I interviewed the president by phone to find out what he wanted to say, completed a first draft by about 10 A.M., and immediately faxed it to my client. My phone rang fifteen minutes later; it was the company's public relations director, with comments on the draft. The PR director and I then worked together over the next few hours, talking by phone and sending drafts back and forth by fax. The fourth and final draft was approved at 2:30 P.M.

That approved version of the letter was in my computer. Using my Smartcom software and modem, I transmitted it to the PR director's computer—faster and simpler than having the letter retyped at the company's offices. The letter was then printed out by the company, reproduced, and distributed to employees before the end of the day.

A drawback of technology is, of course, that it lacks the human element. Free-lance writing is, by nature, an isolating way of life, and technology tends to make it more so, substituting electronic communications for face-to-face contact. Although I still get out of my office quite regularly, the long-term hazard seems to be that technology could turn me into a recluse—a prospect I intend to resist. In addition, because clients know of my technological capabilities, they often demand shorter deadlines and near-instantaneous responses. My work has become far more fast-paced and pressured—the flip side of the higher-fees coin.

I regret these negative aspects of technology but, on balance, I find it a tremendous benefit. Technology has revolutionized the business of free-lance writing, enabling me to work better, smarter, and more creatively.

—RICHARD BLODGETT

6

THE
WRITER'S
BOOKSHELF

Prominent attorneys and famous writers are always photographed against a background of books. The lawyer's books are typically ranks of identically bound volumes containing, one supposes, all the laws ever passed and cases ever decided in that attorney's state or specialty. The writer's books are a motley assortment, not always neatly arranged, and slightly out of focus. What are they? The author's own words? Competitors' titles?

Perhaps they're the books to which that particular writer frequently turns for help and guidance (or just for a hop, skip, and frolic in the endlessly fascinating world of little-known facts and lexicographic lore)—the sort of references recommended here.

Needless to say (it *should* be needless, anyway), the works singled out in this chapter are simply special favorites of the contributors. The cited titles do not by any means represent the writers' entire reference libraries. (*Note:* Some works may be available in later editions than those cited.)

THE WELL-DRESSED MANUSCRIPT

You wouldn't show up for an interview for a highly desirable job dressed in unsuitable clothing, would you? Yet many writers present their work to editors in inappropriate "dress." Unfortunately, the first impression may be the last look, and a worthwhile project may be quickly tossed on the rejection pile.

Two talented veteran writers [and ASJA members], Dian Dincin Buchman and Seli Groves, have created *The Writer's Digest Guide to Manuscript Formats* (Writer's Digest Books). It describes how to prepare and present book manuscripts, magazine articles, short stories, cover letters, proposals, queries, poems, plays, film and TV scripts—any kind of presentation you can imagine. The authors not only provide precise specifications; they also offer examples, as well as suggested work sheets and logs.

This book, with its detailed instructions, is valuable not only to writers hoping to be published for the first time but to professionals who can pick up additional pointers.

—RUTH WINTER

PICTURE DICTIONARIES

What's What: A Visual Glossary of Everyday Objects—from Paper Clips to Passenger Ships, edited by Reginald Bragonier, Jr. and David Fisher (Ballantine, paperback), is an indispensable helper for anyone trying to write descriptive prose. Trying to walk a reader through the steps required to service a bus, for example, or to follow the action of a lacrosse game, becomes a formidable challenge to those without firsthand knowledge of the nomenclature. The book is also handy for technical writers, because it gives the names for generic components of all sorts of commonplace machines and devices. As a cover blurb says: "Now, if you know what it looks like, you can find out what it's called."

—MARVIN J. WOLF

■ ■ ■

What's What is certainly an excellent reference source for our current, modern physical world. But if you want information about European culture, architecture, dress, lifestyles, music, art, etc., the English-language version of *Duden: Bildworterbuch* is the place to turn. It's known here as *The English Duden: A Pictorial Dictionary with English and German Indexes;* I bought my copy at a Crown bookstore. The publisher is Bibliographisches Institut AG, Mannheim. The book is also a treasure trove for the sciences, from atomic reactors to weather and geography, and is strong in such areas as graphic arts, mathematics, flora, and fauna.

—M. LAWRENCE PODOLSKY

WHO? WHERE?

If you have money and space for only two reference books, consider *Webster's Biographical Dictionary* and *Webster's New Geographical Dictionary*, both published by G. and C. Merriam. You'll find a brief answer, complete with pronouncing guide, to practically any question you might care to ask about a person or a place.

—LOUISE PURWIN ZOBEL

■ ■ ■

I have a current atlas, but I also have a number of "outdated" ones bought at second-hand sales. Old atlases can be helpful, because cities and countries change names and boundaries at the drop of a political hat.

—ANA MARCELO

AP AIDS FOR JOURNALISTS

The Associated Press has issued two guides that should be on every writer's desk. They are available in bookstores, or contact the AP at 50 Rockefeller Plaza, New York NY 10020; (212) 621-1500.

The Associated Press Stylebook and Libel Manual is where newspaper reporters and editors turn when they have questions about style. An A-to-Z listing giving guidance on capitalization, abbreviations, spelling, punctuation, and usage is followed by special guidelines applying to particular fields such as sports and business. The libel-manual section at the back of the book also covers the right of privacy.

The Word: An Associated Press Guide to Good Newswriting is a 163-page companion to the stylebook, covering such subjects as introductions, story organization, and the use of quotes. Author Jack Cappon, the AP's general news editor, offers sound advice for journalists and journalists to be.

—DAVE KAISER

■ ■ ■

Of the various stylebooks available, I lean toward the *Associated Press Stylebook and Libel Manual.* Its alphabetical listing includes guides to capitalization, numerals, and all those little things that make your writing comprehensible to your readers.

—DOROTHY SIEGEL

THE ENCYCLOPEDIAS

I couldn't manage without my full set of the *World Book Encyclopedia.* It's not a new set by any means, but updating hasn't seemed necessary, since what you're usually looking for is something so general that an older encyclopedia covers it. I find this encyclopedia clearly written, cleanly designed, and marvelously accessible. Pick one up at a used book sale. It will pay for itself quickly.

—BONNIE REMSBERG

■ ■ ■

My favorite encyclopedia is the eleventh (1910) edition of the *Encyclopaedia Britannica;* it has a wealth of classical material which was omitted from later editions. On a smaller scale, I couldn't be without *The New Columbia Encyclopedia* (Columbia University Press), an excellent one-volume reference. It is often discounted by book clubs as an entry gift or dividend; grab it when you can.

—DIAN DINCIN BUCHMAN

LITERARY LODE

Benet's Reader's Encyclopedia (Harper & Row) is described as the "classic and only encyclopedia of world literature in a single volume." It is just that.

A 1965 edition of the book had been a valuable tool for me for many years, but several years ago, I began to find it sadly out of date. To my great disappointment, no new edition was to be found. Then, in 1987, I read in *Publishers Weekly* an announcement of what was, to me, a major publishing event: a new edition of *Benet's Reader's Encyclopedia.*

Priced at $35, the book lists poets, novelists, playwrights, important literary locations and events, as well as books, plays, and poems by title. The new edition also features large type, making it an easy book to use.

—KATE KELLY

REFERENCE REFERENCE

The New York Times Guide to Reference Materials is a handy aid to deciding where to start looking for information of various sorts.

—MARVIN J. WOLF

SCI/TECH/MEDICAL LEXICON AND LORE

The *McGraw-Hill Dictionary of Scientific and Technical Terms*, edited by Sybil P. Parker (third edition, 1984), is a large, relatively expensive volume, but it is one of the few science dictionaries that include terms from a variety of disciplines. A smaller, easier-to-read dictionary is *The Harper Dictionary of Science in Everyday Language*, by Herman Schneider and Leo Schneider (1988).

For writers new to science, a useful approach to an unfamiliar scientific word is to check an unabridged dictionary for a general definition before going on to a more specialized dictionary. To become familiar with science terminology, it's also helpful to read the weekly *Science News*, available in most libraries or by subscription. A number of the major metropolitan newspapers carry weekly sections devoted to science, and reading these sections regularly is useful, too.

—MARGARET DICANIO

■ ■ ■

As a medical writer, I frequently like to incorporate some historical aspects of the subject into my material. I've found a number of references helpful.

Source Book of Medical History, compiled with notes by Logan Clendening (Dover, 1960), is a wonderful book including original medical quotes ranging from Egyptian papyri (Kahun, Smith Ebers) to the announcement of the discovery of "A New Kind of Ray" by Wilhelm Conrad Roentgen. Sources include Homer, Hippocrates, Syndenham, Semmelweiss, and countless others.

In addition to the wonderful illustrations from the Bettmann Archive, *A Pictorial History of Medicine*, by Otto Bettmann (Thomas, 1962), has an amusing text. The material, again, starts with ancient Egypt and almost ends with Roentgen (it's the next-to-last entry); the material nevertheless complements that of the *Source Book*.

A Short History of Medicine, by Charles Singer and E. Ashwood Underwood (Claredon Press, 1962), is an extremely reliable reference.

It's not only fun to read but also provides birth and death dates for each scientist.

Familiar Medical Quotations, edited by M. B. Strauss (Little, Brown, 1968) arranges its contents by subject matter, ranging from "ability" to "youth." There is an author index as well as an index of first lines.

—SUZANNE LOEBL

■ ■ ■

I write a lot of health material. In addition to books on diseases, drugs, and treatments, a work I couldn't do without is *Dorland's Illustrated Medical Dictionary* (Saunders).

—DIAN DINCIN BUCHMAN

■ ■ ■

Asimov's Biographical Encyclopedia of Science and Technology, by Isaac Asimov (Equinox/Avon paperback, 1976), is a handy and readable reference to science history. Entries are arranged in chronological order, and each of the almost 1200 has a number; they range from #1, the Egyptian scholar Imhotep of the 2900s B.C., to #1195, astronomer Carl Sagan. An up-front alphabetical listing gives the number for each. There is also an index.

As with ordinary dictionaries, medical definitions may vary from one book to another (here, one definition may also be far clearer than another) and it's helpful to have more than one. I like *Dorland's,* but when I'm stumped by a medical term, I check both it and *Stedman's Medical Dictionary* (Williams & Wilkins).   —D.S.

RUNNING THE NUMBERS

At some time or other, most nonfiction writers will have to deal with the correct presentation of statistics. If you write about medicine, politics, economics, or the environment, it's probably inevitable, and it's becoming hard to avoid in many other fields of human endeavor. Help is at hand.

News and Numbers: A Guide to Reporting Statistical Claims and Controversies in Health and Related Fields, by former *Washington Post* Science Editor Victor Cohn, is an understandable, level-headed pathfinder through the numbers thicket. Published in 1989 by Iowa State University Press, it's a project of the Center for Health Communication at the Harvard School of Public Health and is available in paperback.

—VIC COX

■ ■ ■

Another useful and readable reference is *Statistics: Concepts and Controversies,* by David S. Moore (W.H. Freeman, paperback, 1979), which is enlivened by the author's relating statistical principles to the sort of reports one sees and hears daily in the media, as well as a sprinkling of amusing cartoons. Unlike some earlier works, it does not require grounding in higher mathematics.

And when you're looking for statistics to quote—in fields ranging from population to industrial production, from education to energy—look into the annually updated *Statistical Abstract of the United States,* published by the Bureau of the Census of the U.S. Department of Commerce. It can be purchased from the U.S. Government Printing Office, Washington DC 20402, as well as federal bookstores and Department of Commerce district offices.   —D.S.

ME? PRODUCE A NEWSLETTER?

Newsletters are "hot" today; thousands of them, both corporate and nonprofit, are being turned out, many by free-lance writers. Although such work can be both interesting and lucrative, writers often haven't the foggiest idea how to produce a newsletter.

Editing Your Newsletter: How to Produce an Effective Publication Using Traditional Tools and Computers, by Mark Beach, is just what the novice newsletter editor needs. Using jargon-free language, the author walks the reader through the entire publication process: headline-writing, effective sentence and paragraph lengths, type styles, graphic design, dealing with printers, etc. Abundant illustrations depicting designs and formats suggest what you should use and why. The pros and cons of desktop-publishing techniques are also covered, with specific information about computers, software, and printers. This large-format paperback could make you a newsletter professional.

The 1988 edition (the first, precomputer edition appeared in 1981) is $18.50 plus $4 for postage and handling and may be ordered from Coast to Coast Books, 2934 Northeast Sixteenth Avenue, Portland OR 97212; (503) 282-5891.

—PAMELA HOBBS HOFFECKER

THE WRITER AND THE LAW

The thing that has saved me untold aggravation, as well as fair sums of money, throughout the years is not a machine, a device, or a gadget; it is, appropriately, a book. *Author Law and Strategies: A Legal Guide for the Working Writer,* by Brad Bunnin and Peter Beren (Nolo Press, first edition 1983, but updated as the law changes) belongs on every writer's shelf. It should be consulted before negotiating any important deal even if you have an agent, and even if the agent is also a lawyer. It helps you to frame your questions, curb your fears and, above all, set realistic expectations.

In plain, understandable English, this book examines every aspect of the publishing contract for both books and magazines, using lucid (and funny) examples and a sprinkling of cartoons to lighten the reader's way. It also looks at the current status of defamation law, the right to privacy, and the intricacies of copyright. It explains when you need a lawyer and how to find one. It examines the business of publishing. It discusses pivotal relationships in writers' lives—with their collaborators, their agents, their publishers. Finally, it is loaded with sample agreements you can copy, letters you can adapt, and government forms and applications neatly executed so you will be able to do the same.

Legal problems can bedevil writers in all sorts of ways, ranging from late royalty checks to reprint rights, option clauses, rejected manuscripts, and major lawsuits for libel. This volume is a how-to book that will clarify, instruct, and help put your business on a sound footing.

—DENISE SHEKERJIAN

■ ■ ■

The Journalist's Handbook On Libel & Privacy, by Barbara Dill (Free Press), is a series of case studies drawn from the author's years of advising newspapers and magazines on these issues. It makes good reading even if you're not trying to figure out how to call a filthy spade a dirty shovel without getting sued, and it will also serve as a good basic course for all journalists who have to confront issues of libel or invasion of privacy in their work.

—MARVIN J. WOLF

THIS THESAURUS, THAT THESAURUS . . .

As poets feel about Grecian urns, so I feel about my first encounter with a thesaurus as a child. Wow! This was truly a treasure trove. I found I could expand my vocabulary in an instant—yes, yes, that's exactly the word I'm looking for! Thus did my lifelong passion for thesauri begin. But in the way of youth, I met up with the best, discarded it, and then "came home" again.

My first discovery was the "original" *Roget's*. But it is organized in a very idiosyncratic way. So when I came across the "new" dictionary-style version, I thought I had it made. I rashly threw away my worn-out oldie. Over the years, I have purchased other dictionary-organized thesauri, and on my shelf I can reach for the Norman Lewis edition of *The New Roget's Thesaurus in Dictionary Form* (Putnam), *The Double-day Roget's Thesaurus in Dictionary Form,* and the wonderful *Webster's Collegiate Thesaurus* (Merriam). I sometimes use all three, since there are differences in the selection of words offered.

But a few years ago, I started to crave the old-fashioned, non-dictionary thesaurus again. I wanted the phrases, the completeness, the sumptuous servings. I scoured the flea markets and second-hand bookstores and finally found *Roget's International Thesaurus* (Crowell, fifth printing, 1949).

What's the difference? In the dictionary style, you get synonyms (in some instances, also antonyms) as you look up the word in its alphabetical place, as in a dictionary. In the older style, you start with the index. Under the word, you find a list of related words and phrases, each with a number that leads you to a particular section of the book; such a section may be not just a few lines but a lengthy discussion. As an example: Under "remedy" in the index, there are multiple references, the number of one of which, "cure," leads to a section that runs two and a half pages and contains no less than 27 full-paragraph entries.

In addition to this thoroughness, Roget placed relevant quotations at the bottom of every page. One that accompanies the example cited is Franklin's "God heals, and the doctor takes the fee."

—DIAN DINCIN BUCHMAN

■ ■ ■

The Crowell edition of *Roget's International Thesaurus* had always been my stalwart synonym standby. But recently, I discovered another—*The St. Martin's Roget's Thesaurus.* I believe it to be superior.

The St. Martin's is more thorough, the index is fuller, and there are more synonyms. The jacket copy announces that this is "the best thesaurus in the world" and claims further that the book "has more entries, more conveniently and usefully arranged, printed in larger, blacker type on larger, whiter paper." I am in complete agreement with all of the publisher's self-praise.

—HELEN WORTH

■ ■ ■

I have a treasured copy of the 1936 hardcover edition of *The New Roget's Thesaurus In Dictionary Form,* edited by Norman Lewis, and a dog-eared paperback edition published sometime post-1946. Even now that I've got a good thesaurus on my computer, it doesn't have everything, and I still pull one of these out every once in a while.

—JUDI K-TURKEL

■ ■ ■

For years, I've used, depended upon, and benefitted from *March's Thesaurus-Dictionary;* my edition was published in 1958 under the editorial supervision of Norman Cousins. For me, it stands above other thesauruses both because of its exhaustive list of synonyms and antonyms and because of its multiple references for a single word, reflecting slight changes in meaning. "Flat," for example, is included in sixteen listings, among them "adept/bungler," where "flat" means "dunce," and "refuge/pitfall," where "flat" means "shoal."

—JOHN H. INGERSOLL

■ ■ ■

Still another work that can usefully complement your *Roget's* is *The Merriam-Webster Thesaurus* (Wallaby Books/Simon & Schuster paperback, 1980).   —D.S.

. . . AND MORE FINE WORD FINDERS

Among my reference books, I especially treasure *The Word Finder* and *The Synonym Finder.* The latter is called upon for just about every piece I write. When I'm not writing, which is hardly ever, it's fun to read, with fourteen synonyms for the word "cat." Both books are published by Rodale.

—JOAN BARTHEL

■ ■ ■

For looking up synonyms and antonyms, I use a paperback edition of *The New American Roget's College Thesaurus.* But if a nebulous thought is rolling around in my head and I need something to stimulate a certain idea or expression, I find *The Word Finder,* a huge book compiled and edited by J.I. Rodale, a great help. Words are listed alphabetically, with each followed by a list of adverbs, adjectives, and verbs that can be used with it; some listings go on for two or three columns. By the time you've gone through such a list, you're almost sure to come across the one special word that suggests the very thought you wanted to express.

—BERNICE CURLER

■ ■ ■

I have found *The Synonym Finder,* by J.I. Rodale (hardcover published by Rodale Press, softcover by Warner Books), to be invaluable. It's much more thorough than any thesaurus I've ever seen, because its entries are much more complete and detailed. The synonyms offered include everything from current slang to scientific terms, and it's not unusual for entries to go on for half a column or more. It has never failed me.

—KATY KOONTZ

■ ■ ■

As a contributing editor to a Rodale Press publication, *Runner's World,* one of the most valuable perks I've enjoyed is a copy of that publisher's reference work *The Synonym Finder.* A 1361-page work, it offers synonyms of everything from aback (rearward, behind, hindward) to zoom (buzz, whiz, zing). Using a book to find synonyms is no substitute for good writing, but it sometimes helps move you when you're stuck.

—HAL HIGDON

■ ■ ■

The best thesaurus I've found is *The Synonym Finder,* by J.I. Rodale (Warner, 1978). Listings are more current and reflect contemporary American usage better than *Roget's* does, and it is far more comprehensive than any of the skimpy Webster's efforts. It comes in paperback and hardcover.

—VICKY HAY

SYNONYMS PLUS SAMPLES

The second most useful reference book I've found, next to a good dictionary, is *Webster's New Dictionary of Synonyms* (Merriam). Unlike the standard thesaurus and similar works, this book provides definitions and examples for closely related words, enabling a writer to use words precisely. The definitions include special applications and shades of meaning; the examples are quotes from outstanding writers.

New writers in composition classes I've taught find this book the most useful tool for identifying "the right word for the job." When I was starting out, I nearly wore out a library copy. Now I keep my own close at hand.

—ERICH HOYT

ON USAGE AND STYLE

Strunk & White's *Elements of Style* belongs on every writer's desk, true. But I find the late Theodore M. Bernstein equally helpful, especially *The Careful Writer: A Modern Guide to English Usage.* Bernstein, who was assistant managing editor of the *New York Times* and a consultant to major dictionary publishers, was witty and smack on target when it came to advice on precise, colorful, vivid writing. I don't own them, but I've also perused his *Watch Your Language* and *More Language That Needs Watching* and enjoyed them, too.

—DOROTHY SIEGEL

■ ■ ■

When writers are asked to recommend books on the craft of writing, we typically come up with Strunk & White. But I think that *The Golden Book On Writing,* by David Lambuth and others (Penguin), is far superior as an introduction to the craft. First published in 1923 and updated in 1964 with a new chapter on business writing, it is neither old hat nor a business-writing manual but a wonderfully lucid guide, just right for the beginner or for someone who needs to get back on track after trying to make sense of others' meandering prose. This book isn't just about writing; it's about thinking clearly, and God knows we need more of that.

—SHANNON MOFFAT

■ ■ ■

My editor at Dutton once told me she rereads *Elements of Style,* by William Strunk, Jr. and E.B. White, at least once a year. This slim book contains elementary rules of usage, principles of composition, forms, expressions, and a pithy approach to style. Buy it. Read it. Reread it.

But much as I like Strunk & White, I think the Penguin paperback *The Golden Book On Writing,* by David Lambuth, is even better. As

Budd Shulberg says in the foreword to the 1964 edition, it's a book short on pages but long on insights.

Writers should also discover the late Theodore Bernstein. Among his many books are *The Careful Writer: A Modern Guide to English Usage* and *Miss Thistlebottom's Hobgoblins: The Careful Writer's Guide to the Taboos, Bugbears and Outmoded Rules of English Usage.* Everything Bernstein says about language is pithy, interesting, and useful.

And the book *every* writer should have is the great and dependable *Chicago Manual of Style* (University of Chicago Press, 13th edition, 1982). Almost everyone in publishing uses it as *the* authority. It has everything from a list of proofreading marks to advice on preparing a manuscript and includes details on punctuation, names, terms, numbers, quotations, and footnotes.

—DIAN DINCIN BUCHMAN

■ ■ ■

Other style and usage commentaries writers may find inspiring: Wilson Follett's *Modern American Usage* (Hill & Wang, 1966), which was edited and completed by Jacques Barzun in collaboration with half a dozen others after Follett's death; *The Reader Over Your Shoulder,* by Robert Graves and Alan Hodge (second edition, Vintage trade paperback, 1979); *Paradigms Lost,* by John Simon (Penguin trade paperback, 1981); *A Word or Two Before You Go,* by Jacques Barzun (Wesleyan University Press, 1986); any of the several compilations of William Safire's "On Language" columns from the *New York Times Magazine* (Times Books). —D.S.

IN PRAISE OF VERBAL PANDICULATION

"Inspissate" means what? Thicken, of course. How about "abbozzo"? That's a rough preliminary sketch. And "pandiculation"? The act of stretching oneself. All, from one of the more useful and amusing books on my reference shelf: *A Dictionary of Difficult Words,* compiled by Robert H. Hill (Philosophical Library; my edition, 1959). Almost half its listings are not to be found in the more popular desktop dictionaries. It's worth searching for in the stacks of your neighborhood second-hand bookshop.

—JACK COOK

■ ■ ■

I Always Look Up the Word "Egregious," by Maxwell Nurnberg (Prentice-Hall, paperback, 1981), is described as "A Vocabulary Book for People Who Don't Need One." It's a lively read for those who want to use more of their expensively acquired vocabularies but have trouble remembering how to employ (and spell) those high-priced words.

—MARVIN J. WOLF

PURSUIT OF TRIVIA

Whenever I need a lead on an article and haven't an idea where to start, I turn to one of my trivia books, such as Isaac Asimov's *2001 Amazing Facts,* and that usually starts something perking. There are many such books; I pick them up at second-hand bookstores.

—DALE RONDA BURG

CREATIVITY TIPS

Writing Down the Bones, by Natalie Goldberg (Shambhala Publications, 1986), is a gem. The subtitle, "Freeing the Writer Within," says it all. This remarkable little book is full of ideas to help writers be more creative. As Judith Guest (author of *Ordinary People*) says in her introduction, "In this collection of sane and clear-hearted observations on writing, along with its solid, practical tips, there is a vitality that sings and an honesty that makes me want to cry. This is the way writing feels when it is good."

—SALLY WENDKOS OLDS

■ ■ ■

If you tend (as I do) to be a very organized, decisive, clear-thinking, linear writer, your work (like my work) may be missing a whole world of intuitive, connotative, evocative expression. You may do a beautiful job of writing how-to and travel pieces without ever quite breaking the barrier into the highest quality nonfiction—work like Annie Dillard's, Joan Didion's, or Tracy Kidder's.

Gabriele Lusser Rico's *Writing the Natural Way* (J.P. Tarcher, 1983) is a great help in adding layers of meaning to your writing. I take a skeptical view of the simplistic way some current writers are characterizing the right-brain, left-brain division. But Rico's methods for getting at the nonlinear, "pre-writing" parts of writing are excellent. Her technique of "clustering" is particularly valuable, and I use it to explore the possibilities of my research before putting my ideas into a linear outline.

—LEE JOLLIFFE

TRAVELING THROUGH HISTORY

For a quick review of any material in American history that you need to check (through the late 1970s), nothing beats the *Encyclopedia of American History*, edited by Richard B. Morris et al. (sixth edition, Harper & Row, 1982). It includes both a basic chronological section and a topical chronological section, as well as biographies of 300 notable Americans.

—JAMES P. JOHNSON

■ ■ ■

For those of us with no memory for dates, two invaluable cribs are published by Simon & Schuster: *Timetables of American History* and *Timetables of World History*. They display major events year by year under such headings as "Politics" and "Science and Technology" and offer a quick, handy way of checking names, dates, and events. The editions available at this writing end their review of history around 1978 and so often can be found heavily discounted in the Barnes & Noble and other catalogs.

—DAVID BOUCHIER

■ ■ ■

Those of us who write historical travel material find a good historical atlas and historical handbook indispensable for quick reference. The *Atlas of World History*, edited by R.R. Palmer (Rand McNally), and *The New Century Classical Handbook*, edited by Catherine B. Avery (Appleton-Century-Crofts), make a good pair.

—LOUISE PURWIN ZOBEL

JUST FOR A SPELL

Before there were computer programs that could spell-check a document, there were spelling dictionaries. Fortunately, they still exist.

Fifteen years ago, I was given the pocket-sized *Instant Spelling Dictionary*, which lists 25,000 words for spelling reference. The book also indicates how words should be broken into syllables and accented (no definitions are given). Over the years, the book has provided a speedy way of checking words; even now, when I don't have my computer whirring, I turn to it for easy reference. It's a great timesaver.

To obtain the current edition, send $5.95 plus $1 shipping and handling (plus sales tax, for Illinois residents) to Career Publishing, Inc., 905 Allanson Road, Mundelein IL 60060.

—KATE KELLY

■ ■ ■

Although I have a great memory for faces, names, and events, I can't—perhaps won't—remember how to spell certain words. Fortunately, I have a sort of mental light bulb that (usually) goes on and signals "Check it!" If you share the spelling-lapse syndrome, you'll find a bonanza in *Words Most Often Misspelled and Mispronounced,* by Gallagher and Colvin (Pocket Books). I recommend it as an indispensable guide.

—DIAN DINCIN BUCHMAN

■ ■ ■

While most word-processing programs these days have a spelling checker, at least as an option, most will give you a correct spelling if what's on the screen is close—but if you're way off, forget about it. Also, there are times when I want to be alliterative but can't seem to think of an appropriate word beginning with the requisite letter.

To deal with these problems, I keep a common secretary's tool, *Webster's New World Wordbook,* next to my computer. It lists about 33,000 words, including some oddballs. There are no definitions, just words. In the back is a quick guide to punctuation and elementary grammar.

—MARVIN J. WOLF

■ ■ ■

A little book called *Webster's New World 33,000 Word Book* is invaluable. No definitions (you know what the word means, anyway, or you wouldn't be using it), just spellings. Keep it very close. It will save you from getting aggravated when you can't remember, for the hundredth time, whether "accessible" has an "i" or an "a."

—BONNIE REMSBERG

■ ■ ■

For a quick check of spelling, I use the *Instant Spelling Dictionary,* with 25,000 words spelled, divided, and accented. But if I don't know how to spell a word, how can I look it up? Then, I use *The Misspeller's Dictionary,* edited by Peter and Craig Norback (Times Books); it has over 20,000 words with their incorrect spellings in red and is designed for people who spell the way they hear. A similar book is the purse-sized *Webster's New World Misspeller's Dictionary,* with 15,000 words.

—BERNICE CURLER

SCHOLARLY HOW-TO

A writer faced with the rigors of scholarly citations, references, and bibliographies may find that *A Handbook for Scholars,* by Mary-Claire van Leunen (Alfred A. Knopf, 1985), eases the task of mastering those requirements. The author writes with such good humor that her book is fun to browse through even when not faced with scholarly trials.

—MARGARET DICANIO

IN TRANSLATION

My Spanish-English dictionary is nearly indispensable here in California. But as a writer, I find it helpful to have translation dictionaries for other European languages, too, as well as Russian, Tagalog, Hawaiian, and Japanese.

—ANA MARCELO

■ ■ ■

For foreign words, I use the *Seven Language Dictionary,* published by Avenel Books. It has translations for French, Italian, German, Russian, Hebrew, Portuguese, and Spanish.

—BERNICE CURLER

■ ■ ■

For spellings and meanings of foreign words and phrases, the *Dictionary of Foreign Phrases and Abbreviations,* compiled and translated by Kevin Guinagh (Pocket Books), is useful. It includes everything from *roman à clef*—a phrase you can casually drop if you decide to write about real people but give them fictitious names—to *quid pro quo,* something in exchange for something else. President George Bush used the latter no less than four times in one speech. "No, it was not *quid pro quo,*" quoth he.

—DIAN DINCIN BUCHMAN

ALL-PURPOSE WRITER'S REFERENCE

A book I've enjoyed, one that a writer can "grow up" with, from novice to professional, is *The Writer's Encyclopedia,* edited by Kirk Polking, Joan Bloss, and Colleen Cannon (Writer's Digest Books).

As with many one-volume, encyclopedia-style books, most of the entries are short and give an overview of the subject, but the editors have skillfully covered the high points of each topic and provided extensive cross-referencing. They have also thoughtfully included further sources of information whenever possible.

The more than 1200 listings range from the obvious ("unsolicited manuscript") to the obscure ("tautology") and cover the vocabulary and subjects found in the fields of free-lance writing, editing, advertising, broadcasting, film, lecturing, public relations, and more. There are also descriptions of writers' organizations, awards, business practices, and resources.

Undoubtedly the best part of the book is its appendix, filled with sample scripts, book contracts, query letters, book publication costs, copyright applications, and even a stress test for writers.

—JULIE CATALANO

QUOTE / UNQUOTE

In *The Writer's Quotation Book: A Literary Companion,* by James Charlton (Pushcart Press, 1980), the author says, "Writers love quotations. They love quoting someone else's work almost as much as they enjoy quoting their own." He goes on to note that a well-placed quotation "lends weight to one's own opinions by somehow invoking a higher authority."

I agree. As editor of *The Complete Guide to Writing Nonfiction,* another recent work by the Society (Harper & Row, 1988), I began the introduction with a quote from Thomas Carlyle stating that, "The man is most original who can adapt from the greatest number of sources." As a long-time writer and editor, I believe that. I also believe what C.E. Montague penned in *A Writer's Notes to His Trade:* "To be amused by what you read—that is the great spring of happy quotations."

Along with the customary basic references every writer must have— dictionary, thesaurus, encyclopedia, almanac, books on special areas of the craft of writing—I've found my twenty or so quotation books to be not merely interesting and entertaining but informative, educational, and practical. I can't tell you how often I've enlivened, and/or made a specific point in, an article or book passage by turning to my treasury of wise, witty, and engaging quote books.

So get yourself a few books of quotations—taking care not to overlook the latest edition of that indispensable standby, *Familiar Quotations,* by John Bartlett (Little, Brown; 15th edition, 1980)—and put some sparkle and zip in your writing life.

—GLEN EVANS

■ ■ ■

Own books of quotations, as many as you have space for. I keep seven within reach as I work. Quotes are useful creative tools for almost any project you might be working on, fiction or nonfiction. There's nothing like a good quote to hammer home a point, trigger a new line of thought, or qualify you as a scholar in the reader's perception. Appropriate quotes add a note of real authority to your prose.

—RAYMOND DREYFACK

■ ■ ■

One of my favorite reference books is *Dictionary of Quotations,* by the late Bergen Evans. Dr. Evans was one of my professors at Northwestern University, and I find his collection of quotes as delightful as he was as a lecturer.

—ELAINE FANTLE SHIMBERG

■ ■ ■

Consider haunting second-hand bookstores, or sending "search orders," to collect interesting quotation books. I don't mean just the standard (and essential) Bartlett's but other collections as well: *The Oxford Dictionary of Quotations* (Oxford University Press), *Dictionary of Quotations* (Delacorte), *The Penguin Dictionary of Quotations* (Atheneum), *Leo Rosten's Treasury of Jewish Quotations, The Great Quotations* (Pocket Books), and countless others. Buy new and old ones as you find them.

—DIAN DINCIN BUCHMAN

■ ■ ■

The 637 Best Things Anybody Ever Said, by Robert Byrne, is a wonderful three-volume collection of very short, witty quotes. I have the first volume in paper (Fawcett), the other two in hardcover (Atheneum).

—MARTY KLEIN

■ ■ ■

When I was writing executive speeches, I frequently needed a snappy and pertinent quote to augment my own words. I bought four books of quotations. I found one useful: *The Concise Oxford Dictionary of Quotations* (Oxford University Press, paperback, 1982). It utilizes both classical and modern sources. Do not confuse this title with another very like it, but minus the word "concise," from the same publisher; the latter is crammed with thousands of quotes, about 10 percent of which are usable.

—DAVID A. ANDERTON

■ ■ ■

The Great Quotations, compiled by George Seldes (Pocket Books, paperback, 1967), focuses on ideas and concepts and is arranged alphabetically by broad topics (from abolition to youth); there are both author and subject indexes.

Simpson's Contemporary Quotations, compiled by James B. Simpson (Houghton Mifflin, 1988), is limited to the years 1950 through 1987 and is an eclectic potpourri of nearly 10,000 items, including political salvos and advertising slogans, literary critiques and philosophical ruminations, inspiring sermons and quips from stand-up comics. The material is arranged in sections and subsections—e.g., the "Films" section is divided into "Actors & Actresses," "Writers, Producers & Directors," and "Observers & Critics"—with sources listed alphabetically within each subdivision. It's indexed by both sources and subjects/key lines. —D.S.

THE MOVIES

For any writer who specializes in—or would like to specialize in—show business, especially film, *Halliwell's Filmgoer's Companion* can be very helpful. It lists actors and actresses, directors, important producers, etc., with their credits, plus unions, guilds, and celebrated films such as *Citizen Kane* and *Day For Night.*

—DOROTHY SIEGEL

■ ■ ■

Guinness Film Facts and Feats, by Patrick Robertson, is a compendium of historical information on filmmaking and filmmakers; it was updated in 1985. It tells of the inventions that made movies possible, as well as the industry that grew up around them; scripts, performers, music, awards, and credits are covered, as are censorship and the exhibitors. Even television's impact on the movies, as well as the production of the first amateur films, are touched upon.

As might be expected in a book published by Guinness Superlatives Ltd. of Middlesex, there is a great deal of information on the British film industry as well as on Hollywood. Other European contributions are mentioned in passing.

—VIC COX

SPEAKING OF FOOD

Food has a language all its own, and if you're writing about it, it helps to know that *Veronique* denotes a dish made with grapes, and *Florentine* promises a bed of spinach. There are many fine reference books in the field. Among those I use frequently are the *Cook's & Diner's Dictionary* (Funk & Wagnall), *The Nutrition Desk Reference* (Keats), *Dictionary of Gastronomy* (McGraw-Hill), *Food In History* (Stein & Day), *A Concise Encyclopedia of Gastronomy* (Overlook Press), *Larousse Gastronomique* (Crown), *Nutritive Value of Foods in Common Units #456* (USDA) and, for a wonderful historical view, an antique copy of the original edition of the British classic, *Mrs. Beeton's Household Management,* which I picked up in London's used-books district.

—JUNE ROTH

WHICH DICTIONARY?

You'd expect that all dictionaries would define the same words in the same way—but they don't. It therefore pays to shop around among dictionaries for the one whose definitions fit your style of researching and your style of writing most closely.

Some dictionaries list the most current or dominant meaning first. Some provide definitions in chronological, historical order. Some pursue the byways, while others stick to the straight and narrow. And you'll find one dictionary presents its definitions in ways useful to the technologist, another in ways more useful to the romanticist.

Which is best? The real question is, Which is most helpful to *you?* Pick two or three words and compare the definitions in several dictionaries available in the bookstore in which you love to browse and buy. The comparison will be quickly revealing.

If you call on your dictionary just to confirm your recollection of meaning and spelling, a paperback version may do. If you have a real need to make distinctions; to understand a word; to pinpoint the exact, right word—better go to one of the solid hardcover volumes such as *Merriam Webster's Collegiate, Webster's New World, Random House,* or *American Heritage.*

Only if you're determined to track the meaning and spelling of a word to its lair should you choose the big, heavy unabridged volume. Why? You'll be fascinated, distracted, and seduced. You'll forget you went to the dictionary only for help, not for refuge.

And about this guy Noah Webster: He was the first to compile a popular American dictionary of the English language. But Webster died long before Congress passed the first copyright law, and any dictionary may emblazon the word "Webster" as part of its name.

—LOUIS ALEXANDER

■ ■ ■

I keep a dictionary handy wherever I might be writing or reading. On my desk is the *Oxford American Dictionary* (Oxford University Press); the words are in bold print and the definitions in type large enough to read easily. My next most used is *The Doubleday Dictionary for Home, School and Office;* the print is smaller, but there's seldom a word I can't find between its covers, and it has an easy punctuation reference in the front. For bedside reading, I keep on my nightstand a lightweight, easy-to-handle softcover edition of *The American Heritage Dictionary.*

—BERNICE CURLER

■ ■ ■

The New College Edition of *The American Heritage Dictionary of the English Language* is a manageable size for quick reference, but I also often consult the unabridged edition of *The Random House Dictionary of the English Language.*

—DIAN DINCIN BUCHMAN

■ ■ ■

The eighth edition of *Webster's New Collegiate Dictionary* (G. & C. Merriam, 1979) is much superior to the later editions; we suggest writers keep an eye out for it in second-hand bookstores.

—JUDI K-TURKEL and FRANKLYNN PETERSON

■ ■ ■

I rely on the *Oxford English Dictionary* for my nonfiction work much more than I ever imagined I would. It's amazing how many words I want to use are not in other dictionaries.

—LAURIE LISLE

FOR DICTIONARY JUNKIES

Most writers are dictionary junkies, and my bookshelf contains quite a collection. My favorite general-purpose one is *The American Heritage Dictionary of the English Language,* but just about any college-level tome will do fine. For a bit of fun, though, I recommend three other, more exotic items.

The New York Times Crossword Puzzle Dictionary, edited by Tom Pulliam and Clare Grundman, is a 685-page paperback gem. You can use it like a thesaurus; Roget won't tell you that a "beetle" is also a "tumblebug." Or you can use it as a minigazetteer or world almanac: Where else would you learn that in Czechoslovakia they dance not just the polka but also the redowa and the furiant?

My word processor can spell only 50,000 words, so when I need orthographic authority in a hurry, I've found *The Official Scrabble Players Dictionary,* published by Pocket Books, is the best place to get it. This 662-page marvel is designed so that the words really stand out from the concise definitions, making it extra-easy to scan a column looking for the word in question. I especially appreciate the inclusion of the proper spelling of various verb tenses, gerunds, plurals, etc., particularly when consonants must be doubled or vowels dropped. Very few standard dictionaries will tell you that "ickiest" is indeed correct when you mean "the most repulsive."

I don't write poetry, but rhymes can add zest to article titles or subheads, and you can find them in the *Capricorn Rhyming Dictionary,* by Bessie G. Redfield. I doubt that I'll ever have occasion to pair up "metronome" with "palindrome," but it's nice to be reminded that it's a possibility.

—NANCY S. GRANT

■ ■ ■

A Browser's Dictionary: A Compendium of Curious Expressions and Intriguing Facts, by John Ciardi (Harper & Row), a good read for people interested in words, provides an easy and interesting way to build vocabulary without resorting to ponderous conventional dictionaries.

—MARVIN J. WOLF

■ ■ ■

Bernstein's Reverse Dictionary, by the late Theodore M. Bernstein (Quadrangle, 1975), lets you learn the word when you more or less know the meaning and is particularly handy in the solving of double-crostic puzzles (a suitable form of procrastination for writers, since these puzzles offer literary references). It also includes a complete chart of "creature terms," which offers such lore as what to call bunches of beasts (a cete of badgers, a siege of herons), a male swan (cob) or whale (bull), a female ass (jenny) or fox (vixen), or a young eel (elver) or partridge (squeaker).

Two other tomes that may be of interest: Wentworth & Flexner's *Dictionary of American Slang* (Crowell, 1960, and its later edition, the *New Dictionary of American Slang,* edited by Robert Chapman, Harper & Row), which gives dated citations; *A Dictionary of Americanisms,* edited by Mitford M. Mathews (University of Chicago Press, 1951), a fascinating historical tracing of the U.S. version of the mother tongue. —D.S.

EDITORIAL INSIGHTS

An interesting and eye-opening book is Arthur Plotnik's *The Elements of Editing* (Macmillan, 1982). Careful study of it will give you some insight into the editor's job and, by helping you understand why editors sometimes behave the way they do, may improve your professional relations. It's also a useful guide to editing your own copy before you submit it.

—VICKY HAY

WHAT'S IT LIKE?

When William Safire recommended the *Similes Dictionary,* by Elyse Sommer (an ASJA member) and Mike Sommer, in his *New York Times Magazine* "On Language" column, I whistled when I saw the $68 price tag. But then James Kilpatrick raved about the book in *his* column, as well, and I bit the bullet. The book is a delight and, with its hefty 950 pages, the ultimate browsing resource.

Why a dictionary of similes? Of all literary devices, the simile—which describes the resemblance between two dissimilar things, using "as" or "like" to introduce the comparison—is probably the most versatile. Say you're looking up "Writers/Writing." Among its 66 items is the Mae

West remark, "Hiring someone to write your autobiography is like hiring someone to take a bath for you." And Paul Theroux strikes our collective bell with, "Writing is like serving a jail sentence; you're not free until you've done time on the rock-heap."

The dictionary contains more than 16,000 examples, which run the full gamut from classical and current literature to the print and broadcast media. Their arrangement under more than 500 thematic headings, plus the use of many cross-references, makes it easy to look things up. I particularly like the extensive author index and bibliography and the amusing and interesting comments following citations. Another plus is the fact that the dictionary includes similes attributed to many authors not represented in any other phrase and quotation book. I have no doubt that this book will be used by generations of novelists, short-story writers, essayists, journalists, and nonfiction writers, as well as speechwriters.

The *Similes Dictionary* is published by Gale Research, Book Tower, Detroit MI 48226; (800) 223-GALE [223-4253]. At this writing, the publisher is reported to be considering issuing a less expensive paperback edition.

—DIAN DINCIN BUCHMAN

CRAMMED WITH INFORMATION

Among my most handy reference books is *The 1988 Information Please Almanac,* published by Houghton Mifflin. Before purchasing that edition, I had one I bought in the '60s; the binding wore away before the data within did. The almanac is crammed with information, but I seem to use it mostly for proper spellings of colleges and universities and the cities in which they are located. I interview and quote a lot of academics, and the almanac helps me locate them and credit them properly.

—HAL HIGDON

BACK TO (GRAMMAR/PUNCTUATION) BASICS

I write pretty intuitively when it comes to punctuation and grammar, but every so often I have to resolve something like the proper location of a comma, or whether a clause is dependent or independent. When that happens, I find myself consistently turning to one of Karen Elizabeth Gordon's two useful and highly readable books: *The Well-Tempered Sentence: a Punctuation Handbook for the Innocent, the Eager, and the Doomed* (Ticknor & Fields) and *The Transitive Vampire: A*

Handbook of Grammar for the Innocent, the Eager, and the Doomed (Times Books).

Not only does Gordon describe punctuation and grammar exquisitely clearly, she gives some of the most entertaining (if sometimes weird) examples I have ever read. They are accompanied by old-fashioned line drawings and engravings that bring on giggles to accompany one's enlightenment. My grade-school and high-school English lessons were never so much fun. As Edwin Newman wrote of Gordon's first guide, "Punctuation is at least as inevitable as death and taxes, so it might as well be learned and enjoyed. Her little book enables us to do both." I agree completely.

—SHANNON MOFFAT

■ ■ ■

Two grammar references I find excellent are the *Writer's Guide and Index to English,* by Porter G. Perrin (Scott, Foresman) and the *Prentice-Hall Handbook for Writers,* by Glenn Leggett, C. David Mead, and William Charavat.

I have the 8th edition of the *Guide,* published in the early '80s; it had earlier served for years as a University of Chicago textbook, which should be adequate testimony to its authority. The front half of the book discusses specific details of writing. It is followed by the index, focusing on such points as the distinction between "excuse" and "pardon," whether or not to hyphenate "first-rate," and "proved" versus "proven."

I find the *Handbook,* besides being newer, a bit more clearly organized. It includes a glossary of grammatical terms handy for those of us who consult references only to find the explanation so larded with technical jargon that it explains nothing. And it's sparked with pleasant nuggets here and there. An example: H.W. Fowler's " 'Awfully nice' is an expression than which few could be sillier; but to have succeeded in going through life without saying it a certain number of times is as bad as to have no redeeming vice."

Both the *Writer's Guide* and the *Handbook* have worth beyond that of a general reference. Kept near at hand, each offers a rewarding, as well as refreshing, five- or ten-minute browsing break. The sections of general advice are good, too; if you go over them repeatedly, some of that good advice will begin to become second nature for you. Both these guides are essentially college textbooks—but don't sneer. When you write without violating their dictates, you'll have avoided lots of common mistakes.

—ED NELSON

■ ■ ■

I found *The Perrin Writer's Guide and Index to English,* by Porter G. Perrin (Scott, Foresman, 1950), when I was in college; it has been an indispensable item on my bookshelf ever since. It's authoritative, complete, easy to understand, and indexed so superbly that it takes just a minute to find exactly what you need.

—JUDI K-TURKEL

■ ■ ■

The *Harbrace College Handbook* (Harcourt Brace Jovanovich) is a quick guide to grammar, mechanics, punctuation, spelling, diction, and writing effective sentences, as well as creating larger elements within an article or other paper. It's very well organized and makes good use of examples. I use it whenever I'm faced with creating unfamiliar plurals or complex sentences or trying to clean up someone else's first draft.

—MARVIN J. WOLF

■ ■ ■

Write Right, by Jan Venolia (Ten Speed Press), is a good desktop digest of punctuation, grammar, and style.

—FRANCES HALPERN

■ ■ ■

Among the reference books I couldn't live without is *Punctuate It Right!,* by Harry Shaw (Barnes and Noble). I recommend it to beginners and old hands alike.

—MURIEL LEDERER

BARGAIN REFERENCE BOOKS

Many libraries make room for new annual editions of expensive reference books by clearing out old ones at giveaway prices, as little as a quarter. While some of the biggest libraries like to retain their outdated reference books for the sake of completeness, plenty of others simply have no room in their stacks. Library sales are excellent places for secondhand bargains, especially on such annual directories as *Literary*

Market Place and *Editor & Publisher.* Although directories can't be relied upon for current personnel listings, many of the addresses and phone numbers will still be accurate.

A best-buy tip: the U.S. Postal Service's *Zip Code and Post Office Directory.* It can be very helpful if you send a lot of letters. And zip codes aren't likely to change from year to year.

—ANDREW KREIG

■ ■ ■

If you learn of a library sale of used books, don't pass it up. Of course you'll be looking for extra copies of your own out-of-print books but, as important, look for recent reference books the library is discarding because the new volume has come in.

At my local library sale last week, I did acquire another copy of my book *Brotherhood of Money.* But as useful was a 1987 volume of the *Oxbridge Directory of Newsletters*—a great 35¢ buy.

—MURRAY TEIGH BLOOM

REALLY OLD REFERENCE BOOKS

You know that you must have a dictionary, and probably a thesaurus as well, but you needn't necessarily have the most up-to-date version, unless you specialize in something very trendy. I prefer a book I can get lost in when I'm having trouble getting down to writing.

I especially like the first edition of the *American Heritage Dictionary* (Houghton Mifflin, 1969), both for its excellent etymological section and the nifty pictures in the margins. (If you have this book, look up the illustration for "décolletage.") Also good for browsing are really old dictionaries. If, for example, you have a pre-1960s version of the *Webster's Collegiate Dictionary* (and some others), look up "kidney" and "bean" for two really deft circular definitions.

Most of my reference books are out of date but, for most things, it doesn't matter. I have an old encyclopedia I picked up for a song, as well as lots of medical reference books that I got very cheaply because they're out of date. For the beginning stages of research, having this sort of reference on hand can save a lot of time; you'll have to go to the library at some point anyway, and an old book can be a fine place to start.

I do a fair amount of medical and science writing, and I find that these cheapie books are very helpful. And an old anatomy or physiology book won't really be that out of date: the human body hasn't changed that much in the last few decades, nor has our understanding of it on a macro level.

—KATHRYN LANCE

■ ■ ■

Even more absorbing is what was apparently the first single-volume Merriam-Webster unabridged, the 1864 *An American Dictionary of the English Language* (with a lengthy subtitle beginning, "Containing the Whole Vocabulary of the First Edition in Two Volumes Quarto; the Entire Corrections and Improvements of the Second Edition in Two Volumes Royal Octavo; . . ."), by Noah Webster, LL.D., "Revised and Enlarged, by Chauncey A. Goodrich, Professor in Yale College . . . To Which are Now Added Pictorial Illustrations, Table of Synonyms, . . . Etc." (Webster himself had died in 1843.) It was published by George and Charles Merriam, at the time doing business at the corner of Main and State Streets in Springfield, Massachusetts. The copy on my shelf was acquired for $5 in a dusty old Cape Cod bookstore. —D.S.

7

FINDING OUT: RESEARCH RESOURCES

Writers, it has been observed, are perennial students—albeit in an unstructured, nonacademic way. We are gatherers of information—sometimes general information, at other times highly specific data crucial to a book or article or other work. Some information, of course, comes to us from our own observation and experience. But for much of what we need to know, we must turn to others—to books and journals and other published repositories, to the electronic compilations known as databases, to individuals and institutions privy to particular lore. Whatever you need to know, whether on a continuing basis or for a particular project, you'll find good leads here.

LOVE YOUR LOCAL LIBRARY/LIBRARIAN

No matter how poorly your local public library may be stocked, it's bound to have some books that can get you started on your research. And many local libraries have loan agreements with larger libraries and can get you almost anything you need in a week or two (or, maybe, six).

For tighter deadlines, seek out the best library in your area. Many college and university libraries will allow nonstudents to research and even to check out books.

Whatever library you use, don't be afraid to ask for help from the librarian. My experience is that librarians are among the most congenial and helpful of all professional people (next to writers, of course) and see their job as a *service.* For the best service from a librarian, do your homework first, then go in with specific questions. You'll be glad you did.

—KATHRYN LANCE

■ ■ ■

My advice to new writers, especially new nonfiction writers: Cultivate a branch librarian. By "cultivate," I mean *court.* I bring goodies and boxes of candy, give free talks whenever I'm asked, and have even written a letter to the main library commending the work of a particular branch librarian whose help has been both a timesaver and an inspiration. (Not only do I get questions researched and answered in moments, but this remarkable woman has great ideas for articles and wonderful angles to contribute to projects.) I have "cultivated" specialists in other libraries in similar fashion, and I receive equally profitable help from them.

—ANGELA FOX DUNN

■ ■ ■

My local public library is my second home and office. I can find there most of the reference books and magazines I want to consult. I can request any book I need, through an interlibrary loan system that reaches all the way to the Library of Congress. I can find the phone numbers of special libraries in law, medicine, social work, et cetera. I can get access to over 250 electronic databases through the regional library service. There is a handy photocopier; there are even several secluded corners where I can use a tape recorder. And there is a friendly, helpful librarian, who is the best source of information—not only on books but on experts on subjects I'm researching.

—BLANCHE HACKETT

RESEARCH HOW-TO

I admire and make good use of *Finding Facts Fast,* by ASJA member Alden Todd (Ten Speed Press). The subtitle, "How to Find Out What

You Want to Know Immediately," tells all. Included are good shortcuts and insights into library techniques and research methods.

—DIAN DINCIN BUCHMAN

DIAL 800-F-R-E-E

Clip long-distance phone costs by dialing many sources through toll-free 800 numbers. There are two directories of such numbers: *AT&T Toll-Free 800 Directory, Business Edition* ($14.95 plus tax and delivery) and *AT&T Toll-Free 800 Directory, Consumer Edition* ($9.95 plus tax and delivery); both are updated annually.

The business version contains about 120,000 numbers, the consumer book about 60,000. While some numbers are in both editions, it's best to obtain both. Saved costs soon pay for the two volumes.

To order, call (800) 426-8686.

—HAL MORRIS

■ ■ ■

I've found the consumer edition of the *AT&T Toll-Free 800 Directory*, with its thousands of toll-free numbers, extremely useful. Entries are arranged both alphabetically by name of company and by subject in a complete yellow-pages section. I've found a lot of sources through this book, and I didn't have to pay a cent to talk to any of them. New editions come out each October. The book also includes such oddities as a carbohydrate-grams-and-calories chart and a chart of vintage wines.

—KATY KOONTZ

■ ■ ■

Companies with toll-free numbers are great cost savers for the working writer. Although some companies have 800 lines connected just to their order desks, others have them hooked up to the rest of the company, including people you may need to interview. To find out if a specific company has an 800 number, just call (800) 555-1212—toll free.

—BARBARA SCHWARTZ

FINDING FEDERAL EXPERTS

The U.S. Government is an amazing treasure trove of information of every description from the most obvious to the most arcane. But—and this is the rub—the federal bureaucracy is so vast, and its interests so bewilderingly diverse, that homing in on the government's most fruitful source or sources of expertise in a specific issue is a daunting task.

There is a way to sidestep the tedium and frustration of following blind alleys. An excellent signpost leading directly to *the* expert is Matthew Lesko's *Information USA,* published in hardcover and soft-cover by Viking Press and Penguin respectively. In approximately 1000 pages, this source book employs a key-word index to direct the reader to the appropriate entry citing the government's specialist on a subject by name, title, address, and telephone number.

—VERNON PIZER

■ ■ ■

The official handbook of the federal government, *The United States Government Manual,* is a thick paperback covering all three branches and including many addresses and phone numbers, as well as interesting organizational charts of departments, agencies, and commissions. The manual is revised annually; of course it changes most radically at four-year intervals. For information on the latest edition and its price, write Superintendent of Documents, U.S. Government Printing Office, Washington DC 20402.   —D.S.

REUSE YOUR RESOURCES

My desk drawers are lined with metal boxes containing series of three-by-five index cards organized by subject. Each represents an article I have written and includes the name, address, telephone number, and pertinent information about every person interviewed for the story.

Through the years, I've found that a significant number of my physician interviewees have special expertise in other areas. For example, a psychiatrist whom I interviewed for a story on multiple personalities was also an expert in memory problems of the aging; a doctor I interviewed on a neurological condition called Tourette's syndrome turned out to be a specialist in an aspect of genetics focusing on gifted children.

These index cards have become the sources for lots of subsequent articles. I strongly recommend developing such a resource file. For me, it has increased both profits and productivity.

—GLORIA HOCHMAN

PLUMBING THE PAST

If you're looking for historical information, then you may need to look no further than the appropriate local historical society. An event that took place in Missouri, for instance, will likely be easy to trace through the Missouri Historical Society (there are special-interest historical societies, as well).

Letters to such societies will often net you a wealth of research at very little, or no, cost. Some send out a certain amount of material free; others charge copying costs; still others ask a nominal fee, perhaps $25 to $35, in advance before undertaking a special search for you. A few are so small or understaffed that they are unable to handle specific requests but will welcome search visits or will provide you with a list of local researchers who might do the work for you. (Hourly rates for such researchers seem to run from $10 to $30; I've generally paid under $20.)

Most libraries have a copy of the *Directory of Historical Societies and Agencies in the United States and Canada,* which lists the various societies and their addresses. When you write to these societies, allow four to six weeks for reply.

—KATE KELLY

FAMOUS NAMES AND HAPPENINGS

A company called Celebrity Service International has several publications useful to those who write about entertainment-industry "names" and other prominent persons.

The daily *Celebrity Bulletin* updates the activities and whereabouts of newsworthy personalities; the weekly *International Social Calendar* lists "major happenings" such as premieres and fund-raising galas; the twice-a-month *Theatrical Calendar* reports on the theatre world both in and out of New York; *The Contact Book,* issued annually, is an international culture-and-entertainment directory and includes some 7000 listings; the *Celebrity Register,* published every few years, offers biographical material on some 1600-plus current luminaries in the fields of entertainment, sports, the arts, and politics.

Contact the firm for current price information: 1780 Broadway, Suite 300, New York NY 10019; (212) 245-1460 or (212) 757-7979.

—ALMA DENNY

BIOGRAPHIES BY SUBSCRIPTION

Current Biographies, a monthly magazine published since 1940, is a useful source of background information and details on people in the news, including popular celebrities and politicians. It's available by subscription (I've never seen it on a newsstand), and bound copies may be consulted at most libraries.

—DOROTHY SIEGEL

TUNE IN TO WHAT'S UP

I often work in Latin America. When I don't have an assignment there, the cheapest way to keep my ear to the beat is shortwave radio; it's full of information—and provides language practice, besides. I began on the excellent, pocketbook-size Sony IFC 7600D receiver, which isn't great on amateur stations but does a good job on foreign broadcasters. The Sony (or an equivalent) runs about $200 to $300. A good all-band amateur and commercial receiver goes for up to $500.

If you want two-way communication, you need an amateur's license and a transceiver. You're not allowed to do business over the air, but nothing prohibits asking questions, getting educated, or practicing a foreign language. A new transceiver for both receiving and transmitting starts at about $600. Many "hamfests" around the country offer good used equipment for listening and sending.

—WALLACE KAUFMAN

INSTANT PEOPLE

A research treasure: *Instant Information,* by Joel Makower and Alan Green, hardcover edition published by Tilden Press, softcover by Prentice Hall. This volume lists resources for any subject imaginable—addresses as well as phone numbers, and a full description of what each association or institution does and can provide. The listings are by state, but you'll use the meaty subject index more than the table of contents. The book includes everything from the Sherry Institute of Spain and the American Goat Society to the Alternative Energy Institute and the American Physiological Society.

—KATY KOONTZ

■ ■ ■

Instant Information, by Joel Makower and Alan Green, is useful for both writers and idiot savants. It lists thousands (they say nearly 10,000) of institutes, trade associations, nonprofit groups, government agencies, centers and committees for this and that, and special libraries. I've found good sources for subjects ranging from optics to parliamentary procedure.

—NORMAN SCHREIBER

■ ■ ■

Instant Information, by Joel Makower and Alan Green, is a wonderful source of people to interview on every conceivable topic. Like the more comprehensive (and difficult to use) *Directory of Organizations,* this volume lists sources by subject, location, and organization name; unlike the *Directory,* this is a neat, one-volume trade paperback that costs only $19.95.

—JUDITH KELMAN

■ ■ ■

Instant Information, by Joel Makower and Alan Green, is a top-notch source of expertise. I consider this book an absolute must for any non-fiction writer.

—MICHELE McCORMICK

USE YOUR VCR

Your VCR can be handy for far more than taping "Dallas" or running the latest movie from the video store.

If someone you're writing about—or might be writing about—is being interviewed on a talk show, a tape can provide you with a great deal of useful data, recording not only information, but also the person's body language and attitudes. Does the interviewee shift nervously in the chair when a certain topic is broached? Does the subject seem to enjoy discussing his or her past, family, friends?

If you're writing about an athlete or entertainer, you can use tapes to view and re-view his or her performance—and this may be a good opportunity to experiment with some of the controls on your VCR. After hours of trying different ways of slowing down a tennis player's strokes, for example, I found that the frame-advance mode made things clearer to me than any variety of slow motion.

—BARBARA SCHWARTZ

POST-SHOW ROUNDUP

Radio and television are terrific research (and idea) sources. Particularly helpful are National Public Radio (a cornucopia of news and features, it spews out a newspaper's worth every hour of every waking day), PBS (especially "MacNeil/Lehrer"), and, yes, "60 Minutes" on CBS.

As sources, of course, they require that you keep a pad and pen handy while you listen or routinely program your VCR to preserve programs for further study. But if you've missed the episode, so long as you know what you're looking for, you can obtain more information. For instance, if you've been able only to jot down the general sense of a story you've heard and you have the date and time, NPR, which has an ongoing index, will fill in the details for you; call (800) 235-1212.

Similarly, both "60 Minutes" and "MacNeil/Lehrer Newshour," if you've somehow goofed your taping (or find out only later that it's something you should have taped), will provide nominally priced transcripts. CBS is at (212) 975-4321; I don't know the precise transcript fee. "MacNeil/Lehrer" transcripts are $4 from a service in Missouri, (913) 649-6381 (be absolutely sure you have the date right); tapes may be ordered for $25 by phoning WNET in New York, (212) 560-3045.

—JACK FINCHER

LET *THEM* LOOK IT UP

An invaluable research aid that's only a phone call away is the research department of your public library. Usually within a few minutes, a librarian can look up the address of an organization, check out a doctor's credentials, or tell you the name and phone number of a magazine's managing editor. The librarians are virtually always courteous and willing to provide the information. And if it takes a little digging, they'll usually take your name and number and call back when they have the answer.

Here in New York City, I usually call the Brooklyn Public Library rather than the New York Public Library in Manhattan, since the former is less crowded and the line is less likely to be busy.

—MARK L. FUERST

■ ■ ■

I've found that when I need a fact fast, the Brooklyn Public Library can supply it quicker than the New York Public Library. The BPL phone is (718) 780-7700.

—ALMA DENNY

BUT THE BOOK IS OUT OF PRINT

You may find, in the course of research, that you must lay hands on a book or books no longer available in stores or libraries. One Friday afternoon, I found myself in need of several long-out-of-print books. I called around to several book-search services. Most were closed. I left messages on their phone machines. Few even bothered to return my calls.

I was saved by discovering Pomander Books, owned and operated by Suzanne Savrian and her very able staff. They not only smoothed the path of my search but taught me a thing or two. We discussed the fact that I needed the books for research and could therefore get along with copies that were in less-than-perfect condition and consequently cheaper. When I casually remarked that I might even write an occasional note or two in the margins, Savrian commented that I would certainly not need first editions.

Books started coming in within two weeks—other services, those that had returned calls, had promised eight weeks—and on several occasions, Savrian suggested that I hold out for a cheaper copy than the one being offered. I had to rely on her judgment, since I had no idea how rare the books were, but in each such case, she got me a cheaper copy within a few weeks. And on another occasion, when I did want a nice copy of a rare book as a gift for someone, she was meticulous about obtaining a lovely one.

Pomander Books is at 955 West End Avenue, New York NY 10025 and, if you're in the area, is also good for browsing. The collection is eclectic, with special emphasis on art books and cookbooks. Mail orders are welcome, and telephone orders can be placed by calling (212) 866-1777.

—MARIAN FAUX

■ ■ ■

Other sources of out-of-print books may include listings in your local yellow pages as well as classified ads in newspapers, certain magazines (e.g., the *Atlantic*) and journals, and book-review sections of Sunday papers. —D.S.

AUTHORITIES IN ACADEME

An easily reachable, and typically cooperative, source of expert sources is the public relations department at any university that awards the doctoral degree. Such institutions conduct research of all kinds and are therefore rich in experts. Many universities even publish media guides to faculty, listing all their professors by scientific fields; such guides are almost always free for the asking.

—MARVIN J. WOLF

■ ■ ■

If you're seeking authorities on subjects ranging from Africa to zoology, seek them at colleges and universities. Many—ranging from Baldwin-Wallace College (275 Eastland Road, Berea OH 44017) to the University of California at Irvine (Irvine CA 92717)—offer free media guides listing campus experts by category. They're ideal when seeking a quick quote or background for a feature, even on such an esoteric subject as "genetic regulation of eucaryotic cells" (Pennsylvania State University has an associate professor for that one). Most contain direct telephone numbers, and some also list home phones.

—HAL MORRIS

■ ■ ■

Pennsylvania State University's office of public information sends out *Penn State Contacts* periodically. It lists 1500-plus faculty and staff under heads ranging from airline safety and ethics to organized crime, radon, and the stock market. Address: 312 Old Main, University Park PA 16802.

Catholic University of America sends *CUA Experts*, listing 150 of them by subjects from AIDS to trivia. Address: 620 Michigan Avenue NE, Washington DC 20064.

The University of Chicago *Faculty Source List* runs over 100 pages for its subject index, lists many topics under each authority's name and phone number, and offers multiple news-and-information contacts, including their home telephones. Address: 5801 South Ellis Avenue, Chicago IL 60637.

—HENRY and ELIZABETH URROWS

■ ■ ■

Ohio State University—1125 Kinnear Road, Columbus OH 43212— publishes *Info Sources*, an alphabetical listing of topics and experts who can discuss them. Researchers are eager to get accurate information about their work to writers, and many are not only willing to explain their work but to review the completed manuscript as well.

—MARGERY FACKLAM

■ ■ ■

If you'd like to invite academic input on a particular topic, you can do so via *Media Update,* a biweekly newsletter edited by ASJA member Arthur Ciervo; it's circulated to the public relations offices at several hundred colleges, universities, and medical centers across the country. Write or call Arthur V. Ciervo, *Media Update,* 20 West Mt. Airy Road, Dillsburg PA 17019; (717) 766-6163.   —D.S.

THE PHONE BOOK? YES, THE PHONE BOOK

Use the Yellow Pages. They help you find all sorts of specialized services, many of which are more than happy to provide free information, dealing with almost any subject you can think of.

—SUZANNE LOEBL

ASSOCIATE WITH EXPERTS

Do you have a specialty subject, such as medicine, business, or science? If so, there is probably at least one association serving that specialty. If possible, you should belong to such groups—or at least make use of their services.

Because I write about health and fitness, I recently joined the American College of Sports Medicine (annual dues, $120). Previously, I could attend their annual meetings and use the services of their public relations staff. But now, I receive all their publications and notices and—most important—their membership directory. This gives me instant access to thousands of professionals and their addresses and telephone numbers.

Even when you're operating outside of your usual subject area, you can generally contact an appropriate association to obtain leads and help—including, sometimes, research aid and copies of articles from the association's library. Identify such groups by checking the *Encyclopedia of Associations,* available in any public library.

—HAL HIGDON

■ ■ ■

Don't overlook trade and professional association membership directories as excellent resource materials.

For travel writers, for example, the directory of the International Association of Convention/Visitor Bureaus leads to those who can guide you to local interviewees. The Society of American Travel Writers directory lists not only active writers and editors but also associate members who are public-relations executives of hotels, airlines, cruise lines, et al.

And the Public Relations Society of America lists people who would be delighted to guide writers interested in any subject to their clients.

—JOHN MCDERMOTT

DID SOMEBODY SAY "DIRECTORY"?

I find myself benefitting over and over again from the *Encyclopedia of Associations* when gathering background material on issues, and from the *Directory of Special Libraries and Information Centers* when trying to locate manuscript collections on a particular subject or the papers of an individual. And when I start out on a story so ignorant that I barely know where to begin, I turn to the *Directory of Directories.*

These three books have something in common: they are published by Gale Research Company, one of the biggest and most reliable reference-book publishers anywhere. I receive its publications catalog each year in order to keep up with new reference works. Gale's address is Book Tower, Detroit MI 48226.

—STEVE WEINBERG

AUTHOR! AUTHOR!

If you're trying to reach someone, whether expert or popular celebrity, who has written a book, call the publicity department of the book's publisher and ask to speak to the specific publicist handling the author in question.

—JUDITH KELMAN

GET LISTED

Research leads are yours free, just for the asking, by arranging to have your name put on various lists to receive news releases and other materials. The news releases always give the names of individuals, with addresses and phone numbers, who can be contacted for further information.

There are several ways to have your name placed on these lists. One is to be included in the directories of journalists and other writers published annually by a number of companies; check the reference section of your local library. Another is to leave your business card with local organizations, hospitals, business firms, chambers of commerce, and so on, depending on your area of interest, and ask to receive news of their activities. Third, you can write to businesses and organizations, on your letterhead, with such a request; address your letter to the public relations department.

—KAY CASSILL

■ ■ ■

Major universities all have public relations departments geared to promoting the studies and achievements of their faculty members. Send letters to them outlining your subject interests, and you'll receive news releases on a regular basis. Usually, the university updates its list regularly and will send you cards periodically asking if you'd like to stay on the list. If they've been supplying you with good information—just say yes!

—JOAN WESTER ANDERSON

■ ■ ■

You can get advance notice of highlights of each issue of the *Journal of the American Medical Association* via weekly news releases that give synopses of major *JAMA* articles and also include notices of upcoming medical conferences. It's a good way for health and science writers to stay up to date on some of the most important reports. To get on the list, write the department of public information at the AMA, 535 North Dearborn Street, Chicago IL 60610.

—JOYCE BALDWIN

■ ■ ■

A number of other health organizations have similar lists; as with the AMA, requests to be placed on the mailing list should be addressed to the department of public information. Among helpful sources: American Academy of Pediatrics, 141 Northwest Point Boulevard, P.O. Box 927, Elk Grove Village IL 60009; American College of Allergy and Immunology, 800 East Northwest Highway, Suite 1080, Palatine IL 60067; American Academy of Family Physicians, 8880 Ward Parkway, Kansas City MO 64114. —D.S.

SCIENCE/TECHNOLOGY SUMMARIES

We receive two invaluable mailings each year for no cost except our reminding the sources that we relish what they send.

The American Institute of Physics issues a "physics news" compendium covering the field from astrophysics, crystallography, and geophysics to optics and polymers. The AIP is at 335 East 45 Street, New York NY 10017; (212) 661-9404.

The Institute of Electrical & Electronics Engineers issues a "key developments" summary that covers such topics as computers, communications, and medical electronics. The IEEE is at 345 East 47 Street, New York NY 10017; (212) 705-7867.

—HENRY and ELIZABETH URROWS

■ ■ ■

Most industry, business, professional, and technical organizations issue news releases and other informative literature from time to time. Send a letter to the executive director of the group, requesting that you be placed on the mailing list and explaining why you wish to receive the materials.   —D.S.

GOOD SPORTS CONNECTION

Need the address of Mike Ditka or John Elway? How about a telephone number for the Boston Celtics and the name of the team's public relations director? I recently discovered a handy little paperback that delivers a lot of such information and costs only $6.95.

The Sports Address Book: How to Contact Anyone in the Sports World, edited by Scott Callis, includes information on over 50 sports, plus manufacturers, broadcasters, publications, clinics, and more; over 5000 addresses are listed. I haven't found *every* address I needed in this book, but it has certainly provided most of them.

—MARILYN ROSS

MINDING BUSINESS

This may not be practical for everyone, but I recently went to "graduate school" on research methods. Despite 25 years as a journalist, I was shocked by what I didn't know I didn't know.

As part of an assignment, I sat through a one-day seminar sponsored by a group called Washington Researchers Ltd. The topic was "competitive intelligence," a way of helping companies find out about their competitors and their competitors' products. What it was, actually, was a thorough grounding in how to dig up information in the corporate maze, everything from a particular company's hiring practices to the floor plans of its newest plant—all perfectly legal, all perfectly ethical.

In addition to the general seminar I attended, Washington Researchers sponsors similar sessions on researching private firms, foreign firms, corporate divisions (these days, it can be important to know who owns what), and analysis.

The company also offers an impressive—but not inexpensive—array of source books. Sample titles: *Who Knows: A Guide to Washington Experts* ($125), *How to Find Information About Japanese Companies and Industries* ($100), *Business Researcher's Handbook* ($95), *How to Find Information About Private Companies* ($95), *How to Use the Freedom of Information Act* ($40), *Who Knows About Foreign Industries and Markets* ($50), *How to Find Company Intelligence in Federal/State Documents* ($50 each), *How to Find Company Intelligence On-Line* ($50).

Washington Researchers is at 2612 P Street NW, Washington DC 20007; (202) 333-3499.

—KEN ENGLADE

CROSS-COUNTRY PHONE BOOK

The National Directory of Addresses and Telephone Numbers is an extremely handy tool. It is, as the title states, a comprehensive listing, including thousands of leading corporations, universities, media outlets, government agencies (at federal, state, and local levels), law firms, associations and organizations, and more.

The book provides no additional information—simply addresses and phone numbers, as in the usual phone book, and in some instances fax numbers. But the data provided is often essential, and this volume can save the harried writer a passel of frustrating calls to information exchanges.

The *Directory* is published by General Information, Inc., 401 Parkplace, Kirkland WA 98033; (800) 722-3244, except in Washington State, (206) 828-4777. The 1989 edition cost $49.95 plus shipping and handling, with discounts for five or more copies.

—MICHELE McCORMICK

WAS THERE A HEARING ON THAT?

Have you ever had to research a field new to you, fast? Sometimes a great way to get started is to examine the issues as presented in hearings before federal agencies or committees of Congress and state legislatures. Naturally, you'll need personal interviews to flesh out an article. But hearings provide an excellent overview, especially if the deadline is tight.

You'll generally find witnesses with varied views providing opinions, statistics, anecdotes, and prescriptions for reform. The published results may include oral testimony, written statements, research studies, and reprints of relevant articles. Sometimes ordinary citizens will present first-hand accounts of how events affected their lives. Some of the people testifying may have dramatic stories appearing nowhere else. All of this is available at little or no cost.

Hearing transcripts may be published immediately, not for several months, or not at all. Congressional hearings since 1970 are most easily found in *CIS*, an index published by Congressional Information Service (a private firm) and available at major libraries.

—ANDREW KREIG

LET THEM KNOW YOU'RE LOOKING

If you need information on a specific subject, you might get the word out to those ready and willing to offer such information if there's a chance that it will lead to favorable mention of their clients. My wife edits a weekly newsletter, *Party Line;* its subscribers are public relations people across the country, who represent a broad spectrum of industrial firms, associations, nonprofit organizations, and so on.

All you need do is say what you're looking for and how you'd like the information supplied; you can be as cagey as you like about the overall nature of a book or article, or who your publisher might be, so long as your request is worded clearly enough to let the PR folks know what you want. There's no charge to you. You can get a sample of the newsletter to see how items requesting information are usually phrased.

Write or call Betty Yarmon, *Party Line,* 35 Sutton Place, New York NY 10022; (212) 755-3487.

—MORTON YARMON

SURVEY YOUR OWN CIRCLE FOR SOURCES

Editors want to hear the voices of both authorities and ordinary people in articles, and they want to see different regions represented. But tracking down people around the country can take patience and lots of time, and calling strangers with the claim that you're a writer working on a story can sometimes give added meaning to Rodney Dangerfield's famous line about getting "no respect."

It's helpful to set up a research file that includes your own circle of acquaintances and friends; think about it, and you'll realize that almost all of them have some special knowledge or experience that makes them potential interviewees. High-school and college friends, current and former neighbors, co-workers, army buddies, travel acquaintances, members of service clubs and other groups may constitute a mother lode of sources that could add much to your stories. I update my data from Christmas card information, occasional phone calls, quick notes, and visits. When I learn that one has had special success or received a new title, I'm delighted; that new status can add another dimension to my stories.

—JOHN BEHRENS

■ ■ ■

Use your university! Cash in on your college! Your alumni magazine or newsletter is a rich resource. Scan the lists of alumni and their accomplishments to see who might be a good source for product information, opinions, personal-experience tales. And keep up to date on the research projects of faculty members, too.

—MARGERY FACKLAM

NOTE FOR NOVELISTS

The Fiction Writer's Research Handbook, by Mona McCormick (Plume/New American Library), explains how to locate information on costumes, locales, events, weather, manners, morals, and other topics from ancient times to the present.

—FRANCES HALPERN

HIRE A COMPUTER-CONNECTED HUNTER

At this writing, the world's information is doubling every four years, a fact that is both vaulting and wilting to think on for any length of time.

What it means to the working writer is that sooner or later a project will show up, the nature of which is too big, or too technical, or changing too rapidly to handle without help. That's where a researcher comes in. Before you hire one, make sure he or she is skilled in computer database searches.

My researcher, Daniel Starer, has access to more than 1000 databases, covering virtually every subject—information that is, literally, at his fingertips. For a novel about the Vietnam war, he found eyewitness descriptions of village life. For a work set in fifteenth-century London, he located the world's leading authority and negotiated a reading fee to help authenticate the first draft. For a book on cancer, he generated summaries of the latest treatments. For a mystery writer, he tapped into the latest information about forensic methods and interviewed half a dozen homicide investigators. For another piece of fiction, he surveyed turn-of-the-century Parisian fashions, politics, personalities, events, and topics of conversation.

These are the kinds of data that could take a writer weeks, months, or more to compile by combing library stacks the old-fashioned way—complete with paper cuts, dust, and the frustration of missing materials. With the computer, a talented researcher has access to millions of bibliographic citations, documents, reports, articles, proceedings, dissertations. This know-how, coupled with the solid judgment to sift the trash from the worthwhile nuggets, has earned researchers like Dan Starer a prominent place in the operations of many serious writers. In the past ten years, 45 of the books he has worked on have made the *New York Times* best-seller list; let's hope my new one will be the 46th.

Starer is with Research for Writers, 59 West 85 Street, New York NY 10024; (212) 877-5400.

—DENISE SHEKERJIAN

THINGS OF THE MIND
For referral to an expert in any aspect of psychology—including relationships, divorce, adolescence, learning, etc.—contact the American Psychological Association, (202) 955-7600.

—JUDITH KELMAN

SOCIOLOGISTS ALSO SPEAK ENGLISH
Many writers regularly consult such people as psychologists and economists, but few think of talking to sociologists. They're not as dull as you

might think, and many of them even speak English!

If you're writing about family issues, drugs, crime, the environment, or anything that could be considered a social problem, a professional sociologist can usually offer fresh facts and a new angle on the material. Try contacting the sociology department at your local college or university, or write to the press office at the American Sociological Association, 1722 N Street NW, Washington DC 20036.

—DAVID BOUCHIER

EXECUTIVE EXPERTISE

A resource that's proved extremely useful to me is *The Executive Speaker*, a monthly newsletter (usually twelve to sixteen pages) that serves as a clearinghouse and digest of speeches by major business executives.

Don't let the title fool you. It's not just for speakers or speechwriters; it's a valuable reference tool for all sorts of writers, opening doors to experts in a variety of fields and providing a wealth of background material on hundreds of topics. If you're doing an article on the chemical industry, or a book on wildlife management, for example, you can turn to this newsletter and find out who has given speeches in these areas.

The editor, Bob Skovgard, is also a superb source of information. If you subscribe (it's $104 per year), you can call him, explain your assignment, and he'll recommend good speeches on your topic; he'll also provide copies of the full text of those speeches for just a nominal handling fee.

For a free sample copy and a subscription form, write *The Executive Speaker*, P.O. Box 292437, Dayton OH 45429.

—JOAN DETZ

NOTE FOR THE NEW YORK LIBRARY-BOUND

Before you decide that the huge and imposing main branch of the New York Public Library is the only place for proper research, try the Mid-Manhattan Branch, just a few steps south at 455 Fifth Avenue (40th Street). It has a remarkable reference collection and lots of newspaper and periodical files—and the copying machines, at this writing, cost only 15¢ per page versus 35¢ at the main library. You can save a lot of time, too: Hit the main library on the wrong day, and everything—including waiting for books—takes forever.

—MURRAY TEIGH BLOOM

SCIENCE SOURCES

The Scientists' Institute for Public Information is an independent, non-profit organization dedicated to improving the public's understanding of science, health, and technology issues. Its primary program, the Media Resource Service, is a hotline that provides writers with access to sources of information from a database of over 22,000 science, technology, and health and public policy experts who specialize in medicine, the social sciences, criminology, and other science-related subjects.

The Institute also sponsors media briefings on many subjects, usually in New York City; experts are brought in from around the country, and a variety of points of view are represented. The Institute likes to match (but doesn't restrict) writers to their areas of interest—an effort I especially appreciate because it cuts down on the mail I receive. When an invitation to a press briefing arrives from the Institute, I know before I open it that it will be something in one of my areas of interest.

The Scientists' Institute for Public Information is at 355 Lexington Avenue, New York NY 10017. Reach the Media Resource Service by calling (800) 223-1730, except in New York State, (212) 661-9110.

—MARIAN FAUX

■ ■ ■

When I need to talk to an expert about science, technology, or health issues, I use the Media Resource Service of the Scientists' Institute for Public Information. The service is free and extremely helpful.

When you call, try to be as specific as possible. Don't just ask for an orthopedic surgeon, for example; ask for orthopedic surgeons with an interest in the problems of parachute jumpers, or pole vaulters, or whatever. You can also request experts in particular geographic areas, such as electrical engineers west of the Rockies.

The information is provided without bias, unless you specifically request an expert with a certain viewpoint. In other words, if you ask for experts on the disposal of nuclear waste, you'll get all sides of the issue. If you've already talked to several people who believe there's no safe way to dispose of the stuff, and you want to include the other side, explain that you want to talk to someone who can describe a successful disposal site.

I try to call as long before a deadline as possible in order to give the folks at the MRS time to round up a good list of interview prospects. Usually, they call back within one or two working days with names, addresses, and phone numbers. The only stipulation they make is that they like to receive clippings or copies of published articles.

—NANCY S. GRANT

■ ■ ■

The MRS has recently expanded to include specialists in child health and development. This includes not only child and adolescent medicine but also child psychology, child care, child support and related social issues, education, family matters, teen pregnancy, and children and the law.   —D.S.

FAR OUT

Covering stories about claimed UFO sightings, poltergeists, astrology, extrasensory perception, firewalking, spoonbending, psychic predictions? Interested in scientific and logical explanations? Contact Paul Kurtz of the Committee for the Scientific Investigation of Claims of the Paranormal, Box 229, Buffalo NY 14215-0299; (716) 834-3222.

—FRANCES HALPERN

PERFORMING ARTISTS

Trying to reach a celebrity performer? Call the American Federation of Television and Radio Artists (AFTRA), (213) 461-7145, or the Screen Actors Guild (SAG), (213) 856-6741. Most performing artists are registered with one of these two unions. Tell them what periodical you're writing for, and you'll be given the name of the performer's manager or representative.

—JUDITH KELMAN

DC DATA

I have many guidebooks to Washington DC on my reference shelf. These are the most often used:

The Capital Source: The Who's Who, What, Where in Washington packs the most names, addresses, and phone numbers into a compact guidebook of any I've ever seen, from government people to corporations, professionals, think tanks, special-interest groups, clubs, media, and more. This highly useful volume is $30 (plus sales tax locally) from National Journal Inc., 1730 M Street NW, Washington DC 20036; (202) 857-1491.

The United Way Media Factbook is a must if your work involves any public relations efforts in the Capital area. It gives names, numbers, deadlines, circulations, etc., for newspapers, magazines, entertainment and arts periodicals, college and university publications, wire services, and radio and television stations both in the District and in the outlying Maryland and Virginia suburbs. It's $9.50 postpaid, or $7 if you pick it up, from United Way of the Capital Area, Communications Department, 95 M Street SW, Room 306, Washington DC 20024; (202) 488-2060.

—PAT McNEES

PUBLISHED BY THE U.S.A.

Trying to get permission to use already-published charts, graphs, photos, and other visual aids in your own works can be a real hassle. Often, such a request is turned down because your book is viewed as competition. I turn, whenever possible, to U.S. government publications. They are usually in the public domain (i.e., not copyrighted), which means that you can reprint freely simply by citing the source.

The Consumer Information Center—P.O. Box 100, Pueblo CO 81002—is an excellent source of material aimed at the general public. The catalog dated Winter 1988–89, for example, lists about 200 booklets and pamphlets in such categories as careers, children, education, health, housing, money management, and travel. Around half are free (as is the catalog itself); the rest are available for a small charge, usually 50¢ to a dollar or two. Most are well written and contain useful illustrations.

—CHARLES A. SALTER

■ ■ ■

The *Consumer's Resource Handbook,* free from the government's Consumer Information Center in Colorado, is a useful volume that lists major firms with their addresses and individuals to contact on consumer issues; some trade associations and federal agencies are also included.

—DALE RONDA BURG

■ ■ ■

There's a bimonthly publication called, simply, *New Books;* it's subtitled "Publications for Sale by the Government Printing Office." It's free. It lists not only consumer-level material but also more technical resources in subject areas ranging from (thumbing through a recent issue) agriculture, business/industry, and the census, through education, energy/environment, health, and law, to science and transportation. To get on the mailing list, write the Superintendent of Documents, U.S. Government Printing Office, Washington DC 20402-9325.

Not free but a bargain for those who write on health and medical subjects is *FDA Consumer,* the official magazine of the U.S. Food and Drug Administration. Articles are on a nonscientist-intelligent-reader level and, as with any taxpayer-financed publication, material may be lifted without permission or fee. The annual subscription price (ten issues), which has actually dropped in recent years, is $12 in the U.S., $15 foreign, by check (made out to Superintendent of Documents), Visa, or MasterCard; order from the same address as above, except the last four digits are 9371. —D.S.

FOUR FOR HEALTH

Here are four numbers I've found helpful for information on health-related topics, three of them toll-free: the National Health Information Clearinghouse, which is government-funded and covers everything medical, (800) 336-4797; the national cancer hotline, (800) 4-CANCER [422-6237]; the second surgical opinion hotline, (800) 638-6833; and the news branch of the National Institutes of Health, which also provides names of researchers available for interviews, (301) 496-2535.

—TONI L. GOLDFARB

RESEARCH BY COMPUTER I: A LIBRARY LINK

Using a computer and modem, I'm able to search the book holdings at the University of Illinois, Northwestern University, and Chicago's North Suburban Library System. I pay only for the phone call. If your local libraries offer on-line access, they'll provide you with an instruction sheet on how to search by title, author, and subject.

—BARBARA GOODHEART

RESEARCH BY COMPUTER II: FORUMS/BULLETIN BOARDS

The CompuServe Information Service provides a wealth of useful information at reasonable rates; the comprehensive service offers everything from up-to-the-minute news to electronic mail. But for writers, the special-interest forums are invaluable.

The Literary Forum, Journalism Forum, and Public Relations Forum are ideal places to share information with colleagues across the nation. Other special-interest forums focus on topics ranging from computers to health, politics, and religion. These "electronic bulletin boards" allow subscribers to tap others' expertise and exchange opinions and information. Responses are quick; it is amazing how many professionals are willing to share time and knowledge.

Along with the basic message service, each forum maintains extensive data libraries containing documents, software, and information of interest to members of that particular forum.

The basic CompuServe service is relatively inexpensive—$12.50 per hour of connect time at 1200 baud [a unit of modem transmission speed]. There is no monthly minimum. Additional services are extra. CompuServe is at 500 Arlington Centre Boulevard, Columbus OH 43220; (800) 848-8199 except in Ohio, (614) 457-8600.

There is also special software, called *Tapcis,* designed to expedite the use of CompuServe, lessening connect time by allowing users to compose and read messages off line; it also eases the process of sending and receiving information. *Tapcis* may be "downloaded" from its own CompuServe forum and used free on a trial basis for 21 days, when users are asked to register the software and pay a $79 fee. It can also be ordered on disk from Support Group Inc., Lake Technology Park, P.O. Box 130, McHenry MD 21541.

—MICHELE McCORMICK

RESEARCH BY COMPUTER III: COURT CASES AND MORE

Lexis/Nexis is truly one of the greatest database resources around, and it's not complicated to use; after two hours' learning and practice, I was able to find full legal cases quite easily. The manual is also readable, and there is a help line that operates seven days and six nights a week.

In addition to legal material, one can obtain both full texts and abstracts of articles from newspapers (more than 100 of them), magazines, trade publications, newsletters, and wire services. The database also has SEC information, brokerage-house reports, and Congressional information and allows you access to *Medline* and to psychiatry, psychology, and sociology journals. Any text, or part thereof, can be printed out.

—SHIRLEY CAMPER SOMAN

■ ■ ■

Among the databases that I can access from a personal computer hooked up to a modem, one that I've found most useful is Lexis, which contains decided court cases from virtually every federal court and most state courts. The cases go back many decades. For a recent biography of a controversial individual, I searched lawsuits going back to 1920. I found about 300 in less than an hour; in a manual search, I might have found 10 percent of them.

Lexis is from Mead Data Central, 9393 Springboro Pike, Dayton OH 45401; (513) 865-6800.

—STEVE WEINBERG

RESEARCH BY COMPUTER IV: LOW COST, OFF HOURS

A company in California bills itself as the world's largest on-line knowledge bank—Dialog Information Services, 3460 Hillview Avenue, Palo Alto CA 94304; (800) 334-2564. Actually, it offers two distinct services.

The main one, Dialog, is like using a nuclear weapon for research. It has everything from the *Encyclopedia of Associations* to business indexes, AP, UPI, foreign companies and overseas publications, 30 major U.S. newspapers, and 450 magazines. Everything is full text. It's like having the Library of Congress in your computer. If you have to do research on a serious basis, this could change your life.

It's expensive: the time charges (after the one-time start-up fee) can be as high as $200 an hour. A magazine for which you have a major assignment might agree to pick up those costs; you're given a readout showing the charge when your session ends.

The other service is Knowledge Index, an after-hours service which operates nights (6 P.M. until 5 A.M.), weekends, and holidays. This is a compilation of databases that range from *Agribusiness USA* to *Books In Print*, the *Harvard Business Review*, industry indexes, and Standard & Poor publications. If your area is business, there is information on 7800 publicly held U.S. firms, with information on directors, profits, and products. Other subjects include education, economics, engineering, law, and more. Most printouts are abstracts and condensations, with full text sometimes available (or orderable from an outside supplier).

Knowledge Index has a lower start-up fee, with an on-line fee of $24 an hour. There is an easy-to-use workbook.

—SAM GREENGARD

■ ■ ■

Knowledge Index, the low-cost, off-hours version of Dialog, is invaluable. It has more than 70 databases, including *Magazine Index,* indexes to the *New York Times* and other major newspapers, *Medline, International Pharmaceutical Abstracts,* and others ranging from agriculture to philosophy. You can call up, say, *Books in Print,* enter an author, title, or subject, and the computer presents you with a list of bibliographic references. Some databases, such as *Marquis Who's Who, Dissertation Abstracts,* and *Drug Information Fulltext,* provide complete texts.

You have to know what you're doing, because on-line fees add up quickly, but once you learn to search efficiently (instructions are included), you can save hours in the library. And some editors will reimburse reasonable on-line charges.

—VICKY HAY

■ ■ ■

I heartily recommend Dialog Information Services' Knowledge Index. Once you log on, just a few keystrokes and you're into any database that interests you. I tend to be a bit computer-illiterate, but I've mastered it. There are a number of sections, with several databases within each. The sections range from agriculture, arts, books, and business through chemistry, computers/electronics, environment, and history to medicine, psychology, religion, and social science.

Here's an example of a search I did for a book I was writing about the sun and skin. I used such key words and phrases as ultraviolet radiation, skin, skin cancer, sun, ozone layer, and sunscreens to examine a number of databases. First, I checked to see if any books on the subjects were listed in *Books in Print.* I then moved on to *Magazine Index* (to find articles in popular magazines), *UPI News* (which goes right up to the day you're doing the search), *USA Today Decisionline, Newsearch,* and *National Newspaper Index* (which told me about articles in papers like the *Los Angeles Times, Wall Street Journal,* and *New York Times.*)

I then checked out more scientific sources: *Cancerlit, Medline, Nursing,* and *Allied Health and Sport.* All of these revealed a number of citations. With just a few more keystrokes, I could get the whole story from UPI. *Consumer Reports* not only gave me citations on sunscreens and other products but also a summary of each report. A full search like this could take a full hour—but just think of the time it would take to accomplish the same thing in a library. A quick search sometimes costs only a few dollars.

When I finish a search, I save all the data, then I log off. Next, I go to my word-processing program, look through what I've saved, delete what's irrelevant (that happens sometimes!), and print it out. I pull out the citations (duplicates can occur when you use many different databases), categorize them by source, place them in chronological order, and get the actual articles from the library—paying a teenager to find the bound journals and photocopy the articles if I'm pressed for time.

All in all, the cost of a really large search—after paying for on-line time, photocopying, and a student assistant's work—may be upward of $200. But if you've gotten even a small advance on a book, the time you save compared with doing research the old-fashioned way really makes you feel it's well-spent money. I find Knowledge Index to be more complete, for serious writers, than CompuServe (which can divert you with bulletin boards and fun but frivolous extras) and a lot less expensive than some databases used by businesses.

—MARY-ELLEN SIEGEL

■ ■ ■

I use Knowledge Index, the off-hours, scaled-down version of Dialog; it gives access to all kinds of databases in science, social science, education, business, and reference. I use it for two purposes.

First, of course, there is the task of discovering the names and publication dates of books, magazines, journals, and newspapers that carried material about the subject I'm probing. Using my computer and modem and Knowledge Index, I spend five minutes on this at the most, rather than the couple of hours it might take in the library.

I also use it for marketing intelligence. If, for example, I am shaping an article idea, I check out the *Magazine Index,* thereby learning if, where, and how this subject has already been covered; this helps me make appropriate decisions. I can tap into *Books in Print,* as well, and learn what, or what else, is out there.

—NORMAN SCHREIBER

■ ■ ■

Probably the single most powerful and most labor-saving tool I use in my work is Dialog's cut-rate electronic research service, Knowledge Index. It has many of the same databases Dialog has, at a fraction of the price, and the basic $24-an-hour cost applies no matter what databases you search.

In addition to researching topics I'm writing on, when I have an idea, I go first to Knowledge Index to see what's been done, if anything; if my search comes up empty, I know I have an original. If I get a number of citations, I can save them and later take them to my library and get the articles. Most such research is done in less than five minutes; the average bill is $1.50 to $5, and I do it right at my desk.

The trade-off for the low price is convenience. Knowledge Index operates only at off hours, and invoices appear only as a line item on your credit-card statement; Dialog, by contrast, sends you a detailed invoice showing time used in each database and the charges for each search, making it easier to bill clients. To bill clients for Knowledge Index time, I have to submit the service's estimated cost of each search (provided on-line, on request); so far, this has worked.

When you sign up for Knowledge Index, your start-up fee gets you a password and a user's manual. I highly recommend it, especially for beginners. It's much simpler to use than Dialog. And you're far less likely to make costly mistakes when the meter isn't running too fast. I started off with Dialog and was shocked to find myself eating $43 in mistakes in a month.

—PATRICIA MANDELL

■ ■ ■

Knowledge Index, the junior version of Dialog, is a great research timesaver for anyone with a computer and a modem. For the vast majority of research tasks, ten or twenty minutes on the phone brings far more information than an hour or three at the library going through *Reader's Guide* a year at a time. (And there's no travel time, or wear and tear on you.) You can quickly search a very broad range of reference sources, from dissertation abstracts and *Consumer Reports* to more specialized indexes of magazines and journals than you have ever heard of.

You pay (via credit card) for only the computer time you use, at $24 an hour. The better you are at learning and using research shortcuts, the cheaper your search. I can usually dig out plenty for $5 or $10 worth of time (often billable to the client). And when you're through searching, you can type in orders to have journal articles photocopied and mailed to you; this service isn't inexpensive and in my limited experience isn't terribly swift but, for those not near big libraries, it's obviously a nice feature.

The down side: You do have to learn how to search. If you don't use the service often, you'll have to do a certain amount of relearning each time. It's still worth the effort.

—DAN CARLINSKY

▪ PERSPECTIVE: THE RESEARCH REVOLUTION ▪

The personal-computer revolution not only transformed the way writers put words on paper, but also began to alter dramatically the way journalists conduct their research. It introduced the writer to the technique called database searching—which means, essentially, using a modem-equipped computer to extract information stored in a central computer somewhere else, via telephone lines. The process is fast and user friendly.

It's estimated that, as this is written, there are some 2500 databases in the U.S., available from about 300 firms. Some function only as repositories for esoteric information; others contain more general knowledge. A handful are oriented to the consumer market and include such perishable information as current movie reviews, restaurant listings, airline schedules, and stock-market reports. The library at the University of Georgia, where I often work, subscribes to 200 databases, less than 10 percent of the total number available; but according to the librarians, these 200 databases cover nearly 70 percent of the information out there, since there is so much duplication in the services.

Journalists use database searching mainly to gather background, to obtain an overview of a subject—the modern equivalent of the traditional search of the clippings in a newspaper's "morgue." Its speed is awesome; a database search can zip through millions of pages in seconds. It eliminates the tedious work of actual clipping, as well as the possibility that a file will be misplaced. It permits more than one researcher to use the information at the same time.

Databases operate, basically, in one of two forms: bibliographic, or full text. (Some offer both.) Using a bibliographic database is similar to using *Reader's Guide to Periodical Literature,* or *Index Medicus,* or a card catalog. Only minimal details of the original publication are listed, although some citations may supply a short abstract in the form of a one-sentence synopsis. Full-text services can supply the complete story, but at substantially higher cost; you must be sure that the full text ordered is what you need, or you can waste lots of money fast.

The profusion of choices can make finding the potentially fruitful database(s) a bit tricky (the advice of a trained librarian can be very helpful), and there is a certain amount of trial and error. But assuming you've chosen the right database(s), this kind of research will be not only fast but very thorough, turning up most of the available information on the subject. And there are additional advantages.

Databases are by far the most effective way to find certain types of obscure information that might otherwise take an investigative reporter weeks to uncover. Take, for example, the task of finding out what other boards of directors a certain company executive sits on. You can now search business databases, including Security and Exchange Commission disclosures and corporate annual reports, to see if the executive's name shows up. Using traditional methods, such a search would have been like looking for the proverbial needle in the haystack.

The information obtained from a database search is also orderly. Computer printouts are usually organized in a tidy fashion, similar to typed 3- by 5-inch cards, in contrast to the odd-sized clippings and scribbled notes writers often amass from conventional research.

Timeliness is another advantage: Most databases add new entries every day, and newspapers generally have the latest edition on line— available through the computer—the day of publication.

A final advantage is convenience. On CompuServe, the database service to which I personally subscribe, I can get to material any time. I don't have to worry about library hours (or travel).

The major disadvantage of database searches is cost. These information banks were designed for businesses and professionals willing to spend an average of $65 an hour for information. Nexis, the oldest and largest database, charges a $7 per-use search fee, $50 per month for the subscription, and about $35 per hour for long-distance phone lines. CompuServe costs a minimum of $10 per month plus an initial subscriber's fee of $30 and on-line costs of about $6 per hour. (Be warned that one hazard is being unaware of the time you're spending on line. This activity can be seductive. You can be so busy acquiring information that a $50 tab can pile up before you're aware of it.)

One way to control the cost is to set a dollar limit for a search—$25, for example—and pay only for as many citations as that covers. On one search, I learned that there were 328 possible citations; I took a sample of 60, every fifth one, to see how relevant they were. My thinking: if they're particularly useful, I can always get more; if not, I haven't wasted money. (Rarely do editors balk at paying for these services, just as publications have traditionally paid for long-distance calls and other research expenses. The best advice for writers, however, is to make sure up front that these expenses will be covered.)

Be aware, too, that completeness doesn't guarantee accuracy. The problem of lost clippings from an old morgue file no longer exists, but certainly errors occasionally occur in entering the information into the system. And mistakes in the original sources are rarely corrected.

There are some other worries I have about databases.

Searches are specific, discrete. There is little or no opportunity to make chance discoveries. Trails of evidence aren't apparent. Browsing isn't really possible.

I also fret about what I call "groupthink"—that is, everyone tapping into the same set of sources and coming up with the same conclusions. Do common resources restrict the unique approaches writers bring to their craft? I personally have a great appreciation for the offbeat, the small and underrecognized and consistently underutilized sources that conventional researchers might find too unusual or just plain weird. The most interesting ideas often spring from unconventional sources.

Doing database searches from one's office at home also tends to increase a writer's isolation. I wonder how many errors in one's thinking are unknowingly compounded—gaps in logic, or blind spots to alternative interpretations—that could have been caught in discussions with colleagues.

Another of my concerns is the increasing proprietary collection of information; a function of libraries, which have traditionally been free, is thus commercialized.

The database services have great utility for writers when the convenience, speed, and thoroughness make them worth the expense. I'm enthusiastic about them—but my enthusiasm is guarded. Aside from the foregoing concerns, database searches are not going to eliminate the need for other reporting skills and research techniques. They are not, and cannot be, a substitute for aggressive legwork, interviewing, and thinking.

—JOHN W. ENGLISH

8

DO
YOU
COPY?

A long with the fast-food emporium, the copy shop is a ubiquitous presence in urban centers and suburban malls from coast to coast. Still, an increasing number of writers now find they just can't do without their very own copiers. Here's why—and what.

TWO NOVELS AT A TIME

In the early days, the cost of copiers was simply prohibitive for an individual writer. The entry of the Japanese into the market changed all that. Prices dropped dramatically. As important was the change in maintenance, from expensive service contracts to toner cartridges the user can replace. When I decided to get a copier in 1986 and examined the market, I decided on the Ricoh M-10, which then cost $1100.

The copier is especially valuable in sending simultaneous submissions to prospective publishers. Right now, I have two novels ready to submit (I write two at a time; when I reach a block in one, I move to the other). Depending upon the responses I receive to initial query letters, I'll send a synopsis plus the first one to three chapters (whatever's requested) to as many as twenty editors. All will be produced on the copier after I've typed the material just once.

Why not just spin out the copies on my printer? The copier does it faster and cheaper. A plus: While the dots produced by modern 24-pin dot-matrix printers are barely discernible, they can bother some near-sighted editors; copying fills in those almost invisible spaces between the dots.

—ROBIN PERRY

LIVE LONGER, STAY OUT OF CROWDS

My reliable Canon PC-20 copier is exceeded only by my computer in saving time and adding years to my life. In my pre-Canon days, when I needed copies, I'd have to throw on presentable clothes, comb my hair, go out, and walk three blocks to the nearest copy store, where I would invariably find a line of at least twenty people ahead of me. Now, I simply walk across the room.

The PC-20 is ideal for small copying jobs, producing up to nineteen copies at a clip. It's compact enough for the smallest home office, uses plain paper, and includes a manual feed feature. Although I've used only black, cartridges are also available in a variety of colors. And maintenance and handling are truly easy; if *I* can fix a paper jam, *anyone* can.

—FLORENCE ISAACS

HOW DID I LIVE WITHOUT IT?

My favorite piece of equipment, on a par with my Dustbuster, is my copying machine, a Canon PC-25. Comparatively inexpensive, it is a simple machine that makes only one copy at a time (in other words, it doesn't have multiple-feed capability) but, except when I must copy many pages, such as a long manuscript, it's perfectly adequate for my needs. It copies both standard and legal-size sheets; it can also reduce to 68 percent and enlarge to 120 percent. Formerly, I piled up all the papers I wanted to copy and then took them downtown to a copy center every couple of days. Now, I can promptly duplicate whatever I need at the very moment I need it, with my own copier. It's a gadget that makes me wonder how I ever lived without it.

—JOAN RATTNER HEILMAN

INSTANT FILE COPIES

One problem with a dedicated word processor is that you cannot make carbon copies of what you write for your files; you can only save copies of letters and manuscripts on the disk within the machine and, to me, getting ready access to those copies is something of a bother. I eliminate that bother by keeping a copier right beside me in my office when I'm working. I keep it running so that it's instantly available, and I use it several times a day.

—VANCE PACKARD

A COPIER, YES

If anyone out there is wondering whether it's worth buying a copier—yes, yes, yes, it is! My Canon PC-5L is easy to use, cheaper than the local copy-it-yourself shops, and I should have bought it much, much, much sooner than I did. It has never needed repair in over two years. I bought it at 47th Street Photo in New York, at the lowest price I found anywhere.

—TONI GOLDFARB

TIME IS MONEY

My Sharp Z-60 copying machine, for which I paid about $800 three or four years ago, is a low-maintenance, easy-to-use machine and an absolute necessity in terms of convenience. It may be cheaper for a low-volume user to go out to the library or local copy center, and I'm definitely a low-volume user (sometimes I don't even turn on the machine for days at a time). But having my own machine saves me time—and time, trite but true, is definitely money.

It should be added that these small machines are not the world's fastest, and I still use a high-speed copy center for bulk copying.

—GRACE W. WEINSTEIN

MY HOURS, THEIR HOURS

I bought a reconditioned Monroe RL-612 copier for roughly $500 in 1985 and have found it the best investment I've made. While not perfect, the machine copies text flawlessly and black-and-white photos with sufficient accuracy to be understood. It's been repaired once, for around $300.

It's possible that I haven't made back the $800 in savings over the 10¢-per-copy price at the stationery store, although I suspect it's close. But I'd buy it again to gain the saving in time of not driving six miles to the store and back *and* to save the frustration of limiting copies to the most vital documents and timing my copy runs to coincide with the store's hours.

—JOHN H. INGERSOLL

FROM BUSINESS CARDS TO BOOKS

Next to my word processor, the single most useful tool I've acquired is my copier. I have a Canon PC-24, which handles everything from business cards to letter- and legal-size paper, as well as books. It also enlarges to 120 percent and reduces to 78 percent (that's from legal- to letter-size) and 67 percent; the reduction capability is great for compressing oversize tearsheets to more mailable letter size. You can stack about 25 sheets of paper on the tray and make up to 19 copies automatically. At eight copies a minute, it's not as fast as the corner copy shop— but it's oh, so convenient. I get replacement cartridges, which are easy to change and come in several colors, from Staples.[1]

—JOAN SCOBEY

NOW, WHERE ARE THOSE RECEIPTS?

My wife Jinx and I started free-lancing full time in 1976. For the first several years, we spent a small fortune on copying. No writer could afford a professional machine, and the only home models available were slow, employed flimsy thermal paper, and cost more per copy than having it done commercially. Today, things are different. Copiers are available for under $1000. In addition to avoiding the hassle of schlepping your pages to the copy shop and standing in line, you no longer have to worry about saving all those little receipts for the IRS. And if you do a lot of copying, you'll pay for the machine in short order.

One tip: Copiers are sensitive to voltage changes (that's true of all office machines, of course, especially computers). If you live anywhere where the power can be kittenish, investing in an inexpensive surge suppressor can save a lot on repairs.

—JEFF MORGAN

[1]See appendix for a full list of office-supply sources.

AN ANTIDOTE FOR LAZINESS

One of the most valuable, timesaving, productivity-enhancing tools I've ever purchased is my Canon PC-25 copier. I use it almost every day to copy: clips of my published articles to accompany queries to magazines (I believe my sales have increased, because I'm less likely to lazily forget to enclose clips or to send bedraggled ones); correspondence (no more messy carbons); telephone bills and receipts and other records of expenditures that must be documented for reimbursement.

The machine cost me about $800 two years ago at Costco, a membership-only wholesaler in Clearwater, Florida. It's been worth every penny. It's easy to use and rugged; it's needed no repairs. It uses regular or legal-size paper and can also enlarge or reduce (the latter feature is especially useful when copying long newspaper articles).

I used to spend several hours a month running to copy shops. Now, all I have to do is get up from my desk and walk two steps for practically instant copies.

—MAURY M. BREECHER

THOUSANDS OF COPIES, NO PROBLEMS

I got a Canon PC-20 copier in 1986. Since then, I've wondered how I ever got along without it; it has saved me a lot of time and money running down to the local copy shop, which used to be especially onerous when all I needed was a copy or two. It prints only letter-size or smaller. At the time I bought it, I opted not to spend an extra $150 to get the model that reduces and enlarges and handles legal-size paper, and so far, I haven't missed those capabilities; 99 percent of my copying is ordinary letter-size. I've made thousands of copies and haven't had a single problem. Changing the toner cartridge is a snap. A cartridge yields roughly 1500 to 2000 copies, depending on the density of the material being copied.

—ROSEMARY ELLEN GUILEY

ONLY DIVINE

Take my money and take my pearls but please, never take away my Canon PC-3 copier. It weighs in at a very portable 25½ pounds and is designed with this cute little pop-up handle which lets you take it anywhere. The copies are clean and clear. Cartridges come in red, blue, and black. It's reasonably priced at discount stores; I got mine for a little over $300 (the cartridges, which last for about 1500 copies, can be found for about $70). Since it makes just one copy at a time, it's not for book-manuscript-size work—but for copies of articles, bills, and correspondence, it's divine!

—SHERRY SUIB COHEN

FOR QUOTES, CORRESPONDENCE, AND CATALOG ORDERS

I'm never the first to dash for the latest in electronic wizardry. I'm even a member of that minority of American families without a VCR (I might get around to it one of these days). But I did buy a computer fairly soon after word of them got around, a move I've never regretted. And my more recent modern-miracle purchase has been equally welcome.

Not long after I acquired my first computer, I noticed that several of my writer friends had desktop copying machines. A waste of space and money, it seemed to me. My computer printer would provide duplicates of my own work, and what else did I need a copier for? If I did want a copy of a published piece, nothing was easier than to stroll to the nearby neighborhood copy shop, and it got me out of the house for some fresh air.

Then I moved to a remote, rural stretch of Vermont and, more or less simultaneously, began work on a project involving major research. The only copying machines within half an hour's drive were in a library seven miles away, where they did a dreadful job, and in the office of the local town clerk, where they might do you the favor of copying a page or two.

I was using an excellent university library for my research. There, of course, copying machines could be found and, as long as I had the right change, I could copy out any passages I might need to refer to later. But that didn't help when I took books or bound periodicals home and, in reading them, found passages on which I needed to make careful notes. If you've ever done this, you know how long it can take to paraphrase complex ideas, or extract exact information, or decide on the pithy phrase suitable for quotation. How much easier it would be to copy the entire page!

So I went out and invested in a Canon PC-10 copier. It totally fulfilled my expectations. The surprise is how much I use it beyond the original purpose for which the purchase was intended. Now, when I want to send an editor tearsheets, I can pick and choose from my files. I use the copier to make copies of business letters of all kinds. I also use it to make copies of mail orders before I send them.

Given that I'm an hour from everywhere, ordering from catalogs is the easiest way to shop. But some orders arrive within the week, while others take a month or more; by that time, I've often forgotten what I've ordered. Now when I receive a back-order notice asking whether I want to wait, without naming the item, I can turn to my copy of the order. It also helps with the statements for the charge cards one usually uses with mail orders. These statements often designate whatever you ordered simply as "merchandise," which can make me feel like a profligate idiot if I can't remember what it was, or how much it cost, or whether it was returned. The file copies save the day.

These and other uses guarantee that the copier is exercised almost every working day. By now, it's one of those luxuries that have turned into necessities. I have only one complaint. Copiers of the type I own use ink cartridges, just as computer printers use ribbon cartridges. Removal and reloading, in both cases, is easy and clean. But the copier cartridge that cost under $30 when I bought my PC-10 now costs more than $80! Yes, the yen has gone up and the dollar down, and the almost-tripled cost means that each of the 2000 or so copies I get from a cartridge now costs 4¢ or more, a price some of the commercial copying places can almost meet.

There are times that I continue to use commercial copying establishments. My little machine isn't equipped with automatic feed, so when I needed to copy a 1000-page manuscript, guess where I went. Though it cost double what it would have in my home office, it saved me an infinite amount of time, even counting the two-hour round-trip drive.

Now, I notice that some of my writer friends are acquiring fax machines . . .

—CECILE SHAPIRO

PSST! WANNA SAVE ON THOSE CARTRIDGES?

I've found my Canon PC-25 copier has become almost indispensable. But replacing the toner cartridge can be a major expense. I purchased quite a few before discovering that there are services available that will refill the cartridge for about half the cost of a new one. I'm told that a cartridge is good for about four or five refills. A local (Texas) firm that does the work for me charges $39.95, at this writing, for each refill.

—CHARLES BOECKMAN

COLORIZE YOUR COPY

I own a Sharp SF-7200 copier and find it an estimable piece of equipment. It copies same size and also reduces and enlarges. And if you prepare any kind of publicity, which I do from time to time, the color additions can make your news look most attractive.

—HELEN WORTH

SEND THE COPY I: FROM PASTE-UP TO PERFECT

If you use a typewriter rather than a word processor or computer, you don't have to keep retyping to have a nice, clean typo-free final copy. Make all your corrections, using all the paste-ins, white cover-up liquid, or correction tape you need. Then copy the manuscript and send your editor not the original but the perfect copy.

—PAT WATSON

SEND THE COPY II: "HELLO SWEETHEART, GET ME REWRITE"

Here's a way to save time when discussing changes in a manuscript over the phone with an editor, interviewee, or co-author: number your lines of text, so that you can refer quickly and accurately to any line on the page ("the next question is on page 2, line 20"). To do this, type a double-spaced column of numbers and paste it in your copier, along one edge, so that it's picked up as you copy each page of the manuscript; don't forget to make a numbered copy for yourself, too.

—RONALD GROSS

COPIES GALORE

The copier has changed my life.

I used to dread going to my local office-supply store to make copies. I'd stand in line for hours on end waiting for a customer to run off dozens of copies of his family's lengthy genealogy or for a young mother to go through fifteen attempts to achieve just the right reduction ratio on her three-year-old artist's latest masterpiece. Many times, when my turn finally came, people would distract me by talking to me while I was placing documents on the copier or collating the copies, and I'd get home and find I'd copied something all wrong or skipped a part of it. Sometimes, I arrived at the store only to find the copier was broken.

Several hours each week were devoted just to copying.

No more. Now—in my nightgown if I wish, at midnight should the urge strike—I can copy in the comfort of my own home. And copy I do: clips galore, articles by the dozen, tax forms, contracts, recipes for my sister-in-law. I estimate the copier saves me at least six to ten hours a month, not to mention the gas and the wear and tear on the car—and my nerves. In the year and a half I've owned the machine, I've had no mechanical problems and only one or two paper jams; the latter are much more likely with cheap paper, and now I buy nothing but Hammermill Tidal DP.

So far, the big benefit is time savings. I figure my copies are actually fairly expensive to make, since I get only about 1000 copies per $69 cartridge. I attribute this to my copying of many clips and articles with photographs, which uses a lot of ink. By the time I factor in the costs of paper and electricity, I'm probably up to 8¢ a copy or more.

I chose the Canon PC-25, because it's a much heavier-duty machine than the smaller copiers and therefore, in my opinion, worth the higher price. I have written buyers' guides to copiers; the duty cycle is an important factor in the life of a machine, especially if you expect to do a lot of copying. Funny how you can find a lot more things to copy when you own a copier . . .

—PATRICIA MANDELL

SHOP AROUND (AND WRITE TO SANTA)

I can't imagine why any writer would live without a copier, especially for those nights when you finish the job at 3 A.M. and a messenger is coming to pick it up at 8. I use my Canon PC-20 constantly.

Its copies are equal to, or better than, those available in commercial copy shops. The "no maintenance" feature is a joy: the cartridge that contains the ink (or toner) also contains virtually all the parts that could break down; you replace the entire cartridge about every 2000 copies. The worst that can happen to you is that something goes flooey in the middle of a cartridge and you have to replace it early. Cartridges come in black, blue, and brown, and you can put them in and take them out on a moment's notice to do multicolor copying. Two-sided copying is also a cinch. And it uses any paper you have around.

I think the Canon copiers are superior to any others on the market, because of that no-maintenance ease. The company has an ever-expanding line, including some models that are smaller and cheaper than mine; it pays to shop around, too, when you find the one you want, since they are so often deeply discounted. There are also models that are more expensive (but not by much) which do such fancy things as enlarging and reducing, and I *want* one of those; but how can I justify the expense when my five-year-old machine still works *perfectly?*

Santa, are you listening?

—DIANA BENZAIA

BAH, HUMBUG

Having worked in a regular office where we may as well have kept a Murphy bed in a closet for the copy-machine repairman, I'm very distrustful of the things. Since my computer can spit out another copy of anything created on it at any time, and I can get a copy of anything else at the corner drugstore for a ten-minute walk and a nickel, I see no reason to own a copier.

—STEPHEN MORRILL

9

SPEAKING ON THE RECORD

A goodly pro-portion of nonfiction writers (we haven't taken a poll) use tape recorders to preserve the words of interviewees; they are especially careful to do so if there is any fear that the words may later be denied. Many writers, fiction and nonfiction, use these devices for other purposes as well, such as reciting text for an assistant to turn out on a typewriter or key into a computer, or keeping an oral notepad, an on-the-go way to preserve ideas and random thoughts as they occur. Here's what they use, and how.

THE RETICENT RECORDER

Tape-recording an interview sometimes inhibits the person being inter-viewed. Yet a complete recording of what was said, and the precise words used to say it, may be worth its weight in gold—well, silver, at least. I have a way of hiding my recorder (a Sony Stereo Cassettecorder, model TCS 350) even though it is spinning away in plain sight of the interviewee and catching his or her every sigh and whisper.

I arrive with my recorder, a notebook, and a couple of stubby pencils. My recorder is loaded with a 90-minute tape, longer than a good interview is likely to last. It starts when I push a single red button. I push the button. "You don't mind if I tape this, do you?" I ask. I put the recorder down close to my subject. "Well, I guess not," my subject says, not realizing that I already have the permission on tape.

Then I get out my little notebook and my scruffy pencils and make a considerable show of getting set to make exhaustive notes. My subject can see that I don't know shorthand. My pencil lead breaks. I get distracted and seem to forget to put anything down for minutes at a time. It's obvious that my notes are pitiful. And the recorder, which doesn't make a sound, spins on; sometimes my subject thinks I have forgotten to turn it on.

My notes, though smudgy, are not actually as bad as they appear. Those pencilled squiggles enable me, when I get to my desk afterward, to go directly to the key parts of the interview, since the marks on the recorder indicate with considerable accuracy how many minutes of recording time have elapsed. I *never* transcribe an entire tape.

—BRUCE BLIVEN, JR.

DEPENDABLE WORKHORSE

Many years ago, I was a dedicated note-taker and depended on notes to reproduce conversations. When I finally tried a tape recorder, the results showed I'd been missing good quotes, and I converted permanently to using recorders.

My present recorder, a Sony Dictator model B-12, is a dependable workhorse. Not much larger than a pack of king-size cigarettes, the unit records on standard cassettes and, carrying a 90-minute tape, weighs fifteen ounces. The price (in 1987) was over $400, including an over-the-receiver phone tap and a battery charger.

The Sony functions superbly for both phone conversations and on-site interviews. From my seat in the audience at a seminar, I can even tape a question-and-answer session between a speaker and members of the audience. I've conducted interviews on an exposition floor and the recorder accurately picked up a speaker's voice, at a distance of a foot and a half to two feet, amid the din of background noises.

The recorder is tough. I've even dropped it on occasion and, so far, it's survived without missing a beat.

—JOHN H. INGERSOLL

TAG TEAM

I save at least ten hours a week using a Sony system with an Executive tape recorder and Dictator BM-80 transcriber. The system is expensive—it cost me $1200—but, since I value my time at $60 to $100 per hour, it's paid for itself time and time again.

I purchased the system when I was hired to craft a privately subsidized, family-published autobiography of a 94-year-old woman. The project involved extensive interviews and the weaving of as many of her actual words as possible into the story of her life. During the interviews, she tended to ramble and lose the thread of her anecdotes, but the rambling often led to other interesting stories, and I was entranced with her reminiscences and so was loath to interrupt. My patience endeared me to her and allowed development of the rapport that is vital to the success of such a project.

This system, which uses standard cassettes, allows one to put an electronic "pip" or "tag" on a tape as it is being recorded. Thus, it didn't matter if my subject didn't finish one of her stories at that particular time. I would just put the tag on the tape to mark the place. Later, I inserted it into the transcriber, on which one can fast-forward to stop at each of the electronic pips. Thus, I could rapidly sort through hours of tapes, find these points in the narrative, and develop questions, for the next day's interview, designed to gently lead her back to incidents on which I wanted her to elaborate.

This system has also been invaluable when covering complex subjects at medical conferences or interviewing physicians and other experts. It can be connected to one's phone, as well.

—MAURY BREECHER

WORDS, PLEASE, NO MUSIC

Tape recorders can, in very rare instances, pick up powerful nearby radio stations. I discovered this when I did a one-hour interview and then went home to find that the tape had nothing on it but rock music. *That* was kind of a thrill. The next day, I threw my 50-buck compact toy in the garbage can and bought a Sony TCM 5000 EV.

This is a tape recorder measuring about 10 by 6 by 3 inches, with a leather cover, steel front, and steel internal frame. It uses regular cassettes. It will blink a light when you're running out of tape. It cost $400 and is only monophonic to boot. It is also tough as hell, externally and internally. I bought this machine because I'd seen TV field crews using them and I figured anything that could survive their abuse was what I wanted.

The steel frame stops a lot of those nasty radio interference problems. More important, it has a match-needle sound-level meter on the front (and a recording-level knob to let you set the level just where you want it). If my interviewee is talking and the needle isn't moving, I know something's wrong. If my interviewee pauses for a moment and the needle keeps right on wiggling, something's wrong, too; that's how I caught—even before I started the interview—a second instance of radio interference. I moved the recorder a few feet, and the interference vanished (it tends to be very localized). The meter can be set for either source or tape. I leave it set for tape; if it isn't on the tape, I want to know about it.

P.S.: If you can't afford a real top-of-the-line recorder, consider spending a hundred bucks on a "shotgun" microphone. It plugs into your machine, cutting out the lousy built-in mike, and is very directional. No more internal rumbling from the recorder, no more air conditioners, no more humming fluorescent lights; you aim it at the other person's mouth, and that's what you hear. It can even pick a questioner out of an audience at a seminar (try doing *that* with your built-in mike). It's the microphone equivalent of a telephoto lens.

—STEPHEN MORRILL

SOUND QUALITY

I do a great deal of interviewing and, no matter what tape recorders I've tried, I've always come back to Sony—*any* Sony. The sound is never tinny, and the workmanship never disappoints.

—LINDA-MARIE SINGER

SHOPPING TIPS

In our increasingly litigious society, I've learned the value of having irrefutable proof of what someone said in an interview. Too often, interview subjects decide that what they said in the heat of a conversation is very different from what they read in cold type weeks or months later. So although I take notes, I also tape-record every interview. Over the years, I've bought and used a number of recorders and have come to some conclusions about desirable features.

I feel full-size cassettes are preferable. Microcassettes are handy and compact, but they are just about impossible to fix. Regular-size cassettes, while requiring a deft touch, can often be repaired with a Phillips screwdriver, a razor blade or Exacto knife, Scotch tape, and a pair of tweezers.

Machines that use full-size cassettes are also more widely available; almost everybody has at least one. I've been in the midst of, or en route to, interviews when my recorder failed or I decided it was behaving unreliably. I've also found myself needing to play a tape to an editor—or a staff attorney—in a prepublication meeting. In both instances, players were found with little difficulty.

Choose a machine that can use both AC and batteries. (Aside from the expense of batteries, they tend to slowly deplete themselves before total exhaustion occurs, and a tape recorded with weak batteries and played back with fresh ones—or vice versa—can become unrecognizable.) An AC adapter may not be included; Radio Shack sells an excellent model for under $10 which can be used with a wide variety of machines.

Make sure the recorder you buy can accept an external mike. The quality of even a $10 microphone is substantially better than the built-in mikes in most machines. Having four or five feet of wire between machine and mike lets you keep the recorder close to you—where you can switch it on and off (one-hand operation is a must) and check to make sure it's working—while recording close to your subject for maximum quality. Plug-in mikes are also often somewhat directional and minimize extraneous noise.

Don't buy a recorder without automatic recording control—a circuit built into the machine that almost instantly adjusts the recording level to its optimal setting.

"Voice activation" is, in theory, a nice feature which shuts your recorder off after sensing silence for five or six seconds, then switches it on when it "hears" noise. There are two problems. One is that there's a lag between the time the machine senses speech and the turn-on, so that the first word or syllable is lost. Second, if your subject pauses to think about his or her answer before replying to a question, the machine is constantly stopping and starting. That saves tape, but there is a jerky, distorted sound at each start-up.

After using a number of recorders, I've settled on two machines; I use one for field interviews, the other for playback and transcription. I take my GE Fastrac (which cost about $70) with me, and my Sony TCM 848 (about $30) stays home for transcription. I also keep a spare machine in my car (or hotel room, when I'm traveling), and that's either a Sanyo TRC 1550 (about $70) or a Realistic CTR-85 (about $40 at Radio Shack stores).

—MARVIN J. WOLF

COMPACT MICRO, CLIP-ON MIKE

The indispensable tool I've used for several years for interviewing is the Sanyo Micro Talk-Book tape recorder model TRC-5650. It's a microcassette recorder, slightly larger than a pack of cigarettes, with cassettes an inch by an inch and a half. By using Sony MC90 tapes and running the recorder on its slowest speed—plenty adequate for interviews—I can record 90 minutes at a crack, without having to interrupt an interviewee to flip the tape over.

Because of its compactness, the recorder can be easily carried in a pocket for stand-up interviews (I first used it at a ski event in the middle of a snowstorm) as well as the usual across-the-desk talks. Once, faced with the challenge of recording a seminar presentation by a man who constantly moved about the room, I attached a clip-on microphone to his shirt, wired it to the recorder, and stuck the recorder in his back pocket, out of sight and mind.

Because of motor noise, I recommend using an attached microphone instead of relying on the recorder's built-in mike. I've found a Realistic clip-on condenser microphone, sold at Radio Shack stores, is quite good.

—BRUCE W. MOST

LUCKY NUMBER SEVEN

After six casualties (three Olympus Pearlcorders, two Aiwas, and a Panasonic), I thought I would never find a microcassette recorder that would survive more than three months. I finally asked Radio Shack for the cheapest, toughest, smallest machine they had.

I have now been happily and regularly using the Realistic Micro-18 voice-activated recorder, which is under $40, for over a year. I carry it routinely in my tote, "just in case," and use it for oral note-taking. The voice-activated feature (when no one is talking, the device shuts off) works fine for most interviews, too, and I use it for phone interviews with a plug-in telephone mike (also available from Radio Shack).

My cats knock the recorder off tables regularly. I have dropped it about ten times. So far, so good.

—CAROL TONSING

FROM TOGO TO SNOWMOBILE TRIPS

A recorder is very helpful in instances when exact quoting is essential (interviews with cops, lawyers, politicians, and mothers-in-law). I use a Harris-Lanier miniature that has across-the-room pickup capabilities as well as close-in potential. It takes small 30-minutes-per-side tapes. I've used my recorder in the far reaches of Togo, with dust and high temperatures, and on snowmobile trips across northern Wisconsin, when the wind chill was 85 below. No problems in either location.

Four hints for getting the most from your recorder: (1) Always check the batteries before going on a job or a trip. (2) Carry spare (fresh) batteries. (3) Carry notebooks, pens, and pencils for backup. (4) Label each tape with date, place, interviewee(s), and other relevant data as soon as possible after taping.

—MARTIN HINTZ

TWO CRUCIAL FEATURES

I hate using a tape recorder for interviews, because it means listening to a lot of chaff to get to the wheat. But sometimes I need to rely on more than my notebook. My microcassette recorder, the Olympus Pearlcorder SD2, has served me well for years.

Two crucial features: dual speeds, for up to an hour per tape side, and a quite audible automatic shut-off, so you don't have to keep checking to see if you've run out of tape. Not much larger than a pack of cigarettes, it couldn't be more portable—and because it's so puny, it couldn't be less threatening to an interviewee.

—TOM BEDELL

DON'T DRAW A BLANK—AND CHECK SENSITIVITY

Most microcassette recorders don't let you know when you've reached the end of your tape, which means you can "record" hours of priceless information yet have nothing on tape. The ideal is a machine which pops out its record button forcibly and loudly, so you hear and feel it, when the tape ends. A few machines do this, but no salesperson seems to know about this feature, and no catalog sheet mentions it. (Some machines that *lack* it brag about their "silent stop.") To test for it, fast-forward a tape until it's near the end—or flip the cassette to side B and rewind slightly—and record until the tape runs out and see what the machine does about it.

Another important feature is a switch that adjusts the automatic recording-level control's sensitivity. If you can lower the sensitivity when recording in noisy environments, less background noise will break through between the words.

—IVAN BERGER

TAKE TWO; THEY'RE SMALL

I used to carry a small tape recorder and extra batteries to long interviews, seminars, and meetings—until, at a critical time, the tape recorder broke. I now carry a small tape recorder and, instead of extra batteries, an even smaller microcassette recorder. The latter takes up almost the same amount of space as extra batteries but gives me better back-up in case of trouble.

—M. LAWRENCE PODOLSKY

WHY TAPE THE WAITER?

Always remember, when you research a project, whether on microfilm in a stuffy library or in an entertaining conversation, that the material is going to be used later on—by *you*. Today just about everybody, including me, uses tape recorders, but nobody talks about when *not* to use them. Sometimes, they're worse than useless.

At lunch, for example, when all you get is a wisecracking waiter and the loud-mouthed crowd at the next table. Or the time I had a fine talk with Carmen Lombardo on his terrace and wound up with the sound of him eating grapes. Very old people, recalcitrant people, shy people, belligerent people, dumb people—playing back what little they put on the tape just recalls the whole lousy experience all over again and inhibits the writer trying to make use of it.

I no longer take a tape recorder with me when I'm going to talk with a group of people, or for a string of short interviews. What I take is pens (two or three Bic Roller pens with dark blue ink and bold, not fine, points) and paper (a four-by-six notebook—small enough to fit in my pocket, large enough so I don't have to keep flipping pages). I find I can remember conversations with the aid of fairly sparse notes. But there will come a time when the recollection starts to fade; as soon as possible after making the notes, I do make use of a recording machine: I dictate a full account, including descriptions and impressions.

—BOOTON HERNDON

STRICTLY TECHNICAL

In most instances, I've found I spent too many hours extracting messages from tape to make recording really useful. I use a tape recorder only when I'm doing a technical interview and I want to make sure that I have the terminology correct, or when it's important to be able to quote a source verbatim without error.

—JOHN MCDERMOTT

TAKE NOTES OR TYPE—BUT TAPE, TOO

I've saved hours, days, weeks by conducting interviews and gathering information by phone whenever possible. Problem: Your interviewee can't see you taking notes and so invariably talks too quickly. Solution: Tape the conversation. It's the best way to insure accuracy.

—GLADYS H. WALKER

■ ■ ■

When I first began writing, I quickly learned that the most important commodity I had to sell was accuracy. As a writer on money, I interview financial planners, business people, and investment experts all over the country by phone. I must report the results totally accurately, or else I would quickly lose my credibility as a trustworthy reporter.

I tape-record all of my phone interviews. I have an accurate record of what was said, without having to take written notes. Not only do I get quotes exact this way; if an interviewee later questions a quote, all I have to do is play back the tape. I'm convinced that my ability to prove the accuracy of my quotes has been in some measure responsible for my modest success as a free-lance writer.

—DAVID W. KENNEDY

■ ■ ■

Since I'm an extremely fast typist, when I conduct an interview over the telephone, I key the content directly into my computer. That "direct transcription" doesn't mean I don't tape such interviews, however. I do tape all of them, for two reasons.

Often, after a minute or so of typing furiously, I find that the interviewee simply talks too quickly for me. In that case, I just let the tape recorder pick it up and transcribe it later. The second reason to tape every interview is the risk of libel suits. I keep each tape for about six months after the article has appeared and then, if the source shows no sign of suing, I use the tape for another interview.

—DAVID GROVES

ON THE PHONE, ON THE ROAD

You're sitting in a hotel room in Atlanta, and you have a problem. You have to do a telephone interview with a source in San Francisco. You'd really like to tape-record it, but you're a long way from your trusty answering machine, which doubles as your phone-interview recorder back in the office.

Hopeless? Hardly. There's a simple, inexpensive solution—a telephone pickup. These handy devices can be attached to any telephone, such as the one in your hotel room, then plugged into your recorder, to record both sides of a conversation. Essentially, they're suction cups attached to miniature microphones. I picked up mine, the Olympus model TP2, for about $10 a few years ago.

It plugs into the external microphone jack (labeled "mic") of my Olympus Pearlcorder L200 microcassette recorder. The suction cup can be placed on either the handset or the phone itself; the instructions encourage you to experiment with different placements until you find the spot where the electromagnetic field is strongest, which is where the sound will be loudest.

I keep the pickup tucked into a pocket of my briefcase, always at the ready (I often use it in my office as well as on the road). Two warnings, though: Be sure the volume on your recorder is set at zero; if it isn't, there's usually interference. And use only fresh batteries; the quality is fine when you do, but the sound can become almost inaudible when your recorder's batteries are weak.

—DAVID HECHLER

CHEAP PICKUPS

It's easy to record phone conversations with a telephone pickup—a device that attaches easily to the listening end of your receiver with a simple rubber suction cup, while the other end is plugged into your tape recorder. Mine, which is labeled Grecotan T-5 and is made in Taiwan, cost under $5.

—RONALD GROSS

■ ■ ■

You can buy a telephone pickup for under $5 from Radio Shack; at least you could four years ago, when I got mine. It's a 3-foot wire with a small suction cup to attach to your phone receiver at one end; you plug the other end into your tape recorder. The only disadvantage: the suction cup tends to come loose just at the juiciest moments. But if you tape the cup to the receiver, you'll have no problems.

—JOHANNA GARFIELD

■ ■ ■

I tape phone interviews using an inexpensive pickup coil that plugs into the "mic" outlet of a tape recorder and attaches by suction cup to the telephone receiver. Radio Shack sells such a device, model 44-533, for $1.99. The store warns that it "may be incompatible with electronic phones." I find it works well with my old-style rotary phone.

—JOYCE BALDWIN

EVER-READY PHONE RECORDING

No matter how fast you write, it's worth recording interviews. Taping has become routine face to face, and it should be routine on the phone, too. Several scientists once told an editor that I had wildly misquoted them. I told the editor to remind them that the phone interviews had been recorded and to ask if they would like a transcript. Silence. And my honor stayed intact as it could never have done if I had merely produced handwritten notes.

Radio Shack makes telephone taping possible for about $20, if you have a recorder with "mic" and "remote" holes. The module is smaller than a cigarette pack. A wire runs from one end to the recorder, where it splits into two small jacks. The other end contains two standard phone receptacles; you run wires from one to your phone and from the other to the wall phone connection. The device switches one way for record, the other for playback and rewinding. I keep mine plugged in all the time, ready for the unexpected call (be sure it's switched to "record").

Whenever possible, I transcribe a recorded interview right after I hang up. I also keep notes during the interview as a guide to the quotes on the tape and in case technology fails.

—WALLACE KAUFMAN

■ ■ ■

With the Radio Shack recording control, you can permanently hook a tape recorder to your phone line to tape telephone interviews.

I settled on this gizmo after trying all sorts of other methods. The little suction-cup taps for your receiver manage to pop off right in the middle of the most important interviews—and even when they work, the tapes are nearly unintelligible. Heavy-duty answering machines work well and produce good tapes, but the odds are you won't have an empty tape in the machine when you need it.

The Radio Shack control connects directly to the phone line, so the sound is excellent, and it's cheap enough that you can dedicate an inexpensive cassette recorder to full-time interview duty. This can come in very handy. Working on an article for *Ring* magazine on celebrities who'd been boxers, I had spent weeks trying to get hold of Robert Conrad, with no luck. One day, as I was on my way out of the house, the phone rang. Conrad was on the line. I just hit the "record" button and, an hour later, I had all the material I needed.

At this writing, Radio Shack sells two different recording controls. The one that looks like the one I've been using for years is the multiphone model 43-236 and costs $24.95. The other, model 43-228 for single phones, sells for $19.95.

—BARBARA SCHWARTZ

■ ■ ■

A small gadget called a modular telephone receiver amplifier, model MA-20 made by Tone Commander Systems, is plugged into my handset cord and into my tape recorder. This allows me to dispense with attachments to the receiver end of the headset and also gives me the ability to adjust the volume.

—SHIRLEY CAMPER SOMAN

■ ■ ■

For anyone who tapes interviews over the phone, a California mailorder firm, Hello Direct, sells a device called the Tele-Recorder 150. One end plugs into your phone jack, and you connect the other to a cassette recorder with a remote microphone input. When you want to record a call, you just switch the Tele-Recorder to the "on" position (yes, I've forgotten to set the switch at least twice). Hello Direct is at 140 Great Oaks Boulevard, San Jose CA 95119; (800) HI-HELLO [444-3556].

—TONI L. GOLDFARB

EVER-READY II: NO SWITCHING NEEDED

I went to Radio Shack and bought a telephone recording control. I plugged it into a tape recorder with a VAR switch. VAR stands for Voice-Activated Recorder, and the switch can be set to run the recorder only when it hears something on the phone line. The recorder is, thus, always on—but it's in "pause" mode until it's activated; in reality, it starts running when the phone rings and continues for a few seconds after I hang up.

Does this mean every phone call is recorded? Yes. I record every conversation that comes in or goes out. I do this because I interview a lot of people on the phone, and those people often have to call me back. When the phone rings, I never know whether it's going to be a call that needs to be recorded or not. Later, I copy onto other tapes what I need to save and erase the rest.

A legal caveat, when it comes to telephone taping: Most state statutes require only that one party to a phone conversation (you, for example) be aware that a recording is being made in order for that recording to become admissible evidence at a trial—say, for libel. Some states, however, require that you inform the other party, either by a regularly repeated tone or in so many words. Know your state law. And when you advise another party that you're recording, be sure the statement is *on the tape.*

—STEPHEN MORRILL

INFORM AND REASSURE

When I interview people via telephone, I like to use a tape recorder to make sure I have every single word (as well as each and every "er," "um," and "y'know"). Telling people that you are recording them is both courteous and clever. I would hope that the courteousness is obvious. The cleverness has to do with self-preservation. People get pissed when they discover on their own that you have been recording them; visions of secret police dance through their heads.

I have discovered that simply announcing that the tape is rolling, however, can also be a problem, as it can trigger inappropriate but heartfelt invasion-of-privacy paranoia. I have developed a way to both inform and reassure.

"As you might guess," I say, "I'm taking notes." The subject usually makes some pleasant sound of understanding. "And the way I take notes," I continue, "is with a tape recorder. Does that present a problem for you?" It never does bother them, because I've put the recording in the context of accurate note-taking, a desirable end.

—NORMAN SCHREIBER

PLAY IT SAFE

A word of caution: There are laws in some states against taping a telephone conversation without letting the other person know he or she is being taped; in other states, as long as a party on one end of the line knows the talk is being taped, it's legal. I play it safe: I always let the person I'm interviewing know that I'm using a tape recorder. I explain that this eliminates the need for me to take notes, and I can be more certain that all quotes will be accurate. I hardly ever get an objection to this; rather, the interviewee appreciates the fact that he or she will not be misquoted.

There are exceptions. Once, I called an individual at a government institute to ask a follow-up question to an interview I'd done the previous month. I happened to mention to his secretary that the interview had been taped. The fellow came on the line mad as a hornet, warning me that he was going to report to the FBI that he'd been taped without his knowledge.

Expecting to have an FBI SWAT team surrounding my house any minute, I went to my files and pulled the original tape. I played it back for the irate bureaucrat. Clear as a bell was my statement at the top of the interview that I was tape-recording the conversation. Somewhat mollified, the fellow mumbled something vaguely like an apology, but he continued to lecture me on the sins of taping a telephone conversation without advising the other party.

The interview was only to obtain a few statistics available to the public. I was under the impression that my taxes were helping pay the agency's expenses and it was part of its function to supply information to the public, so I never did figure out why the fellow got so huffy. But the incident does underscore the importance of making certain all parties are informed that they're being taped.

Incidentally, in using a tape recorder for telephone interviews, I recommend that you select a model that indicates the recording level, either with a flashing light or a meter of some kind. You can glance at the recorder and make sure that it is, indeed, picking up the conversation. I've used Radio Shack recorders for years and find they've always given me good service (for phone interviews, I use a Radio Shack control between the phone and the tape recorder).

—CHARLES BOECKMAN

CHEAP CAN BE DEAR

I know there are countless cheap (read $1.99) gadgets for taping phone interviews, but I painfully learned that you get what you pay for when I lost a splendid interview because a minuscule wire had pulled loose from one such gadget and the subject had left for Europe right after talking with me. I went to my neighborhood Sony shop, spent $40 for a decent phone bug, and have never had a problem since.

I also made another decision. Now, I always take notes, too, whether it's an in-person interview or a phoner; if, God forbid, the Sony device malfunctions, or the tape recorder's batteries go dead, I'm protected. I might not have the entire interview, with all the pristine quotes, but there will be enough so that all is not lost.

And don't economize on batteries. I buy Duracells, because I've found they last longest, and I keep them in the freezer. There, they'll last indefinitely, so I stock up when they're on sale. If I have the slightest suspicion that the batteries in my recorder might be wearing down, I replace them. I'd rather waste $3 on batteries than lose a $1000 interview. Wouldn't *you?*

—ISOBEL SILDEN

HOW TO COPE WITH A MUMBLER

Ever interview someone who tends to swallow words at the ends of sentences and talks in a mumble the rest of the time? I have, and when I tried to decipher the tape afterward, I was at a loss. What saved the day: a one-watt speaker-amplifier which plugs into a tape recorder and boosts the sound. Radio Shack sells one, model 32-2031, for $17.95.

—JOYCE BALDWIN

SET YOUR OWN PLAYBACK SPEED

My tape recorder—a Realistic VSC-2000, from Radio Shack—has a feature I consider indispensable, variable speed control. It can speed the playback, while maintaining a normal voice pitch level; an hour of tape can be played back in about 40 minutes, and it doesn't sound as if you had interviewed Alvin and the Chipmunks. The current price of my recorder, which is two years old and has given me no trouble, is $79.95, but you may find one for less at one of Radio Shack's frequent sales.

—DAVID A. ANDERTON

■ ■ ■

Listening to tapes to extract needed information used to drive me crazy, because the person on the tape talks and—uh—talks and—er, ah—you get the idea. Enter the variable speed control recorder. Two simple controls let you both double the speed of playback and lower the pitch, so the speaker doesn't sound like Donald Duck. Sounds weird, but it really works. You can hear a one-hour tape in half that time, with better comprehension. I have a General Electric Fastrac; it's small and relatively cheap. There are others.

—WENDY MURPHY

LESS TEDIOUS TRANSCRIBING

One of the main reasons I seldom use a tape recorder for interviews is the odious task of sifting through—or even, God forbid, transcribing—the tape. When it is necessary, however, two little devices make the job much easier.

One is a foot pedal with a connector that plugs into the recorder (I think I got mine at Radio Shack for less than $10) that lets you start and stop the tape at will; since it acts as a "pause" rather than a "stop," there is no need to rewind the tape after each intermission. The second is an inexpensive set of earphones. Together, they truly ease the task of tape-thumbing.

—KEN ENGLADE

■ ■ ■

Transcribing tapes is a tedious job, but I find it more tolerable with a few inexpensive tools.

First, get a tape recorder with cueing features. This means that if you want to re-hear a few words, you simply press the "reverse" button; the tape zips back, then continues forward as soon as the button is released (as opposed to hitting the "stop" button, then "rewind," then "play" to move it forward again). Cueing also fast-winds the tape forward. You can tell a machine that has these features by one or two arrows above the rewind and fast-forward buttons; the word "cue" may also appear above one or more of the buttons. Machines with these features are no more expensive than those without them. I bought one, the Slim Line, at Radio Shack for $30 in 1987.

Second, buy a foot pedal to stop the tape while your typing catches up with the last words you heard; a wire from the foot pedal plugs into a small jack that comes with all but really cheap recorders. It's an absolute necessity for efficient transcribing.

Third, have a set of high-quality headphones, the kind used with Walkmans. Don't depend on any tape recorder's speaker to relay faint voices or confused dialogue. Be willing to pay $25 or so. But these headphones are for stereo listening, and your recorder is mono. Won't you hear the sound in only one ear? Yes—*unless* you get a little adapter, which Radio Shack sells for about $1.50; it's called a mono-to-stereo adapter, and it sends the sound from a mono tape player to both earphones.

—JIM BERRY

MONOPHONIC HEADPHONE

If your tape recorder records monophonically, and you want to use headphones for transcribing, you'll find the usual stereo headphones a needless expense. Instead, use Radio Shack's monophonic headphone set; yes, they really do sell a mono headphone, no matter what the sales clerk says (you may have to special-order it). This assumes that you don't ever want to listen to music on your stereo with earphones; if you do, you may as well use the same ones.

—STEPHEN MORRILL

KEEP YOUR HANDS ON THE KEYBOARD

Tape-recording leads to the onerous chore of transcribing. Though still onerous, that chore is at least 50 percent faster with my microcassette transcriber—the Olympus Pearl model TC1000. It's a far cry from the days when I transcribed directly from the recorder, having to pause frequently to back up the tape. Now, I never have to lift my hands from the keyboard.

Headphones, a foot pedal, variable speeds, and a back-spacer make the difference. The pedal has on, off, fast-forward, and reverse functions. Every time I turn the tape off—by lifting my foot—it back-spaces, as much or as little as I've set on the back-space dial. The speed control lets me slow voices down to a Darth Vader crawl or rev them up to chipmunk level. In its own way, the transcriber is like my computer: I can imagine doing without it, but I'd rather not.

—TOM BEDELL

CUT SECRETARIAL COSTS

I use an Olympus microcassette model 1200 transcriber. It saves time and also increases efficiency if you have to transcribe lots of tapes. The benefit of such a machine over just a foot-pedal system is that the ability to adjust back-spaces and tape speed allows you to gear the playback to your own typing ability. You needn't go back and forth as often—or, if you want to, the machine can do it automatically, overlapping one or two words. The machine also comes with a headset, a vital accessory if you plan to transcribe with others around you who may not want to hear the voices.

I bought my transcriber about five years ago. Even if this specific model number is unavailable now, I have been pleased with this brand. I have gotten back the cost of the machine (around $350 when I bought it) many times over, because I no longer hire secretaries or expensive transcribing services.

—JAN YAGER

WHEN YOU NEED EVERY WORD

Certainly the worst part of any book or magazine article based on interviews is transcribing the tapes. When you need a full and accurate copy of everything that was said, not just a quote or two plucked from the whole, it can mean three-plus hours of transcription time for every hour of tape—and that's if you're a fast typist and the interviewee spoke very clearly and slowly, in relatively complete sentences, and didn't cough or turn away from the microphone too often. The Panasonic microcassette transcriber model RR-900D helps shave the time.

Among its many useful features are a tape speed control, which allows you to shift between two different speeds; a voice speed control; and a tone control that lets you soften particularly shrill voices and clarify muddled ones. The headphones help, too; much of what the naked ear can't make sense of becomes intelligible with the headset. In addition, it operates with a foot pedal linked to a back-space control that ranges from zero to ten seconds. And if that isn't enough—it can also act as a tape recorder, serving as a back-up to your regular equipment.

—DENISE SHEKERJIAN

NO LONGER A DRAG

As a journalist, I use a tape recorder. Taping interviews wasn't a problem, but transcription was—a laborious process of starting the machine, listening, typing frantically, stopping it until my fingers caught up with the voices, starting it again. The whole procedure was a drag.

Then I found out about the Sanyo Memoscriber. This is a commercial tape machine that allows you to record phone conversations using a microphone that sticks to the phone and records with amazing clarity. It will then play back tapes through earphones; you use a foot control to start and stop the tape as you type. The machine also includes a speed control; you can speed up the conversation (everyone sounds like a Disney chipmunk) until you get to a part you want to transcribe, then slow the tape (everyone sounds like a foghorn) and keep the voices in pace with your fingers.

The price is under $300 and, depending on where you shop, deals can be made to reduce the cost substantially.

—PETER LOEWER

RENT A TRANSCRIBER

Whether you're doing your own transcribing or hiring someone to do the chore for you, realize that transcription machines—which are light years ahead of starting and stopping manually—rent for about $35 or $40 a month. Many colleagues are not aware of this possibility. In many instances, they hire typists by the hour to transcribe tapes, don't realize that the typists aren't using transcription machines, and wind up paying a fortune.

—DALE RONDA BURG

FOR WRITING OUT LOUD

I rarely use my typewriter. I don't own a computer or word processor. And although I've published well over 500 articles and ten books, I didn't write them in longhand. I do a great deal of writing at the beach, where my "office" consists of a folding chair, an umbrella, and the contents of my attaché case. Indeed, I write while driving to the beach—usually correspondence, but often notes for works in progress and, occasionally, short fiction pieces. The single piece of equipment to which I have sworn lasting allegiance is my dictating machine.

For my money, there's no other way to write. My productivity is twice what it would be using a word processor, four times that of a typewriter. That's not only because I can talk faster than I can type; I can also scribble changes on hard copy faster than I could make them on a keyboard. Then, while my secretary is making the corrections, I'm on to the next project.

About six months ago, I moved more than a thousand miles from my secretary. We haven't missed a step, although my costs have increased. Dictation tapes containing long articles and book chapters are sent to her by Federal Express; correspondence tapes are played to her over the phone during less-expensive evening hours, and she records them on her end.

I use Norelco dictating equipment. I bought the NT III portable model more than a decade ago, use it hard, and abuse it. (One time, I left it on the roof of my car and heard it hit the pavement when I made a turn in the driveway; it has a small dent in one corner, but it works as well as ever.) It has never needed repairs, nor has my other machine, the 0185, Norelco's least expensive model; the NT III—if still available, which I doubt—is middle-of-the-line. Lanier is actually considered the Cadillac of dictating machines, and if I weren't so heavily invested in Norelco equipment, I might switch. Since the machines aren't compatible, one can't slowly phase from one to the other.

The most common question I'm asked about dictating my material is whether it isn't disconcerting to be unable to *see* the words as one is writing them. The answer is no, although it took some getting used to, just as there are subtle changes required in our thinking when we switch from longhand to typing. Dictation does require thorough preparation, including well-organized notes and a very clear concept of where you're going with the material, even including most transitions, before the writing begins.

I don't think dictating detracts at all from the quality of writing; in fact, it can add spontaneity and a conversational tone. It can pose problems, however, in other contexts. After a few drinks at a party, I've been known to say such things as, "I was down at the beach today, comma, and can you guess what I saw, question mark."

—ROBERT BAHR

■ ■ ■

I do not type (or word-process) any of my writings; I dictate everything. I bought my equipment so long ago I've forgotten why I chose the brand (Lanier) or exactly how much I paid for it. The machines are still working, so they must be okay. To replace everything now would cost about $650, list price.

The dictation machine lists for $250, including a microphone with a switch that records, reverses, and fast-forwards and also has a "conference" setting that lets me lay it down and forget it (the "one person" setting requires you to hold it close to your mouth); a portable costs less, but I have other portables, and I like to have this sturdy office machine set up and always ready to go. The transcriber lists for $400 and has earphones plus a foot pedal with listen, reverse, and fast-forward controls. You can buy one machine for both dictating and transcribing for about $510 list, but of course only one person can use it, in one place, at one time.

My machines use standard-size cassettes, but the equipment comes in a mini version, too. Do realize, however, that they are not interchangeable; if you record an article, or an interview, on one size, you can't use a transcriber that takes the other.

—BOOTON HERNDON

DOUBLE-TALK AND DIALOGUE

If you tape your ideas onto standard audiocassette tapes, you may often wish you could add comments during a later playback without erasing what you had previously recorded. I do this with a Lonestar model K-1 double-cassette "sing-along" system.

This system is intended primarily as a means of playing "duets" with yourself, and I do enjoy using it this way with musical instruments. But I find that it also works well for adding comments to previously recorded voice tracks. While I can usually make out the occasional overlaps when my voice is on both tracks at the same time, I try to remember to pause after my main thoughts when initially recording; in those pauses, I can later add afterthoughts.

Such machines cost about $400, and I wouldn't suggest buying one for this purpose only. But it's also useful for composing dialogue—and, as noted, for playing music. There are some inexpensive versions for children, but be warned that if they run only on batteries, consistent speed is less likely, and some do not use standard-size tapes, making them very likely incompatible with other tape machines.

—DON WIGAL

TAPES: TOO THIN FOR MUSIC, OKAY FOR SPEECH

When I started my writing career, several people told me to use the very best cassette tape I could buy, something like Maxell; nothing's worth a tape failure, they advised. Trouble was, the 30- and 45-minute-per-side good-quality tapes never seemed to be right for my usual one-hour interview sessions. Now, several hundred interviews later, I use Radio Shack's cheap Supertape LN-120, which I buy in boxes of twelve.

This tape runs an hour on each side, which works out well. That length is achieved only by using too-thin tape (too thin for music, that is, but okay for speech). What about all that advice? It's valid, if you're planning to use the tape over and over again. I don't. I save every tape forever, for liability reasons. Each tape is run just four times: twice to record on each side, twice to transcribe each side. I do carry a spare cassette at all times, but I've had just one failure.

—STEPHEN MORRILL

■ ■ ■

I buy the cheapest audiocassette tapes going, usually three for a dollar at Woolworth's, because I don't care about sound quality. This is Joe Doctor I'm recording, not Handel. If I can hear him, that's enough.

For filing my interview tape cassettes, I find that empty facial-tissue boxes—the kind with a large oval opening—are just the right size. A row of such boxes sits on my desk with the openings facing me, each labeled with the name of a project. As I finish an interview, I put the tape in the appropriate box. It's easy to keep projects separated and to file the box of tapes after I've finished each project.

Eventually, the tapes are recycled. I keep a tape for about six months after the story has been published. I then remove the cassette's label, wind the tape back to the beginning (my answering machine does that fast and erases it at the same time), and apply a new blank label (I use self-stick filing-folder labels).

—JANICE HOPKINS TANNE

NON-FLAGGING BATTERIES

Use photo batteries instead of regular batteries in your tape recorder. Not only do they last longer for meetings and lengthy interviews; they also maintain full power until the very end, while ordinary batteries lose power slowly over a period of time.

—M. LAWRENCE PODOLSKY

10

GETTING
IN
TOUCH

Mark Twain, who eagerly took up with one newfangled tool of the writing trade, the typewriter, was far more dubious about another high-tech device. He declined to invest in the gadget when it was first proposed, and when it began to invade the American home, including Twain's house in Hartford, Connecticut, the author—whose office was on the third floor—relegated it to a first-floor closet. Now, of course, the telephone is so necessary a part of our lives that we even have machines to dial it, answer it, and relay its messages to us when we're not around.

MORE THAN ONE PHONE

If, like me, you do many over-the-phone interviews, you need two telephones. (I figured this out when editors complained that it was hard to get through to me.) One of my phones is the incoming line, kept free as much as possible; it's the number listed on my letterhead and in the phone book. I use the second phone for outgoing calls, mostly interviewing; nobody calls me on it, because it's listed in the telephone directory in the name of one of our cats.

The first phone has an answering machine. When I'm on the second line, the taped announcement says, "I'm sorry, I'm on the other line right now. Please leave your name and number and I'll get back to you." When I'm not on the second line, it's available for use by my fax machine.

As a backup, I use my husband's lines, and he does the same with mine (he's also a free lance, but not a writer). His main phone, like mine, has an answering machine, and his second is listed in the name of our other cat.

—JANICE HOPKINS TANNE

■ ■ ■

In some areas, the phone company offers a service called "Call Waiting." When you're on the phone, a special signal lets you know there's an incoming call. Advantage: Callers don't receive a busy signal, and you don't need a second line. Disadvantage: You have to interrupt your conversation (the plunger performs as a hold button) to pick up the other call; if you simply ignore the signal, the caller receives a nobody's-home impression.   —D.S.

ONE PHONE, TWO LINES
Two telephone lines are necessary if you do business from home and another family member uses the phone a great deal, especially if you send data through a modem. I have a Teleconcepts two-line phone with hold button, conference call, ten-number auto-dial, and speakerphone.

—MARTA VOGEL

FUN PHONE
My phone is an AT&T Model 410, with ten-number memory, redial, mute, flash, and hold. It took me forever to give up my old black solid-as-a-rock rotary-dial phone, because the newer phones felt light, chintzy, and cheap to me. But the 410 is fun to use and a real timesaver.

—TONI L. GOLDFARB

PHONE FANCIES: SPEAKERS, ET AL.

Not the fanciest, but the best, phone I've used is the Panasonic Easaphone, with mute button, speaker, automatic dialing for 30 numbers, and redial. Redial and the speaker are the features I most prize—especially the latter, after years of shoulder aches from taking notes with phone clutched by chin. Other features include ring volume control, a tone/pulse switch, and solid construction. And it's easily cleanable.

—BONNIE REMSBERG

■ ■ ■

My handset attachment for recording telephone calls wasn't reliable, so I bought a speakerphone to use with my cassette recorder. With both hands free, it's also easy to take notes, make revisions, and check through manuscripts while on the phone. Useful features of my Panasonic two-line speakerphone, which cost about $100, include hold buttons and automatic dialing of 48 numbers. An added bonus is conference (three-way) calling (a useful feature that I could also get from the telephone company for about $5 a month plus $36 for installation).

—BARBARA GOODHEART

■ ■ ■

A speakerphone seemed like a good idea, but it's been disappointing. The sound quality isn't good, and it seems to confuse the people on the other end. I've stopped using it.

—MARY HARMON

■ ■ ■

I have two AT&T model 420 speakerphones that I bought because I was having trouble recording phone conversations over my old phones and thought these would be an improvement. But the speaker sound is so distorted that whenever I've tried to use them, I've spent most of the conversation explaining why I sounded as if I were at the bottom of a well. Now, I use them as conventional phones—i.e., handset only—and tape interviews by using telephone pickups.

Each phone stores twelve frequently called numbers, a handy feature that saves you time—although you will forget the actual numbers you've stored, so Heaven help you if you have to call your favorite client from a phone booth.

—JANICE HOPKINS TANNE

■ ■ ■

Speakerphones aren't very good to talk on—to the party on the other end, you sound like you're at the bottom of a well—but they're great for waiting. When you call the president of Megaworld Corporation and the receptionist puts you on hold, you can do something besides sitting there like a dummy or getting a crick in your neck from trying to type with a telephone tucked under your ear.

There's a serendipitous effect, too: You can outwait the receptionist. When you're told, "I'm so sorry, Mr. Bigwig is on a long-distance call just now," you say, "That's okay. I can wait—forever." Forever will mean a lengthy tie-up of one of Mr. Bigwig's lines. You will be talking with him soon.

—STEPHEN MORRILL

■ ■ ■

The telephone is my greatest research tool, but I hate the time wasted while on hold. There are a plethora of features on phones out there now, but when I was shopping for a new one, what I looked for was a two-line model with a speakerphone. The Sanyo AD 500 does the job. Now, I just press a button, and the dial tone blares out of a speaker. I punch in the number and then keep right on writing, editing, or paying bills while listening for someone to answer. I could talk without lifting the receiver, too, but callers have told me the fidelity isn't that great. But if I'm put on hold during a call, the receiver goes back in the cradle and I go back to business until I hear the other party return.

Automatic dialing is nice, too (but of course lends itself to forgetting, or never learning, phone numbers). The Sanyo has a 30-number memory for auto-dialing, and I always keep a few slots open for temporary use for numbers called frequently during the course of an assignment. Auto-redial of the last number called is nice, too, and this feature combined with the speaker means I can have busy numbers redialed, once a minute for ten minutes, without ever touching the phone.

Ah, technology!

—TOM BEDELL

NOW, WATCH THIS!

Casio makes a wristwatch, Model DBA80, that not only stores up to 50 entire phone numbers but can actually send out an audio signal that can dial those numbers on command. Unlike telephone answering machines that may also remember and dial automatically, my watch is nearly always with me. It also displays the number, so I can read it to someone or dial it manually.

The audio signal is not accepted by all phones—some types of pay phones, for example, will not heed it. But just having your 50 most frequently dialed numbers in hand is a secure feeling, even when the auto-dial cannot function. And like most Casio watches, this device also does several other handy things: It can be set to ring an alarm at the same time every day, it stores the combination to my club locker, and it stores my credit card numbers. It cost under $70 in 1988.

For office use, if you wish to store many more than 50 numbers, there is the Canon DF-100. It doesn't tell time, but it does work as a full-function calculator. However, when changing its batteries, you must accomplish the task within one minute, or you lose all the stored information. (Imagine reprogramming 80 phone numbers and several dozen addresses just because you took 61 seconds instead of 60 to change batteries! And you thought changing your clocks twice a year was a nuisance.) This device cost about $75 in 1987.

—DON WIGAL

TALK/TYPE AT SAME TIME I: CORDLESS WONDER

Crooking my chin over the phone receiver to hold it on my shoulder while conducting long-distance interviews left my hands free to take notes. It also, in time, resulted in neck and shoulder stiffness accompanied by dull pain in one ear. I feared developing a permanent 45-degree tilt to my head.

To the rescue came Plantronics' LiteSet Wireless Communication System. It's the ultimate in telephone freedom. It consists of a featherlight earpiece which actually hangs from one ear (you make it fit via one of nine different adapters which are included) and includes both the receiver and the microphone; a dial pad, which comes with a belt clip (it's cigarette-package size and can also be dropped in a pocket) and is connected to the earpiece by a four-foot cord; and a "base station," which plugs into the wall and recharges the battery in the portable part when the latter's not being carried around. The manual gives clear instructions for hookup and use.

I hooked up the little gem, gave the battery a 24-hour charge, and then tried it out. Amazingly, the earpiece hung in place despite my head movements. The voice quality, both incoming and outgoing, is excellent. And it has a pager, auto-redial, and volume control and works on either tone or pulse. You can also plug in an answering machine.

I paid $99.90 when I ordered it from the DAK Industries catalog.[1]

—CHARLES BOECKMAN

■ ■ ■

Plantronics' LiteSet cordless phone, which I recently bought from the DAK Industries catalog, is the smallest phone I've ever seen; the "dial pad" is about the size of a 3- by 5-inch index card, and the headset, which contains everything else, is a little fatter and shorter than a Bic pen. The phone, if you can call it that, rests on a "homebase" and charges up when you're not using it. You can look up something in a book or file, clean the house, read the newspaper, or do other quiet kinds of things while talking on the phone, without getting a crick in your neck.

There are a couple of problems: Washing dishes (or similarly "loud" activities) are picked up by the sensitive microphone and will sound like Niagara Falls on the other end. Also, some computers give off a buzz around the phone, so you may not be able to count on taking notes easily while interviewing someone over this phone.

On the whole, however, for $100, I've found it very satisfactory.

—MARTA VOGEL

■ ■ ■

I use the LiteSet by Plantronics to augment my telephone system, especially when I leave my office to spend some time with the children and can't always reach for the nearest telephone. It's completely porta- ble and fits easily into your pocket. The headset can also go into your pocket—or you can wear it around the house, since it's featherweight. It's a terrific advantage to have the phone with you when you're away from your desk; it's easy to use, the quality is fine, and you never miss any calls.

—LINDA-MARIE SINGER

■ ■ ■

The LiteSet, from Plantronics of Santa Cruz, California, is a neat cord- less phone. The headset is light and fits in the ear with no head strap or other encumbrances. It enables a writer to type while talking on the phone and, since it's cordless, it even enables you to go to the mailbox

[1]See "Mail-Order Sources" at end of chapter.

or anywhere up to 1000 feet away and still make and receive calls.

The LiteSet, which works only with single-line phones, is available via several mail-order houses, including DAK, for around $100. Plantronics—(800) 538-0748—will also refer callers to the firm's nearest distributor.

—DAVE KAISER

TALK/TYPE AT SAME TIME II: HEADSETS, GENERALLY . . .

I use a phone-operator's headset, consisting of earphones and a microphone, to conduct telephone interviews. Unlike speakerphones, which often sound as if you're calling from a subway tunnel, a headset sounds completely natural. It leaves your hands free to type notes into a computer and, best of all, eliminates the neck pain that can result from bracing a phone receiver between your shoulder and ear.

—MARIAN FAUX

■ ■ ■

Headsets are cheap these days. If you do a lot of telephone interviewing, especially if you like to type the interview as you're talking, they're wonderful. They're also great if you're hard of hearing, because they're naturally easier to hear (less outside noise), and some of them even have volume controls.

—STEPHEN MORRILL

■ ■ ■

I used to use a regular phone for interviewing, but I started developing minor medical problems from holding the receiver trapped between my ear and shoulder for long periods of time. Now, I use a headset, which fits on my head and frees up my hands. While I conduct the interview, I key the subject's words directly into my computer. I'm unusual in that I type over 100 words per minute and thus am able to get everything keyed in almost verbatim. I also wear my headset, and take notes on the computer, when an editor calls with an assignment, typing while the editor talks; between this and the subsequent assignment letter, I figure I cut down on miscommunication and, consequently, on kill fees.

Obviously, there's a lot to do at once—typing, thinking, coming up with follow-up questions, looking for opportunities to ask the follow-up questions, trying to figure out the spelling of unfamiliar terms your interviewee may use. But you learn to handle it—and you needn't type as fast as I do to use this technique.

One trick is to type everything lower case; that way, you don't have to fool with the shift key. Another is to make sure you get the technical terms right (those are the words that give a quote the flavor of authority) but fudge on the ordinary, everyday words. And don't ever be afraid to ask an interviewee to spell a difficult word or to wait a minute while you catch up.

—DAVID GROVES

■ ■ ■

Immediately after you have thus keyboarded an interview, it is a good idea to do four things, in this order: (1) Save the file on a floppy disk (assuming your system has not done so automatically). (2) Have it examined and corrected by your spell-checking program. (3) Go over it again; correct other kinds of silly mistakes and make missed insertions now, while you remember what your interviewee said; add notes to yourself, e.g. concerning tone of voice. (4) Save it again, and also print out a copy.   —D.S.

. . . AND SPECIFICALLY

A lightweight little headset/microphone is the Unisonic Speak-Easy Headset. The headset itself is connected to a junction box, which clips onto your belt. From the junction box, a 24-foot coiled cord leads either to your phone's wall plug or the base unit, letting you wander around your office while "connected."

A Siamese plug, with two outlets, is provided to replace the wall-to-phone-base cord, so you can plug the lead back in and still have a place for the headset cord; you can still use the regular handset as well as the headset. The junction box has a volume control, as well as a microphone shut-off for times when you want to curse the dog without interrupting the person you're talking to.

For extended telephone interviews, I find this headset nearly priceless. The sound quality is fine. It feels a little flimsy, but given the price, I can replace it easily if need be. I bought it for $19.99 from the Quill catalog.[2]

—ED NELSON

■ ■ ■

[2]See appendix for a full list of order-by-mail-or-phone office-supply sources.

Telephone interviews used to be literally a pain in the neck as I tried valiantly to type quotes into my computer while pinching a receiver between my shoulder and ear. Then I saw the Featherweight Phone advertised on TV and promptly ordered one.

This headset with mike weighs less than a Walkman headset, plugs into a dual socket—so I can transfer from receiver to headset—and came with a long cord that reaches from phone to computer. It works much better than a speakerphone (another possible solution), since it insures privacy and blots out background noise effectively.

The Featherweight costs about $20 by mail from National Teletronics, 16 Industrial Boulevard, Paoli PA 19301.

—CAROL TONSING

■ ■ ■

I've done a lot of interviews over the phone. I've found it extremely useful to use the Duofone 119 headset, available from Radio Shack. I've rigged up my headset along with a jack for my tape recorder, and I tape the interviews while my hands are free to pound out notes on my computer. I then use the tape as back-up or to fill in those spots I missed.

—BRUCE W. MOST

■ ■ ■

I find my Radio Shack Duofone 99 headset invaluable, not only for interviewing but for the many other conversations during which I take notes by hand or work at my keyboard. One caution: This headset cannot be used with touch-tone phones. At first, I kept forgetting to switch my phone to pulse; I consequently ruined two headsets.

—MARY HARMON

■ ■ ■

For anyone conducting lengthy telephone interviews or *giving* extensive interviews, as in promoting a book (I did as many as eighteen radio shows in three days after the publication of my book *Children and Money: A Parent's Guide*), I highly recommend a headset. I use a model called Elite from Radio Shack; it cost $60 when I purchased it in 1985. Just one caveat: I haven't yet figured out how to make it work on a two-line telephone.

—GRACE W. WEINSTEIN

■ ■ ■

It's impossible to cradle a receiver and talk on the phone and still pay attention to your word processing. My last book required 30 lengthy interviews, with 20 being conducted on the phone; without a headset, I would have been lost. My first headset was made in Taiwan, cost $65, and lasted a year. Since then, I've purchased an ACS Dynamate 2000 for $60, which works through a spare desktop phone; by shopping around, I'm sure lower prices could be found.

—PETER LOEWER

■ ■ ■

My headset is the Dynamate 1200. It consists of two parts: (1) a small (2½-inch-long) amplifier (with volume control), which you attach to a wall or piece of furniture near your phone (or the phone itself) using Velcro strips (included); (2) the ounce-and-a-half headset itself—a single foam-cushioned earpiece and attached mike, with a flexible band to hold it on your head. The two parts are connected by a seven-foot cord, which is quite enough to let me reach most of the files in my small office, if need be, while talking.

When you want to use it, you unplug the receiver end of your phone's deskset-to-handset coiled wire and plug it into the amplifier, slip on the headset, and make your call. (You can even, I discovered after fearing to try for some time, transfer the plug after you've placed—or received—the call.) I bought it for $49 (plus shipping) from the DAK catalog.[3] That was in 1987; it has performed admirably and reliably ever since.

The catalog copy included a warning that this device is compatible only with phone-company phones, whether tone or pulse (mine is a Western Electric touch-tone). The maker's instruction sheet that came with the gadget, however, says there are other models (one was mentioned above) and declares that, "There is a Dynamate right for you." ACS Communications, the manufacturer, is at 250 Technology Circle, Scotts Valley CA 95066. —D.S.

MULTIPLE LONG-DISTANCE SERVICES

At least in our area, fierce competition among long-distance dialing services has resulted in very good service with no monthly or hook-up fees—so one can subscribe to several different services. You can have only one service that requires only the 1-plus-area-code kind of dialing.

---

[3]See "Mail-Order Sources" at end of chapter.

But with an automatic dialer, it takes only a second or two longer to dial the additional code numbers when using services that aren't one's primary long-distance carrier.

I use this as a bookkeeping device to help keep expense accounts separate when working on several assignments at once. Rather than having to log calls, I know that long-distance calls made on Sprint are for one account, those made on AT&T for another, and so on.

—JANET GROENE

CARRIERS: WEIGHING THE SAVINGS
The telephone is a basic tool of the writer's business. It can also be an expensive one.

Rule Number One: Investigate the long-distance services in your area and opt for the one that will not only give you the most savings on your long-distance calls but will also indicate those savings on your monthly bill (this assumes you have chosen a carrier other than AT&T). That way, you can monitor your savings and weigh them against the loss of operator assistance.

Rule Number Two: Know how to use other carriers when you need them. Under equal access, phone users designate a primary toll company. The selected carrier handles almost all interstate calls, as well as some within states, that are dialed in the usual manner: 1 + area code + local number. Should you want to make a collect call, or need operator assistance, you will need AT&T. That carrier code is 10288; to place such a call, you dial 10288 + 0 + area code + local number. Codes for other major toll firms: MCI, 10222; All-Net, 10444; U.S. Sprint, 10777; ITT, 10488; Western Union, 10220. But remember that too much use of other access codes will reduce your discount rate with your designated toll company.

A summary of code-dialing rules can be found in the *Long Distance Comparison Chart* published by the Telecommunications Research and Action Center in Washington DC, (202) 462-2520.

—MARY JEAN PARSON

PICKER-UPPERS: PURCHASE POINTERS
We used to employ an answering service; nobody, including us, really relishes talking to a tape recorder over the phone. But when you compare the cost of even the most expensive machines with even the cheapest answering services, the machines come out ahead.

It's important to shop around and gear your purchase to your particular needs and preferences. We prefer machines that are voice-activated rather than limiting callers to 30- or 60-second messages. Check the specifications to find how long a silence the recorder permits before shutting off; if it's too short, it can cut people off in mid-sentence if they stammer or pause to catch their breath.

If you travel a great deal, as we do, you'll probably want a machine that allows remote message pick-up. From a rotary-dial phone, a special beeper must be used for that purpose. But most of the world is, or soon will be, on touch-tone systems, so you're probably safe buying a beeper-less model. The machine we now have, which cost about $100, allows us to call it from any touch-tone phone in the world to collect messages (it holds a total of two and a half hours' worth) and/or change our outgoing announcement.

—JEFF MORGAN

■ ■ ■

Do be sure to buy an answering machine that's voice-activated, not one that faithfully records 30 seconds of silence when someone calls but leaves no message. You'll save yourself several hours a year of waiting to get to the next message.

Also buy one that lets you monitor incoming calls when you're in, so it can function as your robot receptionist. When you hear a call you want to take, simply pick up the phone. But if the caller wants to sell you aluminum siding, let him tell the machine all about it while you keep working.

—STEPHEN MORRILL

MICROCASSETTE RECORDING

I looked for two key features in an answering machine—the ability to record conversations as well as messages, and the ability to do so on microcassette tape so it would be compatible with the rest of my interviewing/transcribing equipment. The Code-A-Phone 3530 does just that. I have noticed a tendency for the sound quality to diminish when I switch on the tape for a phone interview (whether this is a glitch in the machine or in my phone line, I've yet to determine); still, it works better than any other phone-recording system I've tried. And as an answering machine, it has about every feature I could hope for, other than giving me assignments, including remote access.

—TOM BEDELL

SERVICE TO SWEAR BY

I swear by my Sanyo Model TAS-1 answering machine. It's not the current generation and so doesn't offer remote access—but since I'm rarely away, that hasn't been a problem. The Sanyo service people are in a nearby town, just half an hour away, so obtaining parts and service is quite convenient. What's more, on the very few occasions when something wasn't right, I called them, described the problem, and got straight advice on clearing it up, thus acting as my own service person.

—DOROTHY SIEGEL

TRADING UP

My answering machine has been adequate—it's voice-activated and can be accessed remotely without a beeper device—but I've decided to get a snazzier machine, because prices have come down. I'm getting a PhoneMate which also permits changing the outgoing message remotely *and* gives the day and time messages are received, a nice feature when you're out of town.

—ROSEMARY ELLEN GUILEY

EXPECTATION: ETERNAL LIFE

When the then-editor of *Savvy Woman* called to give me my first assignment for the magazine, my then-answering machine failed to record the message. Fortunately, she tried again, but I suffered temporary heart failure.

That system was a rebuilt industrial model of antique vintage. I promptly threw it out. "What's the best machine money can buy, so this will never happen to me again?" I asked a businessman who not only sells such machines but also takes them all apart and fixes them. The Dictaphone Model 757, he said. So I swallowed hard and paid the $365 for the machine, which is made by Pitney-Bowes, one of the nation's premier office-equipment makers.

In three years, the machine has never had a single problem and has never broken down. It not only records messages but also records phone interviews and conference calls and allows me to retrieve messages remotely when I'm on the road. This last feature is especially useful when I'm stranded at the closed Pan Am terminal in New York and my husband is already on his way to Boston's Logan Airport to pick me up. Many times, the machine has been the only way we could communicate.

On occasion, a cassette will fail—but there's never anything wrong with the machine itself. I expect it to live forever, and I feel I've already recouped my investment by knowing I'm certain never to miss another important call.

—PATRICIA MANDELL

YOUR MESSAGE IS THE MESSAGE

Buy the least expensive answering machine you can find that allows you to record your own outgoing messages and to screen your calls by monitoring incoming ones. I use the Record-a-Call 2100, which I purchased from a discount house for about $50.

Above all, be sure your announcement message sounds professional. An announcement that says the caller has reached an *office* serves three purposes: It assures editors, and interviewees who are returning your calls, that you mean business; it turns off telephone solicitors; it discourages crank callers. Eschew gimmicky, froufrou, or bizarre messages.

Single women are wise to imply that more than one person is at the number (use "we," not "I").

—VICKY HAY

"I'M HERE! I'M HERE!"

Answering machines are great, but periodically, you forget to turn the machine off when you return to your office, and the next time the phone rings, you find yourself shouting "Hold on! Hold on!" to a caller through your own recorded message.

The answer is Meyers Electronics' X-cluder, a tiny and inexpensive device that swiftly cuts off the answering machine's recorded message the instant you pick up the phone. Installation takes just seconds: you stick the X-cluder's plug into a baseboard phone-line outlet, plug the answering machine into the X-cluder, and that's it. It works so well that I now leave my answering machine on (which eliminates the problem of forgetting to *turn* it on before going out).

The X-cluder comes in models for one-line and two-line answering machines, at about $15 and $25.

—WENDY MURPHY

MULTITALENTED MACHINE

I've grown quite attached to my PhoneMate series 7350 telephone. It's a sleek little number with an auto-dialer, redialer, hold button, and a built-in answering machine that faithfully takes all calls after X number of rings. (That last is a great feature. You set it once, and that's it. You never have the nagging feeling that you've left the office without turning on your answering machine.)

Further, it lets you record your phone conversations, which is extremely useful when conducting interviews. You just push the button marked "record," and the PhoneMate automatically records the call on the incoming message cassette.

Oh, there's one more wonderful feature. You can set the phone to *talk* to you instead of ringing. A pleasant male voice then says, "You have a telephone call . . . You have a telephone call . . ."

The machine cost me about $180.

—BARBARA NIELSEN

BETTER PLAYBACK

Although my Panasonic VA8045 telephone/answering machine is four years old, I can't imagine any newer model being much better. The special feature of the phone is a recorder that beeps softly every 20 or 30 seconds, but what I especially like is that the sound, on playback, is so clear—sometimes better than what I've picked up in person with a tape recorder and microphone.

—LINDA-MARIE SINGER

THE ANSWERING SERVICE ADVANTAGE

Many callers won't talk to a machine. Far preferable is an answering service, on which a human being answers and is prepared to have a dialogue with the caller. This does mean you have to keep the people buttered up so they act like human beings, and you have to keep them informed so they can track you down. Once, some years ago when I lived in New York, an editor needed a novel condensed over the weekend and started calling writers. I was out, but my answering service talked him into waiting five minutes before going on to the next writer on his list and then tracked me down at Tim Costello's, where I had checked in with the bartender. The $5000 I got for three days' work has paid for many years of telephone answering service.

—BOOTON HERNDON

MAIL-ORDER SOURCES

A good source of phone equipment—phones, plus anything and every-thing for them—is Hello Direct, 140 Great Oaks Boulevard, San Jose CA 95119; (800) HI-HELLO [444-3556].

—TONI L. GOLDFARB

■ ■ ■

The DAK Industries catalog, mentioned several times in this chapter, isn't specifically geared to business but purveys high-tech merchandise of many (leisure and other) types. DAK is at 8200 Remmet Avenue, Canoga Park CA 91304; (800) 325-0800 for credit-card orders, (800) 423-2866 for other inquiries. —D.S.

11

MOVING MANUSCRIPTS AND MESSAGES

‎ime was, there were two choices when it came time to get manuscripts and other materials into the hands of their intended recipients: Hand delivery, assuming geographic proximity, or the U.S. Postal Service. Now, there are many choices—more classes of mail, local and long-distance private delivery services, and electronic methods to transmit your messages.

■   ## FAX IT TO ME   ■

Considered indispensable in a burgeoning number of business offices and, increasingly, by many writers as well, is the facsimile machine—the "fax." Words, pictures, anything on paper can be sent from one fax machine to another, anywhere, over ordinary telephone lines.

NEWS FROM ABROAD

Fax is a dandy way to speed things, especially from abroad; your copy arrives in minutes instead of days, and at much lower cost. I remember covering a scientific meeting in Vienna a few years back; I had to go to the airport to send back copy, and the minimum charge for the service was around $100. But transmitting three pages of copy from Amsterdam, Rome, and Stockholm in mid-1988 via fax cost $10 to $20 (depending on exchange rates).

Federal Express and other couriers are available in some European cities, but they often work through local companies and are fairly high-priced; fax service is quicker and cheaper.

—JEAN McCANN

QUICK QUERIES

For a person better at pitching story ideas on paper than over the phone, when time is of the essence, the fax machine is the perfect solution. An editor may allow your mailed query to sit in his or her "In" box for weeks, and may even neglect to return your phone call for days, but a fax message lands on an editorial desk with an air of urgency. Invariably, you get a quick response. (It's a good idea to check first to see if the editor will accept queries by fax.)

Fax also provides a quick way to follow up on those occasions when you've tentatively sold an editor an idea in a telephone conversation: "May I fax you a fast outline on that?" usually results in an affirmative response to the question and a speedy decision on the proposal.

Editors may eventually begin to react as lethargically to fax as they do to mail and phone calls. For the present, it offers a good way to grab their attention.

—HAL HIGDON

HOW DO I USE THEE?

Fax machines now offer big advantages to writers. Mine is a Sharp 220, which I purchased for about $1200. On it, I have received questions from editors and copy editors at book publishers and magazines and have been able to send back answers immediately. I have sent copies of letters and contracts to my agent. I have received information from research sources in time to meet a looming deadline.

If you've been using express mail service to make sure a manuscript gets to a magazine before the editor leaves—which can be quite quickly, these days—you'll find it's less expensive to use fax. Fax costs only the price of the phone call; express mail costs from $8.75 up. As for modems, which send the copy through the computer, they're good for large manuscripts but harder to use than fax, at least as far as I'm concerned.

—RUTH WINTER

THE COPY SENT 'ROUND THE WORLD

After I became computerized, I wondered how I'd ever worked without a computer. Now, I feel the same way about the facsimile machine.

I've had my fax machine, at this writing, for four or five months, and my ability to get a letter to or from an editor in half a minute is still mind-boggling. I can tell an editor in New York, or in Tokyo, "You'll have the article on your desk when you arrive in the morning" (or, for that matter, "in five minutes")—and it's there, at the transmission rate of a page every 25 or 30 seconds. Most publishers now have faxes—if not in the editorial offices, at least in the advertising department.

I query, market material to foreign countries (and across town), receive data I need for articles, send bills, and beat deadlines by fax. Last week, I faxed a request for some background material I needed that very day for my weekly syndicated column (which is sent to the syndicate by fax); my source faxed through six pages of information 15 minutes later. The week before, I decided to offer a 23-page manuscript to editors in 22 different countries; I did so by fax, a total of 506 pages (I knew a single sale would pay for the overseas line costs ten times over).

Fax is demanding upon the receiver; it demands attention and a fast reply. And an editor can't deny receiving your letter or manuscript: The machine prints out a "receipt" confirming that the message went through, as well as the length of the transmission, the time, and the date.

Fax is usually cheaper than mail or a phone call. Yesterday, I sent an eight-page article, plus an invoice, a cover information sheet, and another page with additional data; the eleven pages got across the country from California to Florida in 4 minutes, 33 seconds, at a line cost of $1.09.

And it saves a great deal of time, aside from transmission speed per se. You don't have the usual mailing chores—preparing labels and envelopes, affixing postage, trundling the package to the post office. Nor do you have the telephone-time expense of normal long-distance niceties ("How've you been?" "Pretty hot there?" "Really great talking to you!").

My machine is an Omnifax G36D, sold by the Telautograph Corporation; it cost me about $1875. What's critical, though, is that any fax you buy be a "Group 3" machine. That means it's capable of communicating with all present general-use fax machines. But that's not enough. At this writing, some such machines retail for around $500, others for $1500 and up. What's the difference? Lower-priced machines have lower-grade scanning ability.

Scanning is the heart of the fax. The scanner inside the machine scans the page and transmits what it "sees" to the machine at the other end of the line. Good scanning delivers a sharp, clear image; poor scanning delivers fuzzy, impossible-to-read text. Good fax machines also do their scanning rapidly. They not only deliver sharp copy to the receiving machine; they deliver it quickly. (The slower the machine, the more you'll pay for the phone transmission time.)

Before you buy a fax machine, insist on a simple test. Have with you a full page (8½ by 11 inches) of single-spaced text, as well as a black-and-white illustration (line drawing or photograph). Ask the salesperson to run them through the machine's "copy" cycle. As this is done, time the process, from the instant the machine begins scanning to the moment the copy appears. You will get out of the machine copies of the text and illustration exactly as they would be transmitted. Check the quality. If the text or line drawing isn't sharp (or a photo at least discernible), and/or it takes over 30 seconds per page, don't buy.

If any reader has questions and would like to ask them by fax, my machine's dedicated line is (213) 826-3676. I promise an instant reply.

—JIM JOSEPH

ORIENT EXPRESS

A facsimile machine is indispensable to me, since about half my writing business is in Japan. With the fax machine, I can send copy there during the early morning hours when telephone rates are lowest. There is a 14-hour time difference between U.S. Eastern Time and Japan, so if I send a fax at 7 A.M., it arrives in Japan at 9 P.M. the same day and will be waiting at the machine when the next workday begins there—and because I'm sending during Japanese nonbusiness hours, I seldom get a busy signal.

I purchased a Murata MT600 and paid extra for an automatic dialer feature. Not only is the auto-dialer more convenient; if a line is busy, it will wait and try again three minutes later. In addition, the auto-dialer assures that you get the right number the first time—an important matter when you're making expensive overseas calls.

I bought my Murata partly because the local dealer from whom I got it gives great service. For example, he installed special phone extension wiring and connections so I could place the fax where I wanted it; he also provided a custom-made carrying case, since I take the fax with me when I spend more than a weekend at our summer cottage. Other features I like: the copy feeds into the machine face up; a digital display shows me the number I've dialed, confirms that the fax has gone through, and indicates how long it took; and it provides a monthly printout of faxes sent and received.

So far, the only "junk" fax mail I've received was some nice Christmas greetings from clients.

—ELYSE M. ROGERS

TWO ON THE ISLE

When Jinx and I first moved to the British West Indies, the telephone system was a quaint antique. Most of the instruments included a variety of handsets, bodies, and dials that had been cannibalized from other phones; the dial on the one in our house bore Arabic characters and the phone itself was the same design as the device Grace Kelly was chatting away on when the guy jumped out from behind the curtains and tried to strangle her in *Dial M for Murder.* Mail to and from the States went the long way around the world and, if it arrived at all, took up to a month.

This state of affairs gave a chilling new dimension to the word "deadline."

For the first couple of years, we bribed ferryboat captains to put manuscripts in the U.S. mail on St. Thomas (where we still keep a post-office box for Stateside mail). If we ran late, we bought a lot of drinks for airline pilots who took envelopes to express mail drops at American airports. When a branch of Federal Express opened in our little corner of Paradise, four weeks became three days—at $35 a shot. Cable and telex rates worked out to about ten cents a word.

Then, in 1988, we unexpectedly found ourselves with viable phone service—a model digital system, North American compatible at that. Now, we use fax constantly, and so do many of the others in the surprisingly large cadre of writers on our little island.

When considering a fax machine, assess your needs carefully and make sure it has the capacity you require. We use the NEC NEFAX Bit-V, which can hold up to 30 sheets of any length paper (even mixed lengths) and has a timer that allows transmission at a preset time; we set it to send after the phone rates go down at 11 P.M. I don't know what this machine costs in the States, but we chose it from those available from the local phone-service firm, Cable and Wireless Ltd., on a hire-purchase arrangement, which means they fix it for free until it's paid for; our final cost will be about $2400. It's expensive, but it has a lot of other features we like (many are also available on cheaper models), including one-touch dialing for frequent destinations and automatic polling for multiple destinations (one magazine we deal with regularly has editorial offices in both New York and Los Angeles).

No matter what machine you get, be sure it's Group 3, which is the present international standard. And if you'll be receiving much fax traffic (we do), get a separate telephone number for full-time automatic reception and make sure your machine will support a large roll of printing paper. One friend of ours hooked his fax machine to his answering machine on his regular phone line and left a message saying, "if you are trying to send a fax message, please touch the star button now," referring to the asterisk button at the lower left on a touch-tone phone, which would send a signal to the fax machine, readying it to receive. But often, people heard "start now," and all he had was an answering-machine tape full of electronic screeching.

A lot of people, both here and in the States, have found that fax is as cheap as, or cheaper than, mail for longish letters. For instance, I once put together a lengthy presentation to a bank manager complete with charts, graphs, and other visual aids. It was twenty pages long, would have cost $1 to mail, and probably would have taken two or three days to arrive. I faxed it for a dime.

Obviously, fax can be invaluable. One word of warning: Fax machines use thermal paper, which has a short shelf life. If you plan to keep a document you've received by fax longer than three or four months, photocopy it as soon as possible after receiving it. (This might be another reason to consider buying a copier. It's insidious how technology feeds on itself, isn't it?)

—JEFF MORGAN

■ ■ ■

And even if you don't plan to keep a faxed document very long at all, don't make the mistake of using a highlighter pen to mark the really important parts; you'll find the print doing an instant vanishing act.

Incidentally, at this writing a few plain-paper fax machines have appeared. They are expensive. But perhaps, as with copiers (the early ones used fast-fade thermal paper), prices will eventually be within reach of writers. —D.S.

"TEN-PAGE" TRANSLATION

I have a Brother 1010 fax bought for $1600 in 1988 at 47th Street Photo in New York City. It is a reliable machine. You should know, however, that there are things they don't tell you.

For instance, the ad may say "five-page document feeder" or "ten-page document feeder." I assumed the latter meant I could load ten pages, send them, then load the remaining eight pages of my story and send them. Not so. What these numbers denote, with many machines, is the maximum number of pages you can send in one phone call. I found this a nuisance, although not as big a nuisance as I first thought— but if I were buying a machine now, I'd go for one with a 30-page document feeder. (Confusingly, *some* faxes are *not* thus limited in number of pages per transmission, and you *can* send a longer document in the same call by just reloading the feeder.)

Most faxes have the ability to send a document of great length, such as an architectural drawing. I'm planning to try to send a printout of a story uncut, as one page, but at this writing, I haven't yet set up the experiment with a client.

Be aware, too, that the same fax machine may be sold under different trade names at different prices; dealers have directories listing them. It pays to ask.

—JANICE HOPKINS TANNE

A "SMART" MACHINE

I wanted a fax machine that would be on 24-hour, seven-day standby, so that clients and editors could fax me material at their convenience, and at low rates, without calling me first to set up a transmission. But I also wanted to put the machine on an existing phone line rather than setting up a separate line for it, since I already had two lines—a home line, and a business line reserved for my business calls, modem transmissions and, when I'm out, messages picked up by my answering machine. I wanted to put the fax on my home line.

The first and second machines I tried functioned in standby primarily as phones, switching to the fax function only after six unanswered rings.

Then I found the Sharp UX-350. It can "tell," on standby, the difference between an incoming telephone call and a fax. After one ring followed by a five-second pause, the machine connects the fax *or* rings again to indicate a phone call. (This works only on single-line phones.)

This machine cost about $1500, compared with $900 for other models, but the "smart" feature is worth it. It also has other nice features: higher-quality reproduction than cheaper models, faster transmission (as fast as eighteen seconds), greater auto-dial capacity (70 numbers in memory), a ten-sheet document feeder, polling, automatic redial and hold buttons, and a speaker.

—BARBARA GOODHEART

FAX ON BOARD

We've installed fax boards in our computers. To send computer-written copy, you just indicate which file [document] you want transmitted; the software formats it into fax code and fires it off. You can also receive faxes via your computer; they can then be printed out on your regular printer.

Most such devices have software that can schedule the time for fax transmissions, so you can transmit at night, when phone rates are cheaper. During the day, the software keeps the fax working in the background, so you can use other computer programs while the fax does its thing.

Quadram makes a fine internal fax board. The firm also makes a portable fax that plugs into the outside of IBM PCs and compatibles, as well as one for the Apple Macintosh; both cost under $600, and there is a deluxe model that includes a modem for folks who don't have one. Apple sells a $700 fax board for Macs which plugs between the computer and the phone line and includes a modem. We can also recommend The Complete Fax (CFAX), made by the Complete PC company for IBMs and compatibles; we prefer Quadram's fax software to Apple's or CFAX's, but the CFAX board is as good as the others.

There is, of course, a drawback to this setup, compared with standalone fax machines: you can't transmit images or type from paper. If you want to do that via a fax board, you must first get the material into your computer, and for that, you need to add a scanner. A number of companies make such scanners; they cost upward of $1000.

—JUDI K-TURKEL and FRANKLYNN PETERSON

CHOICES

Of the various fax machines I've used, the Sharp F0-F10 is excellent. But so is the AT&T internal fax board, run by their program Page Power, in conjunction with Microsoft Windows; the internal fax allows you to dispense with paper almost totally for manuscripts and correspondence.

—SHIRLEY CAMPER SOMAN

FAX IT TO ME—SORT OF

Those of us who don't see the need to buy a fax machine can still use one when necessary. Many local copy and print shops let you send and receive faxes through their machines; they give you their fax numbers for you to give others, and you bring them stuff you want to send out. My local Kinko's [a copy-shop chain], at this writing, charges $2 for the first page received and $1 per page after that, $5 for the first page sent and $2 per page after that. And this particular shop is open 24 hours a day.

It pays to have such a number handy so that any time someone asks about faxing something to you, you can say, "Sure!"

—MARTY KLEIN

■ ■ ■

We'd heard from other writers how handy fax machines were. We'd also heard that some writers found that their machines required service. We took to using machines that belong to others.

The Genovese chain of drugstores has fax machines in most of its stores. Since these machines, like any machines, are subject to malfunctions, we "have" two numbers—one for our local copy shop, the second for Genovese's; both phone us when a fax comes in.

Warning: Fax numbers can bring an avalanche of unsolicited news releases and other materials—with a charge for each page. We avoid giving out "our" fax numbers loosely; we treat them like unlisted phone numbers.

—HENRY and ELIZABETH URROWS

■   NO PAPER NEEDED   ■

But wait—for computer-generated copy, there's also the modem. That's short for "modulator-demodulator," and it's a computer-to-computer communications device. It can also link your computer with "electronic mail" services, to electronic "bulletin boards," and to banks of data to which you might want access (see Chapter 7). It's operated by its own sort of computer program, known as communications software.

OVER THE REGULAR PHONE

So far, I've eschewed the current passion for fax. I can send manuscripts—and receive certain material—much more quickly and cheaply using a $50 modem and an $80 program to operate it. Fax sends a hard copy and may require a dedicated phone line; editors must then keyboard the material into their own systems. With a modem, I send manuscripts directly to the publisher's computer system, on which it is edited, and then typeset, without anyone's having to retype the text. And it goes out over my regular phone line.

—JANET GROENE

NO! GET ANOTHER LINE!

If you use a modem, do *not* have installed on your phone line a feature that notifies you if another call is coming in. If that happens while you're transmitting or receiving material, the tone is going to demolish the data. Either get a separate line for your modem or forget about it.

—KEN ENGLADE

USE THE M WORD

I've found that even some people who have had computers for a long time still have a block when it comes to the M word—modem. I've asked editors, "Do you have a modem?" and a typical response is, "A what? Oh. Uh—the person who knows about that is out to lunch right now." I don't understand why people know what a fax is but don't know the first thing about modems. I'd recommend getting a modem even if you *don't* know the first thing about them. Get someone to teach you. It's really not hard.

Here's another point in their favor: You don't have to have a fax machine yourself to send things to somebody else's fax machine. You can use MCI Mail, an electronic system that costs only $25 a year, and send your letter or article right from your computer. Last time I did this, it went across town in seven minutes; so much for delivery services.

—MARTA VOGEL

INDUSTRY STANDARD

The standard in the industry is the Hayes SmartModem; get one that offers at least 1200 baud [unit of transmission speed], preferably 2400 baud. I recently began paying all my bills through my bank's direct-access system; I found this modem was the only one compatible with the system. And everything *else* is compatible with *it*.

—SHIRLEY CAMPER SOMAN

PROCOMM: FRIENDLY SOFTWARE FOR MODEM USERS

In my tentative steps into the world of telecommunications, I've tried three communications software packages. The one I've found most user-friendly (a hackneyed but useful term) is *ProComm*. It has a wonderful "help" menu which has enabled me to make my way through the complexities of bits, bauds, and parity with very little angst.

When I bought my copy of *ProComm* in mid-1988, the price was $50. The people are also extremely obliging. I needed the software in a hurry. They sent it to me via Federal Express—and called me to assure me it was on its way!

ProComm is available from Datastorm Technologies, Inc., P.O. Box 1471, Columbia MO 65205; (314) 474-8461.

—ANNE L. FINGER

■ ■ ■

One of the best telecommunications software values on the market is *ProComm+*, by Datastorm Technologies. It does everything big-name programs costing up to three and four times as much do, and more. And it's available on electronic bulletin boards, and from vendors advertising "shareware" software in computer magazines, under a "test drive" license; that means people can try it for free and pay the $75 registration fee only if they like it.

One of *ProComm+*'s more unusual features should especially interest writers who regularly submit work electronically to the same publishers. Many publishers' in-house computer systems require users to use specific code words or phrases to "log on." Some telecommunications programs let users automate these log-on procedures, but this usually requires learning the program's own special computer "language" and actually writing a "miniprogram" to handle the log-on routine.

Most writers aren't interested in learning yet another language, and *ProComm+* offers a shortcut around that tedium. It can record a manually entered log-on sequence and put the sequence into a separate file which can be linked with the publisher's phone number in the program's dialing directory. The log-on code is then entered automatically whenever the directory calls that publisher.

Thoughtful features like this make *ProComm+* worth at least a trial.

—THOMAS A. LANKARD

IMP FOR CP/M

If you're using a computer to generate copy, you can also use it, with a modem, to send your copy, to do lots of your research, and to communicate with others—sources of information, people who can give you guidance.

You'll need a communications program (software) as well as the modem itself (hardware). Some of us still use CP/M-based computers, as opposed to the DOS-based IBMs and IBM look-alikes. One of the best communications programs for CP/M equipment can be obtained from many bulletin-board systems for little or no cost.

It's called *IMP* and was written by a Californian named Irvin M. Hoff. The letters stand for *Improved Modem Program,* although many of its users believe, understandably, that the first one denotes "Irv's." Try for a version in the 2.xx series or later. If you join FOG, the computer users' group [see Chapter 3], you can get the program for the cost of a disk.

—ED NELSON

IT'S IN THE (MCI) MAIL

MCI mail service is one of the most reasonably priced around. Subscribers pay an annual fee of about $25 to reserve a "mailbox" (it's not necessary to use MCI long-distance phone service in order to sign up with the firm's electronic mail service). Short messages can be sent for 45¢, longer ones for $1, and extremely long ones for slightly more. There are no additional charges for access or for receipt of mail. The service can also be used to send telex or fax messages, and MCI will send on paper mail, after receipt of your electronic message, for an extra fee.

MCI offers local access numbers in hundreds of cities across the country and seems to be one of the most widely used of these services. It's extremely easy to use. And some publications, preferring that contributors not enjoy direct access to their computers, are accepting manuscripts via MCI "mailboxes."

—MICHELE McCORMICK

■ ■ ■

I cannot sing the praises of MCI Mail highly enough. This electronic mail service allows me to work down to the wire on deadlines as well as to fax my stories to magazines through MCI's central computers—without owning a fax machine myself.

For magazines that also subscribe to MCI Mail, I simply transmit my story—or any message—directly to the editor. It arrives in seconds or minutes, depending on its length. If need be, I can work all night and send my story at 8:55 A.M.

For other magazines, MCI will print out my transmission on a laser printer at the center nearest the recipient and then either send it on via the U.S. mails or, if I wish, deliver it by courier. I have until 11 P.M. to post a piece electronically and have it courier-delivered by noon the next day; this beats Federal Express by five and a half hours, almost a full working day. MCI also has offices in almost 100 countries; letters may be posted via MCI Mail, giving them a head start, and then sent on in paper form through the foreign postal systems.

The firm has also interfaced its mainframe computers with Group 3 fax machines, the fast types that transmit in under one minute. Now, I can fax stories or messages immediately to magazines that don't have computers but do have fax machines. I can't receive fax transmissions, although—at least here in the Boston area—there is a service that will hook you up to receive such transmissions via MCI Mail for $15 a month; to me, it hasn't seemed worth it.

All this power comes pretty cheaply—$25 a year for my "mailbox," 45¢ for short messages, and typical costs of $2 or $3 to transmit stories.

—PATRICIA MANDELL

■ ■ ■

MCI Mail, brought to you by the same people who provide long-distance phone service, is a great bargain in communications. Membership is $25 a year, or $10 a month for up to 40 monthly messages. With a personal computer, a modem, and a telephone line, subscribers can communicate with subscribers to virtually any electronic message service—which include CompuServe, The Source, Delphi, and others—or telex and can even send "mail" to fax machines. If your addressee has none of the above, MCI will print your message and pop it into the mail at the nearest city to the destination.

The service works on a "store and forward" concept: senders and receivers do not have to be on the system at the same time. Senders dispatch electronic messages at their convenience, and receivers check their mailboxes periodically to retrieve material addressed to them. In the case of fax messages, MCI delivers them to the destination fax machine within minutes for about 50¢ per page (there are no phone charges in the U.S.); if the destination number is busy, it will be automatically redialed for up to twelve hours.

In the near future, MCI Mail subscribers will be able to receive fax messages from anywhere in the world. Present capabilities are limited to text messages, but MCI says that by 1990, total graphics transmission and reception will be available. Thus, anyone with a personal computer and an inexpensive hand optical scanner can have all the advantages of a fax machine without owning one (if transmission is limited to computer-produced text, there's no need for a scanner).

I find I can communicate with editors and corporate clients much more conveniently by MCI Mail than by telephone, since there is never any round robin of call-backs because one or the other of us is away from the phone. I also use the service to make and confirm travel reservations and to send the same message to multiple destinations.

MCI Mail is at 1150 Seventeenth Street NW, Suite 800, Washington DC 20036; (800) 444-MAIL [444-6245].

—MARVIN J. WOLF

TANGIBLE DELIVERY

Then again, perhaps you've not only resisted the pressure to purchase a fax machine but the urge to acquire a modem as well (maybe you haven't even computerized). Besides, there are times when what you want to transmit is simply not convertible to something sendable over phone lines (or you'd just rather not). And time—or other—considerations mean the U.S. mails won't do. The consensus among most of our contributors: Check out Federal Express.

VOICE OF EXPERIENCE

I send all manuscripts by Federal Express. I don't use book rate, first-class mail, or even the U.S. Postal Service's own "express" mail. There's a reason for this: experience.

The regular postal system functions well enough for stuff that's not time-sensitive—but only one magazine column has to be delayed for me to lose as much money as I would have spent in a year on postage.

As for express mail: When the post office can't find an address, the mail is sent back—several days later. If the Federal Express driver cannot find an address, the driver or the Fed Ex office phones you for further instructions; that's why they insist on having your phone number on the label (the U.S. Postal Service, you'll note, doesn't know or want to know your phone number). If mail is late, your money is refunded—but only if you wise up to the error (they don't tell you), and only after you fill out all sorts of forms. I'm told that if Federal Express blows it, you'll receive a refund, no questions asked; I wouldn't know about that, since I've only used them a couple of hundred times and, so far, they've never failed to deliver.

Fed Ex costs at least $14, at this writing, to pick up from your office. It's worth it.

—STEPHEN MORRILL

SANITY SAVED

Federal Express helps me keep my sanity. No matter how efficiently I schedule my time, one of my corporate clients always has a rush job when I'm working on a magazine-article deadline. Fed Ex lets me use every possible minute and meet my deadlines.

—PATRICIA HADDOCK

PRECIOUS PICTURES, PLUS

Because I divide my time between two locations and do picture books with a partner, we are constantly sending slides, reference material, and expensive camera equipment back and forth between Nantucket and New York City. Most times, we've relied on United Parcel Service for large cartons and used Federal Express for smaller packages.

But over the years UPS has lost several cartons (last year, one containing a back-up typewriter), and it's inconvenient and sometimes impossible to collect, even when a package is insured. Then we learned that

UPS guaranteed air service is treated as priority, just like overnight Fed Ex, and costs a great deal less. Now, when we have irreplaceable material, this is how it's sent.

—LESLIE LINSLEY

SO FAR, SO GOOD

For last-minute back-and-forth dispatching—knock on wood, cross fingers, and other such superstitious appeasements of the fates—Federal Express has served us reliably and well. It's expensive but, as often as not, we use the client's account number. The biggest advantage: advance arrangement on the Fed Ex toll-free line for pickup at your home or office wherever they have radio-equipped vans. They pick up promptly when promised and, for a small extra charge, they'll pick up on Saturdays.

—HENRY and ELIZABETH URROWS

LOST AND FOUND

For 25 years, while living in the Northeast, I sent thousands of letters and hundreds of articles through the mail with nary a problem. Then I moved to Mobile, Alabama. Within a month, an editor complained that he'd never received an article I mailed first class. By the second month, material was failing to reach *me*, as well.

My method of operation is rather complex, and a great deal of material is sent back and forth. I dictate my material onto cassettes, and my secretary transcribes them. My secretary did not move to Mobile, Alabama; we are separated by 1200 miles. Short tapes are played over the telephone, from my player to her recorder, late at night when rates are low. During my first month in Mobile, longer material—articles and book chapters—went by first class mail, and they weren't getting through.

We decided to use express mail. At about $10 per mailing, it could easily add up to a small fortune. Yet it was preferable to retyping manuscripts. But those trusty carriers who survive rain and sleet failed again. This time it was serious: a chapter for a book. It had taken a month to write. My tape reached my secretary. She typed the rough draft then put it and the tape (a great mistake) in the same package and mailed them to me.

Postal inspectors have determined that, somewhere between Atlanta and Mobile, the package was opened and the contents removed (no doubt thrown away, having no value to anyone but me and my publisher); only the outer envelope was delivered to me. Fortunately, I noticed the damage immediately and pointed it out to the carrier, and it appears that the post office will pay me some paltry amount.

My secretary and I now function under the assumption that material will be lost or stolen; we keep copies of everything. But the biggest change in our system is that my career is now in the hands of private enterprise rather than the U.S. government. We use the services of Federal Express.

The benefits are so great that it's almost worth having lost the manuscript in order to discover them: Second-day service (which, in fact, usually arrives in one day) costs $8.50—less than overnight Express Mail—if the package is dropped off at a Fed Ex center rather than having a driver come to the house. (If I can't do that, pickup is just $3 more.) I have an account, which means that instead of paying each time I send something, I get one bill at the end of the month (my secretary also uses my account number, so I don't have to reimburse her).

And now, Federal Express has sent me preprinted labels with my name, address, and phone number as sender and that of my secretary as recipient. Even my account number is printed on the form. All I have to do is check the box indicating second-day delivery. (I really hated filling out those labels. It's the little, nagging things that drive people crazy.) The company charged me nothing for these labels. Fed Ex apparently doesn't promote this service; I found out about it accidentally. But if you ask, they'll do it.

It has been six months, at this writing, that I've been using Federal Express, and so far—please, God—nothing has been lost or even delayed. And I'm still in business—in spite of the U.S. Postal Service.

—ROBERT BAHR

WORRY NO MORE

For peace of mind and great service, open an account with Federal Express. Their prices are high, but they pick up and deliver with great efficiency, and they provide preprinted forms for you to use and even good, solid *free* mailing boxes. And if you're ever worried about where your package may be, just call them—toll free, of course; they *always* know.

—TONI L. GOLDFARB

SUMMING UP

Anyone can have a Federal Express account at no extra charge. You get preprinted airbills, packaging materials in a variety of sizes, and your information entered in their main computer. They'll pick up packages from you six days a week and bill you monthly. Their number is (800) 238-5355.

—MARTY KLEIN

- # PLAYING POST OFFICE ■

Still, most of us haven't totally abandoned the mails. For those dispatching replaceables, for those for whom time is sometimes not of the essence, for those who simply cling to faith in tradition—there follow some views on getting the most from the U.S. Postal Service.

STAY OUT OF LINES

Spending time in a post-office line and/or wasting postage because you don't know how much to put on an envelope is stupid. And you don't have to do it.

An absolutely indispensable tool for every writer, whether part or full time, is a good postage scale. And don't skimp and get one of those cheap little tin jobs; spring for a really good scale.

Then, next time you go to the post office, don't just buy a few stamps, or a book of scamps. Buy a whole roll (or sheet) or two of the first-class, first-ounce denomination (25¢, at this writing), plus a supply of the kind covering the charge (20¢, now) for each additional first-class ounce. [Stamps in the amount covering two first-class ounces are also usually available.] Get an additional assortment of stamps in odd denominations—1¢, 2¢, 10¢—plus a few 50¢ and $1 stamps. Buy a bunch of prestamped postcards for follow-up.

Then get a listing of current postal rates for first class, fourth class, and foreign mail. Use your scale, determine your own postage, and never again serve time as a slave on the long post-office lines.

—KATHRYN LANCE

■ ■ ■

Buy a postal scale. I've saved countless hours and trips to the post office because I can figure out for myself just how much it costs to mail manuscripts. And since stamps can now be purchased by mail and even in many supermarkets, there's even less need to brave those lines.

—CAROL WESTON

■ ■ ■

An inexpensive postal scale has saved me hundreds of precious hours. My petite scale, a Pelouze, cost only $10.95 and includes a handy chart listing ounces with corresponding first-class and third-class mailing costs. When rates change (I've had the scale for five years), I simply tape updated rates (from a free post-office booklet) over the old ones.

I keep a supply of stamps in the denominations I use most often—at this writing, 25¢, 45¢, and 65¢—next to the scale.

—PAMELA HOBBS HOFFECKER

■ ■ ■

You don't really need an elaborate postage scale. In fact, I don't use a scale all that often. Years ago, I took a bunch of paper and envelopes and performed a scientific experiment. The results, now known as Morrill's Postal Laws, are as follows.

Assuming normal-weight envelopes and 20-pound bond paper (paper clips are a judgment call): (1) One number ten envelope, plus up to five sheets of paper, equals one ounce. (2) One 9- by 12-inch envelope, plus one sheet of paper, equals one ounce, and up to six additional sheets of paper add up to another ounce. (3) One number nine or number ten s.a.s.e. weighs the same as one sheet of paper.

One advantage of abiding by the Laws is that you don't have to recalibrate anything when the rates go up. Just remember to use the first-class stamp for the first ounce, then turn to your additional-ounces stamps for the rest. At this writing, were I to mail a 9- by 12-inch envelope with a 15-page manuscript, I'd automatically use one 25¢ stamp and three 20¢ stamps.

In five years of using this system, I've mailed, probably, several thousand items. None has ever been returned for more postage.

—STEPHEN MORRILL

STAMPS BY MAIL

Did you know that the post office will fill stamp orders by mail? All you need is one order form to get you started (pick up at your post office) and, with the exception of parcel post, you need never visit their counter again. International reply coupons and postcards can also be included.

—JOAN WESTER ANDERSON

■ ■ ■

You can now buy stamps of any denomination, in any quantity, by mail from the U.S. Postal Service. There's a special order form (or you can use a blank piece of paper), and you simply make your check payable to "Postmaster" and send the order—if you use the official envelope that accompanies the order form, no postage is needed—to your local post office. A new form will be sent with your order, which usually arrives within three days. You can even get a receipt if you ask for it.

—MARTY KLEIN

NO STAMPS NEEDED

My Pitney-Bowes postage machine is a great convenience; I should have gotten it much, much sooner. But wait to buy one until you receive a direct-mail introductory offer, or call Pitney-Bowes, (203) 356-5000, and ask to be put on the mailing list for special offers. They include such bonuses as a period of free use, free delivery, and a free message plate. If the machine ever malfunctions (mine has, twice), they send a repair person at no charge.

—TONI L. GOLDFARB

DON'T MISS THE MS. RATE

Many writers still don't know that the post office offers a special rate for manuscripts—at this writing, 90¢ for up to one pound. On the envelope, write: Special 4th Class Rate—Manuscript. Many postal workers don't know about this rate and have difficulty looking it up in their schedules, but I use it daily and have never had a manuscript returned for postage.

—JANET GROENE

ELEPHANT-RESISTANT ENVELOPES

Tyvek is a DuPont material (technically, it's something called spun-bonded olefin) used for envelopes. A Tyvek envelope is said to be four times as strong as one made of 28-pound kraft but to weigh 40 percent less, and it's resistant to water and chemicals. It's such good stuff that most of the overnight express services use it for their own envelopes;

it's also used for the jackets of 5¼-inch computer diskettes, so you know it won't shed on your valuable photos.

I've had many paper envelopes mashed into disaster by the elephants that the post office hires to dance on packages, but I've never received a Tyvek envelope with any significant damage. It does cost more than paper, but it's worth it if you're mailing anything important. You can get Tyvek envelopes from Quill and many other office-supply houses, blank or with return addresses imprinted.[1] I use 10- by 13-inch envelopes (Quill's catalog number S-R-1590) with a border of green diamonds that signifies first-class mail. That helps the postal workers pick it out from the great mass of third-class mail and gets you the special treatment you're paying for.

—BARBARA SCHWARTZ

DOUBLE-DUTY MAILERS

White cardboard mailers look better than manila envelopes, especially after the post office gets through with them; they also save the weight and hassle of separate cardboard backing inside a regular envelope. I stamp mine PLEASE OPEN CAREFULLY AND RECYCLE, which saves enclosing a second envelope for material I wish returned, and I enclose a return address label, along with a check for return postage. (Three out of four times, a check for return postage will be returned to you. Stamps *never* reappear.)

I've been pleased with mailers from Calumet Carton Co., P.O. Box 405, 16920 State Street, South Holland IL 60473; phone, (708) 333-6521. At this writing, though, their price appears to be slightly beaten by the Mail Safe Division of Chicago Packaging, 4340 West 47 Street, Chicago IL 60632; phone, (800) 527-0754, except in Illinois, (708) 872-6677.

—PAT WATSON

SATISFACTION CERTIFIED

For many years, we've employed what is still the safest and most accountable mail channel—certified mail with return receipt requested. Next best is "priority" mail, which costs $2.40 for up to two pounds.

—HENRY AND ELIZABETH URROWS

[1]See appendix for a full list of order-by-mail-or-phone office-supply sources.

EXPRESS MAIL MAY MAKE SENSE

This is a pitch for the post office's express mail service. You may, considering the source, have presumed it was a dog. Or you may simply not have been aware of it. But the price is right—better, the last time I looked, than the competition. And, in some locations, they deliver overnight while the other big boys are still lacing their shoes. I'm not saying they're the be-all; I'm just saying, check 'em out.

—WENDY MURPHY

■ ■ ■

Here it is Friday night—or Saturday, or Sunday. It has to be there on Monday. You don't have, or have access to, a fax, or they don't. Many messenger services either don't work on weekends or charge exorbitant fees. Try express mail at the post office. It's usually slower than Federal Express, delivering before noon rather than before 10 A.M. But in many cities, a central post office accepts packages for Monday delivery as late as Sunday evening.

In New York, for example, the general post office at Eighth Avenue and 33rd Street accepts express mail until 8 P.M. on Sunday and gets it to my client in New Jersey before noon on Monday for about $8 to $10 (depending on weight). There's no private service that would do that for me on a Sunday—and for Saturday pickup with Monday delivery, private services charge around $30 or $35.

—JANICE HOPKINS TANNE

MAILING CASSETTES

A nifty way to send a cassette through the mail is in a clear plastic box. The Radio Shack stores sell a pack of three such boxes plus gummed mailing labels for under $1. You just slip the tape in the box, stick the addressed label on it, tape the sides closed, and add postage.

—JOYCE BALDWIN

BIG-TIME MAILER?

Writers who self-syndicate—submitting the same manuscript (such as a short travel piece) to many non-overlapping markets (such as newspapers across the country)—may benefit from buying a bulk mail permit. Get details at your post office, then decide if it would save you money. You must mail at least 200 pieces of mail at the same time and do some presorting; you must also allow some extra transit time, because bulk mail travels slowly.

If you want undeliverable bulk-mail material returned to you, be sure your envelopes or labels say "Return Postage Guaranteed"; such mail will be returned at your expense. If you don't want it back, mark it "If Not Deliverable, Abandon."

—JANET GROENE

IN DEFENSE OF THE POSTAL SERVICE

While negativism about the United States Postal Service abounds, I'd like to suggest that writers maintain faith in the system. I run a successful mail-order business; for ten years I have been mailing books all over the U.S. (and some internationally), and I have rarely had "lost book" complaints or gripes about delivery.

What's more, the price is right. Book rate is a very good deal: Imagine paying only 90¢ for any type of service, let alone for having a one-pound book delivered to a specific home or office anywhere in the country! And for the flat priority-mail charge of $2.40, you can send by first-class mail anything weighing two pounds or less; that, too, is a bargain.

At times, the Postal Service can even beat the competition. Recently, someone in Colorado mailed two packages to me on the same day—one by book-rate mail, the other via a well-known parcel delivery service. The package sent by mail arrived in five days, the other two days later.

I did business from New York City for many years. Now, I'm based in a small community not far from there. In both locations, I've found that a personal touch is helpful. I make a point of meeting new mail carriers and, since I'm so dependent on the mail, I write a "thank you" letter to the local postmaster at the end of each year. While that can't improve the service once my package or letter leaves my post office, I speculate that it does explain why, even in New York City, mail sent to me with only the correct zip code and no street address still managed to get delivered.

The U.S. Postal Service was designed to serve the largest of cities and the smallest of hamlets, and you have to marvel that, despite the incredible growth of our country, it still continues to do a pretty good job. Yes, I've stood on seemingly endless lines, and I've encountered rudeness— but on the whole, I've been very impressed with the service I receive.

—KATE KELLY

BARGAIN SHOPPING AT THE POST OFFICE

The U.S. Postal Service offers two bargains that many writers might find useful.

First: For those who can afford to buy a box of 500 stamped envelopes (or multiples thereof), the post office will print not only a return address but also a few additional options such as a phone number and some descriptive language (the limit for all the printing is seven lines, with no line longer than 47 characters, including spaces). They come in two styles, regular or window, and in two sizes.

Besides doing away with the labor of licking stamps and writing or typing a return address, the printed, stamped envelopes cost less per envelope than I've paid to buy plain envelopes and stamps separately. A box of 500 regular number ten envelopes cost me $136.90 (1989); other kinds are comparably priced. The order forms, which can be picked up at the post office, say to allow four weeks for delivery; my orders have arrived in about two weeks.

Second: When the post office is closed and the zip-code-information phone line is shut down for the night, it's a comfort to have on hand a post-office-sized zip-code directory. At this writing, that luxury costs only $9.

—MARGARET DICANIO

■ ■ ■

Prestamped envelopes printed with your name and address by the post office are a real bargain. Prices for 500 envelopes range from $134.90 for the 6¾-inch size to $137.50 for number tens with windows. Since the postage alone amounts to $125 (at 25¢ per envelope), this is a very small price to pay for the printed envelopes, which are useful for paying bills, sending for information, and other purposes where your letterhead isn't needed. Soon, it may be possible to order fewer than 500. For more information, write U.S. Postal Service, U.S. Stamped Envelope Agency, Williamsburg PA 16693-9989.

—LOUISE PURWIN ZOBEL

P.S.: INSIDE INFO

A warning: Even though some mailboxes still have uncorrected schedules on their inner lids, the national U.S. Postal Service rule—perhaps aimed at keeping the Lord's Day sacred—is not to make Sunday collections.

A tip: When you get down to the wire, and the front door of the post office has firmly shut for the day just moments before you arrived, sometimes going to the back door will turn up a Samaritan who will accept your mail.

And a few little-known facts, from our experience, about foreign correspondence:

Mexico. For messages to Mexico from the U.S., airmail takes longer than surface mail, since it's always routed via the Federal District, where people hate their jobs. For mail *from* Mexico, don't rely on domestic mail if you can find a northbound traveler who will drop it in a U.S. mailbox.

Brazil. Unless things have changed, Brazil will not guarantee mail deliveries unless you insure them.

France. Post-office people in central Paris are most accommodating. They take mail and cable texts in the middle of the night.

U.K. and Ireland. Both U.K. and Irish post offices, which are often concealed in small shops, have strict hours, but they are staffed by helpful people.

—HENRY and ELIZABETH URROWS

12

GET
THE
PICTURE

n certain cases, pictures may be worth not merely the proverbial thousand words apiece but may be the clinchers in sales of many more words worth many thousands of dollars. Some writers are also photographers; for them, cameras and film are as much implements of their craft as their writing machines—although published pictures aren't always what the writer has in mind.

INTERVIEW ICEBREAKER

My favorite interview tool is a good camera. Even if I don't plan to use it, I walk in with a camera over my shoulder and set it carefully on a desk or on the floor. It's amazing how subjects will start to open up when they see that camera.

—PAT WATSON

SAVE BY MAIL

Shop for, but don't buy, cameras and other photography gear at your neighborhood retail store. Buy from mail-order houses; you'll find their listings in all the popular photography magazines. You'll save half the cost. Do realize that there is sometimes a long wait for delivery, though, so don't order by mail if you need the equipment right away.

—STEPHEN MORRILL

I MUST REMEMBER THIS

A camera is my research tool. It will not only record a beautiful scene—a towering mountain, or a golden sunset. It will also record the furnishings of a room, the shabbiness of a financially depressed town, the character and condition of transportation in another country, people's clothes and hairstyles. Pictures can help a writer recall a mood (and may trigger ideas for other articles, too).

Any camera will do—the simpler, the more efficient. An automatic is best. I use an old instant-load Magimatic that cost about $30 many years ago. All I have to do is point it and click the shutter. It saves me writing a thousand words when I'm researching a story, and it records the information in vivid detail.

—BLANCHE HACKETT

■ ■ ■

Although I do take pictures with the intention of selling them, I also use photography as a form of note-taking. If I haven't time to copy an inscription, for instance, I shoot it for later reference. The camera is useful in industrial plants, too, when it may be inconvenient to take notes or even to record your impressions, since a tape recorder has a bias for ambient sounds and all you'll be able to hear is the whir or clatter of machinery. My favorite camera is a Minolta X700 with a 28-135mm lens and macro capability.

—JOHN RAVAGE

■ ■ ■

With a pocket-sized 35mm autofocus camera, you can take photos of people and places that can jog your memory when you sit down to write your article. (Sending an interviewee a flattering photo is also a nice way of saying thanks and will leave a good impression should you need to contact the individual again.)

It's helpful if the camera has a backlight compensation lever. This opens the lens diaphragm to let in more light for photographing a subject that is lit from behind. You can also put more light on the subject by using the flash that's built into almost all autofocus cameras. To make the flash work manually, simply hold your hand over the lens while you depress the shutter button slightly; when the flash pops up, snap the picture.

I've been using a Nikon L35-AF for years and, although it's been discontinued in favor of more advanced models, it's still available at some stores and at a far lower price than originally. I find it more than adequate and prefer its simplicity to the frills found on many of the new cameras on the market.

—ARTHUR HENLEY

■ ■ ■

A camera is a most useful note-taker if you write about tangible things. A quick walk around, maybe half a dozen shots, and you've recorded operation, shape, color, and details. There are probably a dozen point-and-shoot cameras on the market costing between $100 and whatever is burning a hole in your pocket or purse. Cameras used for this purpose should have (if not, don't buy) automatic focusing to 16–18 inches or so, automatic exposure, a moderately wide-angle lens (35–40 degrees), and built-in flash.

—DAVID A. ANDERTON

A LOOK AT LENSES

Of the dozen or so lenses in my collection, I find I use three zoom lenses almost exclusively. A "zoom" lens is one that pulls in and out to allow for a range of focal lengths, allowing you to frame your subject just the way you want at the time you take your picture.

A 35–70mm lens is perfect for most portraits (50mm is considered "normal" and is the stock size on most retail cameras); a 70–210mm lens, good for people and birds that happen to be not too far away; my 500–800mm lens is used only when there's no other choice (which is the case with some of the outdoor nature stuff I shoot).

Some zooms, usually at the lower end of the range spectrum, come with "macro" settings, which allow you to take a picture of an ant from a range of one foot and make that ant look huge.

A word of warning: All telephoto lenses compress the depth of field. At long ranges, your depth of field may be a matter of inches, requiring extreme care and precision on your part since, when a 35mm slide is enlarged to magazine-page size, the slightest fuzziness becomes an insurmountable problem. For long-distance photography, a heavy-duty tripod and remote shutter release are essential.

In lieu of extra lenses, you might look into "doublers," which let you get more out of the ones you have. A doubler, which looks like a lens itself, screws into the camera, and you then screw your lens into *it*. The effect is to double the focal length—e.g., turning a standard 50mm lens into a 100mm, or a 70–210mm zoom into a 140–420. This arrangement results in slightly lower quality, but it's cheaper than buying more lenses.

—STEPHEN MORRILL

■ ■ ■

A photographer's loupe is usually advised for checking out the sharpness of slides. You don't need to buy one. Just use your camera's 50mm lens—backward—as a magnifier. Works great!

—PAT WATSON

PORTRAIT OF A PROFILEE

I have a suggestion for those who, like me, must often provide photos to accompany interviews. This usually means two or three lenses are needed for a portrait, a shot of the subject in an office or other setting, and possibly a close-up of some object, as well. If you've found your glasses are necessary to see the read-out on the camera (they don't make print as large as they used to), and you have to change lenses and shift focus as you move around, I'd recommend one of the newer, programmable cameras.

I bought a Maxxum 5000 with automatic exposure and automatic focusing. The zoom lens I chose ranges from 30 to 200mm and also includes a macro attachment which produces one-quarter life size. Once the lens has moved into focus automatically, it can be pulled in or out to compose the picture. (If I were to choose now, I'd settle for a 30 to 100mm zoom; it's really all you need unless you do nature photography.) The programmable flash gun reads the amount of light needed, so you can continue talking to your subject without the distraction of changing lenses or exposures.

You will almost always get a good picture, even if it's not of salon quality. Changing the setting from "program" to "manual" gives you more control when you want it.

Nikon and Canon make similar cameras. Warning: As with a computer, you must spend some time learning to use the buttons that dot the camera.

—GEORGE DELUCENAY LEON

ALL A NON-PRO NEEDS

When I recently worked on a children's book about San Francisco, I shot some photos. I'm not a professional photographer, and I don't want to become one. But I do enjoy taking pictures, and I wanted to grab some "people" shots that captured the character of the city without being "touristy." Not only were six of my photos used in the book; four were also used to illustrate a magazine article on living and working in the city.

The friendly folks at the camera store recommended an autofocus 35mm camera. The model I chose was a Yashica, but any good brand would have worked. Unless you need to shoot portraits or close-ups, or you face lighting challenges, a good autofocus 35mm camera is all a writer needs.

—PATRICIA HADDOCK

TWO EXTRA TOOLS

You can improve the clarity and quality of your photographs dramatically by using a lens hood and a tripod. The hood prevents "flare," caused by excess side light. The tripod cuts down on camera movement.

—PAT WATSON

THE FILM IN THE FRIDGE

When I get an assignment calling for photos as well as words, I don't worry about running out and buying film. Nor do I use some film I have around and then try to find that old receipt to support my expense statement. I simply open my refrigerator, grab what I need from my ever-present supply, and I'm out the door. When I turn in my film for processing, I replace precisely the stock I've used and have the lab include that cost on its invoice.

The refrigerator? Yes, I refrigerate my film, just as the professional supply shops where I buy it do. I also put it into a securely closed plastic bag, so the refrigerator won't dry it out. And because I live in Florida, where the humidity is world class, I let the film warm up before I open it, to avoid condensation.

For black-and-white shooting, I use Ilford ASA 400. If I'm going into an extremely iffy lighting situation, I'll use Ilford XP-1, an oddball film that permits you to change your ASA in mid-roll, anywhere from about 50 to 1500. The results can be a bit grainy at times, especially at the high end—but if it's pitch-dark one minute and brilliant sunshine the next, you do what you gotta do and pray for brilliance in the film lab.

For color, I usually use Fujichrome ASA 400-D or 100-D ("D" designates film intended for professional use, and it's been closely monitored at the plant for chemical balance). Don't ever think about using color print film; transparencies are a must.

I don't do my own processing, because a professional film lab knows more about it than I ever will. And I use the best film lab in the city, the same one the advertising agencies and professional photographers use; it costs more, but it's worth it to get their expertise as well as the assurance that fresh processing chemicals are used for every batch. Professional labs, by the way, will imprint your name and copyright information on the frame of each color slide, if you so request; mine does it for free.

—STEPHEN MORRILL

FIRST, LOAD THE CAMERA

I'm totally unmechanical, and I don't use my cameras often enough to do the right things automatically. Here's what I've done to help prevent problems that could occur when I need to take pictures.

I have two identical 35mm cameras, with identical flash attachments. I use only two lenses, an 80mm (it could be 90mm) on one camera and a 28mm (it could be 35mm) on the other. Before leaving the house to go out on a story, I load both cameras and check all settings, usually using color film in one camera and black-and-white film in the other (I'll exchange the lenses halfway through each roll). *Important:* Each time you load your camera, trip the shutter twice and check to see if the film-winder turns; if you do this religiously, you'll never come back with a blank roll of film.

These setups are more than adequate to illustrate almost any story. Leave variations to art photographers; you don't need to be burdened by them.

—JUNE GRAYSON

GOOD SHOTS ON THE GO

Two special tips for taking photos to accompany travel stories:

(1) Try to avoid dating your pictures, so they'll be usable for years to come. Clothing, hairstyles, autos, and billboards advertising trendy items can all pinpoint the year the picture was taken. Be aware that clothing styles change less often for men and small children than for women and teenagers, and less often for older than for younger women. If cars appear in the scene, it's sometimes possible to compose the picture so they can be cropped out later.

(2) Be careful when shooting a person framed by a famous landmark. Focus on the person, and you can't tell whether that looming structure is the Eiffel Tower or the Empire State Building. Focus past the person on the landmark half a football field away, and the human subject will appear as a skinny black stick. Solution: Back off until the background object exactly fills your viewfinder. Then, bring the subject forward until his or her head and shoulders fill about a third of the frame. Zoom in on your human subject, letting the background fall just slightly out of focus, and you have your perfect place-plus-person picture.

—LOUISE PURWIN ZOBEL

DON'T LOSE A LEG (OF YOUR TRIP)

As you take photos on a trip, use a write-everywhere pen to label your film canisters with locations or dates (preferably both) or, at the least, consecutive numbers. When you return from your trip, don't send your film to be processed all at once. Film can get lost. Instead, line up the canisters in the order in which the rolls were shot, and count off by fours (one, two, three, four, one, two . . .). Send the "ones" out for processing in one batch, the "twos" in a second batch the next day, and so on. That way, even if one batch is lost, you haven't lost an entire section of your trip.

—PAT WATSON

EDITOR'S CHOICE

When submitting black-and-white pictures to accompany articles, I send "proof" (contact) sheets along with the manuscript, circling the shots I think may be most appropriate. The choice, of course, is the editor's, and this is a lot less expensive than sending along prints that may or may not be used. When the editor has made a selection and we've agreed on payment amount for the photos, I make and send the enlargements. *Never send negatives.* The loss of contact sheets or prints is no big deal; lost negatives are irreplaceable.

—M. LAWRENCE PODOLSKY

CHECKPOINT POINTERS

I don't believe for an instant those cheerful assurances, by minimum-wage guards at airport checkpoints, that their X-ray equipment won't damage my film. The common advice, in the United States, is to demand that your camera bag be inspected by hand. In other countries, your request may be ignored, usually by a person with a machine gun.

I don't burden myself with lead-lined camera bags. What I do is take all my film out of those cardboard boxes and put the canisters into a transparent plastic food-storage bag. I place this on top of the camera in my camera bag. When I get to the checkpoint, I pull out the plastic bag, hand the camera bag to the X-rayologist, and walk through the metal detector, plastic bag in hand.

The metal detector will *not* affect your film and, oddly enough, metal film canisters rarely set off alarms; if they do—and you need about 40 cans of film to get enough mass to do the trick—you need only show the plastic bag to the guard.

—STEPHEN MORRILL

■ ■ ■

Before going through a checkpoint with cameras and film, unload your cameras, writing the exposure number on the tag end of the film, so you can rewind to that position. Then, allow your cameras to be X-rayed. This is much more efficient than a hand examination of your cameras, and you don't have to worry about some clumsy ox dropping them or fingerprinting your lenses.

Carry your film in a separate bag and insist on hand examination. Remember that X-ray effects are cumulative, and the faster the film, the more sensitive it is to X-ray fogging.

—PAT WATSON

■ OTHER PHOTO SOURCES ■

There are also other sources, besides your own photographic skill, for pictures to accompany articles, books, and other projects.

PICTURES FROM THE PAST

Sometimes a photographic illustration will add just the saleable slant for an article. I've found several good sources:

(1) For pictures taken from the 1950s on, a good source is Bettman News Photos (Bettman bought United Press International several years ago). The cost is roughly $85 for single use of a black-and-white print, with charges varying according to the size of the order, number of pictures, and types of usage. Bettman News Photos is at 48 East 21 Street, New York NY 10010; (212) 777-6200.

(2) For pre-1950 photos, try the famed Bettman Archives, 136 East 57 Street, New York NY 10022; (212) 758-0362. Charges are similar.

(3) The Library of Congress has an extensive photo collection. Write its Photo Duplication Service if you know the picture you want, and its number; otherwise, query Free Lance Researchers, Library of Congress, Washington DC 20540.

(4) For photos dating from 1860 to 1960, the National Archives is excellent, and charges are extremely reasonable, currently just over $4 for an 8- by 10-inch black-and-white print, but delivery takes eight to ten weeks. You must be able to identify the photo you want; check out *An American Image, Photos from the National Archives,* which can be found in most libraries. Then phone (don't write) and request an order form: (202) 523-3236.

—M. LAWRENCE PODOLSKY

UPDATED HISTORY

If you have an old photograph you want to use, perhaps to illustrate an historical piece, what you need is a copy negative and a new glossy print. For many years, I've been highly satisfied with the work done by a mail-order firm called Custom Quality Studio. Prices are reasonable— at this writing, $2.50 for a copy negative and 90¢ for a 5- by 7-inch print—and they are very good at following directions for cropping. For a current price list and more information, write the studio at P.O. Box 4838, Chicago IL 60680.

—JOYCE BALDWIN

ART AND ARTISTS

For me, as an art historian and critic, finding illustrations has sometimes been a formidable challenge. The chief sources, if you have the money, are museums and photography and film archives, which have varying fee schedules, often according to whether you're writing for a scholarly journal or a mass magazine. For a scholarly piece, you may be asked for a minimum of $25; if the article is deemed "commercial," fees can range from $125 to $350.

But for profiles of living artists, I simply go directly to the source. An artist may already have photographs of his or her work; the gallery that shows the artist's work may have had the work (and perhaps the artist, as well) photographed for advertising or publicity purposes. And these transparencies are free.

—CASSANDRA L. LANGER

■ ■ ■

Whenever your subject involves an entity seeking fame, fortune, or both, you can usually assume there are public relations people who are able to provide pictures of the people, products, or institutions they represent. This is also sometimes true of special-interest and professional groups seeking to raise public awareness of an issue or cause. —D.S.

13

WRITER

EN

ROUTE

Perhaps you're
a travel writer—or perhaps, just a writer who travels. Either way,
technology has entered the picture; a number of contributors en-
thuse, in Chapter 3, on the topic of take-along computers. (If you
carry cameras and film, find advice in Chapter 12.) Here, some
lower-tech suggestions.

MAKE A LIST

Whether a writer travels a lot on assignment or for leisure, you'll still
be writing. Creating a list of basic tools ahead of time helps, especially
if you sometimes find yourself packing an hour or two before a three-
week trip. I've not only developed such a list, but also a little "map" of
where everything goes in the one carry-on bag that enables me to travel
lightly, comfortably, and fast.

Everybody's list will reflect personal needs and habits. Some items on
mine: extra pens, address book, steno pad, manuscript-size pad, large
envelopes to use for local clippings and for sending things home, busi-

ness cards, ID cards (and extra ID photos for foreign documents), a few clips of my work, U.S. stamps (for mail entrusted to others to be carried back and posted Stateside), expense-record book, international phone credit card.

—WALLACE KAUFMAN

■ ■ ■

I can't tell you how many times I've been in Big Fork, Minnesota, at midnight looking for a roll of Tri-X film. Not many drugstores are open that late in Big Fork. Not many of the drugstores that are open carry Tri-X.

Now I have an all-purpose list of just about everything I've ever found necessary on a trip to anywhere. Included, in addition to such working needs as pens, notepads, tape recorder (and tapes, batteries, and an auxiliary mike), and camera (and film, flash, filters, and close-up lenses): suitable clothing and toiletries, scuba gear, passport, pilot's license, sleeping bag, credit cards, aspirin, money, foreign money, addresses and phone numbers, flashlight and fresh batteries—and much more.

I go over the list as I prepare for a trip; as I pack each item (or decide I don't need it for this particular trip), it's checked off. Just before I leave, I scan the list again to be sure there are no empty spaces.

—ROBERT GANNON

CREATE A KIT

Airplane flights, rides on surface transportation, waits anywhere needn't be "dead" time. I carry a small kit that contains everything I need for productivity away from the office. Included: notepads, pens and pencils, highlighters, a small dictionary, calculator, scissors, tape, paper clips, Post-It notes, envelopes, stamps, return-address labels, a miniature stapler, a six-inch ruler, correction fluid, and a small address book. I add to these basics as assignments or current projects demand.

—MARILYN ROSS

■ ■ ■

You can write *anywhere*—even on a plane wedged between two overweight fellow passengers—with a truly portable kit of writing/editing supplies. Get a leather or plastic zippered 8- by 10-inch case. Fill it with writing pad and instruments, seven-inch scissors (they'll pass airport security), an Etona disposable stapler (1 by 3½ inches), a small tape dispenser, Post-It cover-up tape, rubber bands, and paper clips. Bingo: you're set to write or edit (cut, paste, staple, delete) anywhere! Total cost, under $15. Such kits are available preassembled, but the stuff is usually gimcrack even if color-coordinated. Putting your own together is more fun, and it will be more serviceable.

—RONALD GROSS

LIGHT LUGGAGE

An item I find absolutely necessary is a briefcase that doesn't weigh a ton empty. It may not be as elegant as crocodile, but my Lands' End Square Rigger can accommodate not only pads, pencils, and file folders, but camera, tape recorder, and other bulky items such as a fold-up umbrella and even a change of shoes. But the best part is that it's light. And it comes with a shoulder strap so that, even when loaded, it's easy to carry.

—JOHN RAVAGE

■ ■ ■

I'm a travel writer; my research is in the field and on the road. Fifty percent of my time is spent away from home. My main travel tool is my purse—well, let's call it a "press bag." In it: a standard reporter's notebook, dark glasses, reading glasses, several pens, passport wallet with cards, money, traveler's checks; there's also room for a 35mm camera or a small tape recorder. A side pocket carries keys, change purse, stamps, et al. My jacket pockets are empty, and my trouser pockets do not bulge in several directions. How does any traveling male writer get along without such a bag?

—JOHN McDERMOTT

FLIGHT GUIDE

While it's designed for travel agents, anyone can subscribe to the *Official Airline Guide,* which lists flight schedules (not fare information) for all North American flights; it also includes information about airports, gives airline phone numbers, and so on. Not only does it help in planning trips before (or without) calling a travel agent; you can carry it with you to cope with unexpected changes. Subscription is currently $71 per year; there is also a separate overseas edition. Orders/information: (800) 323-3537.

—MARTY KLEIN

INTRODUCE YOURSELF

Traveling writers will find it very helpful to have business cards printed on one side in English and on the other side in the language of the country they're visiting; it works like magic when it comes to making friends and gathering information. The printing can usually be arranged inexpensively through the airline of the destination country.

—LOUISE PURWIN ZOBEL

TAP TRAVEL CONTACTS

Wherever you go, make good use of personal contacts. As you travel, get names and addresses; keep a file of them, with dates and brief descriptions of the circumstances. No matter how much material you've brought back from a trip, there's often something you missed or that seemed unimportant while you were on the road—but you have a second chance if you've kept good records of your contacts.

You can write to verify a fact, get an extra quote, or take that picture you realize only after you get home is really vital to your story. I kept the name of Ahmed, who drove the van in which I traveled on an African trip; for a self-addressed envelope and postage, he obtained a release from a subject I'd photographed in the savanna. Mary, a tour guide in Switzerland, sent me the best recipe for wiener schnitzel from a restaurant on her tour.

I like to mail these contacts greeting cards or otherwise keep in touch at least once a year. And of course a copy of your article is always welcome, especially when they are mentioned.

—BLANCHE HACKETT

NOW NOTE THIS

If you're taking a foreign trip and expect to take lots of notes, you needn't take lots of notepaper. Literally everywhere in the world except the U.S., you can buy inexpensive children's school notebooks. They're usually about 16 by 21 centimeters (a bit over 6 by 8 inches), completely flexible (they can easily be folded in half and slipped into a pocket), often with an illustration on the front and a multiplication table on the back. The pages, generally either 32 or 64, may be blank, lined, or have little squares, like graph paper. You can buy ten or twenty of these handy notebooks at a time. If you run out, you can always get more—even in the remotest little town in Switzerland, India, Ghana, Peru, Tasmania, or Vietnam.

—PETER WHITE

JOIN THE CLUB

If you travel by air, on business or pleasure, more than once or twice a month, and you haven't joined an airline club, you probably aren't maximizing your time on the road. The club facilities at airports typically contain soft chairs with telephones on tables next to them, desks, sometimes computers, and a pleasant atmosphere away from the terminal hubbub—in short, a place where you can work. Anyone willing to pay the annual membership fee can join; the work you can accomplish during one missed connection may more than pay for the fee.

Often, the clubs have conference rooms, which can sometimes be borrowed for interviews (they must be reserved in advance). While talking to a Boston physician in connection with an assignment for *American Health,* I learned that he was planning to go skiing in Colorado and that he'd be changing planes in Chicago. We agreed to meet at the airport, which is within driving distance of my home, and his airline club (Delta) provided use of a conference room for the interview.

On another occasion, I learned that a particular scientist was going to a scientific conference in Las Vegas. So was I. I had been trying for two years to get him to sit still for an interview but, until now, he had always been too busy. Now, I booked myself onto the same American Airlines flight he was taking from Chicago. Alas, we were assigned seats far apart. I appealed to the public relations department of the airline. While we were in the American club awaiting the flight, the PR people arranged for us to have seats together—upgrading us to first class without extra charge. The scientist was charmed, and we talked for three hours.

In picking a club, choose one on an airline you fly frequently or that has lounges in cities to which you travel often. (The fact that an airline flies to a city doesn't necessarily mean it has club facilities there.) I belong to American's Admiral Club, because the line has lounges in two dozen cities.

American charges $150 to join and $100 per year to renew; a lifetime membership is available for $1550. Adding your spouse costs an extra

$30. Most other airlines' charges are similar. To request full information, just call the airline's 800 number.

—HAL HIGDON

HEAR THE CLASSICS

If you need to drive some distance, take the opportunity to improve your education and polish up your writing style at the same time. There's a wonderful selection of classic literature available on tape from Recorded Books. The quality of the reading is almost always outstanding. You can "read" all those things you never quite got around to, like *Moby Dick* and *Walden;* your driving time will become a treat; and every mile, you'll learn something new about the art of writing.

The prices for 30-day rentals are reasonable. You can get a catalog from Recorded Books, Box 409, Charlotte Hall MD 20622; (800) 638-1304.

—DAVID BOUCHIER

REGIONAL ADDRESS BOOKS

You're about to leave—to research a project, to give a lecture, to attend or participate in a writers' conference, to carry out an assignment, to vacation. There are relatives, friends, business associates, professional colleagues, editors, and/or agents you anticipate contacting. You start scrounging through files and address books to make a list covering just your destination area(s). It's aggravating. It's time consuming. But there's a solution.

Buy a bunch of address books no bigger than about 4 by 6 inches. Divide up the country (or the world) into sections or areas you visit frequently. At odd moments—while you're watching TV or listening to the radio—gradually fill your small address books according to location.

I, for example, have separate Florida, East Coast, and northern California books, among others. When I'm packing for a trip to New York, the first thing that goes into my carry-around case is the East Coast address book. And in addition to addresses and phone numbers, I have cards and notes on favorite restaurants and various services I might need tucked into each regional book. This tiny tool is a great timesaver and tension reducer.

—FRANCES HALPERN

TRAVELING TYPEWRITERS

I don't take a computer on research trips, since I never write while I'm out interviewing and gathering information. What I've done for two decades is type my handwritten notes at the end of each day—expanding and embellishing, deciphering the sometimes almost illegible scrawls resulting from interviews.

For this job, I've found a lightweight thermal typewriter invaluable. I use a Brother EP 43, a model that works either with a tiny ribbon on conventional paper or with no ribbon at all on special heat-sensitive paper. It's cheap, $150 or so. Most important, I come back from my trip with *paper* in hand, never fearing that three days' or three weeks' worth of work has gotten mysteriously zapped.

—ROBERT KANIGEL

■ ■ ■

I have about $12,000 worth of computers lying around my home office—but when I pack my bags and head for the airport, do I take with me the latest in "laptops" to handle the writing I'll do en route? I do not. I take a twenty-year-old portable manual Olivetti typewriter that I bought for twenty bucks in a Goodwill store.

Why? I go to places where the absence of electricity or batteries is balanced by an abundance of thieves. I could leave my portable typewriter on top of a bar in the worst hellhole in Haiti and know it would still be there when I came back for it three days later. And if it weren't, I wouldn't care; I could buy a replacement locally for $3 American.

What do I do when I come home? What about all the retyping I'd save by dumping copy from the memory of a little computer into my big computer? Well, I figure I'm going to do some rewriting anyway, so I start the process as I copy the stuff from the paper into my computer.

And if I want to send stories from the field, I can do so, assuming a nearby post office or a friendly pilot who'll fly copy out. To do that with a computer, I'd need a printer. (Normally, there's no frantic rush with my stories. If there were, I'd take a computer and file material via a modem.)

—STEPHEN MORRILL

A TYPING "TABLE"

Wire-service writers who used to travel around the world were often stuck in dubious hotels or motels and required to get some copy together. Writing with a portable typewriter (or computer) on your lap is not a pleasant task; you're too cramped to let the words flow. If you're staying in a plush room with a coffee table, it's much too low. Other tables are typically too high for comfort. And we don't normally pack folding typewriter tables.

Those old wire-service people devised a solution. If you pull the second drawer out of the usual hotel-room bureau, then re-insert it about six or eight inches but *upside down,* you're likely to find that the inverted drawer will hold your typewriter (or computer) at just about the right height.

—ED NELSON

RENTALS: BE WELL CONNECTED

If you need to write while on a trip to Great Britain or the Continent, it may be easier to rent than to schlepp your own portable battery-powered equipment. (It has to be battery-powered; your plug-in equipment won't work on their DC current.) Many shops that repair typewriters (or portable computers) have rental machines available. But not all of them do, and once outside London or other major cities, you may wonder where to turn.

A quick way to discover equipment renters in a particular area is to stop in at a local bank and ask to see the manager. A bank manager knows the district and can usually either quickly direct you to a specific rental firm or tell you who can quickly locate it for you. This route may also offer another advantage: rather than coming in off the street as a foreigner on your own, you're there on the referral of a (presumably) respected local business executive. The result may be better price and service.

—SHIRLEY SLOAN FADER

---14---

FURNISHING
THE
WORKSPACE

A few of us enjoy the luxury of a spacious place to work, a large room set aside just for our literary or journalistic endeavors. Most of us feel we're fortunate if we have a *small* space, separate room or not, to call our own—and some of us must just make do with a corner carved from living room, kitchen, or bedroom. Here, the office furnishings our contributors have found conducive to productivity—or at least to wrestling writer's block in relative comfort.

TAKE THAT STEP

For too long, I worked either at the dining-room table or in my bedroom. Each day, I spread my papers out, got organized, and went to work. And each night, I packed up everything and set it aside. Hours were lost tracking down mislaid papers. Annoyance turned to frustration—and, finally, provoked action. I converted unused space in the basement into an office.

It's a simple, well-lighted, white-walled area with all-white furniture;

a desk—two-drawer file cabinets supporting a formica top—and a book-case have organized my life. Windows, though small, give me a glimpse of trees and sky. And for those pauses that refresh, I have an antique bent-willow rocker outfitted with a patch of bright quilt.

The message: Don't wait too long to set up your own office area. Not only will it improve your efficiency; it will bolster your professional self-image, as well.

—JOYCE BALDWIN

BEHIND CLOSED DOORS

If you have the opportunity to design your own office, you might want to include a walk-in storage area with a door. I find such an area in my basement office especially useful not only for research materials and office supplies but also for picture files, photographic equipment, and field gear. Just closing the door (actually, in my case, double folding doors) gets a lot of clutter out of sight.

I also gained office space by putting a row of four-drawer file cabinets in an adjoining utility room and removing a section of the wall between so that the file drawers open into my office. Sliding doors on a track hide the entire file-cabinet section from view when desired.

—GEORGE LAYCOCK

■ ■ ■

My office has a walk-in closet filled with heavy-duty cardboard file boxes piled four high. Atop the file boxes are scattered an assortment of briefcases, camera bags, and boxes of stationery supplies. Above are two levels of open-wire closet shelving, holding about 50 cardboard maga-zine-storage boxes. It's not a pretty sight, but it's efficient. And when I don't want to look at it, I close the door.

—STEPHEN MORRILL

PROFESSIONAL HELP

For years, I used one bedroom in our four-bedroom house for my office. It was comfortable, but it was small. With our three children out of the nest, I decided to rip out a wall and reclaim one of their former rooms to expand my office. The most important decision I made was to do so with the help of a local architect, who analyzed the space available plus my work habits and created a master design. I accepted some of his ideas and rejected or modified others.

I'd used architects on previous remodeling projects such as kitchen and basement and found that their greatest value is in coming up with ideas that may not have occurred to you. In the case of my office, it was a skylight, a great idea which I'd never have thought of. Whether or not it makes me write better, or faster, I enjoy much more the environment in which I spend my working hours.

Even if you don't plan to rip down walls or add skylights, you may want to seek an architect's advice if you're thinking about reallocating your space. Architects vary in price anywhere from, say, $75 for a few simple ideas to $500, $600, or more for a grand plan. You probably should choose an architect used to designing offices as well as houses, but most important is that the person be creative.

—HAL HIGDON

BUILT-IN OFFICE-CUM-BEDROOM

Short on space? Need an office to double as a bedroom? Here's a solution I've used in three different locations in the U.S. and Canada. It requires only elementary skill with a saw and hammer and nails. The bed doubles as a working surface and accommodates a bank of file cabinets.

The surface of the bed frame is a sheet of at least ⅝-inch plywood, with a two-by-four frame around the perimeter to rest the plywood on and keep it rigid. The frame is set on an arrangement of three to six two-drawer file cabinets (depending on the shape of the room and the configuration you'd like, preferably in a corner and fastened to the wall). A piece of foam or a futon serves as a mattress and can be rolled up or removed during the day.

I also have a conventional desk or table beside the bed, at the same height, to provide a place for my computer and printer. A swivel chair on wheels, adjustable to the height of the work surface, completes the setup.

—ERICH HOYT

CORKING GOOD IDEA

A cork bulletin board is a wonderful invention that can make a room look like an office immediately. Get a large one. Put up a list of your projects and deadlines as well as all the notes, letters, and other bits of information that are worth keeping readily available and not filing away. Add some fancy postcards from distant places, so it looks as if you have affluent friends. And stick up a couple of encouraging epigrams like "The art of being wise is the art of knowing what to overlook" (William James) and "Minds are like parachutes; they only function when they are open" (attributed to James Dewar).

—EVELYN KAYE

■ ■ ■

It is also helpful to post a time-zone map scissored from your phone book so that you will know instantly when not to place a call to a person on the opposite coast. Outsize plastic paper clips can be hung on push-pins. Rolls of packaging tape can be hung on extra-large pushpins. Any scrap of paper, business card, or what you will that would quickly become lost in or on your desk should be pinned to your bulletin board. When things begin to get lost on your bulletin board, it is time to start over.   —D.S.

■ ■ ■

It's simplicity itself—and also attractive—to panel one whole wall of your office with sheet cork. Such cork, available at most large hardware stores and many lumber-supply outlets, comes in small squares and larger strips that can be easily cut to size and cemented to the wall. Although the choice is usually limited to "natural," the cork can be painted if you like. Select cork thick enough to take long pushpins as well as thumbtacks to make your wall-to-wall bulletin board most use-ful.

—WILBUR CROSS

■ ■ ■

But do not—repeat, *not*—use the self-adhesive cork squares found in many hardware and home-furnishings stores. They are easily cut to size to fit your wall. They look terrific—at first. Then, small sections begin to crumble and tumble off the wall. Whole chunks start to slip slowly floorward. You replace them. You replace the replacements. Finally, when you have at last decided after untold years to grit your teeth and let a painter into your office, you decide that you will simply remove the remaining squares and start over.

That is when you discover that there are, in fact, two distinct breeds of these cork slabs, although they all seem identical; those that did not spring or slide off the wall are clinging to it with steel-trap tenacity. After you and the painter, armed with chisels, have managed to pry the larger pieces loose, you are left with a gluey expanse, flecked with fragments of permanently imbedded cork, over which five coats of special material must be applied to create an entirely new wall surface before any paint can be laid on. There is now a nicely framed cork bulletin board, purchased from my local stationer, hung on the brightly painted wall above my desk.   —D.S.

THE REAL THING

Stationery stores now sell something called a "Crate-a-File," made of brightly colored plastic; it resembles a milk crate but has built-in metal rods along the sides to support hanging file folders. A real milk crate also makes a good substitute for a file drawer, as well as a good container for files that have to be transported; all the ones I have were purchased for a dollar or two at yard sales. Presumably, they were discarded by their original owners.

Milk crates can vary slightly in size. If they're too wide, the folders will slip off the sides. If they're too narrow, the folder edges get frayed. I usually bring along a folder to test the size. But even milk crates that are the wrong size for files can be good buys; they can be stacked on their sides to be used as bookcases.

—MARGARET DICANIO

GOVERNMENT SURPLUS

The best desks, the sturdiest and by far the cheapest, are old government desks. If you don't live in Washington, where these things are snapped up by people in the used-desk business, check out government auctions. My oak desk with a pull-out typewriter table (it holds my computer monitor and keyboard) and several file cabinets (much sturdier than new ones) were government surplus. And when you're shopping the used-office-furniture places, keep an eye out for library card-index cabinets; they make great files for stamps, envelopes, cassette tapes, disks, et al., and each drawer can be labeled.

—MARTA VOGEL

FOLD-AWAY SPACE

Was there ever a writer who had enough table space for papers, manuscript pages, open reference books, closed reference books, correspondence, etc., etc.? Not in my experience. Consider making your own compact work tables. I did, and it's *simple*.

Get two sets of folding legs from a big hardware store (they may have

to be specially ordered) or from a hardware mail order firm; my favorite
is Northern Hydraulics, (800) 533-5545. Then get from a lumberyard a
4- by 8-foot sheet of plywood, at least ⅝ inch thick. Cut it in half the
long way (or beg or pay the yard to do it for you). Attach a set of legs
to each half. You now have two 8-feet-long, 2-feet-wide fold-away tables.

If you want something a little fancier, some lumberyards sell the
same size plywood sheets with a formica surface.

—WENDY MURPHY

96 FILES AT HAND

What writer can do without filing cabinets? I have several throughout
the house. They're fine for filing less-current materials that I'm unlikely
to need at once. But for items of immediate interest, which I'm likely
to want at a moment's notice, I have a different piece of furniture.

It resembles a bookcase and stands—right next to my desk—some 6
feet high, 3 feet wide, and a foot deep; that may sound huge but, pressed
against a wall, it doesn't take too much space. It contains 96 separate
compartments, each capable of holding about as much as a fat folder in
a filing cabinet (the papers lie flat). Instead of having to get up and slide
out drawers, I can grab the papers instantly.

Such constructions are known in office-equipment stores as "letter
sorters" or "letter organizers." They come in a variety of sizes, with
different numbers of compartments, and range from about $150 up-
ward.

—CHARLES A. SALTER

THE CHOICE OF CHAIR

I spend long hours at the keyboard, but I no longer suffer the kinks and
backaches that were frequent before I discovered the importance of
getting the proper chair. Office chairs can look alike, but cheaper ones
have only two adjustments—up and down, in the back and the seat. In
a better chair, you can adjust the back not just to hit you in the right
spot; you can also vary its tension. My chair adjusts so easily that I may
change positions several times during a long workday.

—JANET GROENE

■ ■ ■

While each person must choose his or her own favorite chair, I recommend seeking out a furniture store that distributes Steelcase. I paid about $325 for a Steelcase desk chair four years ago, and I've been delighted with it. It still looks almost new, and I find it comfortable for working at the computer, making notes, or talking on the phone.

You might also consider a small footstool. I find that my chair has to be at a certain height for me to be comfortable at the computer keyboard, and a footstool improves the situation for my legs. There's nothing like being able to put your feet up while you're working!

—KATE KELLY

■ ■ ■

I can't overemphasize the importance of a good quality, ergonomically designed office chair. For a number of years, I used a kitchen chair with a pillow; I'm surprised I still have a back left. I finally invested in a good-quality chair from a local dealer, Regan of Westchester. I bought the top of the line, for close to $400, several years ago and can now work long hours at the computer without fatigue. (I bought one with arms, since I wouldn't like using an armless chair.) IBM also makes an excellent ergonomic chair, but it is in the $500-plus range. Much cheaper chairs are also available—but when it comes to one's back, I believe it's important to get a well-designed chair, one that may be easily adjusted at various points and is sturdily constructed of good materials.

—ROSEMARY ELLEN GUILEY

■ ■ ■

Check out the art-supply stores that carry what's known as "drafting furniture"; some of the better chairs (and lamps) can be found there. My chair is a gem on an asterisk base with smoothly rolling casters at all five points, 360-degree swivel, vertically and horizontally adjustable back support, pneumatically changeable seat height, and a suspended-from-the-seat footrest (essential if your feet don't rest on the floor when you're seated). The legend on the back reads "Charvoz Dauphin, Made in West Germany." It came from Lee's in New York City and cost a little over $300 in 1981. —D.S.

HAVE A KNEEL

If you're a back-pain sufferer, look seriously at those oddly shaped "back chairs" which have you half-squatting, half-kneeling at your desk. This writer endured back pain for twenty years and started using kneeling chairs five years ago.

Try to buy a model that swivels or moves on castors, because these are easier to rise from in a hurry or in a confined space. If possible, avoid very cheap versions sold through catalogs, because they can be badly made and have inadequate padding. The best kneeling chairs are made in Scandinavia or England and cost $100 to $200 or more.

When you first start using such a chair, your knees may get a bit sore from the unaccustomed pressure. But this discomfort soon goes away, and it pays to persist, because these chairs really work. Even if you *don't* have back pain, you'll find them very comfortable for long writing sessions.

—DAVID BOUCHIER

TRY A TOOTSIE ROLL
I have a foam cushion, shaped like a Tootsie Roll, which I place between my lower back and the back of my desk chair. It makes a world of difference.

—MARY HARMON

BACKING AT HOME OR AWAY
Unless you do most of your writing lying down, you'll be doing more sitting than your back can stand. The absolutely best back support—fitting any seat you may be forced to occupy away from home, and turning any seat at home into an orthopedically proper chair—is a device called the Back Machine.

It's a pillow of sorts, 12 by 17 inches, but with internal steel ribs to provide support and an adjustable roller bar that makes it truly your own. It relieves and prevents lower-back stress like nothing else I've tried, weighs only two pounds, and comes with a carrying bag. The cost is $35 plus $4.95 shipping from Norm Thompson, P.O. Box 3999, Portland OR 97208; (800) 547-1160.

—ELLEN PERRY BERKELEY

THE ROUND FILE
Absolutely indispensable for every writer's office: an extra-large wastebasket that won't tip over.

—JANE MARKS

■ ■ ■

Chaos is the biggest battle I face as a writer—the chaos of debris that flows through my mailbox like lava. I can run away from it at first, but then it solidifies and becomes very tough to move. So I have a *big* wastebasket, and I use it to throw away 90 percent of my mail as soon as it arrives.

—TOM BEDELL

CUSTOM CONSTRUCTION

My desktop is an inch-and-a-half-thick piece of butcher block, 6 feet long and 25½ inches wide (available at any lumber-supply store). Most desks are 30 inches high. My desktop is 33 inches from the floor—I find those 3 inches make a world of difference—and rests on two free-standing units which I had specially built.

The left-hand unit has four compartments: In the top slot, I keep my typing paper (I'm still using a typewriter, and I see no reason to change); in the next compartment, I keep stationery, envelopes, and carbon paper; a third compartment holds the files of stories I'm currently working on; and the lowest compartment is a letter-size file drawer. The right-hand unit has three drawers plus another full-size file drawer. Thus, I have the equivalent of a two-drawer file cabinet, plus a variety of slots and drawers.

I should add that this tailor-made unit was constructed by my son, who happens to be a skilled builder/carpenter, and I paid him $500 for it.

Since my desk is unusually high, I needed a special chair. To be exact, it's an architect's stool. The seat is pneumatically adjustable and can be set anywhere from 22 to 28 inches from the floor; I use the latter position almost all the time, which allows me to sit with my legs fairly straight under me. (For me, this happens to be a necessity, since I have a surgically fused right hip—but I think people with normal hip joints would find it advantageous to sit up high, too.) My chair was made by an outfit called Designcraft, and I bought it for about $70 fifteen years ago. I don't know if Designcraft still exists, but I'm sure there are other chairs like this on the market.

A virtue of a separate desktop, whether custom-designed or not (such desks are also available commercially) is mobility. An office can thus be moved from room to room, house to house, or state to state more easily.

—RICK BODE

DRAFTING-TABLE DEVOTEE

I don't use desks. I have three architectural drafting tables that can be adjusted for height and for slope. The one I use for my computer is covered with Borco, a clear rubberized-plastic material available from architectural-supply dealers; it eliminates the need for a stupid "mouse-pad," considered essential if you use a mouse with your computer, and lets me roll my mouse anywhere I want.

—STEPHEN MORRILL

DESK INVESTMENT

Mattress salespeople often like to point out that we spend nearly a third of our time in bed, so we might as well be comfortable. That sort of logic applies to home-office equipment, too.

One day, I saw a new roll-top desk in an office furniture store. I just had to have it. All those convenient cubbyholes and drawers, devised when roll-tops were invented in the 1830s, are *still* perfect for creating order out of the stationery, stamps, and other supplies that clutter desks.

Fortunately, I took a moment before buying it to consult an experienced friend. She warned against immediately purchasing it. She then helped me find a well-preserved Meekins, Packard & Co. oak roll-top, circa 1910, at an auction—for only $200 more than the cost of the brand-new model I'd seen in the store. "A new desk," she advised, "will start going down in value the moment you buy it. But an antique will give you more pleasure—and will become more valuable every day you own it."

Now *there*'s a comforting thought!

—ANDREW KREIG

NO CRICKS IN THE NECK

When I first got my computer, I placed it on my desk. But then I had nowhere to study research material, make notes, or do anything else. So I turned my typewriter table around 90 degrees, put the computer monitor at the center, and the keyboard at the end where I could sit comfortably. It's right by my desk, so I can roll my chair there in a second.

I don't warm to those fancy computer work-stations where you have to peer upward at the screen on a little shelf. I'm looking down at the same angle at which I was looking when I had the typewriter on the table, not up where neck-cricking can occur.

—EVELYN KAYE

LOOK OUT BELOW!

Although I use standard letter-size file folders, I've found that the wider legal-size cabinet is desirable, for several reasons: (1) Many news releases are printed on 8½- by 14-inch paper; I can file them unfolded. (2) The wider cabinet accommodates my collection of sample issues of magazines, many of which exceed standard size. (3) Even when searching for the usual 8½- by 11-inch items, the extra space means fewer smashed fingernails.

I advise that, unless you're a lot taller than I am (5 feet, 11 inches with my cowboy boots on), stick to a maximum of three drawers. That way, the top of the cabinet will still be at a convenient height for a to-be-filed tray, with space behind it for a postage scale or a group of reference books.

An important safety tip, whatever size or height your file cabinets: *Always* begin filling the drawers from the *bottom*. And put the heaviest, bulkiest stuff (like those magazines) in the bottom drawer, to add stability.

When you're ready to buy a second cabinet, consider distributing part of the contents of the first one into the corresponding drawers of the second, so that similar subjects are side by side instead of atop each other. Why? Because then you won't be tempted to have two drawers of the same cabinet open simultaneously, a practice which makes file-searching nearly impossible and could put an abrupt end to your career anyway if the laws of gravity decide to demonstrate themselves by impelling the whole shebang to crash down on you.

—NANCY S. GRANT

ROLLING STOCK

Rolling carts can be useful for all kinds of things. If you thumb through office-supply catalogs, you'll see page after page of rolling carts, with prices that can start you rolling, as well. If you look in your local hardware store, you can find so-called utility carts (Cosco is one reliable brand name) that cost in the $20-to-$35 range.

The only drawback is that they're sold unassembled. My local full-price hardware store assembled one for me, and it was probably a bargain considering that the bargain-priced one *I* assembled ended up costing $100—$20 for the cart, and $80 for the doctor's fee and the X rays after I smashed my finger.

—BARBARA SCHWARTZ

■ ■ ■

Stacked plastic baskets on wheels, available in housewares stores, are great for clippings to be filed, mail to be answered, and work in progress. I have two three-basket sets, which roll under my desk and out of the way.

—GRACE W. WEINSTEIN

MADE FOR TV

Thank God for TV stands. I have one of those inexpensive wooden ones with casters on the legs, and I use it constantly. It holds, more or less permanently, the two floppy disk storage boxes I always seem to need even with a hard drive in my computer. It holds the material I'm working with at the moment. I stack the envelopes that are going to the post office on it. It's a great place for my cup of coffee, because it reduces the chance of spills on my computer keyboard. And when I'm not using it, it rolls out of the way, under my worktable.

—KEN ENGLADE

SORTING THINGS OUT

I've worked in various locations—in our Connecticut house, in our summer house on Martha's Vineyard, in a place we rented for twelve years in San Miguel de Allende, Mexico. A feature of every work area I've used has been a bed, preferably two beds at right angles to each other.

Much of my work involves sorting large amounts of research materials into piles as part of coming up with a working structure for whatever book or article I'm preparing. It's a waste of money to have places for spreading out such materials constructed when beds serve ideally. They're even an ideal height for reaching and viewing what you have.

—VANCE PACKARD

SEE-THROUGH BULLETIN BOARD

Many writers find a bulletin board next to the desk essential. What to do if your desk is next to a window? Buy sturdy cafe curtains, and pin your notes and reminders on them. Your memory-joggers are right at hand—along with a view of the great outdoors.

—ROBERTA ROESCH

PRESSED INTO SERVICE

A writer often needs a temporary extra work surface for such tasks as collating or spreading out reference books. A sturdy ironing board can be pressed into service (sorry!) for this purpose. Most ironing boards have the added advantage of being adjustable to various heights. In a pinch, an ironing board can be used, too, to hold a lightweight type-writer or computer keyboard (of course there's the small problem of how to arrange your legs around the board's legs).

—MARGARET DICANIO

DESK DOOR

Why do many beginners assume that they must spend money on "proper" furniture before launching into the business of writing? For three years, my "office" consisted of a portable file cabinet that accom-panied me to whatever space in the house I found usable from time to time. When I graduated to a "desk," it was actually two two-drawer file cabinets (seconds, due to dented tops) covered by a painted-to-match door with knob removed.

—JOAN WESTER ANDERSON

■ ■ ■

Some desks can cost as much as a *Reader's Digest* paycheck. I bought a 3- by 6-foot birch door from the lumberyard (about $40), sanded it lightly, stained it, and brushed on polyurethane to seal the surface. (Smaller or cut-to-size doors can also be purchased.) Two two-drawer metal filing cabinets serve as sturdy "legs."

—PAMELA HOBBS HOFFECKER

THE LIGHT STUFF

After years of making do with an old floor lamp, I acquired a bright, sturdy desk lamp. It makes a world of difference. Don't skimp. Your eyes will appreciate it.

—EVELYN KAYE

■ ■ ■

The "banker's" lamp, with its green glass shade, is a perennial cliché of mail-order catalogs. For reading and writing by hand at your desk, however, it's still about the best-designed lamp you can buy. It throws a bright patch of light on your work, but the short stem and green shade keep the light out of your eyes. The banker's lamp, cliché or not, also brings a warm, traditional touch to the home office.

—DAVID BOUCHIER

■ ■ ■

Fluorescent light plus video terminal equals headache. There are ill effects on the eye and the brain when the frequency of fluorescent light interacts with that from a computer monitor; black-and-white and green-on-black screens appear to be worse (as opposed to the amber-on-black many users prefer). Play it safe: If you use a computer, use only incandescent light in the room where you do your writing.

—M. LAWRENCE PODOLSKY

■ ■ ■

It's easy to overlook the obvious when you're engaged in a field as precarious as free-lance writing. Be *sure* you're working in good light. Murray Teigh Bloom, one of the Society's founders, told me this. You would think I might have been intelligent enough to figure it out for myself. I went out and bought a better lamp. It helped.

—BONNIE REMSBERG

■ ■ ■

The best desk lamp I've found is a Luxo with an incandescent light *and* a fluorescent ring, on a movable and bendable arm.

—GRACE W. WEINSTEIN

LOOK UNDER THE BED

For those whose offices are at home, and whose homes are crowded, one of the smartest space savers is a storage bed—a platform bed with large drawers underneath. They're commonly made by built-in-furniture specialists, in either one-tier or two-tier configurations.

My queen-size "high dresser" version has, on each side, one bottom drawer running the length of the bed and, above each of those, a pair of drawers each 40 inches wide. Yes, I imagine such drawers are commonly used to hold sweaters and underwear, but any writer with a home office knows that half the drawers in the house end up sheltering stray files and piles of paper that you're going to get to later.

One caveat: Cheapie beds may be tempting but, as with file cabinets and many other things, it pays to go for quality. Anything that has moving parts and will be subjected to much use is worth the extra investment.

—DAN CARLINSKY

GETTING THE LONG VIEW

One stage of structuring an article or book is getting a "fix" on how it works as a whole. I've found that 2- by 4-foot corkboard panels, available from most lumber suppliers, are ideal for pinning up copy and getting this fix. One panel accommodates eight to ten pages, roughly 2000 to 3000 words, the length of an average article.

The first complete draft of my first book, *Orca: The Whale Called Killer,* came to about 500 pages. After three years of writing, I had only a dim sense of where I was repeating myself and how the book worked as an entity. I rented another office, installed corkboard panels all around the room, and pinned up the entire book. I spent two months in that room, moving around on a swivel chair with casters, comparing, editing, and rewriting.

—ERICH HOYT

PENS AND PENCILS AT HAND

I used to keep pens and pencils in the middle drawer of my desk, which meant opening the drawer every time I wanted one. Now I keep a

dozen of each in a souvenir metal cup right in front of me; it makes
things quicker and easier.

—EVELYN KAYE

∎ ∎ ∎

Other useful containers for this purpose (you might want several—black
pens in one, colored pens in another, pencils in a third): amateur-made
ceramic mugs (not good for coffee, because the glazes might leach lead),
plastic 8-ounce yogurt cups, 8- to 10-ounce cans covered with pretty
paper such as wallpaper samples.   —D.S.

A NOD TO THE PAST

I'm a firm believer in recycling. Thus, my office furnishings include
many old items converted to modern use. Among them:

An old-fashioned armoire is my supply closet. I sit in an antique
Windsor chair when I'm at my computer. An old wooden, hinge-lidded
cigar box (which sits next to a Rolodex) holds index cards with the names
of sources for the two columns I write. An old ceramic crock is my trash
can. Old baskets serve as "In" and "Out" boxes. An old, small pickling
jar holds pens and pencils. A Tetley tea advertising tin, circa 1925, holds
my postage stamps, and a Louis Sherry tin holds assorted small items.
An old clothes-drying rack holds current newspapers and magazines.
Computer disks reside in a dainty wire egg basket. An antique wooden
ironing board serves as an extra lamp table and is often a work table
when I need a bit of extra room.

Many such items may be purchased inexpensively at garage sales and
flea markets (which are, incidentally, also excellent places to find used
file cabinets and other heavy-duty office equipment at incredible bargain prices). I like this kind of eclectic mix. I can reach for the future,
never forgetting to bow to the past.

—GAIL GRECO

CORPORATE-MOVE BOON

Filing cabinets—good ones, that is—can be fiendishly expensive, as
anyone who's shopped for them has surely discovered. The secret is
to keep your ears open for news of a company's imminent move.
Often, a corporation that's moving will completely redecorate, and

they'll sell unwanted furniture. That's how I acquired two four-drawer, super-heavy-duty files for $10 each. They're a little beat up, but they're superbly built, and I keep them in a back bedroom now known as the file room. Had I wanted them in my office, covering them with paint or stick-on paper would have been an easy cosmetic job.

—ISOBEL SILDEN

SKIRTING THE ISSUE

Two problems: (1) You could use an extra working surface or a place to put such frequently used items as your computer disks. (2) You have a couple of unsightly piles of research material for in-progress projects, really ugly but necessary to have nearby for ready reference until the projects are completed. The single solution: Add an old table. Cover it with bright felt or other colorful material that reaches to the floor (like the old "skirted" tables that used to be fashionable parlor mainstays). You have at once an attractive addition to your office and a place to tuck those research materials so they're out of sight but still accessible.

—ROBERTA ROESCH

RACK 'EM UP

If you usually have a certain number of "active" file folders on your desk representing pending projects, chances are those folders frequently get buried and lost. You can't put them in the filing cabinet; they'll be forgotten. A simple solution is a metal or plastic stepped file-folder holder or rack, available (often in a choice of attractive colors) from any office-supply store. It lets you keep about ten files upright on your desk in the space of one lying flat, and with all the labels clearly displayed.

—DAVID BOUCHIER

DISHPAN HANDY

I always hated metal filing cabinets. I now have, on a large table in my office, an array of plastic dishpans in which I keep my files. This dishpan tip is one I picked up from fellow ASJA member and good friend Muriel Lederer, who used them for toys when her children were small and then made the wondrous discovery that they were a perfect size to hold file folders. Once I learned that, I became Rubbermaid's best customer.

And you can easily pick up your project and take it with you. I used to embarrass a co-author by dragging my dishpan of folders to luncheon meetings. What did I care? The book got written.

—BONNIE REMSBERG

FILES ON WHEELS

Rolling file carts with open hanging folders are a great help. Because they're so accessible, they encourage you to do filing instantly, instead of putting it off until you have a mess accumulated on your desk.

—DALE RONDA BURG

■ ■ ■

Plastic bins on wheels, holding Pendaflex hanging folders, are wonderful for current projects, for pending projects, and for things you need to reach when you're on the telephone. There are several types and sizes; I found mine at Ideal Stationery in New York City.

—SHIRLEY CAMPER SOMAN

■ ■ ■

I found a classy version of this kind of thing in a mail-order catalog called Hold Everything, a Williams-Sonoma spinoff which mostly shows such household stuff as shower caddies, wine racks, and closet accessories but offers a few office-oriented items as well.

My rolling file cart holds anywhere from 25 to 50 hanging folders, depending how much you cram into them, at a perfect level for thumbing through while I'm seated; down below the file rack is a handy shelf. It's made of lacquered wood, not metal or plastic. Less than 23 inches high, it fits neatly under my desk (actually a built-in desk-height counter) when not in use. It cost $45 plus shipping in 1989. The Reliable catalog (see appendix) offers something similar.

To get the Hold Everything catalog: P.O. Box 7807, San Francisco CA 94120; (415) 421-4242. There are also Hold Everything stores in San Francisco and several other California communities, as well as in a few locations in other states. The maker of the cart is Fanta Furniture, Tulip and Westmoreland Streets, Philadelphia PA 19134; (215) 289-3665.   —D.S.

NEW USE FOR OLD FRIDGE

Thinking of throwing out an old refrigerator or small freezer? Don't, if you have room enough for it in the basement or a storage closet. It may not be as efficient as a costly fireproof safe—but it will protect computer disks and one-of-a-kind manuscripts from flames, smoke, and a considerable amount of heat should you have a fire in your home, God forbid, while you're away.

—WILBUR CROSS

15

FOR
WRITERS
WHO
LEAVE
HOME

Many—proba-
bly, most—of us delight in working within our houses or apartments,
never needing to brave the elements or bother about rush-hour
crowds or other nuisances on the way to our desks. Some of us,
though, like (or even psychically need) to go *out* to work. And others
find that, for various reasons, the home office isn't working out, or
a special project demands different arrangements for a period of
time. Commercial rents are beyond most solo writers. There are
alternatives.

ALTERNATIVE I: RENT WITH A FRIEND
This is a joint recommendation for writing efficiency—and enrich-
ment—from two ASJA members who were once neighbors in Birming-
ham, Michigan. Both of us wrote at typewriters (it was way before word
processing on computers) in offices in our respective homes.

There were problems with those home offices.

Mary often felt she should be polishing the silver or baking a cake instead of writing—particularly when the writing wasn't going well.

Julie felt no such compulsions. But she was often distracted from her work. Her teenagers liked to turn the stereo to ear-piercing volume when they arrived home from school. The doorbell's chime set off the dog's howls, often just as she was talking on the phone to an editor or client.

We found peaceful writing environments when we rented small offices together a few blocks away. Rents have risen, and the distance from home has increased, but we have shared office space ever since (one large room or two small adjoining ones; we've moved several times)—for more than 25 years.

The arrangement provides many benefits, aside from a place free of doorbells and household concerns (but with amenities including hot water for coffee or tea, a small refrigerator, and a microwave). Sharing space helps keep costs down—and offsets the loneliness that most writers feel. We bounce ideas off each other, ask advice on difficult leads and transitions, exchange interesting clippings, share resources and reference books, borrow stamps and mailing envelopes.

Best of all, we've remained friends.

—JULIE CANDLER and MARY AUGUSTA RODGERS

ALTERNATIVE II: THE WRITE SPACE

For those who can't cope with the endless series of distractions or interruptions that go with writing at home, or who find cramped living quarters too confining, there are affordable alternatives to renting prohibitively expensive private office space.

Writers in the New York metropolitan area can find one such refuge in the New York Public Library's central research building at Fifth Avenue at 42nd Street, where the Frederick Lewis Allen Memorial Room provides free space to writers with book contracts, generally nonfiction. The elegant marble and wood-panelled room, 17½ by 32 feet, has eleven carrels, each with enough shelf space for typewriter or computer, manuscript, and research materials. One advantage of working here, of course, is that you can draw upon the library's millions of books, periodicals, and other reference materials on its 88 miles of shelves—and keep them in the room for a month at a time. The room also has a special computer terminal which will give you catalog numbers for all the books acquired by the library since 1972.

Since the room was established in 1954, with a donation from the Ford Foundation, more than 500 writers have used it. Books that have been written, at least in part, in the room include Betty Friedan's *The Feminine Mystique,* Susan Brownmiller's *Against Our Will,* Theodore White's *The Making of the President, 1964,* Nancy Milford's *Zelda,* Robert A. Caro's *The Power Broker,* and my own *The Right to Bear Arms.*

Because as many as 25 people have keys to the room at any one time, none has exclusive use of a carrel (although some writers manage to establish sovereignty over one for a period of time). Use of the room is for a six-month term, with a maximum of two consecutive terms before a writer must return to the waiting list. Waiting time is seldom more than a few weeks or months (thanks to the emergence of other spaces around the city, lessening demand for the Allen Room); often, there is no waiting time at all.

Another NYPL space is a walled-off section of the Main Reading Room known as the Wertheim Study; it was created in 1964 by the late author-historian Barbara Tuchman in memory of her father. There are seats for 36 people at the room's three 12-foot-long tables, but the room is seldom crowded and, because typewriters are prohibited (laptop computers are permitted), it is generally quieter than the Allen Room. Use of the room is for an initial term of three months, with renewals allowed for two additional three-month periods. There is generally no waiting time, and it is not required that the writer have a book contract.

Applications for use of the NYPL rooms are available from the Office of Special Collections, New York Public Library, Fifth Avenue and 42nd Street, New York NY 10018; (212) 930-0740.

Among private libraries in New York offering space to writers are the New York Society Library, which ties the privilege to library membership ($100 for one year or $65 for six months), and the Mercantile Library Association, which charges "published or aspiring" writers $300 for a three-month rental of one of the eight partitioned-off areas in a large room. The New York Society Library is at 53 East 79 Street, New York NY 10021; (212) 288-6900. The "Merc," as it is known locally, is at 17 East 47 Street, New York NY 10017; (212) 755-6710.

Use of library space is restricted to the libraries' hours. The nonprofit Writers Room, in Greenwich Village, offers the unique advantage of being open 24 hours a day, 365 days a year. Something of an urban writers' colony, founded in 1978 by several exiles from the NYPL's Allen Room, the Writers Room has 27 desks (with three others in a separate room for smokers). Eighteen are for "floaters," who pay $150 for three months and occupy any available desk when they come in. "Permanent" desks can be had for $200 per quarter, renewable for up to two years. There are also six private offices for $200 per month. (Fees cover only a third of actual costs. The enterprise is supported by the New York State Council on the Arts and other public agencies, as well as by foundations and other private sources.)

Amenities include a kitchen with a constant supply of coffee, a lounge, a small reference library, storage space for typewriters and research materials, and phones for outgoing calls. Writers who are willing to work nights or weekends can usually be accommodated immediately; for others, the waiting time may range from weeks to months. Although the Room is used by many established writers (Judith Rossner wrote her best-selling novel *August* there), beginners with a "serious commitment" to writing are also accepted.

For an application, write or call The Writers Room, 153 Waverly Place, Fifth Floor, New York NY 10014; (212) 807-9519.

Some other cities offer comparable facilities. In Boston, for one, the Artists Foundation Writers' Room, open twenty hours a day and seven days a week at City Place in downtown Boston, has eleven desks, available for $225 per quarter (or $125 if shared), plus two private offices at $250 per quarter ($175 if shared). Accepted writers (a "serious writing commitment" is a requirement for consideration) may be permitted to renew for up to two years. There are a reference library, a cafeteria, and coin phones on the premises.

For an application, write or call Writers' Room of Boston, Artists Foundation, Eight Park Plaza, Boston MA 02116; (617) 227-ARTS [227-2787].

The intangible benefit of these rooms, of course, is that they foster a certain camaraderie, serve as an inspiration, and help assuage the anxieties inherent in one of the world's loneliest professions.

—CARL BAKAL

16

KEEPERS,
FINDERS

$\mathbf{W}$hatever happened to the prediction, heard in some quarters a decade or so ago with the advent of the personal computer, that paperwork would simply vanish? No such luck. The papers are still very much with us, from research to receipts, from notes to ourselves to necessary correspondence with others. Here are some of the tools writers use to get that material under control, or at least make a valiant effort. (Notes on financial records and calendars—often kept together—are in the latter part of the chapter.)

ALL TOGETHER

To avoid losing important bits and pieces, I set up a separate, sturdy folder for each magazine article or column. In it, I put all pertinent correspondence, receipts for expenses, notes from interviews, relevant brochures or literature, lists of resources, early drafts (if I think they're worth saving), contract with the magazine, and a list of dates—when mailed, when paid, when published.

I write important sources' phone numbers directly on the front of the folder. Then, when the fact-checker calls or if I need more information in a hurry, it's not a frantic search.

Eventually, I put a set of tearsheets in the same folder. At that point, I weed through it and toss those early drafts and anything else that's no longer needed.

—JANE MARKS

TRACKING RESEARCH

When I undertook an historical project that meant gleaning research material from over two hundred books, I had to find some method of keeping track of my notes. The system I found works best for me:

I use a clipboard holding loose-leaf paper. The first entry is the title, author, publisher, and date; in a corner, who owns the book or where I obtained it (if it's a library book, I note the call number). As I read the book, instead of taking extensive notes or making copies of several pages, I simply list page numbers with brief notes on data, so I'll know exactly where to return for that information. Each book receives a number, and the sheets go into a loose-leaf binder.

Then, for an instant checklist of my source material, I set up an index-card file. Each card carries a specific topic—e.g., food, clothing, education. On the card goes the book number, page number(s), and very brief description of the reference.

—BERNICE CURLER

AFTER THE FACT

Once you've written a book on a subject, you're generally alert to related items in newspapers and magazines. I keep a file folder for each book I've written—not stashed away, but right in my office so it's convenient to clip an item and put it in the appropriate folder right then and there. I'm probably not going to be doing another book on lawyers or on Wall Street—but one never knows, and the item might still turn out to be useful for an article or other project.

—MURRAY TEIGH BLOOM

WHAT COLOR ARE YOUR FILES?

If you're working on more than one project, or kind of project, at a time, color-coding can help. File folders are available in a number of colors.

I use red ones for medical articles, blue for nonmedical articles, and green for public relations projects. Then, when I dig into a pile of folders, I can quickly spot what I want.

—ELAINE FANTLE SHIMBERG

PERTINENT AND PORTABLE

I'm not sure why it took me so long to discover accordion files, with many compartments inside. I now love having all the pertinent letters or articles I need for a book neatly organized, by chapters, in one filing system. And accordion files are portable!

—CAROL WESTON

SQUIRREL NO MORE

For years, I stuffed notes, clippings, articles, and other valuable bits of information into drawers and boxes or tossed them onto shelves. My chances of retrieving them on demand were no better than a squirrel's of finding its buried hazelnuts.

Then, somebody put me onto the Day-Timer Fingertip Filing System. Now, everything goes into manila folders, each for a specific subject or item. The folder is numbered. The number is recorded on an alphabetical subject key. When I want to refer to the subject, I look it up in the key, get the number, and—presto—I have the folder.

For more information: Day-Timers Inc., One Day-Timer Plaza, Allentown PA 18195-9987; (215) 395-5884.

—JOHN RAVAGE

READY FOR ACTION

Everyone knows that papers multiply geometrically. I've found that the only way to control this growth is by sorting into action files—"Phone," "Write," "Awaiting Reply," "Ideas" (for future proposals). One called "Slush" is for letters, clippings, or ads of indeterminate use; they are either dealt with or discarded within a few weeks.

—FLORENCE TEMKO

ROPE IT ALL IN

Keeping research material organized when you're working on a project is a prime requisite. My first step after receiving an assignment is to set up a large, heavy-duty 10- by 15-inch accordion envelope that expands to 5¼ inches; this kind of envelope is known among lawyers as "Red-weld" or "Red Rope." I label the outside flap with the subject or title and place inside file folders (legal or letter size) labeled according to the needs of the project—contracts, correspondence, interviews, notes, photographs, etc. Everything is in one place while I'm working on the story, and it's easy to retrieve the material intact after the story is completed.

—ELISE VONS ULRICH

■ ■ ■

I've found that the best way to organize magazine-article material for reference and storage is legal-size accordion files, such as Smead's 1526E envelopes. They're available for about $1.50 to $2, depending on quantity, and they can store everything from thick government reports to newspaper clips (full-size newspaper pages folded horizontally in thirds fit easily).

For each assignment, I subdivide such an envelope with letter-size tabbed manila folders; a routine article might contain just four of these— say, "Clips," "Interviews," "Correspondence," and "Finished Story"—while a complex, in-depth piece could require an envelope stretching out four inches thick, with nine or ten file folders inside. It's great to have this kind of flexibility, because the scope of research is seldom entirely predictable at the outset.

And extra organizational effort can pay off handsomely. A prompt answer to an editor's frantic last-minute question encourages future assignments. Moreover, systematic filing paves the way for recycling the research later for other publications—and paychecks.

—ANDREW KREIG

THE LOOSE-LEAF WAY

I always keep several loose-leaf notebooks and a supply of paper on hand. When I receive an article assignment, I take all relevant material—until then, collected in a file folder—and put it into a notebook. A three-hole punch makes everything fit; odd-size pieces of paper such as newspaper clippings are attached to loose-leaf paper. If necessary, I separate the material into sections by using a set of tabbed dividers.

The notebook is both sturdy and portable, the contents are easily rearranged, and it's easy to keep adding new material. Once the article is finished, I take everything out of the notebook. A copy of the final draft, the contract, and any other material I want to save are held together by paper fasteners inserted through the holes, and this clutch of papers is tucked into a folder, which goes into my file cabinet. And the notebook is ready for another assignment.

—SUSAN J. GORDON

KEEPING CARDS IN ORDER
I meet many vendors of goods and services in the course of my work and need to keep track of them for future reference, but entering them in my Rolodex phone index would be useless, since I sometimes can't recall their names or even their companies. Since they invariably give me their business cards, I've solved the problem by setting up a business-card file in a small plastic box made for this purpose and sold in most stationery stores; it's just the right size and comes with alphabetical dividers.

I don't use the dividers to sort out names of firms or individuals, but for categorical divisions; printers, for example, are under "P," typesetters under "T," and messenger services under "M." If I'm interested in a copier, I look under "C," where I'm likely to find a number of people in that business, which facilitates comparison shopping. This method beats the yellow pages, since all of these people initially contacted me.

This neat little box has saved me hours and hours. The system could be easily adapted to other special categories—types of experts, for example.

—ALEXANDRA S.E. CANTOR

IT'S ALL IN THE BOOK
Step One, when I begin work on a new book, is to set up a 6- by 9-inch spiral notebook. The bulk of the notebook is divided into chapter sections. For each chapter, I record details on interviews, library references (including call numbers), and other sources. This notebook becomes a permanent record in case I ever need to recheck the source of anything in the book.

But the most heavily used part of the notebook is a typewritten summary sheet pasted inside the front cover. Each chapter is assigned a horizontal line. In addition to the chapter number itself, there are five columns, headed "Subject," "Length Projected," "Words Actual," "Disk #," and "Hard Copy" (a date is entered in the last column). As the first draft of each chapter is completed, I mark that chapter number with red pencil. This sheet tells me at a glance the current status of the book and its chapters and keeps me on track throughout the project.

—GEORGE LAYCOCK

Q AND A

I always keep on hand a huge supply of 3- by 5-inch index cards plus pads of paper in that very same size. I use them in an organization system for questions and answers that I've found invaluable for massive research jobs in which questions seem to keep arising endlessly. Here's how it works:

When I'm planning to conduct an interview, or write a letter seeking information, or visit a library or archive, I jot questions, just as they occur to me, on the pads of paper, one per page; each page is paper-clipped to a card with the name of the interviewee (or library, or correspondent) I hope will provide the answer. Just before the interview (or library visit, etc.), I organize the questions—e.g., by subject or chronology. If I obtain the information I seek, I throw out the question slip: if I don't, the slip of paper is attached to another card, bearing the name of another source.

—LAURIE LISLE

TRACKING QUERIES

A 5- by 8-inch yellow pad helps me keep track of the article proposals—queries—I send to magazine editors. This could be done by computer, but I like to have the tablet on my desk where it constantly reminds me to follow up on queries and send out new ones.

Each month, I flip to a new page and write the month at the top. The page is then numbered down the left-hand side and divided into four columns, "Date," "Publication," "Idea," and "Response." With this method, I can tell at a glance the status of each query, as well as the number of queries I've sent that month; if it's the 20th and I've mailed only five, I know it's time to get cracking.

I also have a record at year's end showing queries sent and which ones and how many landed assignments; a review of that information can prove very instructive.

—BARBARA NIELSEN

GETTING MONEY BACK

To facilitate reimbursement for telephone expenses (most magazines cover them for assigned articles), I keep a homemade log with columns for date of call, phone number, person called, disposition (contact made, message left with secretary, message left on phone machine, etc.), and the piece in connection with which the call was made. When the phone bill arrives, it's a simple matter to match my log to the charges, copy the pertinent records, and send an expense invoice to the editor.

—JUDITH KELMAN

■ ■ ■

When I get an assignment, I immediately open a file for it—specifically, a legal-size hanging Pendaflex folder. The first thing that goes into the hanging folder is an ordinary letter-size manila file folder labeled "Project X—Expenses" in red. Into that folder I put taxi receipts, airline tickets, marked-up photocopies of my phone bills, and evidence of anything else I've spent on the article or other project. When the project is completed, it's easy to put together my expenses to bill the client.

—JANICE HOPKINS TANNE

ALL CALLS

In the eternal battle to get and stay organized, I find something I call a "desk book" to be extremely useful. I use a spiral-bound 6- by 9-inch standard secretarial notebook; another format would do. In it, I note all phone calls, both in and out, with the person's name and number and a few words on the substance of the call—references, dates, appointments made, and so on.

It may seem very obvious but, if you're like some of us who note things on scraps of paper, margins of newspapers, or any writable surface that comes to hand, you can have a very hard time reconstituting the trail by which you reached a certain source or tracked down a certain person. Calls come in at odd times, when you're writing or whatever, and the scribbled notes one takes tend to disappear.

Keeping a desk book, and keeping it handy at all times, solves this problem. It provides back-up evidence for phone costs incurred in research. And it can be taken on trips, with all the relevant names, dates, times, and places noted as they were taken down when appointments were made.

I keep these books after they're filled, with inclusive dates marked boldly on the covers. I find them useful references when it's necessary to reconstruct past researching exercises.

—JUDSON GOODING

■ ■ ■

I've heard of writers who keep a phone log with notes on every call they make or receive. I tried it, but I never kept it up. I do keep an outgoing phone-call notebook, however, where, day by day, I list the people I have to call, with their phone numbers.

After each call, I make a note in the margin to remind myself what happened. A check mark means I reached the person and we talked. "WCB" denotes the dubious promise that the person couldn't talk then but "will call back." "LM" means I left a message with a human being. "LMM" means I left a message on the (answering) machine. "NA" means "not available": the person is on vacation, has moved to another city, or has left the company.

—EVELYN KAYE

TRAVEL-LOG

Yes, I have a computer, a copier, and other high-tech tools—but let me say a few words about the old reliable 3- by 5-inch index cards, especially useful if you sell travel pieces to newspapers. The travel pieces I self-"syndicate" are usually sent out on speculation (unfortunately, that's how newspaper travel pages work) and go to many regional papers simultaneously.

Each story has a card, on which I list the newspapers to which I send it, with the editor's name and the date mailed. As responses come in, I update the card. I can tell at a glance where the article has been sent; who has responded and how; how much each paper paid; and—in the case of competing dailies in the same area—where I can submit the piece after a rejection.

I also keep a separate card file of the markets, where I can instantly find addresses, phone numbers, editors' names, and history of story use and rates paid.

—JOAN SCOBEY

IN SIGHT, IN MIND

The desk in my office is normally overrun with the books and papers related to my current writing project. Everything else in one way or another current—letters to be answered, a book I'm reviewing, a pile of receipts for preparing an expense statement, an address to which I want to write for information—I keep three steps away on a large table, measuring about 2½ by 6 feet, where I can see everything at a glance.

For me, if I can't see it—which is to say, if I file it—I forget it. This way, what I need to do lies staring me in the face, in neat little piles, ready for action. When I want a short break from work on a long project, a glance at the table tells me what needs tackling next. (That's where I just found a reminder to submit something for this book.)

—ROBERT KANIGEL

INTERIOR DECOR

You can always learn something from just about anyone. When I complained to an interior decorator that I couldn't seem to find anything in my closetlike study, he passed along one of his secrets, which I now pass along to others.

I'd been using many file folders for each book, marked "Book X Correspondence," "Book X Promotion," "Book X Jacket Blurbs," etc. There was such overlap that I never knew which folder had the letter or list I needed. My decorator suggested buying large loose-leaf notebooks and turning the tabbed file designators into interior dividers. Now, everything pertaining to one book or other project is within my grasp, nestled in one notebook.

—ELAINE FANTLE SHIMBERG

IN THE CARDS

A stack of 3- by 5-inch index cards comprises what I call my "portable office." Each client, magazine, and book publisher has its own card; the front lists address, phone, editors and others I've worked with (and personal notes about their special interests, personalities, etc.), while the back lists projects, with delivery and billing dates, and check-offs for payments received. Clipped-on cards list projects under discussion. A top-of-the-stack card is my daily "to do" list.

—JUDITH H. McQUOWN

COLORFUL NOTES

Twice, recently, I've had assignments where the research material was voluminous; I had stacks of information, a huge pile of notes. Here's how I handled the problem of almost-too-much research.

First, I photocopied the typed-up notes. Then, I used variously colored marking pens to denote connected material, scissored up the notes, and pasted them in the order I felt fit the story—this part here, that part there—and the piece was practically written. All I had to do was type it, rewriting and editing as I went.

I use a similar system when doing a personality profile for which I have scads of quotes from different people. Each person gets a color—green for Mary, blue for John, pink for Amy, and so on. Then, when assembling the piece, which will cover a number of different topics, I can put each individual's quotes in context more easily.

—ISOBEL SILDEN

USEFUL CATEGORIES

Here are some special files I've found useful:

In a "Directions" file, I toss instructions for getting to somewhere after I've been there. Then, when I have to make a repeat visit, I can fish the directions out instead of asking for them again.

In a "Books to Read" file, I toss the names of books and authors people have recommended to me, as well as reviews of books I may want to read. Then, three or four weeks before I go on a trip, I pull out the list and put reserves on books at the library, or pick them up at a bookstore, to take along for travel or vacation reading.

In a "Quotes" file, I toss noted bon mots for possible later use.

In an "Ideas" file, I toss title phrases, random thoughts, and clips I suspect might suggest or contribute to article or book ideas.

—PAT McNEES

TOO FAT FOR A FOLDER

The most useful filing tools in my office are inexpensive cardboard open-front file boxes, the kind libraries buy for temporary magazine storage. I order the 8½- by 11-inch size by the dozen; widths range from 3 to 5 inches. They're shipped flat and take up no room until they're needed.

Such boxes are ideal for files that get too thick for manila folders in your file cabinet. They can be filled with a fat jumble of the odd-size items—brochures, booklets, maps, photographs, miscellaneous notes— that sometimes accumulate while researching an article, then placed on a shelf. If you don't spot them in office-supply catalogs, ask a librarian about a good source of storage supplies.

—JANET GROENE

■   TAXING TEDIUM   ■

The sorts of records most writers find most tedious are the kinds that can land us in jail, or at least in heavy debt to the Internal Revenue Service, if they aren't kept in an acceptable manner. They want to know about the money coming in—how much, when, what you did to earn it. They want to know about the money going out—how much, when, where you spent it and on what and with whom. And then prove it. Here's how some of us cope.

BOX PLUS NOTEBOOK

I've religiously calculated all my allowable expenses and filed diligently with the IRS. The heart of my admittedly low-rent system is a cardboard box and a spiral notebook.

Every expense receipt is numbered on the back, then tossed in the box (they're emptied out, checked, and kept at year's end). The number on the receipt matches a line in the spiral notebook. On that line, I note the date, the amount, and the category of the expenditure; the categories I use match those suggested by the IRS on Schedule C, Part II (dues and publications, travel, etc.) or are relevant categories I've devised for use under "other" on the return.

This system hasn't been tested with an IRS audit, so I can't guarantee it. But I did consult a professional about it and got an okay.

—BILL LONDON

RED FOR WRITING

I've been told that the IRS prefers that we keep track of appointments, trips, etc., related to our writing in date-book form. For a while, I kept two separate appointment books, but that became too cumbersome. Now, I simply circle writing-related activities with a red pen. They stand out clearly, and I have a ready reference for myself as well as the government.

—GLADYS H. WALKER

BINDER ORGANIZER

After spending a few frustrating years trying to adapt my records to preprinted diaries and ledgers, I finally developed my own personal organizer. It may look rather high-schoolish, but it's cheap (under $10), it works great, and no one but me (and possibly—horrors!—the IRS) will ever see it. The basic elements: a standard three-ring binder; a black felt marker; a package of three-hole "pocket pages"; a package of notebook subject dividers with attached index tabs, to fit the notebook; a package of extra index tabs (the self-adhesive kind with inserts); a pack (at least 30 sheets) of ruled three-hole paper.

First, put the current year on the spine of the binder. Next, affix the index tabs to the pocket pages and make labels. My six pocket pages are labeled for my major expense categories: postage; office supplies, furniture, and equipment; photocopies; books and publications; meals and travel; and miscellaneous (which covers repairs, professional services, dues, business gifts, et al.).

Place the pocket pages in a group in the front of the binder. Then add the dividers, one designated "income" and the others reflecting your own categories of activities of which you need a record—e.g., telephone, submissions, mileage. (I actually carry a clipboard with several sheets of notebook paper in my car and record my mileage there; the pages go into the binder at the end of the year.) The telephone record should show date, person called, project involved, and cost of call. The income page should show the date, source, amount, and project for each payment received.

Whenever you come home with a receipt, jot the name of the item right on the receipt (if it's not obvious) and shove it into the appropriate pocket. The same goes for cancelled checks. Remember to record every check received and every long-distance phone call. (I keep the binder open on my desk to the telephone section, since I seem to spend half my life making calls that begin with the number "1.")

At the end of the year, totaling the receipts and records is a simple matter. I record the totals right on the front of the pocket pages and on the dividers; I then transfer the figures to the worksheet my accountant sends me in January so that he can figure my taxes. After tax time, you file the binder on a shelf with its predecessors.

One writer friend who liked my binder idea enough to make his own has added sections for appointments and for addresses and phone numbers (the latter, of course, is transferred to the following year's binder). This is a good idea unless, like me, you prefer to keep these in separate, more portable books that can be stashed in purse or briefcase.

—JACQUELINE SHANNON

A SET OF ENVELOPES

Once a year, I set up my financial files, using 9- by 12-inch envelopes from publicity mailings (I cut open the long flap side, leaving the other three sides intact). Using a different color marking pen each year, I label the envelopes with all pertinent categories: among others, billing (invoices plus a list showing dates of bills and payments), expenses billed to magazines and other clients, each credit card, each bank account, telephone, professional dues and publications, postage, office supplies. At the end of the year, I store all the envelopes in a box (a carton from your local liquor store is about the right size).

—JANICE HOPKINS TANNE

INCOME HISTORY

On one page of my record book, I keep track of my gross income from writing by months and years; the years are listed at the left, with twelve columns set up for the months of the year. This single page now has summaries of income for the past ten years and, if there are another ten, these figures will be added to the same page. The record is *cumulative;* the entry for March 1990 shows my gross income from the beginning of the calendar year through the end of that month. This tells me at a glance how my income at any given time of the year compares with similar periods in other years, as well as how the years' total incomes compare. It also quickly tells me if I need to file an amended tax estimate for the current year with the IRS.

—GEORGE LAYCOCK

LITTLE BY LITTLE

In order to take legitimate business deductions, you must keep accurate and detailed records. First, of course, keep a daily log or diary and carry it with you, jotting down expenses as you incur them—right after you leave the bus or taxi, right after you get off the pay phone, even before you leave the copy shop. Then, save all checks and receipts.

Perhaps you've been obsessively passionate about these tasks. Then comes February or March, and you're dealing with hundreds of tiny receipt slips, canceled checks, and chicken scratches in your journal. You dread attempting to add all this up. What should you do? I've evolved a method of easing the shock. I call my record-keeping system the Basket On the Piano Method. The IRS has approved of it. Here's how it works.

I throw all my receipts, including credit-card slips, into a basket on my piano, even before I take off my coat. Every two weeks or so, I haul this basket, along with my daily diary and checkbook records, over to my computer or typewriter and update my financial records. These are simply 8½- by 11-inch sheets of paper, each headed with a different category of business expense—e.g., stationery, postage, business entertaining. Each entry is explicit, including date, amount, and precise nature of the expenditure, e.g.: "$2.65—03/25/89, typewriter cartridge, Jay's Stationery"; "$8.00— 04/12/89, breakfast with agent"; "$60.00—04/30/89, business cards, Franz Printing." When I've typed up the expenses, I put the receipts, credit card records, and canceled checks in an envelope marked with year and category.

Before visiting my accountant, I simply photocopy my financial record sheets and then hand them over at our meeting so he can prepare my Schedule C. Because I've done small amounts of record-keeping each month, it takes me about an hour to gather the picture together, not two to five days of misery. Should I be audited, the receipts, canceled checks, and credit-card records are bundled together under appropriate categories and, of course, my journal entries correspondingly strengthen my assertions.

—JANICE PAPOLOS

STORE-BOUGHT RECORD KEEPER

I used to throw all my receipts into a file folder and have to sort out the mess at tax time. Now, I use the Dome Simplified Home Budget Book, available in office-supply stores, and it has eased my worries about keeping business records and receipts.

There's space, each month, for listing both income and outgo. Day-by-day separate listings for telephone, entertainment, insurance, etc., make it simple to keep track of monthly expenses; I added a few categories of my own, such as office expenses and supplies. In the back of the book, there are four envelopes for receipts; I keep three months' worth in each pocket.

—ANTONIA VAN DER MEER

COMPLETELY CODED

I keep all papers relating to a particular article (or other project) in a single folder; these folders are filed by number. If I've just completed my tenth project in 1990, it is designated "90/10." Whenever I complete an article or other assignment, it is entered on my income record form for the year. That sheet has space to enter, for each item, its code, the nature of the material, the magazine or other client, the publication date, my payment and date received, and agent's commission if any.

The codes aren't always in order. The 1990 page, for instance, might start out with 90/1, 90/2, and 90/3. But then "85/8" might appear, representing a royalty payment on a book completed in 1985. That might be followed by "86/17," denoting a foreign-periodical reprint, or inclusion in an anthology, of a 1986 magazine article.

This form has a number of uses. It is, of course, a complete record of my gross income for the year. If I'm trying to track down information related to an article I did in—maybe—1984, I flip to the 1984 page; if I don't find it, I might try 1985 and 1983, where I discover it was project 83/14—and there's the folder, number 14 in my 1983 drawer. I can look at last year's record and see when this year's royalty checks are likely to arrive. And the date of publication is good to have, because I'm always losing tearsheets of stories and having to get copies from the library; this way, I can locate them fast.

—ROBERT GANNON

DATEBOOKS AND DIARIES

Classic House sells a line of desk and pocket loose-leaf diaries called the Classic Diary Systems; they range from the "Mini" (page size slightly under 3 inches by slightly over 4) up to the Executive (6¼ by 8¼ inches), with annual refills available for all. The refills include a daily section, a monthly section, an address-book section, a cash-record section, and a storage box. There are also other forms available ("Things To Do," "Car Expenses," etc.). I've used Classic's Standard (roughly 3 by 5 inches) notebook for many years; it's light and fits neatly in purse, bag, or pocket.

Classic House is at P.O. Box 15507, Santa Ana CA 92705; (714) 541-3613.

—BARBARA SCHWARTZ

■ ■ ■

I'm disorganized, I admit it. I'm fighting it. I've tried a lot of "organizing" methods in my years of writing, and none of them work. But some of them don't work better than others.

For the big picture, I like the Four-Month Planner pad from Caddylak Systems. It measures 17 by 24 inches—big enough to leave right on my desk like a blotter, and its thick pages stand up nicely to coffee mugs. The format is essentially four large boxes broken up into days of the week. The rest is blank; you fill in the months and dates. If an editor calls with an assignment, I don't have to flip through calendar pages. A quick glance tells me how close I am to missing yet another deadline. There's plenty of white space for doodling, too—no small asset. Caddylak also has a variety of 8½- by 11-inch time and project management pads, 100 thick sheets to a pad. I like to play around with the This Week and Project Planner pads.

Caddylak puts out a Today pad, too, but for daily minutiae, I turn to my One-Page-Per-Day Pocket Day-Timer, Senior Size, which is a 3½- by 6½-inch wirebound two-month notebook. I write down appointments in the "Appointments" section, try to prioritize the day's activities in the "To Be Done Today" section, and log in long-distance calls in the "Diary" section.

Caddylak Systems Inc. is at 201 Montrose Road, Westbury NY 11590; (516) 333-8221. Day-Timers Inc. is at One Day-Timer Plaza, Allentown PA 18195-9987; (215) 395-5884.

—TOM BEDELL

■ ■ ■

I've relied for years on the National Diary #55-047 (that number appears on the spine), distributed by Keith Clark (Sidney NY 13838) and available at most stationery-supply stores. It's 5 by 8 inches, with a full page for each day, and everything goes on that page from little things to do, to long-distance calls to make (a check mark says I've made it), to actual appointments (instantly visible because they get colorful stickers—sold by the sheet or strip at paper-goods stores and published in books by Dover). In front of the diary pages are a clutch of alphabetized pages for addresses and phone numbers; I rip them out, since I keep that data in a loose-leaf binder.

This appointment book has several terrific features. Up front, there's a full-page calendar for the whole year. At the very back, there's a full-page calendar for *next* year. Immediately preceding that, there's a list of U.S. legal holidays and observances, both nationally and state by state; since free-lance writers don't get any holidays, this is the only way to know when the bank's closed, there's no mail delivery, and editors and others are unlikely to be available.

And immediately preceding *that,* there's a key part of my financial record-keeping system. A two-page spread is allotted to each month. There are columns headed "Date," "Item," "Received," "Paid," and "Balance." I use all but the last. Every payment I receive is entered here, without exception. The "Paid" column is used strictly for *cash* expenditures, with a check mark next to the date signifying that I got a receipt (for some things, such as local bus rides and magazines and newspapers, you won't have receipts); the receipts themselves—along with *all* paid bills—go into an accordion file with category-labeled compartments.

At tax time, I find it not too stressful to check the contents of the accordion file against the back-of-the-diary cash-outgo record. Other writing-related expenses are picked up by going through cancelled checks and credit-card statements for the year (my copy of the transaction record, which ends up stapled to the paid statement, always bears an appropriate notation). The year's diary, together with a fat envelope containing the stuff from the accordion file, goes into a file drawer, where it's kept for several years.

My husband (also a free lance) and I have been audited, and this system proved acceptable to the IRS. I did learn a lesson from that audit, though: When you deposit checks, make a note on your copy of the deposit slip of the source *and purpose* of each check. Tax examiners do not like to find sums in bank deposits that do not appear in your income lists. Sometimes you yourself will not remember that your friend gave you a check to reimburse you for laying out the full cost of theater tickets. And if a hefty check from a magazine wasn't a fee but reimbursement for a slew of long-distance calls, it's important to so note. —D.S.

GET FREE HELP FROM THE FEDS

The Internal Revenue Service provides a variety of aids for no charge. For starters, there's an annual publication called *Your Federal Income Tax;* for a free copy, call (800) 424-3676 (allow ten working days for mailing) or visit your local IRS office.

This publication can be of invaluable assistance, because it furnishes far more information about specific situations than is supplied in the instructions that routinely accompany your return. Its several hundred pages contain numerous examples, as well as sample filled-out forms that take you on a line-by-line journey through the perplexities of the return and the ever-growing number of other forms and schedules you may have to submit.

There are also available other IRS publications focusing on specific subjects—deductions for computers, for example, or office-at-home expenses. They're listed in the instructions that come with your return—or, again, visit your local IRS office. In addition, the Form 1040 instructions include a list of IRS toll-free telephone numbers you can call for answers to specific federal tax questions.

Be aware, though, that IRS surveys have revealed numerous errors by its employees in responding to inquiries—and such mistakes do not excuse goofs on your return. You're still fully responsible for paying the correct tax, and the law permits the IRS to disclaim all responsibility for inaccurate information you may have received from the agency itself.

—JULIAN BLOCK

17

SELLING YOURSELF AND YOUR WORK

Many of us feel
that, ideally, we would do absolutely nothing but *write.* We are, after
all, *writers.* Shouldn't such crass pursuits as selling our words and
services be left to agents, publicists, and the like? Unfortunately, it
doesn't always work that way in the Real World. Literary agents do
market book- or movie-length works, but not articles or your services as a preparer of brochures or annual reports. A publicist may
be able to book you on a radio or TV show to promote your just-
published book, but can't tell you how to approach the inter-
viewer—or see that your books are available in stores.

ALL-KINDS-OF-MEDIA LISTING

Whatever your field of writing interest—and whether you're seeking
markets or publicity outlets—you'll find the *Pocket Media Guide* a
valuable reference. This handy directory contains addresses and phone
numbers for more than 700 major consumer, trade, and technical publications, as well as major-market newspapers and television and radio

stations. Obtain the current edition *free* by writing on your letterhead to Media Distribution Services/PRA Group, Department P, 307 West 36 Street, New York NY 10018.

—GLEN EVANS

BACKUP "BROCHURE"

When you're sending a query to a magazine, you need to present proof of your experience in order to secure an assignment. Here's an impressive way to present that backup.

First, select two to four published articles you feel represent your best work. Then, draw up and type a one-page résumé. Finally, design a cover page, which should include your name, address, telephone number, perhaps brief descriptive copy and even a logo (the latter should be relatively conservative). If you have a computer and printer with graphics capability, and some knowledge of design, you can do your own typesetting and layout; or, you can have someone else do the design.

Photocopy your cover page on nonwhite paper (I use an ivory beige, but any pale color will do). Arrange copies of your résumé and clips in a pleasing order following your cover page, and have your print shop spiral-bind the result. Mail a copy of the "brochure" with each query letter.

—VICKY HAY

REJECTED—BUT BY WHOM?

You sent your manuscript off two months ago to the acquisitions editor at Simon & Schuster listed in *Writer's Market.* Finally, the reply arrives: "Sorry, not right for our needs." You've been rejected by Simon & Schuster and should move on to try another publisher—right? *Not necessarily.* Herein lies one of the greatest delusions of hopeful authors, the belief that rejection comes from "the publisher." In truth, you've been rejected by *one person* at Simon & Schuster.

A writer's rejection by a publishing house is, in fact, relatively rare. It does occur with very small firms where the editor is, for all intents and purposes, the entire company. It can happen, too, when an idea has made it past an initial screening in a larger house and then is turned down by an editorial committee. But in most cases, "rejection" is rejection by a single individual only.

Let me illustrate. Once upon a time, I had what I thought was a marketable idea for a humor book about cats. I sent the idea to two publishers, Holt, Rinehart & Winston *(101 Uses For a Dead Cat)* and Workman. Both rejected it, but the rejections were personal notes, not form letters, and both indicated that the idea had generated some interest. That gave me some hope. I next sent the idea to Ballantine, publisher of the best-selling "Garfield" books. That generated only a form rejection.

But then I had another thought. I was still convinced the idea was right for Ballantine. How about sending it to a *different* editor there? Originally, my suggestion had gone to the contact listed in *Writer's Market* (Writer's Digest Books). That person, I realized, was probably swamped with submissions and would be unable to give an individual proposal a great deal of time or thought. I reasoned, too, that a more *junior* editor might be more motivated to give a good idea serious attention: if the editor could convince higher-ups to publish the book, and it sold well, that would be a terrific career credit for the editor.

I turned to another directory, *Literary Market Place* (R.R. Bowker), and found the name of a Ballantine assistant editor. I sent the idea to her. She loved it. She convinced the house to take it on. *Weight Training for Cats* was published by Ballantine in 1982 and, while it was not another "Garfield," it did make both me and Ballantine a respectable amount of money.

So don't assume an entire publishing house has turned you down if you're rejected by one editor listed in a popular writers' publication. *LMP* can be a most valuable resource for finding an editor who's less likely to be deluged and perhaps more likely to give your idea the kind of consideration you'd like it to receive.

—ANTHONY SERAFINI

■ ■ ■

Literary Market Place, which can be consulted at the reference desk of many libraries, now also includes an appendix listing book publishers with toll-free (800) telephone numbers. Some of the numbers go to order departments only, with no transfer to editorial offices possible, but many others go to someone who can switch you either to the extension of your dreams or to the publisher's main switchboard. It's always nice to save a few pennies.

—DAN CARLINSKY

■ ■ ■

Writer's Market (Writer's Digest Books) is updated annually; it is available in most bookstores. *Literary Market Place* is also updated annually and contains every pertinent name, address, and phone number in book publishing; it may be found in many libraries or may be ordered from the publisher, R.R. Bowker, 249 West 17 Street, New York NY 10011; (800) 521-8110, except in New York State, (212) 645-9700. Bowker also publishes *Publishers Weekly,* a magazine often called the bible of the book industry; anyone may subscribe.

—DIAN DINCIN BUCHMAN

■ ■ ■

Addresses and telephone numbers of book publishers can generally be relied upon to remain the same from one annual update to the next. That is not necessarily true of editors; a game of musical chairs seems always to be in progress. Unless you have seen an editor's name and title in a very recent issue of *Publishers Weekly,* it's a good idea to confirm that the editor is still there, with a call to the publisher, before mailing off a manuscript or proposal.   —D.S.

GOOD TIPS FOR GLOBE-TROTTERS

April 1989 marked the tenth anniversary issue of *Travelwriter Market-letter.* We aren't primarily travel writers, who write mainly about resorts, tours, hotels, restaurants, and so on. But a fair amount of the legwork for our business, science, technical, and education articles is done in other countries, and so we subscribed. We're glad we did.

The monthly ten-page newsletter, edited by [ASJA member] Robert Scott Milne, is well worth the cost of $60 per year. The market information is second only to that which we receive in the members-only ASJA newsletter. We've had a number of assignments resulting from queries to publications we first learned about from this source. And as important are the frequent caveats about slow- and no-pay periodicals and other forms of grief, with consequent waste of precious time, from which Bob Milne's advice has rescued us.

Subscriptions may be ordered from Milne—Waldorf-Astoria Hotel, 301 Park Avenue, Suite 1850, New York NY 10022; a sample copy is $6.

—HENRY and ELIZABETH URROWS

■ ■ ■

The monthly *Travelwriter Marketletter* is one of the most indispensable tools available to the working writer. Its news is up to the minute and, although it's geared mainly to the needs of the travel writer, it covers a broad range of publications and provides information that's extremely useful to any magazine writer. In addition to its several dozen market listings in each issue, it offers news of sponsored trips available to established travel writers and also reviews books of interest. There is no other publication that can begin to match its practical usefulness. It really is a must.

—MICHELE McCORMICK

SEEKING UPSCALE CLIENTS

In addition to authoring books and articles, I undertake assignments ranging from speeches to promotional copy, annual reports, and other projects for business firms, audiovisual scripts, and editorial consulting jobs. I decided a brochure promoting my professional services would be helpful, and I decided to have the brochure professionally designed and produced. The graphic-artists firm I selected, and which I highly recommend to those in the Washington DC area, was Wickham & Associates.

I gave Wickham's Jane Firor and Tom Jones copy and described roughly what I had in mind, adding that I usually enclose samples when approaching a prospective client. They suggested a folder that would enclose such samples and came up with a wonderful design. Their fees for such designs range from $400 to $1000. I spent an additional $495 to have 1000 copies of the slick-looking result printed in black, white, red, and gray.

It's too soon, at this writing, to tell how many upscale clients the brochure will attract but, so far, I feel it has definitely been worth the expense. I seem to land clients primarily through my credentials and samples, but the brochure does seem to catch their attention.

Wickham & Associates is at 1215 Connecticut Avenue NW, Third Floor, Washington DC 20036; (202) 232-1921.

—PAT McNEES

PUSHING BOOKS

If your publisher doesn't seem to be pushing your book successfully, you might consult a firm called Sensible Solutions, Inc., 275 Madison Avenue, Suite 1518, New York NY 10016; (212) 687-1761. This consultation company offers practical advice on maximizing sales; its services are available on an hourly fee basis, or it will plan and implement a full-scale promotion program.

—HELEN STUDLEY

■ ■ ■

Judith Applebaum and Florence Janovic of Sensible Solutions can plan the kind of book promotion and advertising that authors dream about but publishers rarely provide. Yes, it does cost money—but better to spend it up front than watch your book sink quickly into never-never land. The firm also offers a variety of materials for sale, including a handbook, with worksheets, on getting published; order forms to hand out to bookstores who don't carry your book; and a calendar and planning guide.

—EVELYN KAYE

START-TO-FINISH BOOK-PUSHING HELP

While ghostwriting a self-published book for a businessman, I came across a consulting service that was extremely valuable in getting the book produced and, more important, also getting it promoted across the country.

The service, About Books, Inc., handles everything from analyzing the merits of a proposed book project to copy-editing the manuscript to production (they turn out a quality product that compares favorably with any book you see in the stores) and marketing—or, if you like, it can be hired to answer only a specific need. These people work primarily by phone and mail, so location is no problem, and I found them energetic, fair in their pricing, and extremely knowledgeable about marketing and public relations.

The service also helps authors promote (non-self-published) books their publishers may be ignoring, including arranging for interviews, reviews, and other exposure.

About Books, Inc., is at P.O. Box 1500, 425 Cedar Street, Buena Vista CO 81211; (719) 395-2459.

—BRUCE W. MOST

QUICK CREDITS RUNDOWN

If you belong to a group that publishes members' credentials, that succinct listing can be handy. I used to send extensive résumés along with my query letters to magazines for which I hadn't written before. I learned, however, that editors have little time for such lengthy treatises. Now, I simply send a copy of my listing in the ASJA membership directory along with my queries and clips; it works as well or better.

—M. LAWRENCE PODOLSKY

LET THEM KNOW YOU'RE AVAILABLE

Promoting a book—or a product, service, cause, organization, opinion, or point of view—on radio and TV can be easier when you advertise your availability in a magazine called *Radio-TV Interview Report,* which was recommended to me by another, very successful, author. According to the publisher, the magazine is used by more than 4500 talk-show producers, newspaper book reviewers, and feature editors throughout North America to find interesting guests for live and telephone interviews.

Placement of two ads for my co-authored book *Playing God: The New World of Medical Choices* resulted in appearances on three TV talk shows and 45 (live and taped) radio interviews. Ad rates vary; typesetting is free, and for a small extra fee, staffers will write your ad for you.

Radio-TV Interview Report is published by Bradley Communications Corp., 135 East Plumstead Avenue, Lansdowne PA 19050; (215) 259-1070.

—CELIA G. SCULLY

"NO" BEATS NO ANSWER AT ALL

An unanswered letter or phone call is irritating—but when your livelihood depends on a response, the lack of one can be devastating. I've learned that "no" is better than no response at all: you know, at least, whether to keep hoping or to submit your article idea, for example, elsewhere. I use a form letter to elicit answers from those often forgetful folks.

My form letter reads, "I know that you're very busy. Although I haven't heard from you since I last wrote, I'd rather not burden you with a response if you're not ready to reply. I've therefore prepared the following form for your convenience. Simply check off the appropriate box and return it to me. Thanks."

The form that appears below this message offers four choices: (1) "I'd like to respond, but things are hectic now. I'll get back to you within" (I suggest periods ranging from two to six weeks). (2) "I'm interested in replying but never get around to it. Give me a call, please, within" (again, I offer a choice of times). (3) "I'm interested in replying but I'm not in a position to do so now. I will get back to you, or you get back to me if you don't hear in two months." (4) "I'm not interested in replying to you now or ever. Get off my back." A postscript reads, "I fall behind on my mail. I wish someone would send me a form."

It works. In about eight out of ten cases, I've received a reply and, in over half, it's been positive. Remember that not everyone is as efficient as you are. Sometimes, all it takes is a light, tongue-in-cheek jab to get things moving again.

—ALVIN H. REISS

DON'T COUNT ON A SINGLE SOURCE

Beginning writers often suppose *Writer's Market* to be the last, complete word in guides to magazines. Not so. While it's useful, several caveats should be kept in mind when using this deceptively handy guide.

One is that turnover in the publishing industry occurs at a breathtaking pace. The editors listed may have left a magazine by the time *Writer's Market* reaches your bookstore—or even, for that matter, before the book is off the press. Check the masthead of a current issue.

Another is that payment figures are often misleading—in either direction. Editors usually give their lowest fees, and a writer with solid experience and/or special expertise can often command more. But sometimes, hoping to attract top talent, they list what they'd pay a Famous Household Name—with no intention of paying the average Joe or Jane that much.

Third, be aware that skimming *Writer's Market* is no substitute for reading the magazine.

And fourth, know that it does not list every magazine; its categories are not comprehensive, and there are many unlisted magazines that may be potential markets for you. Two other reference works available at public libraries, Ulrich's *International Periodicals Directory* and Gale's *Directory of Publications,* list many magazines not found in *Writer's Market;* for newspapers, consult the *Editor and Publisher International Yearbook,* which includes names and titles of department editors.

—VICKY HAY

NO BOOKS IN THE STORES I: GET A JOBBER

If you're a published author whose publisher is less than reliable in seeing that stores are supplied with books during your personal-appearance promotion tours, you might wish to arrange for an independent distributor to handle the task. Such distributors are known as book jobbers. One such jobber, which specializes in children's books, is BMI Educational Services, reachable at (800) 222-8100.

—VIC COX

NO BOOKS IN THE STORES II: PHONE AHEAD

One little trick I've learned has to do with promoting a book in scattered locations. In many instances, a publicist will have arranged radio interviews with stations around the country; often, these interviews are actually done from the author's own home, via telephone. Unfortunately for the author, such interviews will frequently be in vain, since there will be no copies of his or her books in the local stores.

There is a remedy. The author should invest in a volume called the *American Trade Book Directory* (R.R. Bowker). It lists just about every bookstore in the U.S. and Canada, including type (general, religious, children's, et al.), names of manager and buyer, and telephone number. Be sure interviews are set up at least two weeks in advance. Call the stores in cities or towns within range of the radio station's signal and alert them to the forthcoming interview. Offer to say, on the air, that the book is available at particular stores—*if* (and this is important) the stores will agree to order copies. Most will.

This simple effort on the author's part will greatly increase the effectiveness of a radio "tour" and will result in extra sales. Trust me.

—LEWIS BURKE FRUMKES

ON-TARGET PUBLICITY

As more and more authors find they need to publicize their own books, publicity skills and tools are becoming increasingly important. In my experience, newsletter publicity has been one of the best ways to increase book sales. Because newsletters go to very specific audiences, and their editors select only those items that will be of interest to their readership, publicity can be sharply targeted, and reader response tends to be strong.

Of course the tool needed to make this work is an up-to-date directory of newsletters. One of the best is the *Oxbridge Directory of Newsletters* (Oxbridge Communications). It offers more than 17,000 listings of subscriber and trade-association newsletters focusing on topics from fund raising to college life, safety, and photography, and the editors seem particularly diligent about thorough updating, crucial to any directory.

The directory is currently priced at a steep $195, but each year there is a substantial prepublication discount, so you can save if you purchase the book at that time. The publisher is at 150 Fifth Avenue, Suite 301, New York NY 10011; (212) 741-0231.

—KATE KELLY

PUBLICITY BASICS

Want to promote your books, and/or yourself, but don't know how? Have I got an idea for you!

There's a book called *The Publicity Manual,* written by a pro in the field, [ASJA member] Kate Kelly, that is a super do-it-yourself guide to fame and fortune. Kelly has encapsulated her years of experience in a fine manual that gives the neophyte publicist step-by-step guidance, sample news releases, even a resource directory to get you started. Any author who wants to sell books had better be prepared to toot his or her own horn. This book shows you how.

For information on the latest edition: Visibility Enterprises, 11 Rockwood Drive, Larchmont NY 10538; (914) 834-0602.

—MARILYN ROSS

LISTEN AND LEARN

Do you like to learn by listening? *Book Promotion and Marketing: Success Strategies to Increase Your Sales* is a set of audiocassettes representing six hours of concise, invaluable marketing and publicity advice particularly useful for authors. It's by Tom and Marilyn Ross, the latter an ASJA member, who have put their extensive advertising and public relations experience on tape and have also included a useful workbook. The set is $69.95 from Communication Creativity, P.O. Box 909, Buena Vista CO 81211; (719) 395-8659.

—ALAN CARUBA

WHAT DOES YOUR STAMP SAY?

When you're writing an editor or prospective client about an assignment, it sometimes makes a good impression to use stamps that have particular appeal. The Postal Service will provide, and put you on its mailing list for, its *Philatelic Catalog,* which lists and illustrates hundreds of currently available stamps.

If you're seeking an assignment in the environmental field, for example, you'll have a virtual gold mine—stamps showing all kinds of flora and fauna that need protection. If your addressee is an historian, you might want to use stamps showing old sailing ships, early steam locomotives, or noted personalities of the past. While most people pay little attention to the postage on envelopes they receive, you can mention a particularly interesting or significant stamp in a postscript.

Envelope flaps can also be sealed with special-interest (nonpostal) stamps, of which there are hundreds of varieties on every imaginable subject.

—WILBUR CROSS

BOOK PROMOTION/PLACEMENT POINTERS

A book filled with many tips and suggestions is *1001 Ways to Market Your Books,* by John Kremer. In addition to discussing advertising, publicity, and bookstore promotion, this guide includes suggestions for special sales, information on how to sell books to schools and libraries, and ideas on getting placement in non-bookstore retail outlets. Whether you've self-published or are working with an established publisher, this book can be a handy one to have around.

It can be ordered for $14.95 plus $2 shipping and handling from Ad-Lib Publications, P.O. Box 1102, Fairfield IA 52556. Ad-Lib also sells a number of other publications of interest to writers. When you order, you'll get their literature; check it out.

—KATE KELLY

PICTURE PROFITS

Many writers take pictures to illustrate their writings, but few are knowledgeable about marketing the results. One of my most profitable investments has been a book called *Sell & Re-Sell Your Photos,* by Rohn Engh. An updated version is available for $16.95 plus $3 shipping and handling from PhotoSource International, Pine Lake Farm, Osceola WI 54020; credit-card orders only can be phoned to (800) 624-0266; for other information, call (715) 248-3800.

—PAT WATSON

HELP FOR THOSE UNACCUSTOMED TO PUBLIC SPEAKING

Fear of public speaking was a serious handicap for me. I was frequently asked to appear on talk shows, go on personal-appearance tours to promote books, speak at club meetings and book-and-author luncheons, participate in workshops, teach classes. I always refused.

After many years of dodging these opportunities, I signed up for a weekend workshop specifically designed for people with this problem, which had literally become a phobia for me. I found I wasn't alone. One woman was so undone at being asked to stand up and tell the rest of us her name and occupation that she burst into tears. But by the end of the weekend, we were giving short speeches to one another—not brilliantly, but adequately.

The leader strongly urged us to join an organization called Toastmasters, which would give us more practice before we actually went out and attempted to speak to audiences. This international organization has chapters almost everywhere in the U.S. Each chapter meets weekly, with members volunteering to give short talks at upcoming meetings; the speeches are evaluated by the other members. At each session, there are also "table topics," surprise subjects about which each member must speak spontaneously for one to two minutes. Some of the members join, as I did, to overcome anxiety; the majority want to learn to speak more effectively.

After attending meetings for six months, I felt secure enough to accept an invitation to give my first outside talk (choosing, for security, the local garden club). I managed to speak without falling over. I even enjoyed myself. Public speaking still makes me extremely anxious—but at least I know I'm capable of doing it.

For more information, contact a local Toastmasters chapter or write Toastmasters International, 2200 North Grand Avenue, Santa Ana CA 92711.

—JOAN RATTNER HEILMAN

THE CONVENTION CONNECTION

The annual meetings of the American Booksellers Association (ABA) are held, usually close to Memorial Day, at convention centers in different parts of the country. They are very well attended by representatives of publishing firms and have presented me with some of my best selling opportunities.

After my first book was published, my publisher took me to the ABA (as the event is also known in the trade). I autographed books at specified times at the publisher's booth and remained there to talk up the book at other times. It was hard work. But I sold my next book to another publisher as a result of a casual meeting in a coffee shop during the convention.

Since then, I've attended other ABA's, either with expenses paid by a publisher or paying my own way. One year, I sold a three-book series plus two others. I'm always careful not to take up much time talking to editors at booths when they're busy with buyers from bookstores; I make initial contacts, then follow up later by mail or phone.

If you hope to attend under your publisher's sponsorship, begin making arrangements at least two months beforehand.

—FLORENCE TEMKO

KIDS' BOOKS PUBLISHERS

For those who'd like a current, free list of firms that publish books for children, there are two good sources. The Society of Children's Book Writers publishes such a list, available to members only. *Anyone* can receive a list of the publishers who are members of the Children's Book Council by requesting it from the Council—located at 67 Irving Place, New York NY 10003—and enclosing a stamped, self-addressed number ten envelope.

—BARBARA SHOOK HAZEN

THE WHOLE YOUTH MARKETPLACE

If you want to make a name for yourself writing for children and young adults, a good reference guide is *The Children's Writer's Marketplace,* by S.F. Tomajczyk (Running Press).

Want to know what magazines are published for this age group, which book publishers target this market, which agents work in this area? This book tells you who they are and what kind of material they seek. As the book's cover promises, it "reveals dozens of little-known outlets for such specialized projects as alphabet books, coloring books, TV scripts, how-to hobby guides, teen romances, and preschool picture books." There's also a list of prizes, awards, and professional organizations—in short, everything you wanted to know about writing for children but didn't know whom to ask.

—JOYCE BALDWIN

NOT JUST A BUSINESS CARD

A business card can convey more than your name, address, and telephone number. As time went by and the number of books I'd had published mounted, I decided to display those accomplishments. I designed a two-sided business card. One side, in black on white, has the usual information. On the other side is a full-color photograph of my most recent books, posed in a row with each overlapping the next (part of the title, and at least part of my name, can be seen on each); I started with four, and the number has grown, but I've limited it to eight, since more would look crowded. The card has been enormously successful in getting me quick recognition as a professional author, since my credentials are instantly apparent.

—ROBIN PERRY

RECYCLE A LIBRARY THROWAWAY

At the end of each year, your local library discards its paperback copies of the monthly *Reader's Guide to Periodical Literature* when the annual hardbound volume arrives. Ask your librarian to give you the paperbacks instead of throwing them away. One listing of year-old magazine articles in hand is better than two trips to the library.

—MARGERY FACKLAM

GET THE WORD OUT—ON STICKERS, BALLOONS . . .

When I was promoting my book *Girltalk About Guys,* my publisher's publicity department was able to give me an overrun of the cover; I used them, as oversize postcards, to let people know about the book. I then spent my own money on stickers, which I sent to my hundreds of teenage pen pals in the hope that they would use them and thus help me spread the word.

One place from which you can order such stickers—or rulers, pens, bookmarks, balloons, or anything else printed with your book title—is Think Ideas, 38 West 32 Street, New York NY 10001; (212) 736-1215.

—CAROL WESTON

PUBLICITY: WHAT WORKS, WHAT DOESN'T

I'd like to recommend an excellent book geared to getting publicity for *your* excellent books—*Publicity for Books and Authors,* by Peggy

Glenn, a large-format paperback geared to both authors and small publishers.

It's full of specific examples (news releases, cover letters, etc.), case histories, mistakes (made, recognized, and described to spare the reader from making the same ones), and all sorts of practical suggestions (clothes to take on tour, coming up with visuals for TV, handling newspaper interviews). Finally, there's that section we all hope we'll need—"Dealing with Fame."

Not only is the book helpful. The author comes across as someone you can identify with and would like to know, so it's also fun to read. In short, it's terrific. It may be ordered for $13.95 from Aames-Allen Publishing Co., 1106 Main Street, Huntington Beach CA 92648.

—SALLY WENDKOS OLDS

I'M IN THE BOOK—AT LEAST TWICE

I have a three-name name. Because people who want me to write for them might look under either Hopkins or Tanne (despite the fact that my byline always includes both), I'm listed in the phone book under both. The extra listing is available for minimal cost, less than $10 per year. This would seem to multiply the chances of receiving strange calls but, although I get occasional calls from readers of my articles, I've never had a call from a true weirdo.

My two cats also have phone-book listings—that's another story [told in another chapter]—and the listings do land you on some interesting mailing lists. My cats have been offered dancing lessons and terrific deals on certificates of deposit.

—JANICE HOPKINS TANNE

DON'T BLOW YOUR BIG CHANCE

If you're promoting your book on radio or TV, of course you want to make a great impression. You might consider special media training, which is available from Ailes Communications in New York City. Although Ailes is primarily known for its work with politicians (including the Great Communicator himself, former President Ronald Reagan), the organization also trains authors for media tours and special appearances.

The author training is conducted on a one-on-one basis by Ailes senior vice president Jon Kraushar, who is co-author with company president Roger Ailes of *You Are the Message: Secrets of the Master*

Communicators (Dow Jones). Fees vary according to the scope of the training, which is custom-designed to meet each author's needs.

Ailes is at 440 Park Avenue South, New York NY 10016; (212) 685-8400.

—JOAN DETZ

HOW TO SELL—AND PUBLISH—YOURSELF

Sometimes, the way to purvey your ideas is to publish them yourself. Self-published books have been known to go on to astounding success, both critical and financial, and some have been eagerly adopted by mainstream publishers.

If you're considering self-publishing, *The Complete Guide to Self-Publishing*, by Tom and [ASJA member] Marilyn Ross (Writer's Digest Books) is an invaluable step-by-step handbook, offering full information on everything from design and production to advertising, distribution, publicity campaigns, and the selling of subsidiary rights. I wish it had been around when I first self-published; I do refer to it now, especially for its sales advice. A revised and expanded edition was published in 1989.

Ten years ago, when I started, the guide that was around, for which I was most grateful, was *The Self-Publishing Manual*, by Dan Poynter. It's still around in updated form and is now rightly considered a classic; it covers everything from writing to printing, promotion, and distribution. While both these titles cover what you need to know, I find that reading about a subject from different perspectives gives me greater insight. Poynter's book is available for $19.95 plus $2 for shipping from Para Publishing, P.O. Box 4232-842, Santa Barbara CA 93140.

Another guide by the Rosses, more specifically focused, is *How to Make Big Profits Publishing City and Regional Books*. If you've thought about marketing your area expertise by writing and publishing a directory of local restaurants, or a parents' guide to area activities for children, check out this advisory. It explores the many aspects of city/ area books—tourist guides, regional cookbooks, nature guides, historical books, and more. It's available for $14.95 plus $2 shipping from Communication Creativity, P.O. Box 909, Buena Vista CO 81211; (719) 395-8659.

—KATE KELLY

IS THE PRICE RIGHT?

A book titled *How to Set Your Fees and Get Them,* by [ASJA member] Kate Kelly, can be of great help to anyone who puts a price on his or her writing services. As a free-lancer who also sells to other than magazine and book publishers, I've found this unique book extremely helpful in gauging what to ask so that the client and I can strike an equitable arrangement. It shows how to choose the right fee structure (per day, per project, etc.), points out common pitfalls, and gives guidelines for preparing agreements.

For ordering information, write Visibility Enterprises, 11 Rockwood Drive, Larchmont NY 10538, or call (914) 834-0602.

—MARILYN ROSS

SELLING YOUR ARTICLES OVERSEAS

Markets Abroad, a quarterly newsletter, is an excellent source of overseas magazine markets, listing current editors, rates, and tips on selling to foreign markets. These periodicals, many of which pay on publication, are not very suitable for selling original articles but are often splendid outlets for reprint material.

An annual subscription to *Markets Abroad* is $25. It may be ordered from Strawberry Media Inc., 2460 Lexington Drive, Owosso MI 48867.

—MICHELE McCORMICK

SHOW AND TELL

The first project I tackled when learning to use *Pagemaker,* a computer program for desktop publishing, was a brochure about myself and the kind of writing I do. It slips into a number ten envelope. In addition to selling my writing services, it illustrates the kind of brochure I can produce. More recently, I created a brochure for one of my books, which (typical tale) is not in every bookstore; it describes the book, lists the retail price, and gives the publisher's name and address. When people call or write to ask where they can find the book, I mail them a copy of the brochure.

—ELAINE FANTLE SHIMBERG

PEDDLE SECOND RIGHTS TO THE PAPERS

Many travel writers fail to tap a broad second-rights market: newspaper travel sections. Most of us now work with word-processing programs, on computers. This means that you can send each potential secondary market not a carbon copy or a photocopy of your article but a "typed" original—without doing any retyping yourself and without springing for return stamps.

When an article done for a major outlet ages, send it to your computer's printer with an order for a dozen copies. Send them to likely (non-overlapping) markets, and *don't* include a costly self-addressed stamped envelope; the postage to return the piece is more than it costs to print out another copy. Tell the editor, in your cover note, that there's no need to return the typescript. Enclose a self-addressed, stamped *postcard,* with statements (they can be rubber-stamped) for the editor to check off: "No," "Yes, I'll use it" and, if applicable, "Send photos." (There is no need to duplicate and send pictures unless they're specifically requested.)

With this system, you save much money and time. You also keep up with who is buying what, as well as who is too rude and lazy to bother to check off a box on a stamped, addressed card and throw it into the "Out" basket. Be sure to scribble your own code on each card, so that on its return, you'll know who sent it back to you and which article it concerns.

Faithfully followed, this program can turn up as much as $400 to $500 a month until your backlog of old articles runs out. The work involved is negligible, because your printer will be grinding out the copy while you're out planting radishes in the spring sun.

—BERN KEATING

YES, THE S.A.S.P.

If you write on a word processor or computer, there's no need to supply the traditional self-addressed stamped envelope (s.a.s.e.)—with its heavy postage toll—for return of an unsolicited manuscript. Instead, enclose a regular, prestamped post-office postcard. Address it to yourself. On the correspondence side, type, "Ms. is on disk; no need to return. Please check:" Then add boxes for the editor to check off various replies, e.g., "Your submission is accepted," "I need more information," whatever applies. Leave a space for the editor's name and signature. Add a "Thank you," and your signature or initials, at the bottom.

—HELEN WORTH

■ ■ ■

Self-addressed stamped postcards (s.a.s.p.) are great not only for elicit-ing replies to submissions and queries but also for interview responses, quick notes to editors, and confirmation that your book manuscript or assigned article reached its destination safely. You can make your own using 4- by 6-inch index cards, or buy them at the post office for the same price as a stamp, 15¢ at this writing.

I order professional-looking, personalized white postcards from the American Stationery Company.[1] They are 3½ by 5½ inches and framed with a thin colored border, with my name and address printed (in the same color) on the message side; the cost is $4.95 plus shipping for 50 cards.

I neatly print a variety of appropriate options, such as "I'd like to hear more" and "Your idea doesn't suit our editorial needs." At the bottom, I ask for the editor's signature and the date. The card is ad-dressed to me with a transparent label that has my name and address printed in black (same source as the postcards, $8.95 plus shipping for 450).

Then I smile as I reach past my 25¢ stamps for a 15¢ stamp.

—PAMELA HOBBS HOFFECKER

TO MARKET, TO MARKET

When I have a story idea, I immediately set up a file folder for it. Into the folder go all notes, clippings, doodles, and copies of query letters to magazines on the idea. On the outside of the folder are listed potential markets for the article. Then, if a query is rejected, I already have a plan for the next positive action I can take; this generally lessens my ego's shrinking reaction and gets my second-string query into the mail sooner. Of course, I still spend some time thinking about my approach and the quality of my query, to see if I need to make changes before I launch it again.

—LEE JOLLIFFE

CHRISTMAS IN MARCH

If you wish to write pieces appropriate to particular seasons or holidays, you need to plan ahead, since magazine editors do: "theme" issues are generally planned nine to twelve months in advance. But how can you

[1]See appendix for a full list of order-by-mail-or-phone office-supply sources.

produce a sparkling query, or a reflective essay, about Christmas in mid-March?

Set up a special seasonal calendar for this purpose; make one, or use one of the free ones available from banks and local merchants. Write that query or story during the season or holiday, while you're in the mood. Then place it in the calendar for submission at the appropriate time.

—KAREN O'CONNOR

FINDING FUNDING

If you're seeking funding for a major writing project, there's a practical handbook that may help: *Foundation Fundamentals.* The current (third) edition, priced at $12.95, provides information on the best ways to approach foundations and includes worksheets, checklists, and illustrations designed to assist you in your search for hard-to-come-by foundation funds. Order from the Society for Non-Profit Organizations, 6314 Odana Road, Suite 1, Madison WI 53719.

—GLEN EVANS

SELLING TO THE SELLER

We all receive announcements of new magazines, inviting subscriptions and often promising the first issue free; a bill will follow, but if you don't like the magazine, you simply mark the invoice "cancel." For a free-lance writer, such "junk mail" can be a valuable marketing tool. When I receive such a mailing, I always return the card saying I want that free issue. (The minute the bill comes in, I cancel the subscription, unless it's something I'm totally enchanted with.)

Usually, somewhere in the literature is the name of the editor—and, sometimes, the magazine's actual address (the return postcard frequently, though not always, goes to a fulfillment center in Ohio or Colorado); if not, it will be in that first issue—which I'll be sure to see, since I've reserved a copy. I write to the editor—a professional yet friendly letter, letting him or her know who I am and what I do, with samples.

I have received many, many assignments as a result.

—RUTH PITTMAN

18

REAL
NEAT
GADGETS

There are com-
puters, of course, and the things that go with them. And fax machines. And copiers. (All covered in earlier chapters.) There are also
other irresistible devices, some high-tech and others decidedly not,
that draw writers to the doors of office-supply (and hardware and
housewares) stores and the pages of mail-order catalogs.

AN END TO PROCRASTINATION?

You need one of those battery-powered electric pencil sharpeners on
your desk. I bought a Lyon LB-10 for about $20 six or eight years ago.
If you get in the habit of automatically putting a pencil into the sharp-
ener before sticking it back in your pencil jar, you will always have a
sharp pencil. You will also have eliminated the time-honored thing for
writers to do instead of writing the story, sharpening all your pencils.

—JANICE HOPKINS TANNE

QUICK CORRECT SPELLING

The Franklin Spelling Ace is an absolute necessity for writers like me who don't know all their "ables" from their "ibles." Spell-checking software on your computer obviously works, but it's helpful to have something separate right next to you as you work, and it's faster than a dictionary. In fact, I use it along with my spell-checking program, since my software takes longer to spew out options for misspelled words than my Spelling Ace takes to tell me the correct spelling.

—KATY KOONTZ

TIME'S UP!

One of the most helpful tools I use in my work is a kitchen timer. I find it's difficult to get started on an article, or the next chapter of a book, after I've finished doing the research and collecting information. But I've found a miracle technique that always works: I set the timer for one hour. That's a short time, and I promise myself that after those 60 minutes, I can break for a cup of tea.

When the dinger rings, I'm always surprised. By that time, I'm deeply involved and don't *want* a tea break—so I set the dinger for one more hour. At the end of hour number two, I may stop or I may not, depending on the momentum I've gained. I repeat the process as long as needed.

—BEVERLY ANDERSON NEMIRO

■ ■ ■

If you suffer from a painful, stiff neck after hours at the computer, try this: Set a timer to ring every half hour. When it rings, rise from your chair and rotate your head gently three or four times.

—ROSALIE MINKOW

■ ■ ■

A kitchen timer can be extremely useful. I have one that goes up to 99 minutes. Use it to get yourself to work for a certain amount of time—*or* to make sure you don't spend too much time on something that isn't worth it!

—MARTA VOGEL

■ ■ ■

All of us need an occasional reminder—to return a phone call after lunch, to make a long-distance call after the rates change, to pick up a print or copying job before the shop closes. The typical kitchen timer can be set only for an hour—and can handle only one reminder at a time.

We found a multiple-event timer in a discount store for only $15. It can handle three reminders at once, up to 24 hours in advance, and is easy to set. Best of all, it's only a few inches square, not more than a quarter of an inch thick, and has a magnetic back so it can be stuck on a file cabinet.

—GORDON and JANET GROENE

MAGAZINE KEEPER

Sometimes, I want to save the entire issue of a magazine in which one of my articles has appeared. I use large loose-leaf binders and buy magazine binder strips, plastic strips three-hole-punched to fit the standard binder; you simply open the magazine and slip it through the lengthwise slot in the strip, then place the strip in your binder. The strips are available from the Miles Kimball Company's catalog, called the Business Book; I've also seen them in other catalogs.[1]

—GAIL GRECO

BREATH OF FRESH AIR

Those who have allergies, pets, or computers, or must share quarters with a smoker, may find that the comfort and quality of life are vastly improved by an ionizer—a device that cleans the air and removes smoke, pollen, and pet dander, not to mention other villainous fumes and particles that come floating through city windows.

A visit to my next-door neighbor, a chain-smoking film director with a large Dalmatian, converted me immediately. His apartment had previously reeked of deeply imbedded doggy/smoky odors. The fresh, sparkling, crystal-clear air in his home office was a dramatic change: plumes of smoke magically vanished, and the dog was a welcome, odorless presence. It was all the work of a small, quietly humming machine, an ionizer.

My neighbor had bought it to cure persistent headaches that came

[1]See appendix for a full list of order-by-mail-or-phone office-supply sources.

on after he worked with his computer; he reported great improvement. He explained to me that computers and other appliances emit something called positive ions—electrical charges that can make the atmosphere oppressive, causing fatigue, headaches, and overall malaise. The ionizer emits negative ions, which recharge the air, while attracting and trapping foreign particles in its filters.

I ordered the same machine he has, the Neo-Life Consolaire. It seems to be one of the more costly ionizers available (about $190) and requires a change of filters every three months. But it has been well worth the expense. Visitors who were allergic to my two cats now report complete tolerance and no catty smells. I can clear the air of smoke or cooking odors in a flash. The air in my small apartment is always fresh, and I seem to be able to work at the computer for longer stretches.

I bought my ionizer through one of the several Consolaire distributors in the New York area—Beth Anderson, 26 Second Avenue, #5F, New York NY 10003; (212) 777-6787. There are others available—brand names I've seen include Bionaire and Pulsar—from stores and upscale catalogs.

—CAROL TONSING

KEEP OR TOSS

When submitting queries, proposals, or manuscripts, it's often necessary or desirable to send along other materials such as clippings, background papers, copy prints, or biographical data. Sometimes such materials needn't be returned to you; editors appreciate it if you specify what they can retain for further reference or toss out.

A simple way to do that is with a rubber stamp. Mine reads, "Expendable—No Need to Return This Material to the Author." Such stamps can be self-contained, with a built-in ink supply in whatever color you might desire to call proper attention to the message.

—WILBUR CROSS

FIGHT FATIGUE AFOOT

To help overcome the fatigue and poor circulation that can so easily result from sitting for hours at the computer, I use a foot roller. It's a uniquely shaped piece of wood which I place on the floor under my desk, pressing one foot at a time on it and rolling it back and forth to stimulate the soles of my feet. Plastic rollers break easily, and a Coca

Cola bottle (although its shape is appropriate for the purpose) could also break, with disastrous results. Foot rollers are available in some health-food stores and through some mail-order houses. A safety note: Put the roller away after each use; don't leave it on the floor to be stepped on by mistake.

—DON WIGAL

WORKOUT I: CROSS-COUNTRY COGITATION

A brief session with an exercise machine can help get rid of writer's block—and also provides a perfect excuse to procrastinate, since exercise is good for you. I swear by one called Fitness Master. It supposedly simulates cross-country skiing; since I've never been on skis, I can't vouch for that. But it is enjoyable to use, and I've experienced no muscle strains. Sometimes, I think through a rewriting problem while I "ski" for 20 or 25 minutes. Sometimes, to be honest, I listen to a favorite radio program.

The model I have, which cost $400 plus shipping, is the firm's least expensive; other models are more elaborate, some including pulse-monitoring equipment. Mine requires only a bit over four feet of floor space when in use and rolls under the bed for storage at other times.

Fitness Master, Inc. is at 504 Industrial Boulevard, Waconia MN 55387; (800) 328-8995. The firm offers a 30-day money-back trial period.

—SYLVIA AUERBACH

WORKOUT II: RIDE AND READ

A terrific antidote for the sedentary spread that can plague writers is a stationary bicycle. A plastic book rack, available at sporting-goods stores (mine cost $9.95), turns the bike into a work-station. I use mine, a moderate-priced Tunturi, while I edit or catch up with my reading.

—JUDITH KELMAN

FAST FOOD, "FRESH" COFFEE

There's something to be said for a leisurely, contemplative lunch hour, an abeyance of the day's labors, a scheduled respite to recharge the batteries. In the hustling writer's life, that something is usually "Forget it." Lunch is more likely to be on the wing, or at the desk, in the form of a hastily-slapped-together peanut butter and jelly sandwich and yet another cup of coffee.

I therefore laud the microwave oven as a critical, if not absolutely essential, tool of the writer's trade. With a microwave and leftovers, you can serve the interests of variety and presumably better nutrition, without sacrificing any of the inherent speed of constructing a p.b. & j. Is my microwave second only to my computer as a great timesaver? Maybe.

The microwave will not, of course, solve the problem of food dropped onto your keyboard.

—TOM BEDELL

■ ■ ■

A microwave oven is especially valuable for those of us who drink coffee all day as we write. Before the days of my "nuker" (as the yuppies refer to these gizmos), I made a big pot of coffee in the morning and turned on the flame to reheat it every time I wanted another cup. By the end of the day, I was drinking something like mud. Now, I make the big pot as usual, but all that coffee no longer gets repeatedly reheated. For the second and subsequent cups, I pour one mugful from the pot, zap the mug into the micro for 50 seconds, and have the closest thing to "fresh" coffee all day.

—DIANA BENZAIA

THE ONE THAT GOT AWAY WON'T AGAIN

We've all had those marvelous ideas for stories that come to us either in our dreams or in a semi-awake state. We always suppose that of course they'll still be in our brains when we're fully awake and can jot them down. We all know better; I know I've lost many fantastic (I think) ideas that way.

In a gift shop, I bought a lifesaver. It's a 4- by 6-inch memo pad on a small stand with attached pen and a light, powered by two AA batteries, that goes on as soon as the pen is removed from its holder. I can't tell you how many good ideas have been jotted down on this pad between 3 and 6 A.M., when I'm seemingly most creative.

If you can't find this or a similar gadget, just keep a memo pad, a pen, and a small flashlight on your night table. Trust it rather than your somnolent memory.

—ISOBEL SILDEN

RUN BY THE SUN

Writers need small calculators to figure taxes, balance checkbooks, and occasionally check a percentage or do other simple math. Low-cost calculators are so dependable that there's little point in buying an expensive one. Mine is solar-powered and cost about $10 at Radio Shack.

—DAVID A. ANDERTON

■ ■ ■

Solar—which means that any light, not just sunlight, provides performance power—is super; no more of those nasty little miniature batteries to replace. Mine, with big easy-to-hit buttons and the display slanted slightly upward for clear viewing, is Texas Instruments' model 1795 and is priced, at this writing, at $11.49 in the Quill catalog (see appendix). —D.S.

STAPLE IT

Staplers are cheap, but the teeny-weeny dime-store kind are more trouble than they're worth. You can buy sturdy, reliable ones for $8 or $10 from stationery stores and catalogs. Keep them both on your desk and near the place where you go through magazines, newspapers, or journals, clipping out what you want to keep—and staple on the spot.

—JANICE HOPKINS TANNE

PUNCH IT

If you punch a lot of holes in a lot of paper—if, say, you keep a lot of things in loose-leaf files—go out and buy the most expensive paper punch you don't think you can afford. The best ones have some sort of handle around which you can wrap your fingers, instead of just banging on the thing with the heel of your hand. The best ones also have removable, super-sharp punches that can be switched around for different kinds of paper and different hole configurations.

—STEPHEN MORRILL

TIME IT

Digital watches with built-in stopwatches are dirt cheap these days. The stopwatch can be very handy for timing phone calls, as well as keeping track of time worked on a project. (If you suspect that some of your assignments are taking more time than they're worth, you can find out for sure—and raise your rates!)

—BARBARA SCHWARTZ

INK IT

You can save money on ribbons for your computer printer with a ribbon inker, which allows you to reuse the ribbon several times. It's electric and it's easy to use; while you'll probably get ink on your hands the first time, experience and a set of plastic gloves (included) will solve that problem. Mine cost about $40; with ribbons averaging $7 a shot, this little machine is well worth it. I got my Mac Inker from Computer Friends of Portland, Oregon; (503) 626-2291.

—MARTA VOGEL

SPIKE IT

For inveterate note-writers, there is nothing like the old-fashioned copy spike, called a "spindle" by fancy-talking office-supply people. I'm constantly writing notes to myself: people I need to call—today, tomorrow, next week, next month; things I need to pick up; places I'm supposed to be and directions on how to get there; books I want to buy; receipts; bills; rarely, checks that need to be deposited. My desk and worktable were disappearing under little piles of paper.

Then I remembered that great newsroom organizer, the copy spike. It took visits to three stores, but I finally found some for about $2.50 each, complete with protective plastic nipples that fit over the pointed steel rods. I now have a whole row of them sitting side by side across my worktable, each holding a different kind of document. They have made my life considerably more ordered.

—KEN ENGLADE

NOT JUST FOR CLOTHES

Hardly high-tech but nonetheless useful are spring clothespins. I have them handy in my office, and I carry some with me, as well. They can hold open the pages of a book. They can pin reminder notes to folders or calendars. And affixed to a wall with mounting tape or Velcro strips, they can serve as "clipboard" adjuncts to your bulletin board.

—MARGARET DICANIO

FOR THE RECORD

The old-fashioned, changeable-date rubber stamp is still a useful item for writers who receive a great many press releases, which are seldom dated. We often file them for use in connection with future articles. If you date them as they arrive, you'll know how fresh they are when you refer to them again.

—JANET GROENE

SSSSSSSHHH!

If you've ever tried to write while horns blared and engines revved just outside your window, or a baby cried endlessly in the next apartment, or children played raucously in the hall, then the Marsona 1200A Sound Conditioner is for you. This device can produce a variety of soothing sounds that mask the din and clatter so destructive to creativity.

You can select the kind of sound you like, and you can also adjust its pitch and tone. One setting provides a rising and falling sound of surf. Another mimics rain. My favorite is the so-called "waterfall" sound; it purrs steadily, like the hum of a fan or an air-conditioner. Whatever you choose, the steady sound blots out intruding noises from outside, allowing you to concentrate rather then be driven to distraction. (It could also help you to sleep by blocking out noises that keep you awake.)

The Marsona is available for about $140 from a mail-order firm, The Lifestyle Resource, 921 Eastwind Drive, Suite 114, Westerville OH 43081. I've also seen similar devices in stores.

—CHARLES A. SALTER

CARD CARRIER

If you receive, and need to refer to, a great many business cards, get a Rolodex phone directory with plastic sleeves. You can simply slip the cards into proper place, eliminating the need to type the information.

—GRACE W. WEINSTEIN

PAPER TRAIL

We all know everyone needs a calculator. But just one tiny slip of the fingertip, or a weak battery, changes everything—and if you're not super-sharp, it's easy to miss mistakes. The answer: a calculator that spins a paper tape. Check the tape, and you'll be sure all the figures have been entered correctly.

—DIANA BENZAIA

BUILD MUSCLES, PREVENT PROBLEMS

Carpal tunnel syndrome is a sometimes serious problem that may strike writers because we use repetitive wrist movements when typing. Wrist and forearm developers, beloved by golfers and tennis players and available at sporting-goods stores, helped me deal with a minor case of the syndrome by strengthening those muscles. The devices are available in several strengths. I keep a pair near my keyboard, stopping every once in a while to squeeze off 50 compressions of the springs.

—DAVID A. ANDERTON

■ ■ ■

As an advertising giveaway, I received a hand exerciser—one of those coiled springs with plastic handles, which you press together to strengthen your grip. I keep it alongside my computer and use it for two purposes.

First, at regular intervals, I use it to exercise my hands. Second, when I can't think of a word, or a thought is elusive, or I'm wondering how to phrase something, I pick up the exerciser; somehow, a couple of squeezes often serves to squeeze an idea from the subconscious to the conscious.

It also prevents nail biting.

—M. LAWRENCE PODOLSKY

19

THE
NUTS
AND
BOLTS

These are the basics—the pens, the paper, the letterheads. The tape. The glue. Plus, for those who use computers, the floppy disks, the printer ribbons, the perforated paper. All those things that go under "stat. supp." in the list of expenses you keep for use at tax time.

THE NOTEBOOK . . .

My favorite notebooks for travel note-taking and interviewing are called, simply, Reporter's Notebooks. They measure 4 by 8 inches and fit nicely into the back pocket of jeans. They're very hard to find in most stores, but you can get them from the Tanner-Durso Printing Company, 581 Broadway, New York NY 10012; (212) 226-0001. The notebook number is 568G.

—APRIL KORAL

■ ■ ■

One of the professional touches that caught the eye of journalists view-ing the movie *All the President's Men* was that reporter Woodward (Robert Redford) used a reporter's notebook to take notes and slipped it into his pocket.

These notebooks are slim, wire-spiral-bound books measuring 4 by 8 inches; they fit easily in purse or pocket. The source that supplies many newspapers and other media outlets is Portage, P.O. Box 5500, Akron OH 44313-0500; (800) 321-2183. There's a minimum order of two dozen, and the price at this writing is $18 postpaid.

Portage also has smaller "pocket" notebooks, as well as steno-size notebooks for those reporters and writers who prefer them.

—CLAUDIA M. CARUANA

■ ■ ■

When conducting interviews anywhere other than at my own desk, I rely on the slim spiral-topped reporter's notebooks from Portage, in Ohio. You can choose from two different line spacings, half-inch or quarter-inch.

—ELLEN ALPERSTEIN

■ ■ ■

Living far from the rich resources of New York office-supply stores, I find it hard to locate the classic, narrow, spiral-bound reporter's note-books that fit so conveniently in a jacket pocket and hold so much information. But a mail-order source for them is Stationers, Inc., P.O. Box 755, Richmond VA 23206; (800) 446-3002 except in Virginia, (804) 282-7000. They've been willing to send such notebooks to me all the way to Paris, so I doubt they will boggle at other requests. But you pay the postage.

—JUDSON GOODING

■ ■ ■

If you're looking for a notebook small enough to tuck into a pocket, briefcase, or camera bag yet sturdy enough that it won't self-destruct, I recommend the original spiral-bound reporter's notebook, available from Stationers, Inc. Each book contains 80 sheets, ruled on both sides in either wide or narrow style.

The cover is the best part. It's heavyweight (28 point) kraft, provid-ing a firm writing surface. It's so firm you can put several wide rubber bands around it to make a convenient temporary storage spot for maps, assignment letters, release forms—anything you might need to take along to an interview or photo session. I keep rubber bands on the back cover, as well, so I have a place to put press releases, business cards, and other little handouts that often turn up on the scene.

The notebooks are 4 inches wide and come in 6½- and 8-inch lengths. Call or write Stationers, Inc. for a descriptive brochure.

—NANCY S. GRANT

. . . AND OTHERS

For taking notes during client meetings and interviews, I use spiral-bound 5- by 7¾-inch notebooks with brown cardboard covers; each has about 80 sheets of lined paper. The most recent batch I bought is style number 45482, made by Mead; I paid $1 each at my neighborhood stationery store. This size is handy and unobtrusive, with about the same height-and-width dimensions as a cassette tape recorder, and you can hold recorder and notebook together with a rubber band.

Before I use notebooks, I number them—1990 #1, 1990 #2, and so on. I also number the pages. I stick one of my address labels on the front cover (I lost a notebook only once, for fifteen minutes, and it came back to me because of the label). As the notebook fills up, I enter a "table of contents" on the front cover—pp. 1–4, discussion with client A; pp. 5–35, interview with Smith (who had a lot to say); pp. 36–40, interview with Jones (who didn't); and so on. Usually I clip the interview notes and put them in my story file; the remaining notes stay in the book, which stays with my current diary until the end of the year, when they're filed together.

—JANICE HOPKINS TANNE

FREE SCRATCH PAPER

Since I regularly receive a 5-inch-high stack of mail each day, I often use the back sides of letters, news releases, etc., as scratch paper. How do I know it's scratch paper? I tear off a corner, which is a lot faster than crossing out the text on the other side. When I see a piece of paper with a corner torn off, I know I can write on the clean side without fear of destroying something of importance.

—LOUISE PURWIN ZOBEL

■ ■ ■

And here's what to do if you want smaller, padded scratch paper: Remove staples (with a staple remover; for this, you don't want torn corners). Using a paper cutter, cut those 8½- by 11-inch sheets in quarters. When you have a pile of 4¼- by 5½-inch sheets that's about the size you want—say, half an inch high—stack them up very neatly on a sheet of expendable paper, so all the edges are carefully aligned. Be sure all the blank sides are facing up (or down). Put something (like your stapler or your tape dispenser) on top so they don't shift around. Then slather some Elmer's Glue-All on the edges at one end. Let it dry. You have a scratchpad.   —D.S.

STAMP OUT FINGER LICKING

For anyone who collates anything, leafs through anything, or reads, a product called Sortkwik is a find. A nongreasy, waxlike substance, it comes in a little round tub to keep near your page-turning hand. Instead of licking your finger, simply rub it across the surface of the stuff, and your finger becomes tacky enough to effortlessly turn pages, leaf through articles, separate papers in files; it's particularly helpful for handling small pieces of paper such as checks or receipts. Sortkwik lasts longer than saliva, doesn't stain, and really doesn't feel icky. Added bonus: It prevents newsprint-ink ingestion!

—ALEXANDRA S.E. CANTOR

YOUR BASIC BALLPOINT

I have a lawyer friend who, when he needs to jot down a note or sign a letter, makes a great ceremony out of doing so with a flourish of his $200 Mont Blanc fountain pen. He lives in fear of losing that pen or, worse still, laying it down where someone else might actually pick it up and write with it; the different angle and degree of pressure from another hand would ruin the nib, don't y'know.

I have enough to worry about just getting words from the brain to the paper. That's why I have a whole coffee mug full of basic blue Bic medium ballpoint pens. I buy them in bulk, usually at a cost of less than 20¢ each, and I've left a trail of them across two continents.

When I'm not losing them, I'm using them for a surprising number of tasks: to pry out stubborn staples; to mark my place in file folders, dictionaries, and magazines; to gnaw on while trying to remember how many O's there are in Toowoomba;[1] to dial the telephone; to tighten

---

[1] A city in Australia.

an audiocassette reel; to scratch that tense spot between my shoulder blades. Oh, yes—I do actually *write* with them from time to time.

I use ballpoint for field notes, for outlining first drafts, and for memos to myself, because it won't smudge. I use it for bookkeeping chores; the IRS and the bank frown on pencil. I sign my letters, though, with a black Bic Rollerball. I doubt that any editors have mistaken it for script from a fountain pen, but at least the color matches my letterhead.

—NANCY S. GRANT

YOUR UN-BASIC BALLPOINT

If, in your research, you like to mark up newspaper clippings or other source material, you might like to use a four-color ballpoint pen, which lets you "code" the material. Such pens have been made by Parker, Mont Blanc, Lamy, and others, but they haven't always been easy to find in the U.S.

Now, there's something even better, and it's readily available here: the Niji Quad-Point 4-in-1 pen/pencil. In one regular-size pen, you have black, blue, and red ballpoints, *plus* a 0.5mm automatic pencil (good for marking up books, if you're addicted to that and still want a hope of erasing the markings later). Because blue and black are pretty similar, I've substituted a green refill for the blue, so I now have black/red/green plus pencil. Refills aren't hard to find; many stores carry them for Lamy pens, but they will fit the others, too.

If you can't find the Niji Quad-Point where you are, you can order it by mail or phone from Fahrney's Pens, Inc., 1430 G Street NW, Washington DC 20005; (202) 568-6551. The price in early 1989 was $28.

—PETER WHITE

YOUR BASIC PAPER

Buy your 20-pound rag bond paper from a printer instead of from a stationery store. You'll save 25 to 50 percent.

—PAT WATSON

■ ■ ■

For those still using typing paper rather than tractor-feed computer-printer paper, be advised that a ream of 20-pound copying machine paper costs about a quarter to a third the price of 20-pound bond typing paper and, except for a slightly shinier surface, has the same nice features. I've been using it for years, and I've never had a complaint from an editor.

—JOAN WESTER ANDERSON

YOUR BASIC LABELS

Plain white self-adhesive file-folder labels, about 3½ inches long and a little over half an inch wide, available at stationery stores, are handy for relabeling regular file folders you're going to use again. They're also handy for relabeling audiotape cassettes you're going to reuse; they're just the right size to fit over what you wrote on the original label.

—JANICE HOPKINS TANNE

NICE PRINT PEOPLE

If you should need something printed—letterheads, business cards, a brochure—there's a fine resource that's maybe right in your neighborhood. I'm talking about the storefront franchise printing outfits. There are a number of them. I use PIP; it's a national chain with many hundreds of centers. My local PIP people knock themselves out to get just the right paper and shade of ink for me (at no additional charge), then deliver the finished work on time and looking gorgeous—and, at a better price than any standard print shop I've checked.

—WENDY MURPHY

STOCK UP ON ENVELOPES (ONE WAY OR ANOTHER)

I always buy envelopes by the box, which is much cheaper than getting them piecemeal, and in several sizes. In addition to regular business size (number ten) and smaller white envelopes, I keep on hand a supply of 6- by 9-inch and 9- by 12-inch brown envelopes. And although I don't buy them by the box, I try to have on hand book mailers of several sizes, as well. It took me a few years of free-lancing to realize that there actually would be times when I needed a certain size of envelope at three in the morning.

—KATHRYN LANCE

■ ■ ■

If you buy 9- by 12-inch or 10- by 13-inch kraft envelopes, the cost can add up. The junk mail frequently arrives so clad. If those already-used envelopes are in relatively decent shape, and it's not urgent to put a good "face" on a mailing, use the used envelopes. Just cross out the return address, place a new address label over the one addressed to you, and cover the metered postage marking with your own stamps.

—DOROTHY SIEGEL

FOR THE LONGHANDERS
Legal pads with narrow spaces between the lines instead of the usual wide ones give you twice as much writing for the money. They're a bit harder to find, but they're worth the effort.

—JOAN BARTHEL

■ ■ ■

As I do my first drafts in longhand, one of my favorite writing tools is ruled 8½- by 11-inch paper with narrow spaces between the lines, on which I invariably get 250 to 260 words per page. If I have a 1500-word article to write, I just fill six pages; I never have to count words.

—JUDITH H. McQUOWN

HANG IT ALL
If you're still using the old-fashioned folders that flop all over each other, please switch right away to the folders that hang in place on rails. These hanging folders stay in place neatly, and you can push them back and forth without causing an earthquake.

They're available in every imaginable size and most colors, in paper or plastic. They also come with box bottoms and closed sides for things that could fall out. There are even special-size plain folders, called "interior folders," that fit into hanging folders without sticking out at the top (you can use these to further sort the contents of each hanging folder).

If your file cabinet wasn't set up to use hanging folders, you can get frames. They are—let's be frank—not that easy to put together, but they eventually yield to brute force and a hefty screwdriver.

Brand names for hanging folders include Pendaflex and Vertiflex. Many office suppliers, including Quill, have house brands.[2]

—BARBARA SCHWARTZ

[2]See appendix for a full list of order-by-mail-or-phone office-supply sources.

GET IT ON TAPE

I've found a set of handy helpers that go by the name Rollfix, made by a company called Pelikan; they bring you glue or white correction "fluid" in tape form, so you needn't worry about spilled liquids. The adhesive, available in both temporary and permanent versions, coats one side of a roll of tape, which you simply press to the paper, then lift off the tape. The whiting-out stuff is applied exactly the same way.

—FREDA GREENE

LETTERHEADS: CUT-RATE BUT CLASSY

Since letterheads are often a free lance's opportunity to make a good first impression, quality stationery is one of the most important tools of the trade a writer can buy. And aye, there's the rub: quality 20-pound rag bond letterheads can cost an arm and a leg. There's a solution, however.

Letterheads, envelopes, and business cards so beautifully embossed that they appear engraved are available for prices that usually beat what you'll find in your own home town. Write to Keystone Process Printing Corporation, 175-30 Liberty Avenue, Jamaica NY 11433, or call (718) 523-6425, for a price list. They don't charge a setup fee and usually deliver within three weeks or so.

—RUTH PITTMAN

ON DISPLAY

I find a supply of clear plastic 9- by 12-inch envelopes (they're open at one end) useful for several purposes. They're available at stationery stores in my area, and maybe yours, as the Sturdi-Kleer Multi-Use Pocket, made by Angler's Co., or the Utili-Jac Heavy Gauge Vinyl Jacket, made by Joshua Meier Corp. I've been paying 80¢ or 89¢ apiece for them.

The main role they play in my office: An editor calls and says, "This is Jane. I have a question on page three of the eggplant piece." I need to lay hands on my copy of that story fast. I don't want to dig through my entire working file. I reach up to the shelf just above my desk, where there's a row of those clear plastic envelopes. I find the one with the page facing out on one side reading, in large, handwritten letters, "Eggplants and You, *Veggies Quarterly.*" It takes me only a moment. Facing out in the other direction is my copy of the manuscript.

These envelopes are also useful for holding other frequently needed information, such as the telephone area-code map and a local zip-code map, for ready reference.

—JANICE HOPKINS TANNE

CLIP TIPS
Buy plastic paper clips. The metal ones rust. Go back to metal-paper-clipped papers years later, and you'll find rusty, clip-shaped marks.

—BONNIE REMSBERG

■ ■ ■

Plastic clips are also more colorful. But be aware that they'll snap if you try to hold too many sheets with them. Also widely available: plastic-coated metal clips in a rainbow of hues and in at least two sizes.   —D.S.

THE BIG PICTURE
The most useful tool in this writer's life comes from the art-supply store, where I buy large—14- by 17-inch—pads of newsprint. When I'm starting to work on an article, I take a fresh sheet and write a tentative title, plus a one-sentence subhead describing what the article is about, in the middle.

Then I start making notes all over the paper, in a roughly circular fashion, of what should or could be in the article. This keeps me from thinking linearly and having the article jell prematurely; it also allows fleeting ideas to be jotted down here and there, without waiting until I "get to" that section or having to shuffle pages back and forth.

When the sheet is filled, I have a survey of the article content. I can then start organizing the material in conventional fashion.

—JO COUDERT

OFF THE SHELF
One difficulty of free-lancing is getting some idea of one's working schedule in the weeks and months ahead as well as when money will be coming in to balance the steady flow of bills to be paid. My solution: I keep a long strip of plain shelf paper taped across a wall in my study, marked off in blocks about 4 inches wide. Each block represents a week, and each strip is long enough to display about four months.

This is my "time line." Due dates for assignments are noted in red marker, with the amount of money expected. The weeks no assignments are due are then blank, and I know I can—and should—accept assignments deliverable in those "off" times.

Since, with few exceptions, neither magazines nor other clients pay up promptly, this is an imperfect picture of when payments will actually arrive. But it does better enable one to achieve continuity of income and a positive cash flow. And those blank spaces do push you to actively seek assignments, often a writer's least favorite activity.

—LEE JOLLIFFE

NEVER TYPE ANOTHER ENVELOPE

Computer magazines spend endless pages telling readers how to print envelopes on their computer printers. If you aren't too picky and don't demand elegance, using two-window envelopes can solve the problem, putting both your return address and the name and address of the person to whom you're writing behind see-through windows; you just experiment with your word-processing program until the addresses fall in the right places and then save that form as a template, calling it up whenever you write a letter.

I use the Du-O-Vue #771 from NEBS (New England Business Service) [see appendix]; the price, at this writing, is $17.50 for 250. If you'd like something fancier, NEBS also sells printed letterheads and envelopes with a single window in the envelope for the addressee.

—BARBARA SCHWARTZ

BYPASS THE RETAILER

I'm able to get all my paper, manila envelopes, padded shipping bags, and most other office supplies for half the retail price by making direct purchases from manufacturers and/or their jobbers (many manufacturers sell exclusively through jobbers). Minimum quantities are normally quite reasonable.

My routine is to go into a retail store and take the manufacturer's name off the products I want. Then, through the *Thomas Register*, which is available in most public libraries (although I have my own set), I look up the factory's phone number. It usually doesn't take more than one call to place a direct order or get the name of the firm's nearest jobber. Some jobbers give free local delivery service.

If the minimum quantity available from a manufacturer is too great, consider making a joint buy with other writers under one name.

—RICHARD C. LEVY

COPIES THE OLD-FASHIONED WAY

Carbon paper. I can just hear the groans from those old enough to remember smudged papers and fingers and the tedium of trying to use correction strips or fluid on a blurry carbon copy. Those who don't remember probably think that computers and copiers rendered carbon paper a quaint relic of the past. Copiers are handy, but I don't have one in my office, and daily trips to the copy shop waste too much time. With carbon paper, I can make inexpensive copies any time.

Of course it's not actually called carbon paper these days, but it's the same principle. The brand I use is called "carbon film"; it's made by Ko·Rec·Type and is available at most stationery stores. It's an 8½- by 11½-inch sheet (the extra half inch makes it easy to remove after use) of polyester coated with a multi-release ink that lasts and lasts, making clear, sharp, nonsmudge copies. I don't have to worry about making corrections on copies, because I've already previewed, reviewed, and re-reviewed my text on my computer screen.

Why don't I just keep "copies" of letters, manuscripts, etc., on disks and eliminate the extra papers? Because I've found that when I'm busy writing something new, it's actually less cumbersome to pull out a carbon copy to answer an editor's telephoned question. There's no need to leave what's currently on screen, try to find the disk with the relevant material, retrieve it to my screen, and totally interrupt my train of thought. And carbons, unlike disks, can be taken along to interviews or photo sessions for easy reference, even coming in handy as a place to jot down notes.

—NANCY S. GRANT

■ ■ ■

A similar product is Burroughs' Super Nu-Kote, which that manufacturer refers to as "film carbon." A plus: the nonworking side is silver, so you will never slip your carbon in backward, something many of us used to do all too often back in the old days.   —D.S.

■ ■ ■

Before Xerox and Canon, there was carbon paper. It's still useful. If you're printing (or typing) a letter, invoice, or other short document, try using carbon paper and a second sheet. They come paired as Copy-settes, made by Huron and available at stationery stores.

—JANICE HOPKINS TANNE

DRAFT ON DRAFT

I don't know about you, but I absolutely have to have hard copy to edit. Since I go through a number of revisions, this adds up to a lot of paper for each article or book. Several years ago, when I still wrote on a typewriter, I started typing new drafts on the backs of old drafts. Not only does this ease my conscience about adding to the world's wastepaper load, but it's kind of fun, sometimes, to reread some of the really old things.

—KATHRYN LANCE

HOW DID WE LIVE WITHOUT THEM?

I couldn't imagine running my office without Post-It notes. These self-adhesive reusable papers come padded in a staggering variety of shapes, sizes, and colors. They are great for keeping track of expenses (notes on phone calls et al. can be stuck on the inside cover of your research folder), marking places in a manuscript that need revision, leaving yourself reminders of things to do, and on and on. (You can turn any piece of paper into a Post-It, by the way, by applying a special adhesive called Tack a Note.)

—JUDITH KELMAN

■ ■

Carry a wide-tipped fluorescent highlighter pen and several pads of small yellow (or other) Post-It notes in your purse, pocket, car, or brief-case at all times. Use the pen to highlight a map route or important passages in magazine or newspaper articles. Use the sticky-back notes as bookmarks, as notebook flags, or for reminders attached to your notebook cover or your dashboard; as a writing teacher, I've also used them as inexpensive last-minute name tags.

—KAREN O'CONNOR

■ ■

Post-It notes are God's gift to writers. Use them for quick notes to editors, to point out something on a particular page. Their cousins, Post-It Tape Flags, are especially good for marking pages of manuscripts with questions to an editor or a co-author; you can color-code them for different people—the typist, the illustrator, the typesetter, etc.

—MARTA VOGEL

■ ■ ■

Paper clips often leave an imprint on an otherwise pristine manuscript. One way to avoid that is to use one of the larger-size Post-It notes folded in half lengthwise to hold the pages lightly together.

—MARGARET DICANIO

■ ■ ■

Where would we be without Post-Its? We all use them for everything from phone memos to bookmarks, but you might be interested to find out just how many different items are available in this form. I also use Post-It calendars (monthly and biweekly) and Post-It folder labels; the latter are available in both one-third- and one-fifth-cut sizes for use with both hanging folders and the regular kind. For hanging folders, the labels are much handier than those devilish little pieces of cardboard you have to stuff inside the folder tabs—and on regular folders, you don't end up with an unsightly mountain of labels as the folder is reused.

—BARBARA SCHWARTZ

▪ SUPPLYING THE COMPUTER ▪

Just as we used to—and some of us still do—supply our typewriters with paper and ribbons, we now supply those items to the printers hooked up to our computers. And for the computers themselves, we need a steady supply of disks to store the words we and our word processors turn out daily.

DISKS: BRAND NAMES VS. GENERICS

Floppy disks are now selling for way under a dollar, and mail-order houses, listed in the computer magazines, offer great bargains every once in a while; I've obtained some double-sided, double-density 5¼-inch disks for as low as 29¢ in quantities of 100. If there isn't a special sale, the 59¢ or 69¢ you might pay is still a bargain. If you make backups of all your work, as you should, 100 disks will not last a lifetime—but if you feel that's still too many to use in the foreseeable future, share the order with someone.

How do these low-priced disks compare with standard brands? I've tested at least 200 and have yet to find one that didn't check out perfectly. (Even if you find one or two bummers in a batch of 100, the price is still good.) To make certain there are no faulty sectors on a disk, format it at once (this should also be done with standard brands); faulty sectors will be indicated, and the disk can then be returned or discarded.

One order-by-phone source I've used is called, simply, 1800 Floppies; the phone is (800) FLOPPYS (356-7797). When I last placed an order, the price for 100 disks was $39.90; sleeves and labels are included.

—GEORGE DELUCENAY LEON

■ ■ ■

I pay about 25¢ each for 5¼-inch floppy disks. If you've been laying out a dollar or two per disk, you may be thinking, "She's buying junk." Not so. Of the 100-plus low-priced disks I've used over the past three years, not one has ever lost even a single word of text. A leading computer magazine that compared full-price disks with cheapies found that they tested about the same, and the best performance of all was turned in by one of the cheapies. So start saving money.

A dependable supplier is MEI/Micro Center [see appendix]; they also sell the newer 3½-inch disks used in laptop computers.

—WENDY MURPHY

■ ■ ■

When you're buying any kind of magnetic media, including computer disks, buy quality, name brands. The money you'll save on bargain-basement specials isn't worth the anguish you'll feel when your computer refuses to read the disk with your latest notes on it. You'll also save money in the long run, since better-made media will take better care of your machine's innards. Trade publications usually have periodic issues rating media, but you can't go far wrong using brands like Maxell, Sony, IBM, etc.

—BARBARA SCHWARTZ

RIBBONS I: BUY BY MAIL

No matter how much you pay for your printer, chances are that the cost of ribbons over its useful lifetime will exceed the purchase price of the hardware. One way to reduce the price is to buy by mail. In general, the larger the purchase the lower the unit price.

For several years, I've done business with BC Computer Company, Box 246, Summersville MO 65571; (800) 648-2759 except in Missouri, (417) 932-4196. Their prices are 25 percent or more below those of office-supply retailers, their delivery is fast and efficient (they ship, by UPS, within 24 hours), and they accept credit-card orders.

—MARVIN J. WOLF

■ ■ ■

A computer maven of my acquaintance assures me that some of the best buys on printer ribbons (and disks) are available from MEI/Micro Center [see appendix]. For my Epson LQ850, the ribbons were $2.27 each in packs of six (plus shipping and handling). If you have a Hewlett-Packard printer, which I'm now using, you're unfortunately out of luck; at least at this writing, they don't carry H-P products.

—ANNE L. FINGER

■ ■ ■

In the past, I erred on the cautious side about buying such products as printer ribbons. I am now selectively cautious. After eight out of twelve expensive single-strike Xerox ribbons for my Diablo printer turned out to be defective, I bought half a dozen of the same type from Quill. [Again, see appendix.] Not only were the Quill ribbons half the price; they turned out to print more, too. Quill also sells a decent ribbon for my IBM Correcting Selectric typewriter.

—PAT McNEES

RIBBONS II: RE-INK, REFILL

When I acquired my first computer, I innocently plunked down the cost of a new ribbon cartridge every time my printer demanded one. Then, I found out about ribbon re-inking. There is almost no limit to the times a ribbon can be re-inked, and the savings are considerable.

There may be a re-inking service in your community. The one I use, which accepts mail orders, is Systems/Ink, 3208 Azores, Corpus Christi TX 78418; (512) 937-1537. Prices vary with different ribbons but are usually half the cost of a new ribbon. They do an excellent job. You get the ribbon back sealed in plastic; they even thoughtfully include a little towelette you can use to clean your fingers after installing the ribbon. The smart way to use their service is to wait until you have several ribbons that need re-inking, to cut shipping costs.

If you use one-time-use carbon ribbons, these cartridges can be *re-filled* (*not* re-inked) at a fraction of the cost of new ribbons. For several years, I've had prompt, professional refill service from the Ben Torres Ribbon Company, 590 East Industrial Road, Unit 13, San Bernadino CA 92408; (714) 796-5559.

—CHARLES BOECKMAN

■ ■ ■

A ribbon replacement service can save both time and expense; you mail in the used cartridges, and you receive the same number back within about ten days (at least within California). An order of six refilled Diablo Hy-Type carbon ribbons costs about $16.50 from the Ben Torres replacement service. If the ribbons are defective, the service promptly and graciously replaces them. A wide variety of printer ribbons are handled, and the same is probably true for typewriter ribbons.

—ELLEN ALPERSTEIN

PRINTER PAPER: CHOICES
Continuous, tractor-feed paper has those perforated strips along the sides that must be torn off once the printer has done its job. It comes in two types, coarse perforation and micro-perforation. The former being cheaper, I bought a big bunch of it. My advice: Don't. If you have a number of pages, it requires a lot of muscle to tear the coarse-perf strips off, and they leave unsightly stubs all along the paper's edges. Next time, I'll spend a little more and get neater, easier-to-tear micro-perf paper.

—WENDY MURPHY

■ ■ ■

If you've been taken, as I have on more than one occasion, by the promise of continuous-feed paper that tears clean, only to get home and find it tears clean only if you tear it two sheets at a time, you will want to know about Disaperf paper. It tears very clean and can be torn in chunks of twenty or more pages. A respectable 20-pound weight, it was priced at this writing at about $27 for a carton of 2500 sheets. A minor complaint is its slightly grayish cast; if this bothers you (it doesn't bother me), you can buy a higher quality, for about double the price.

Disaperf is available from Lyben Computer Systems [see appendix].

—MARIAN FAUX

■ ■ ■

Just as Wall Street tycoons wear pinstripe suits, our computer-generated manuscripts should dress for success. I use a dignified 20-pound watermarked paper called Oxford Executive Smooth Edge; 1000 sheets cost about $40. Because the perforations are laser-produced, you get neat, not jagged edges. Southworth makes a slightly better quality watermarked paper, with 25 percent cotton fiber content, at a little over $50 for 1000 sheets. Either brand has to be special-ordered through my local office-supply store and usually takes about five days to arrive.

I sometimes cut costs by using cheaper paper for rough drafts. But I never send it off to an editor.

—PAMELA HOBBS HOFFECKER

■ ■ ■

When placing orders for printer paper, it pays to shop around. You can do so without leaving home, if you review current offerings in the office- and computer-supply catalogs listed in the appendix. Most offer a range of qualities and prices. It also pays to order in quantity (at least 1000, preferably over 2000, sheets at a time); if necessary, share an order with a friend. —D.S.

20

BIRDS
AND
MUSIC

The invitation to ASJA members to share their thoughts and experiences for this book was open-ended. Tell us, we said, what's worked for you, what tools you've found terrific. We expected to hear about pet word-processing programs, favorite file folders, best-loved reference books. We *didn't* necessarily expect some of the comments in this chapter— although you may well find many of them no less useful than leads to the latest in ergonomic furniture and fax machines. We cannot live by computers and copiers alone.

ON SONGS OF WING

Sometimes, a two-minute break is all you need to recharge your writing batteries. I've discovered a tiny (2½-inch) device called the Audubon Bird Call. It costs a mere $4.95 and consists of a red birchwood chamber and a pewter insert which, when twisted in different patterns, creates many kinds of chirps. Its maker, Roger Eddy of Newington, Connecticut, claims it will attract a variety of wild songbirds. I can't attest to that, but it *is* a quick refresher. Now, get back to the computer and meet that deadline!

—JOYCE BALDWIN

IT HATH ITS CHARMS

I used to write in total silence. Then, another writer suggested it was helpful to have a radio on your desk tuned to your favorite music station. I would never have believed it was true—but I tried it, and I've kept it up. The background music seems to calm some special spot in the mind and let you work more effectively.

—DIANA BENZAIA

■ ■ ■

I don't know about you, but I find my writing tasks divide pretty neatly into "hard" and "easy" categories. "Hard" is actually composing prose, organizing notes, editing. "Easy" is writing letters, keying something into my computer, or proofreading.

For the hard stuff, I need silence. But for the easy stuff, I find music is essential; otherwise, it begins to fall into the category called "boring." If you've never worked to music, give it a try, especially for the easy stuff. I've found a radio best; getting up and changing a tape or record makes it hard to keep my mind on the task.

—KATHRYN LANCE

SIMPLE THINGS

I write on the same big table I wrote on 30 years ago. For many years, I used the same typewriter (which actually was used when I bought it); I hated to give it up, and it took a long time to accept the way of the word processor. But the table is my old friend and a reminder of accomplishments of the past; it tells me that I will do it again.

I like to have music on the radio while I work. My preference is classical music. Other music tends to interfere or distract, whereas serious music is always there with pleasant sound but never gets in the way. I listen to it on a simple, inexpensive radio.

The point is that precious little gadgetry is really needed. Much wonderful work has been produced without it. I can't imagine Henry David Thoreau or John Muir writing their inspirational and challenging pleas for nature with anything but the simplest tools, to match the simple style of their lives.

A writer's workshop should be a place he or she likes, a congenial place for that writer. I've always been lucky in the view. Where I live now, in northwest Washington, I look out on big trees and ferns along the creek. And sometimes, when I'm lucky, two or three deer will come by.

—MICHAEL FROME

GET OUTDOORS

My secret weapon for keeping my sanity is my garden. For those who can get access to a small plot of earth, balancing cerebral work at a word processor with physical, intuitive, expressive work outside is perfect.

—LAURIE LISLE

BRING THE OUTDOORS IN

Rocks from the beach or garden can play several roles in an office. Among other things, they can prop up a book being read, hold down papers in a summer breeze from your open window, be used as book-ends—and serve as reminders that there is a world away from the keyboard.

—MARGARET DICANIO

CALL TO CONSCIENCE

A master of time-wasting stalls, I can always find good reasons to avoid sitting down at the keyboard. I must therefore devise counterbalancing tricks to keep myself working in long, productive stretches. To that end, I employ my ancestors.

The walls of my office/study are hung with the faces and artifacts of departed family members—to a man, and woman, hardy nineteenth-century Scotch-Irish souls whose work ethic was notorious. Surrounded by this gritty, no-nonsense crowd, none of whom would have given the time of day to a family sloth, I am shamed into gainful activity. Thus, every time I complete a saleable manuscript, I give a nod of thanks to my silent gallery.

Harnessed to a kind of Scotch-Irish Shintoism, the conscience is an amazing dynamo.

—JAMES S. WAMSLEY

OFF TO WORK WE GO

Free-lance writing is a difficult business; any little gimmicks you can use
to psych yourself up are useful. One that many free-lancers, including
me, have found useful: Get up early. Get dressed. Go *out* to breakfast.
Do your newspaper reading, or your list-making, at the coffee shop.
Then, come back to your office *as if it were not in your home.* You are
at *the office.* Do not wash dishes. Do not do laundry. Work as if there
were a boss looking over your shoulder. At the end of the day, go
out—for errands, or just for a walk. Then come back *home.*

—BONNIE REMSBERG

SENSORY CUES

A goldfish, swimming in a little tank that sits on a filing cabinet in front
of my desk, is one of my most valuable writing tools. What my fish does
is get me relaxed and able to turn my full concentration to my work.
I watch him lolling around in there, slowly waving his fan-shaped tail,
and I ease into the comfortable state that I associate with writing.

This frame of mind, very ordinary and familiar, the same automatic
concentration that goes with interstate driving, results from a sort of
self-hypnosis. I find that I get into this "writing mode" most easily if I
begin with watching my fish. I also have a music tape in my tape
recorder that has the same effect on me.

What's important is not the choice of a thing to watch or listen to but
the repetition of it. I now associate watching my fish, or listening to that
piece of music, with writing easily—so when it's time to write, this
relaxing ritual makes it easier to turn out pages once again.

I read somewhere once that Balzac required the smell of rotting fruit
in the room while he was writing; that smell was linked in his mind with
doing good work. I'd rather choose a more pleasant cue. But I'm very
convinced that for all of us, some sensory cue, whatever it may be, is
a very valuable aid to getting in fullest touch with our story-telling
powers.

—PEGGY PAYNE

■ ■ ■

I have an aquarium in my office. When my eyes are tired, and I'm
uptight, frazzled, or befuddled, I stare at the tank and the small finny
things languidly moving about. Three minutes' worth relaxes my soul

(as well as my tense shoulders); I suspect the bubble-sounds have a soothing effect on the psyche, as well.

—JOAN WESTER ANDERSON

■ ■ ■

A special tool of my trade is Jovan's Misty Tea Rose spray cologne, which I spritz on while pacing the room trying to think of what to write next; I buy it by the case. For inspiration, I stare at lovable Garfield the Cat, a stuffed toy given to me by my son, or at a wood-and-plastic nameplate reading "Ruth K. Witkin, Author," given to me by my daughter.

—RUTH K. WITKIN

COFFEE WITH A COLLEAGUE

Nearly every Friday, I meet with a fellow writer at a local coffee shop. We drink café au lait, discuss ideas, critique each other's manuscripts, and share information on everything from potential markets to which post office has the shortest lines. I've come to regard these meetings as my "week in review," a summary of what I've accomplished over the last seven days. Our talks are useful, inspirational, and morale-boosting. They're also fun.

—BARBARA NIELSEN

BLOCK-BREAKING TRANCE

Self-hypnosis is a great tool for breaking writer's block. I put myself into a trance and visualize the block as something or someone I can talk to, such as an animal, a person, or a mythological figure (gremlins, goblins, and dragons come frequently to mind). Since trance uses the right side of the brain, I often gain interesting and valuable insights into how I view the work. The dialogue process then reveals ways I can either vanquish the block or work around it.

—PATRICIA HADDOCK

FELIS FELICITOUS

You don't have to grow up with animals (I didn't). You don't have to write a book about cats (I did). You don't even have to follow the recent research showing what boons domestic critters can be to human beings (lowering blood pressure, among other things).

A beloved pussycat will sit on your lap companionably while you pound away at the lonely work of writing. A beloved pussycat will safely receive your mutterings about editors and publishers. A beloved pussycat will listen to your latest paragraphs with nonjudgmental interest.

And a beloved pussycat can *probably* be taught not to sit on the latest page you've turned out, not to play with your loose pencils, not to walk across your keyboard. But if not, you're still ahead.

—ELLEN PERRY BERKELEY

■ ■ ■

A good remedy for the isolation of the free-lance writer, at least for me, is to have two cats. One sleeps on top of my computer (don't tell my computer repairman), the other on the floor beside me. Cats are perfect writing companions: They're there when you want to gripe about editors, and they never ask, "What have you been doing all day?"

—MARTA VOGEL

■ ■ ■

Every writer should have cats. They interrupt you and force you to stop work when you're getting too intense and need a break. Your writing gets better after the refreshment of a purr and a hug.

—DIANA BENZAIA

ENCOURAGING WORDS

Every time an editor—or anyone—sends you a complimentary note on something you've written, pin it up on a bulletin board near your desk. You'll be amazed how encouraging it will be when you're sitting and staring into space trying to get over writer's block. (If people only knew how much even one word of encouragement spurs writers onward . . .)

—LUANNE PFEIFER

SETTING THE SCENE

I believe that setting and ritual are necessary for all truly important events—and writing is an important event. Reassurance is one important element: I like to have on my walls some framed copies of my best published work; they remind me that I've done it before and can do it again.

I also keep on my walls poster-size pictures of a couple of my favorite places in the world, such as ski slopes and the Piazza Navona in Rome.

My office is windowless; these pictures evoke fond memories and also remind me that there is a world out there.

Offices and the usual office tools—books, computers, answering machines, file cabinets, in and out boxes—are also straight-lined. On my desk, I always have a few toy pandas. They make my workplace a little less high-tech and a little more warm-fuzzy.

As to ritual: Each writing session begins, for me, with some kind of mind-settling meditation, whether prayer or unfocused reflection. I find it calms the turmoil and sharpens the senses.

—CHARLES AUSTIN

TAKE A NEW VIEW

A whimsy I enjoy is a small optical device dubbed the "dragonfly," referring to its simulation of an insect's multifaceted view of the world. When you're in need of inspiration, take a look through it; as you turn it, even the dullest item of office decor will be transformed, repeated over and over to form a fascinating quiltlike design. The "dragonfly" is made by Van Cort Instruments; I've seen it in museum shops, galleries, specialty stores, and gift catalogs, selling in the $11 to $13 range.

—JOYCE BALDWIN

CONSTRUCTIVE PROCRASTINATION

My wife and I once embarked on a foolish and unhappy book collaboration. Her honest workaholic conviction is that if she's not working, God is going to get her. My honest playboy attitude is, if I don't feel like working, let's have some fun. Our marriage held together, which proves that love conquers all, but we learned two things from the experience that are worth passing on.

One is that if you are unhappy not working, try something other than writing. The other is: Don't push it. What you write when you are forcing yourself to put words on paper can be worse than not putting down anything at all. Next day—or some day—you have to read it again and revise it, and if it is boringly bad, you may not want to have anything to do with that material ever again.

What do you do when you should be writing? Of course you can do other jobs—research, write letters, read your notes again. Lots of people play with their computers or their sound systems. Some clean out closets or files or fix something around the house. I used to head for the companionship of a bar.

Today, after researching and writing a couple of books dealing with physical fitness, I recommend exercise. Twenty minutes of exercise not only invigorates the physical body, but emotional and mental states as well. Much about endocrine activity is still to be discovered, but one thing is scientific fact: Exercise stimulates production of the feel-good hormones.

I'm not talking about organized games, which are difficult to get up on the spur of the moment. I mean things you can do all by yourself and fairly quickly. Run, jog, walk fast, swim if you live near a pool. Indoors, you can follow an exercise video or use a stationary bicycle or a rowing machine or other gadget. There is some kind of exercise for everybody.

After exercise, you'll probably feel like getting back to work. Give it a try. But if the words still don't come, just remember that words written when you don't really want to write read like words you don't want to read. Go do something else.

—BOOTON HERNDON

21

HIRED
HANDS

We're inclined
to think of writing as rather a solitary pursuit. And we *don't* tend
to think of ourselves as employers—or other people as tools of our
trade. Perhaps, sometimes, we should.

HIGH-SCHOOLER SAVES HALF A DAY

Basic clerical work can be a drag, whether you're just starting out or
you've been making your living as a writer for years. Why not set aside
the things that cut into your creativity and pass them on to someone
who is willing and able? Hire a high-school student part time for a dollar
or so over minimum wage. I have a girl who works for me four to six
hours a week. She does whatever I ask, including laundry, but most of
her work consists of filing, stuffing and labeling envelopes, preparing
mail, sorting paperwork, and so on. This simple shift in tasks has opened
up over half a day of time I didn't have before.

—KAREN O'CONNOR

A "GOFER" FOR ALL THE NITTY-GRITTY

Throughout my writing career, the greatest help I've had is from high-school or first- or second-year college students who are willing to run annoying errands and handle a variety of necessary chores, personal and professional.

They have schlepped for post-office and writing supplies, as well as food, dry-cleaning, and drugstore items; picked up children; gone through bills to be paid, written checks for my signature, and balanced my checkbook; renewed magazine subscriptions; made follow-up phone calls; and handled routine clerical work. They've saved me enormous amounts of time and frustration, as well as reassuring me that the nitty-gritty was being taken care of as I worked on articles or books.

The role they've played is essentially that of the "gofer" on films, a person who does whatever is required, including fetching lunch.

Clues to using high-school and college students successfully: Interview carefully to be sure they really want regular work; set specific work hours and hold them to the schedule; stress that they'll be doing a variety of jobs, including dumping the garbage (or whatever other unpleasant chores you have in mind), and be sure that's acceptable; be sure they have the requisite typing or word-processing skills, on *your* type of equipment.

To find such help, call the student employment offices of high schools and colleges in your area.

—HARRIET HARVEY

SUBURBAN RESOURCES

I've had great success in hiring part-time helpers to type, transcribe taped interviews, perform a variety of office tasks—organizing files and books, handling correspondence and phone calls, preparing manuscripts—and even take over some personal errands. Advertising in a suburban weekly paper, I've found an abundance of bright, underemployed people, mostly women who, because of family obligations, want to have a flexible schedule. I prescreen by letter and telephone and have found some wonderful helpers.

—SALLY WENDKOS OLDS

THRILL A JOURNALISM STUDENT

The more successful you become as a writer, the more important efficiency becomes, especially if you're producing a substantial volume of articles, books, and/or commercial work. I've found it useful to hire area college students, preferably English or journalism majors, to work several hours a week for me performing secretarial duties, basic library research, and those other mundane but necessary tasks that steal from a writer's creative time.

Contact the job-placement offices or internship programs at your local colleges; they'll usually be more than happy to post your name and needs. Some students will be eager to receive credit for working for you; others just need the money (I pay slightly above minimum wage, plus mileage if I send them on errands). Usually, students are thrilled at the opportunity to work with a professional writer.

Cautions: Be patient breaking them in, e.g., learning to use your computer or other devices. And you must be flexible with students: their class hours change, and many will have other jobs in addition to yours, if you can't guarantee them enough hours.

—BRUCE W. MOST

THE OLD SCHOOL TIE

Can you and your own alma mater do each other a favor?

Yale, for one, has an "externship" program in which students can apply to spend a week or two of their spring vacation with alumni who are working in a field that interests them. For three years, now, I've been able to select a student out of dozens of applications and then have that student spend a productive week with me. I like having a bright undergraduate edit, proofread, and inspire me and, in turn, the student learns a lot about the pros and cons of free-lancing.

Check your college's career counseling office or your alumni association to see if there might be an aspiring novelist, or a columnist on the campus daily, who would like to help you while learning what it's like in the Real World.

—CAROL WESTON

FIRST, WHAT KIND OF AIDE?

I free-lanced for six years before I hired an assistant for more than occasional help. Still unsure that I needed a "real" assistant, I hired a fourth-year journalism student. When she left a year later, I wasn't sure I could get by without her. Like many a luxury, she had become a necessity.

Do you need an assistant? Maybe not. But if your work load is steady and full time, your business—and your life—will probably run more smoothly if you have someone to tend to details while you spend your time writing. In an average of under ten hours a week, my assistant relieved me of the chores of filing, photocopying, buying office supplies, tabulating and invoicing telephone bills to magazines and other clients, setting up interview appointments, and numerous other errands and office tasks I would have put off. I paid her $7 an hour, with occasional bonuses when she worked especially hard on a project.

My assistant was enormously helpful when assignments required library research, involving copying materials and highlighting pertinent facts. She collected information for several sidebars to accompany articles. When I compiled a directory of self-help groups, she mailed a form letter to more than 100 agencies to gather information, then kept the project organized when we were inundated with packages of data.

If you think you need an assistant, it's important to decide just what kind of person you need. Do you need someone simply to help you with purely clerical tasks, or someone with minimal journalistic or research abilities *and* a willingness to do clerical work, or a beginning writer to whom to subcontract some work? I prefer to hire a person who falls into the first or second category, then hire a more skilled writer as a subcontractor when my workload requires it.

When interviewing potential candidates, be honest about the amount of clerical and other "grunt" work the job will involve. It's just not fair to hire a journalism student with big dreams, then saddle him or her with a year's backlog of filing and no opportunity to learn. If you simply need a secretary, hire one.

But if you need an eager research assistant who can also pitch in with some clerical tasks, head to your nearest university journalism or English department. Most such departments allow students to receive college credit, as well as income, for internships with professional writers.

College students often have the research skills, flexible hours, and computer literacy you need. They're enthusiastic about getting real work experience, college credits, and pay that's above minimum wage. And I've found that having a twenty-year-old around the office broadens my knowledge of current trends, provides me with a base of young interviewees when I need them, and is just plain fun.

—MARCIA HIBSCH COPPESS

BOTTOM LINE FOR A BOOK

Although computers are indeed wonderful, near the end of work on my last co-authored book, we hired a good old-fashioned typist to enter the corrections I made on paper. There's definitely a difference between what you see on the screen and what you see on paper—most notably, what's missing; nothing beats the stark truth of black on white, and almost every human eye is less discerning when staring at a video display.

It's also very nice, especially when you are exhausted from working on a book, to have someone else care about the picayune details. I plan to factor a typist into my next book contract.

—MARTA A. VOGEL

WHY TYPE (OR PROCESS) WORDS—EVER?

The best tool any writer could possibly have in getting words on paper is not some gadget but another human being. I have not typed—or word-processed—*any* of my books, *or* my last few hundred magazine articles. Fooling around with mechanical or electronic equipment is a time-wasting indulgence. To get your words down on paper quickly and efficiently, *dictate.*

Get all your research together so that you can reach it with both hands (they're not tied to a keyboard). Look at it, or out the window at the birds and the trees, or at the pleasant picture on the wall (your eyes are also free). Turn on the mike. Start talking.

You'll never see, and be threatened and depressed by, a blank piece of paper. The first paper you see is paper bearing your words that someone has put there for you, your first rough draft. To make those words better, sit down with them and a broad ballpoint pen with dark blue ink (black is okay, but dark blue is prettier), Mozart in your headphones, and your mike. Make marks with your pen, larger changes with your voice. If you want the second paragraph on page 16 to shift to Where Marked on page 3 of Insert A, just say so. What do you care whether it's moved by shears and Scotch tape or by word processor, as long as you don't have to mess with it yourself?

I'm amazed at the time and trouble some writers go to in researching, shopping for, buying, using, keeping up with, and repairing word processors and computers. In contrast, I've *never* had *any* trouble finding intelligent *human beings* to help me. (And although they may break down once in a while, an apology and a smile usually work a lot more quickly and cheaply than a repairman.) I've had a string of delightful young women (I've got nothing against men, but none has ever applied) who have more or less materialized when I needed them.

Some just typed. Some became more interested and helped in various other ways, such as calling people for information. One figured that if I could do it, so could she; she's now a member of ASJA. All learned a lot working for me, eventually went on to better things, and are still friends.

Most of my assistants have handled all the work I could give them in two short days a week. I've usually provided a fairly comfortable work room within shouting distance, just down the hall from my own office; my current aide prefers to work elsewhere, where she has access to a word processor, and that's perfectly okay with me.

My work is neither better nor worse because it's dictated. The important advantage is that I can put the time and frustration I would spend typing into more productive work—or enjoyable play.

—BOOTON HERNDON

22

PROFESSIONAL
CONNECTIONS

Membership in
state, regional, and national associations can be a key tool for writers. Some such organizations focus on subject matter, others on style or medium. Many writers join two, three, or more groups, depending upon their interests, location, and experience (some groups, like ASJA, are restricted to those who can offer particular credentials; you'll find a bit about us at the back of the book). After the general comment that follows, those organizations cited by Society members as particularly helpful are listed in alphabetical order. Contact each group directly for details of membership requirements, costs, and benefits.

A FEW OF THE BENEFITS

Most such groups publish newsletters giving reports about prospective markets for your work and other information important to your occupational survival. Many have regular meetings. Some sponsor workshops and seminars which enable you to hone your skills and mingle with others in your field. All offer a channel of communication with writers like yourself, a way to discuss problems and seek solutions.

A list of writers' organizations is published annually in *Writer's Market* (Writer's Digest Books).

—DAVE KAISER

AMERICAN MEDICAL WRITERS ASSOCIATION
9650 Rockville Pike, Bethesda MD 20814; (301) 493-0003

Members receive an excellent quarterly journal as well as chapter newsletters (there are regional chapters throughout the U.S.); there is also a great annual meeting.

—TONI L. GOLDFARB

AUTHORS GUILD/DRAMATISTS GUILD
234 West 44 Street, New York NY 10036; (212) 398-0838 (Authors Guild), (212) 398-9366 (Dramatists Guild)

The two guilds are siblings, both part of the Authors League of America; members of either guild are members of the League as well.

The Authors Guild represents thousands of published authors, of both fiction and nonfiction, throughout the United States. It has created recommended guidelines for book contracts, especially helpful for authors who do not have agents. Its quarterly bulletin provides information on editorial changes at publishing houses as well as transcriptions of periodic seminars on a variety of topics (e.g., remaindered books, contracts, finding an agent) and discussions of current issues. There is an annual meeting in New York City. Dues changed, as of 1989, from a single amount to a sliding income-linked scale, with a $90 minimum.

The Dramatists Guild is an important organization for playwrights. Members are provided with contract guidelines, and the Guild is an excellent information center, publishing a list of agents who represent playwrights, a monthly newsletter with news of playwriting contests and production companies seeking new plays, and a quarterly. There is an annual meeting. Documentation of your work is required, and there are two levels of membership: active members, whose work has seen production at a certain level (current dues, $75), and associate members ($50).

—JAN YAGER

INDEPENDENT WRITERS OF SOUTHERN CALIFORNIA
P.O. Box 34518, Los Angeles CA 90034; (213) 969-1663

Founded in 1982 by six professional writers who banded together to seek better pay and improved contracts and to deal with other concerns, IWOSC has since grown to nearly 500 members. It publishes a monthly newsletter; conducts monthly general meetings as well as half-day craft sessions; and sponsors a variety of specialized groups dedicated to particular interests such as health writing, scriptwriting, and public relations. IWOSC also offers medical and dental insurance; a credit union; and discounts on legal, accounting, and financial services.

Membership is open to anyone interested in writing—i.e., beginners are welcome—but, because of the emphasis on professional training, the organization tends to retain only those pursuing writing as a career. The cost of joining is currently $110, with dues $55 per year thereafter.

—MARCIA HIBSCH COPPESS

INTERNATIONAL FOOD, WINE AND TRAVEL WRITERS ASSOCIATION
P.O. Box 1532, Palm Springs CA 92263; (619) 322-4717

This is a very spirited group of writers, both free-lance and staff, in the food, wine, and travel fields; it also includes associate members who provide services—travel agents, publicists, hotels, airlines. One recent effort was a compilation of the favorite restaurants, hotels, and travel destinations of its members, published as a book entitled *Windows to the World* (free to contributing members, for sale to others). A monthly newsletter provides information on firms and places offering assistance to writers with bona fide assignments. There is an initiation fee, and yearly dues are currently $50.

—JAN YAGER

INTERNATIONAL SCIENCE WRITERS ASSOCIATION
c/o Howard J. Lewis, 7310 Broxburn Court, Bethesda MD 20817

You're traveling to India and would like to research a story on the long-term results of the Green Revolution. Where do you start? For this and other international science stories, a good source of contacts is the directory of the ISWA, along with back issues of its newsletter. It's an organization of professional science, environment, technology, medicine, and health writers in about 40 countries (the newsletter is in

English); encouraging cooperation and exchange, it can help you develop a worldwide network for researching and planning stories. Membership currently costs $20 a year.

—ERICH HOYT

MYSTERY WRITERS OF AMERICA
236 West 27 Street, New York NY 10001; (212) 255-7005
An organization for mystery writers and those who are interested in mysteries, MWA offers active membership to those who have already published (fiction or nonfiction) in the crime/mystery/suspense field and affiliate membership to those working toward publication. There is a monthly newsletter, and local chapters hold regular meetings and publish their own newsletters. All members, published or unpublished, are invited to submit short mystery stories to *The MWA Anthology*, which is published annually.

—MARGARET DICANIO

NATIONAL ASSOCIATION OF SCIENCE WRITERS
P.O. Box 294, Greenlawn NY 11740; (516) 757-5664
NASW has three categories of membership: Active members are newspaper, magazine, broadcast, and free-lance writers who primarily report on science to the general public. Associate members are employees of associations, corporations, foundations, hospitals, public-relations firms, research laboratories, and universities. Student members are enrolled in college-level science-writing programs and are not yet eligible for active or associate membership.

There are regional and local chapters. A quarterly newsletter includes essays on ethical issues, announcements of national and chapter events, and news of fellowships, grants, and employment opportunities.

NASW requires that new members be recommended by current members. For those who do not know any members (or don't know whether they do or not), the national office can provide the names of members in a particular locale.

—MARGARET DICANIO

NATIONAL WRITERS CLUB
1450 South Havana, Suite 620, Aurora CO 80012; (303) 751-7844
The first writers' organization I joined was the NWC; I'm still a mem-

ber. Founded with the motto "You Are Not Alone," the Club offers a variety of services for free-lancers, all designed to make working independently more enjoyable. Members include both fiction and nonfiction writers; the mixture adds perspective. There are two levels of membership, professional and associate, depending on the writer's published credits.

The Club's publications include *Authorship,* a general newsletter; several market-news advisories, each with detailed information on editors, payment rates, etc.; and the *Professional Freelance Writers Directory* (listing is available only to professional-level members), distributed to magazine editors. Among the many free or reasonably priced services the Club offers are manuscript criticism, marketing advice, research reports, workshops, a complaint/collection service and, not least, friendship—in person, by phone, or through the mail—with other free-lancers.

—NANCY S. GRANT

PEN AMERICAN CENTER
568 Broadway, Fourth Floor, New York NY 10012; (212) 334-1660
The U.S. branch of this prestigious international literary organization is open to published authors, editors, and translators who meet the group's guidelines and committee review for acceptance [it's not limited to the Poets, Essayists, and Novelists for which the acronym originally stood]. Most important is its collective voice for writers throughout the world, including those in prison or in any way hampered by political oppression; the group has also sponsored special projects for charitable causes.

PEN holds an annual reception for new members, as well as an annual party, and sponsors frequent readings and seminars. News is transmitted through a regular newsletter. There are also special committees reflecting particular interests, such as children's books. Annual dues, at this writing, are $60.

—JAN YAGER

SOCIETY OF AMERICAN TRAVEL WRITERS
1155 Connecticut Avenue NW, Suite 500, Washington DC
20036; (202) 429-6639
This organization is wonderful for travel writers, although you must demonstrate considerable success in the field before you may join. You

must also have two sponsors from within the organization; request a membership list to find out whom you might know in your area. Membership offers a helpful newsletter, a national annual convention with excursion options, local meetings throughout the year, and a subgroup for free-lancers.

—KATY KOONTZ

SOCIETY OF CHILDREN'S BOOK WRITERS
P.O. Box 296, Mar Vista Station, Los Angeles CA 90066
An organization for both writers and illustrators of children's literature, SCBW has two membership categories—active members who have already published works for children, and associate members who are working toward publication. A bimonthly national newsletter includes regional activities and events, advice on writing techniques, and a substantial section on market possibilities; the regional chapters have their own newsletters and can usually direct writers to local groups.

—MARGARET DICANIO

SOCIETY OF PROFESSIONAL JOURNALISTS
53 West Jackson Boulevard, Suite 731, Chicago IL 60604;   (312) 922-7424

This organization includes staff reporters in print and broadcast media, free lances, and those engaged in the teaching of journalism, as well as those studying journalism at the college or postgraduate level; it speaks for all journalists on such issues as freedom of information. Local chapters across the country—the one in New York City is known as the Deadline Club—are terrific resources for meeting others in the field. Members receive the national SPJ magazine, *The Quill*, which discusses censorship, ethics, and other journalistic concerns, as well as chapter newsletters.

—SHIRLEY CAMPER SOMAN

P.S.: REMEMBER YOU'RE A BUSINESS PERSON, TOO . . .
Writers sometimes forget that they are business people and need to network, just like other self-employed people; networking puts you in contact with potential clients and gets you known in your community. Small-business people who aren't writers always need professional writing help.

I joined a local networking organization about a year ago, and I've become the group's "resident writer." I've written brochures, newsletters, speeches, and book proposals for fellow members, and I've received referrals to do work for my clients' clients. About a third of my income now comes from my connection with this group, and I plan to join a second, similar organization to widen these contacts.

—PATRICIA HADDOCK

. . . AND CHECK OUT THE CHAMBER OF COMMERCE

If you're a self-employed writer and cannot find group health insurance, look into membership in your local Chamber of Commerce; in many cities, membership costs are affordable and insurance plans good. And if you write in a field where local networking can be useful, your membership can offer additional benefits.

—GORDON and JANET GROENE

APPENDIX:
MAIL-ORDER
SOURCES

These are the companies that offer either computer-related products or general office supplies (generally including computer-connected items) that may be ordered by mail or phone, often at substantial savings. It's smart to obtain catalogs from several and comparison-shop when you need supplies.

The listing is by no means complete (and no criticism is implied by, or should be inferred from, omissions). Firms are included here because contributors have volunteered comments about them; because they have been mentioned elsewhere in the text as sources for various items; or simply because their catalogs happen to have recently crossed the editor's desk. (Except as specified here or elsewhere, members of the Society have not necessarily dealt with the listed companies.) Most accept credit-card orders.

American Stationery Company, Inc., Peru IN 46970 / (317) 473-4438. Mentioned in Chapter 17 as a source of personalized postcards and labels.
The Business Book, Miles Kimball Company, One East Eighth Avenue, Oshkosh WI 54906 / (800) 558-0220 / Fax (414) 426-1132. Strong on personal-

ized, printed items, as well as some handy gadgets that aren't necessarily found in the larger, more inclusive catalogs. *(D.S.)*

Central Computer Products, 330 Central Avenue, Fillmore CA 93015 / (800) 456-4123 / Fax (805) 524-4026. Software (mainly) and accessories.

CompuAdd Corporation, P.O. Box 200777, Austin TX 78720 / (800) 627-1967 / Fax (512) 335-6236. Computers, printers, software, accessories. Also has some 90 retail stores, in Texas and many other states.

Computer Direct Inc., 22292 North Pepper Road, Barrington IL 60010 / (800) 289-9473. Computers, printers, software, accessories.

Dartek Computer Supply Corp., 949 Larch Avenue, Elmhurst IL 60126 / (800) 832-7835 except in Illinois, (312) 832-2100 / Fax (312) 941-1106. Computer furniture, software, accessories, supplies.

Editor's Choice Software, 4224 24th Avenue West, Seattle WA 98199 / (800) 641-1116 / Fax (206) 282-8135. Programs for IBM-compatible computers.

Fidelity Products Co., 5601 International Parkway, Minneapolis MN 55440 / (800) 328-3034 except in Minnesota, (800) 862-3765 except in Minneapolis-St. Paul, (612) 536-6500 / Fax (612) 536-6584. General office supplies and equipment, some furniture.

Frank Eastern Co., 599 Broadway, New York NY 10012 / (800) 221-4914 except in New York State, (212) 219-0007 / Fax (212) 219-0722. Office furnishings, including computer-related items.

Global Computer Supplies, 11 Harbor Park Drive, Port Washington NY 11050 / (800) 845-6225 except in New York State, (516) 625-6200 / Fax (516) 625-6683. Computer and printer furniture, accessories, supplies, as well as some software. Also ships from centers in California, Georgia, Illinois. This was the first mail-order source to stock ribbons to fit a new model printer the ASJA office purchased in mid-1988 (Inmac wasn't far behind, though).

Inmac, 2465 Augustine Drive, Santa Clara CA 95052 / (800) 547-5444.

A high-quality computer/printer supplies and accessories dealer with super-fast service, Inmac has fifteen distribution centers and can guarantee over-night shipment to a fairly large part of the country if you order before 3:30 P.M. If you order before 11 A.M. and don't mind paying $14.95 extra, you can even get six-hour service within 50 miles of the eight regional distribution centers (to which mail and fax orders are sent). Inmac gives you up to *one year* to decide whether you like something and then offers a minimum two-year performance warranty (some products have even longer guaran-tees). Then again, Inmac's products are so good, you may never have to use the warranty. I once had a flaky computer that wrote and read data only when and if the spirit moved it; when I saved information, I never knew if I'd see it again. Inmac's Plus disks were the only brand with which it never had a problem. *(Barbara Schwartz)*

I've found Inmac's Good Impressions printer ribbons consistently, de-pendably problem-free. If you've ever been stuck with a batch of "bargain" ribbons that jammed, one after the other, when you had an assignment overdue, you know how important that can be. *(D.S.)*

Lyben Computer Systems, P.O. Box 1237, Troy MI 48099 / (313) 589-3440 / Fax (313) 589-2112. Lyben is a dependable, all-around computer supply house that sells brand-name products at discount prices. It isn't the cheapest supplier around, averaging about a quarter off (compared to a third to a half from some mail-order sources), but what it doesn't offer in discounts it more than makes up for in service. Orders are routinely shipped the same day they are placed and arrive within three working days. Best of all, the phones are manned by friendly, knowledgeable souls who want to help you get exactly what you need. In addition to a broad selection of ribbons and disks, Lyben stocks a large line of computer-related furniture and accessories ranging from dust covers to power supplies. *(Marian Faux)*

Markline Business Products Company, P.O. Box 171, Belmont MA 02178 / (800) 343-8572 except in Massachusetts, (617) 891-8954 / Fax (617) 899-1833. Off-price brand-name fax machines, phones and answering machines, recorders, transcribers, a huge assortment of calculators.

MEI/Micro Center, 1100 Steelwood Road, Columbus OH 43212 / (800) 634-3478. Mentioned in Chapter 19 as a good source of disks and printer ribbons.

MISCO, One Misco Plaza, Holmdel NJ 07733 / (800) 631-2227. A good source of computer supplies, though not a discounter. Orders are shipped promptly via UPS. *(Rosemary Ellen Guiley)*

NEBS (New England Business Service), 500 Main Street, Groton MA 01471 / (800) 225-6380 or (800) 225-9550. Envelopes, letterheads, business cards, computer paper—just about everything you might find in the finest stationery and office-supply stores is available here. The service is fast and reliable and the prices are competitive, sometimes even low. I've used this company for eight years and have never been disappointed. *(Carolyn Janik)*

Power Up! Software Corporation, P.O. Box 7600, San Mateo CA 94403 / (800) 851-2917 except in California, (800) 223-1479. Programs published both by this firm and by others, mostly for IBMs/compatibles, some for Apples.

Public Brand Software, P.O. Box 51315, Indianapolis IN 46251 / (800) 426-3475 except in Indiana, (317) 856-7571. One of the best suppliers of public-domain (free) and shareware (pay only if you like it) software for IBMs and compatibles. Their catalog is particularly attractive and well written, carefully explaining the pros and cons of the programs and rating them for quality and ease of use. They also offer a selection of disks packed with their own combinations of programs, compacted so that more can fit on a disk (instructions for "unpacking" them are included). Another touch I particularly like is that the catalog tells you whether a program is public-domain or shareware and, if it's shareware, the amount of the registration fee. (Some other dealers sidestep this question, implying that you're getting everything for just the disk copying charge.) PBS ships the same day your order is received. The programs are on quality disks sent in disk carriers so they don't get mangled in the mail. They also seem to ship the latest versions; on my last order, one of the programs had had a major update less than a month before. The free catalog is an easy-to-read introduction to the whole field of free/low-cost software. If you have any interest at all in software, I think you'll find something you'll like. *(Barbara Schwartz)*

Quill Corporation, 100 Schelter Road, Lincolnshire IL 60069 / Rockies and East (708) 634-4800 / West of Rockies (714) 988-3200 / Fax (312) 634-5708. Big semiannual catalog, plus frequent sale catalogs.

Quill is a dependable office supplier that always tries to please. They get your order out fast and, if it's over $45, pay for shipping it anywhere in the continental U.S. Customer service is first rate, and you have 30 days to pay and 90 days to decide if you're really satisfied. Prices are generally good, but be sure to pay attention to deals such as special freebies with bulk orders; some appear in the sale catalogs, while others are listed in the regular catalog. Recently, I ordered four boxes of hanging file folders ($27.96 for the total of 100 letter-size folders); with them I got a box of 100 colored interior folders, a pack of Post-It labels, and a sample hanging file jacket free. Quill also sells a computer program, *Quill Service Link,* with which you can order by modem. I haven't used it, and I have to admit that one of the reasons I'm skeptical about it is that they say it provides "a list of previously ordered items, quantities, and past order dates" so that "you can transfer the 'old' items onto your 'new' order without retyping everything!" I'm more concerned with sale prices than with the convenience of using old numbers. If you use this program, make sure you use the special-deal numbers that will get you the best bargains. *(Barbara Schwartz)*

I swear by Quill. After about a year and a half of dealing with them from my small town in Pennsylvania, I've yet to swear *at* them. I've ordered plastic mats to place under my desk chair, printed stationery, plain paper for my computer printer, big and small yellow tablets, file folders, mailing envelopes, and ballpoint pens. The service is fast and the order-fillers accurate—thank heavens, since there are few torments more hellish than trying to straighten out a loused-up order. Quill's prices compare favorably with the local stationery store. You do have to order in quantity to get the best prices—e.g., a dozen tablets—and unless your bill is over $45, exclusive of taxes, you pay the freight. I keep a "wants" list and order when it adds up. *(Sylvia Auerbach)*

I live and work in the heart of the Colorado Rockies, a good two-hour drive to a well-stocked office-supply store. I rely on Quill for fast, courteous service and products delivered right to my door. They carry a wide variety of economically priced supplies, machines, and office furniture—just about everything you could need. The few times I've experienced problems, they were cheerfully and promptly resolved. A little-known fact: Quill will accept collect station-to-station calls if you are placing an order. Other conveniences include a 24-hour fax-order number and an after-order inquiry hotline. *(Marilyn Ross)*

Reliable Corporation, 1001 West Van Buren Street, Chicago IL 60607 / (800) 735-4000 / Fax (800) 326-3233. Annual catalog, plus periodic sale books.

Reliable provides discounts on office products coupled with the convenience of shopping by toll-free phone. I've had excellent experience with them; my order usually arrives within two days of my phone call. Offering everything from staplers to printer ribbons, copier paper, and office chairs, they promise great savings. It's worth a look at their catalog. *(Kate Kelly)*

This excellent mail-order source of discount office supplies lives up to its name, offering a wide selection at prices considerably below retail rates. Orders are shipped quickly, for a nominal UPS charge, anywhere within the continental United States. Updates on special sales are mailed frequently. *(Michele McCormick)*

In my opinion, Reliable is the best discount mail-order supply house (just one exception: don't buy their own brand of printer ribbons). To get the best prices (and free shipping), one must buy in quantity; the amount needed for free shipping depends on your geographic location. Reliable has an unconditional customer satisfaction guarantee policy. I had no trouble returning a box of printer ribbons for a full refund, even though two of the ribbons were partially used. Customer service is prompt and courteous. *(Rosemary Ellen Guiley)*

Schiller & Schmidt, Inc., 3100 North Elston Avenue, Chicago IL 60618 / (800) 621-1503 except in Illinois, (312) 463-1060. I recommend this office-supply company for reliability, competitive prices, and fast service. *(Jan Yager)*

Selective Software, 903 Pacific Avenue, Santa Cruz CA 95060 / (800) 423-3556 / Fax (615) 867-5318. Programs for IBMs/compatibles.

Staples, P.O. Box 160, Newton MA / (800) 333-3330 / Fax (617) 558-5158. A catalog and chain of discount office-supply stores in the Northeast which, at this writing, is expanding west and south.

Staples is perfect for small-business people and independent workers like writers. They have just about everything you could think of in the line of office and computer supplies—and a lot more that you couldn't (like coffee and other things that keep an office running). They also provide services like photocopying. And they do everything at low prices. *(Sally Wendkos Olds)*

Best office-supply store to date: Staples, the Disneyland of office supplies. In my neighborhood, it took over a Safeway supermarket and filled every inch. The prices and selection are the best. *(Marta Vogel)*

Staples, "The Office Superstore," is super. You'll find discounts, some of them very deep, on all kinds of items—copiers and paper, fax machines and supplies, disks, telephones and accessories, etc. If you're in the Northeast, call and they'll tell you where to find the store nearest you; if there isn't one near you, ask for a catalog. *(Joan Scobey)*

If you're the kind of writer who dreams of a supermarket of stationery supplies, Staples is the store for you. It provides you with a shopping cart— and anyone who loves pencil and paper will find it hard to leave without filling it. Offerings range from desks and answering machines to paper clips, envelopes, markers, and labels. The savings are substantial, and you can also apply for a free "membership" that gives you even deeper discounts. *(Kate Kelly)*

Stationery House, 1000 Florida Avenue, Hagerstown MD 21741 / (800) 638-3033. A good, reliable source of custom-printed items such as letterheads and labels. *(Jan Yager)*

Tiger Software, 800 Douglas Entrance, Executive Tower, Seventh Floor, Coral Gables FL 33134 / (800) 888-4437 / Fax (305) 444-5010. Programs for various computers.

UARCO Computer Supplies, 121 North Ninth Street, DeKalb IL 60115 / (800) 435-0713 except in Illinois, (800) 345-4335. Mentioned in Chapter 3 as a source for desktop printer stands.

ABOUT THE AUTHORS

．

Louis Alexander has been a *Newsweek* correspondent and is a former chairman of the University of Houston's journalism department. He now free-lances for national and regional magazines and newspapers, covering topics ranging from business to space flight, and does technical writing and editing.

Ellen Alperstein, a former editor of Continental Airlines' inflight magazine, writes on travel, adventure, sports, health and other subjects for *Islands, Outside,* the *Los Angeles Times, Women's Sports and Fitness,* and a number of the airline publications; she is also a photographer.

Joan Wester Anderson writes about family life, from marriage and children to retirement, for such periodicals as *Bride's, Catholic Digest, Modern Maturity,* and the *Christian Science Monitor;* she is the author of *Dear World, Don't Spin So Fast, Teen Is a Four-Letter Word,* and five other books.

The late **David A. Anderton** was the author of eight books on aviation and aircraft, including *United States Fighters of World War II, Hellcat,* and *The History of the U.S. Air Force.* Formerly European editor and technical editor of *Aviation Week,* he also wrote many informational publications for NASA.

Sylvia Auerbach has written for periodicals ranging from *Cosmopolitan* to *Barron's* and is the author of *An Insider's Guide to Auctions* and other books. She is currently director of the Publishing Institute at the University of Pennsylvania and adjunct professor of journalism at Temple University.

Charles M. Austin, formerly religion reporter for the *New York Times,* covers that and other topics of current interest for various periodicals in the U.S. and Europe. His latest book is *Desktop Publishing for Congregations.* He is also the author of *Let the People Know* and a variety of curriculum materials.

Robert Bahr is co-author of *The Hibernation Response;* his other books include *The Blizzard, The Virility Factor,* and *Least of All Saints,* a biography of Aimee Semple McPherson. His articles on health, medicine, and psychology have appeared in *Playboy, Smithsonian, Glamour, Parade,* et al.

Carl Bakal has published in *Esquire, Fortune, National Geographic, Reader's*

Digest, Harper's, Town & Country, and other leading magazines and is also a speechwriter, photojournalist, and public relations specialist. His books include *Charity U.S.A., The Right to Bear Arms,* and works on photography.

Joyce Baldwin writes on topics ranging from education and health to antiques and crafts. Her work has appeared in the *New York Times, Newsday, Americana, Current Biography, Collectibles, Science Activities,* the *Franklin Mint Almanac,* and a number of education publications.

Joan Barthel's books and articles have garnered many honors, including the Society's 1986 Outstanding Article Award and the American Bar Association Gavel Award. Her most recent book is *Love Or Honor;* two earlier books, *A Death in Canaan* and *A Death in California,* became TV movies.

Thomas Bedell, immediate past (1989-90) president of ASJA, has written on a broad range of subjects—from books to beer, from sports to music—for a broad range of publications, including *Cosmopolitan, Reader's Digest, Air & Space, Adventure Travel, Newsday,* and the *New York News Magazine.*

John C. Behrens is an *Elks* magazine business columnist and has written for a variety of other periodicals, including *Editor & Publisher, Minorities in Business, Financial Weekly, Career World, The Quill,* and *Writer's Digest.* His books include *Typewriter Guerrillas* and *Magazine Writer's Workbook.*

Diana Benzaia's most recent book is *Protect Yourself from Lyme Disease.* She has published articles on medicine and related topics in *Harper's Bazaar, Saturday Evening Post, Family Circle, Self, Health,* and other magazines and currently serves as a consultant to the National Institutes of Health.

Ivan B. Berger's articles on electronics and photography have appeared in the *New York Times, Village Voice, Newsday,* and many magazines, including *Video, Road & Track, Working Woman,* and *Home Mechanix.* He is the author of *The New Sound of Stereo* and technical editor of *Audio.*

Ellen Perry Berkeley is the author of *Maverick Cats* and *Architecture: A Place for Women;* she was formerly a senior editor of *Architectural Forum.* Her articles have appeared in the *New York Times, Country Journal, Cat Fancy, Vermont Life,* the *Village Voice,* and other magazines and newspapers.

James R. Berry's most recent books are *Magicians of Erianne,* a fantasy novel, and *Kids On the Run.* He has published articles in periodicals ranging from *Parents* to *Popular Science,* as well as technical journals, and is presently science broadcast coordinator for the American Institute of Physics.

Bruce Bliven, Jr.'s many books include *New York: A History, The Finishing Touch, Volunteers, One and All, Under the Guns, The Story of D-Day, Battle for Manhattan,* and *The Wonderful Writing Machine.* His articles have appeared in the *New Yorker,* the *New York Times,* and other periodicals.

Julian Block has written on money management for most of the major magazines and also bylines a syndicated column, "The Tax Report." His *Julian Block's Year-Round Tax Strategies for the $40,000-Plus Household* is updated annually. He has been a frequent guest on the "Today" show.

Richard Blodgett, a former reporter for *Business Week* and the *Wall Street Journal,* is the author of *Photographs: A Collector's Guide, The New York Times Book of Money,* and other books. His articles have appeared in *New York, McCall's, Reader's Digest, Smithsonian,* and other leading magazines.

Murray Teigh Bloom, a co-founder and past president of ASJA, has published hundreds of magazine articles in major magazines. His many books include *Brotherhood of Money, The 13th Man, Rogues to Riches, The Trouble with Lawyers, The Man Who Stole Portugal,* and *Money of Their Own.*

Richard Bode writes on business, economics, technology, and other topics and has contributed to many magazines, including *Reader's Digest, Good Housekeeping, Families,* and *Sports Illustrated,* as well as such industry publications as IBM's *Think.* He is the author of *Blue Sloop at Dawn.*

Charles Boeckman writes both fiction and nonfiction, for both children and adults; his work has appeared in *Success, Family Circle, Modern Maturity, Writer's Digest, Alfred Hitchcock's Mystery Magazine,* et al. His books include *Surviving Your Parents' Divorce* and *Cool Hot and Blue.*

David Bouchier is the author of *Radical Citizenship, The Feminist Challenge,* and other works dealing with the issues and events of our times. His articles and essays have appeared in the *New York Times,* the *Chicago Tribune, New Statesman & Society,* and many other periodicals in the U.S. and Britain.

Maury M. Breecher's articles on health and behavior have appeared in a variety of magazines, including *Health, Reader's Digest, Mademoiselle, Woman's World,* and *Ladies' Home Journal,* and in many newspapers. He serves on the board of advisors of the Florida Freelance Writers Association.

Dian Dincin Buchman, a past (1978–79) president of ASJA, writes on subjects from health to writing itself. She is author or co-author of many books, including *Superimmunity for Kids, The What If Book, The Complete Book of Water Therapy,* and *The Writer's Digest Guide to Manuscript Formats.*

Dale Ronda Burg is a columnist for *Woman's Day* and has written for many other magazines, including *Cosmopolitan, Glamour, Harper's Bazaar, Working Woman,* and *Ladies' Home Journal.* Her latest books are *What's Stopped Happening to Me?* and *How to Stop the One You Love from Drinking.*

Julie Candler, author of *Woman at the Wheel,* has written on travel and other topics for both trade and consumer periodicals, including *Woman's Day, Nation's Business, Detroit Monthly, Michigan Woman,* and *Advertising Age;* she is also a photojournalist and specialist in public relations.

Alexandra S.E. Cantor is executive director of ASJA.

Dan Carlinsky writes for many magazines and newspapers and has published a lengthy list of books, including *Little Sports, Stop Snoring Now, The Status Game, Do You Know Your Husband/Wife?, Are You Compatible?, The Great 1960s Trivia Game,* and *The Complete Beatles Quiz Book.*

Claudia M. Caruana's articles have appeared in *McCall's, New York, Parents, Consumers Digest, Working Mother,* the *New York Times,* the *Christian Science Monitor,* and other periodicals. She is a past president of the Deadline Club, the New York chapter of the Society of Professional Journalists.

Alan Caruba is the author of *Boring Stuff: How to Spot It & How to Avoid It* and *People Touch.* A public relations counselor as well, he is author of *Power Media Selects.* He also writes for the *New York Times Book Review* and other periodicals and is a member of the National Book Critics Circle.

Kay Cassill is a special correspondent for *People* and has written on travel, health, and other topics for *McCall's, Ladies' Home Journal, Smithsonian,* and other major magazines. Her books include *Twins—Nature's Amazing Mystery* and *The Complete Handbook for Freelance Writers.*

Julie Catalano is the author of *The Peoples of North America: The Mexican-Americans.* Her articles on subjects ranging from health and psychology to the arts and entertainment have appeared in *Modern Bride, Beauty Digest, Vista, Amtrak Express, Country Home, Ultra,* and other periodicals.

Sherry Suib Cohen, an ASJA Board member, is the author of *Tender Power, The Magic of Touch, The Looks Men Love, About Face, Cristina Ferrare's Style,* and other books. Her articles have appeared in *Redbook, Reader's Digest, New Woman, Playgirl, Mademoiselle, Glamour,* and other major magazines.

Jack Cook, a former copy editor of the *Boston Globe,* has written on rural life, gardening, nature, backpacking, and the out of doors for many regional and national magazines, including *Country Journal, Harrowsmith, New England Monthly, The New Englander, Vermont Life,* and *Horticulture.*

Marcia Hibsch Coppess's articles have appeared in *American Health, McCall's, Woman's Day, Child, Family Circle,* and other magazines. She is co-author of *Get Published,* a guide to magazine writing, and author of *Fodor's Guide to San Diego* and *Fodor's Guide to California,* 1983–86.

Jo Coudert's articles and essays have appeared in *Reader's Digest, McCall's, Family Circle, Woman's Day, Cosmopolitan,* and many other magazines. Her books include *Advice From a Failure; Go Well, The Story of a House; The Alcoholic in Your Life;* and *The I Never Cooked Before Cookbook.*

Vic Cox writes about nature, travel, and the sciences for a wide variety of periodicals that have included *Final Frontier, National Wildlife, Omni, The Nation, Newsweek, Los Angeles, Science Digest,* and *Us.* He is the author of *Whales and Dolphins* and *Ocean Life: Beneath the Crystal Seas.*

Wilbur Cross, a former associate editor of *Life,* has published in *Reader's Digest* and other major magazines and is the author of more than 40 books, including *Investor Alert, Space Shuttle, Portugal, The Conway Twitty Story, The Weekend Education Source Book, Presidential Courage,* and *Kids & Booze.*

Bernice Curler's articles on personalities, travel, crafts, and historical subjects have appeared in many magazines and newspapers, including *McCall's, American Girl, Modern Maturity, House Beautiful,* the *Christian Science Monitor, Success, Real World, Sacramento,* and *Writer's Digest.*

Alma Denny has written on lifestyles, psychology, and family relations for *Good Housekeeping, Ms.,* the *New York Times, Forum, Parents, Playbill,* and other periodicals. She has also published fiction and humor, and her light verse has appeared in magazines and newspapers and in several anthologies.

Joan Detz is the author of *How to Write & Give a Speech* and *You Mean I Have to Stand Up and Say Something?;* the latter, a guide for young people, received a Notable Children's Trade Book Award for Language Arts. She is also a speechwriter herself and frequently teaches workshops and courses.

Margaret DiCanio specializes in writing about medicine and health, science, lifestyles, and the social sciences. She is author of *The Encyclopedia of Marriage, Divorce, and Family, The Facts On File Scientific Yearbook 1988,* and *The Facts On File Scientific Yearbook 1989.*

Raymond Dreyfack writes for both general and business periodicals. His non-fiction books include, among others, *Business Perks & Benefits, Making It in*

Management the Japanese Way, The Complete Book of Walking, Zero-Base Budgeting, and *Sure Fail.* He has also published a novel, *The Image Makers.*

Angela Fox Dunn writes on many subjects, including celebrities, health, pets, and lifestyles; her articles have appeared in a variety of magazines and have been distributed internationally by the New York Times Syndicate. She is author of *Mathematical Bafflers.*

Kenneth F. Englade, recipient of ASJA's 1988 Outstanding Article Award, is an investigative reporter whose articles on law, politics, and business have appeared in *Forbes, Atlanta, Southern, Harper's Bazaar, Madison Avenue,* the *ABA Journal,* and other periodicals. He is the author of *Cellar of Horror.*

Eloise Engle has written on subjects from food to travel to military history for consumer and government publications. She is the author of *The Winter War, Man in Flight, America's Maritime Heritage, The Finns in America, Of Cabbages and the King, The Baltimore One-Day Trip Book,* and other books.

John W. English, an ASJA Board member, teaches journalism at the University of Georgia. He has published ten books, including *Slices of the Peach, When Men Were Boys,* and *Criticizing the Critics.* His articles have appeared in the *New York Times, Atlanta, American Film,* and other leading periodicals.

Glen Evans, a past (1987–88) president of ASJA, is co-author of *The Encyclopedia of Alcoholism* and *The Encyclopedia of Suicide* and editor of *The Complete Guide to Writing Nonfiction.* His articles have appeared in most of the major magazines, and he reviews books regularly for several periodicals.

Margery A. Facklam is the author of *The Trouble With Mothers, Partners for Life, Spare Parts for People, So Can I, But Not Like Mine, Changes In the Wind,* and other books; her children's books have won a number of awards. She has written for *American Baby, Cricket,* and other magazines.

Shirley Sloan Fader is a columnist for *Ladies' Home Journal, New Idea,* and *Woman;* her articles have appeared in *Reader's Digest, Redbook, McCall's,* and most other major magazines. Her books include *Successfully Ever After, Jobmanship,* and *From Kitchen to Career.* She has also published fiction.

Marian Faux focuses on social issues, career guidance, and subjects of interest to women. Her books include *Roe v. Wade, Crusaders: Voices from the Abortion Front, Childless By Choice, Entering the Job Market, Successful Free-Lancing, The Complete Résumé Guide,* and *Executive Etiquette.*

Ruth Duskin Feldman's books include *Communicoding, Human Development, Rematch, Whatever Happened to the Quiz Kids,* and *Chemi the Magician.* She has written articles for *Better Homes & Gardens, Woman's Day, Travel & Leisure, USAir,* the *Chicago Sun-Times,* and other periodicals.

Jack Fincher has written on a wide variety of subjects for *Reader's Digest, Smithsonian, McCall's, Geo, Esquire, Sport, Saturday Review,* and other magazines. His books include *The Brain: Keeper of Life, Human Intelligence,* and *Sinister People: The Looking Glass World of the Left-Hander.*

Anne L. Finger is co-author of *One-Day Plastic Surgery: A Consumer's Guide to Savings and Safety.* Her articles, on topics ranging from medicine and mental health to business and social issues, have appeared in *Health, New Body, Parents,* the *New York Times, The Record,* and other periodicals.

Blythe Foote Finke, a former United Nations correspondent, is the author of twenty biographies and other books for young adults. She has published articles in the *New York Times*, the *Christian Science Monitor*, the *Baltimore Sun*, the *Los Angeles Times*, and many special-interest magazines.

Mitch Finley's books include *Time Capsules of the Church, Catholic Spiritual Classics, A Special Way of Being Alive*, and *Christian Families in the Real World* (with Kathy Finley). He writes on similar topics, and reviews books, for many magazines and newspapers.

Katharine Davis Fishman, 1990–91 president of ASJA, is author of *The Computer Establishment*. She has written on the arts, education, business, and technology for a variety of publications, including *Atlantic, New York, Town & Country, Manhattan inc., Family Circle*, and *Woman's Day*.

Michael Frome's conservation writings have earned many honors, including the Society's 1981 Outstanding Article Award. He is a columnist for *Defenders of Wildlife* and a faculty member at Huxley College of Western Washington University. His latest book is *Conscience of a Conservationist*.

Lewis Burke Frumkes is the humor columnist for *Penthouse* and writes for many other periodicals, including the *New York Times* and *Punch*. He is the author of *Manhattan Cocktail, Name Crazy*, and *How to Raise Your IQ by Eating Gifted Children* and co-author of *The Mensa Think Smart Book*.

Mark L. Fuerst, an ASJA Board member, writes on medicine and other sciences for both lay and professional publications, including *American Health, Parents, Woman's Day, Discover, Medical World News*, and *Physician's Weekly*. He is co-author of *The Couple's Guide to Fertility* and *Computer Phobia*.

Robert Gannon is a contributing editor of *Popular Science* and has also written for *Reader's Digest, Saturday Evening Post, TV Guide, Science Digest*, et al. He is author or co-author of eight books, including *Half Mile Up Without An Engine* and *Why Your House May Endanger Your Health*.

Johanna Garfield's articles on relationships, education, and other subjects have appeared in *McCall's, Reader's Digest, Seventeen, Ms.*, the *New York Times, Newsday*, the *Christian Science Monitor*, and other periodicals. She is the author of *The Life of a Real Girl* and *Cousins*.

Toni L. Goldfarb is editor and publisher of the *Medical Abstracts Newsletter*. She also writes on medicine and health, as well as family relationships and the social sciences, for a wide range of periodicals, including *American Health, Parents, Redbook, Self*, and a number of professional publications.

Barbara Goodheart writes on medicine and related topics for both lay persons and physicians and is also a medical editor and scriptwriter. Her articles for consumers have appeared in many magazines, including *Better Homes & Gardens, Discovery*, and *Westways*. She is the author of *A Year on the Desert*.

Judson Gooding, author of *The Job Revolution*, has written on a broad range of subjects for a variety of periodicals, including the *New York Times Magazine, Reader's Digest, Fortune, Travel & Leisure, Sport*, and *Money*. His work has won several honors, including the coveted Penney-Missouri award.

Susan J. Gordon writes on travel, literature, children, families, and topics of special interest to women. Her articles and essays have appeared in such periodicals as *Ladies' Home Journal, Good Housekeeping, McCall's, Woman's Day, Seventeen, New York Newsday*, and the *New York Times*.

Nancy S. Grant writes on subjects ranging from music to rural life and crafts. Her work has appeared in many national and regional periodicals, including

Symphony, Frets, Kentucky Living, Louisville Magazine, Keyboard, and the United States Information Agency magazine *Topic.*

June Grayson's subject specialties include gardening, business, antiques and collectibles, health, and home decor. She has written for *Best Report, Glass Collector's Digest, Off Hours, Sunday Woman, Good News America, Victorian Sampler, Vista,* the *Chicago Sun-Times,* and other publications.

Gail Greco focuses on business and entertaining and is the author of *Secrets of Entertaining from America's Best Country Innkeepers* and *Bridal Shower Handbook.* She has written articles for many national, specialty, and corporate magazines and is a monthly columnist for *Entrepreneur* and *Innsider.*

Freda Greene, former regional editor of *Changing Homes,* is co-author of *How to Get a Job in Los Angeles.* Her work has appeared in many periodicals here and in Britain, including *Travel & Leisure, Travel Holiday, Financial Weekly, The Observer,* the *Boston Globe,* and the *Los Angeles Times.*

Samuel Greengard covers subjects of current interest ranging from media to medicine for many periodicals, including *Playboy, Family Circle, American Health, Travel & Leisure, Los Angeles, Kiwanis, Barrister, Ford Times, American Way, USAir,* the *Chicago Tribune,* and the *Los Angeles Times.*

Janet and Gordon Groene write on recreational travel, boating, and how-to topics. Their columns appear regularly in *The Homeowner* and *Family Motor Coaching;* their books include *Cooking On the Go, Cooking Aboard Your Recreational Vehicle, How to Live Aboard a Boat,* and *Dressing Ship.*

Ronald Gross is the author of *The Independent Scholar's Handbook, The Great School Debate, The Lifelong Learner, Megalearning,* and *The Children's Rights Movement.* His articles and essays have appeared in *Parents,* the *New York Times Magazine, Harper's, TV Guide,* and many other magazines.

David Groves has written on health and fitness, sports, travel, and people for periodicals including *American Health, Good Housekeeping, McCall's, Psychology Today, Sport, Working Woman, New Woman, Harper's Bazaar, Seventeen, Self, Health, Woman,* and the *Los Angeles Times.*

Rosemary Ellen Guiley's books include *The Encyclopedia of Witches and Witchcraft, Tales of Reincarnation, Lovelines, Career Opportunities for Writers,* and *Psychic Spawn.* Her articles have appeared in *Health, Writer's Digest, Working Woman,* the *New York Times,* and other publications.

Blanche Hackett writes on a wide spectrum of subjects from travel to nature, crafts, health, and consumer concerns. Her articles have appeared in many periodicals, including *American Heritage, Parents, Reader's Digest, Ms., National Geographic, Travel Holiday,* and the *New York Times.*

Patricia Haddock is the author of *City Watch: San Francisco* and *Standing Up for America: A Biography of Lee Iacocca,* both for young readers. She has published articles for adults and children in such periodicals as *Better Homes and Gardens, Woman's Day, Ranger Rick,* and *3-2-1 Contact.*

Frances Halpern's column, "Bookmarks," appears weekly in the *Los Angeles Daily News;* she also hosts a weekly radio program on KTMS in Santa Barbara and is the author of *Writer's Guide to Publishing in the West.* Her articles have appeared in *Los Angeles, Seventeen,* and other magazines.

Mary Harmon writes on business management, careers, psychological topics, self-help, and issues of interest to women; her articles have appeared in *McCall's, Working Mother, Ladies' Home Journal, MD, Woman, Medica, Mademoiselle,* and the career supplements of the *New York Times.*

Harriet Harvey is a writer and editor who focuses on health, psychology, travel, and business management; her articles have appeared in the *New Yorker,* the *New York Times, Vogue, Woman's Day,* the *Boston Globe,* and other periodicals. She has also produced documentary and instructive videos.

Millicent V. (Vicky) Hay is associate editor of *Arizona Highways;* she has also written, on topics from business to lifestyles, for other magazines including *Editor & Publisher, Saturday Review,* and *Private Clubs.* She is the author of *The Essential Feature: Writing for Magazines and Newspapers.*

Barbara Shook Hazen is a prolific writer of both fiction and nonfiction for children and young people. Among her recent books are *The Knight Who Was Afraid of the Dark, Very Shy, You Can't Have Sunbeams Without Little Specks of Dust,* and *Have Yourself a Merry Little Christmas.*

David Hechler, a former English teacher, is the author of *The Battle and the Backlash: The Child Sexual Abuse War;* his articles on education, law, and social issues have appeared in the *New York Times* and other periodicals. He was the recipient of a 1985 grant from the Fund for Investigative Journalism.

Joan Rattner Heilman's books include *Unbelievably Good Deals & Great Adventures That You Absolutely Can't Get Unless You're Over 50, Estrogen: The Facts Can Change Your Life,* and *The Complete University Medical Diet.* She writes for *New Woman, Glamour, Parade,* and other magazines.

Arthur Henley is the author of *Phobias: The Crippling Fears, The Difficult Child, Yes Power, Don't Be Afraid of Cataracts,* and other books. His articles have appeared in many leading periodicals, including *Grandparents, Ladies' Home Journal, Saturday Evening Post,* and the *New York Times.*

Booton Herndon has published many magazine articles and 23 books, including *Racin', Tubex, How Life Insurance Companies Rob You and What You Can Do About It, Mary Pickford and Douglas Fairbanks, The Great Land, Over the Hump,* and *The Sweetest Music this Side of Heaven.*

Hal Higdon, a finalist in the NASA journalist-in-space program, has written for *Air & Space, Reader's Digest, American Health, Hippocrates,* and other magazines and is the author of two dozen books, including *The Masters Running Guide, Fitness After Forty,* and *The Crime of the Century.*

Martin Hintz's fourteen children's books include *Living in the Tropics, Computers in Our World,* and *Tons of Fun: Circus Workin's.* His articles have appeared in *Home & Away, Midwest Living, Sailing, Scouting, Trailer Life, Milwaukee Magazine,* the *Chicago Sun-Times,* and other periodicals.

Gloria Hochman's long list of honors includes the AJSA's 1986 Outstanding Article Award. She has written for *American Health,* the *New York Times Book Review, Ladies' Home Journal,* the *Philadelphia Inquirer Magazine,* et al. and is the author of *Heart Bypass: What Every Patient Must Know.*

Pamela Hobbs Hoffecker has written on parents, children, the family, and sports for a variety of general and specialized periodicals, including *Woman's Day, Parents, Child Life, Tennis, Highlights for Children,* and *Christian Writer.* She also writes videoscripts and edits newsletters.

Erich Hoyt, author of *The Whale Watcher's Handbook* and *Orca: The Whale*

Called Killer, received a 1985–86 Knight Science Journalism Fellowship at MIT. He is a field correspondent for *Equinox* and has written for many other magazines, including *Reader's Digest, National Geographic,* and *Oceans.*

John H. Ingersoll, a past (1983–84) president of ASJA, is a former senior editor of *House Beautiful.* He has written for *Consumer Reports, Family Circle, Home Mechanix, Omni, Popular Mechanics,* and other magazines and is the author of *We Can Save Ourselves* and *How to Sell a House.*

Florence Isaacs, 1990–91 executive vice president of ASJA, writes on health, family relations, human behavior, the arts, and other topics. Her articles have appeared in many leading magazines, including *Reader's Digest, Good Housekeeping, Parade, Savvy Woman, Mademoiselle,* and *New Woman.*

Warren Jamison is co-author of a number of books, including *Screw: The Truth About Walpole Prison, Ed McMahon's Superselling, The Official Guide to Success, How to Master the Art of Selling,* and *How to List and Sell Real Estate.* He has also written several corporate histories and business books.

Carolyn Janik's articles have appeared in *McCall's, Inc., Redbook,* and other leading national magazines. She is the author of a number of books, including *Money-Making Real Estate, Positive Moves, All America's Real Estate Book,* and *The Complete Guide to Co-ops and Condominiums.*

James P. Johnson is the author of *New Jersey: A History of Ingenuity and Industry* and *The Politics of Soft Coal.* He has written for many periodicals, including *Historic Preservation, New Jersey Monthly, American Heritage, Smithsonian, Journal of American History,* and the *Washington Post.*

Lee Jolliffe received a Ph.D. degree from Ohio University in 1989 and is currently an assistant professor of journalism at the University of Missouri. Her articles have appeared in *Ohio Magazine, Living Single,* and other magazines and newspapers; she also writes proposals and corporate reports.

Thomas H. Jones's books include *Heirloom Furniture You Can Build, Furniture Fix and Finish Guide, How to Build Greenhouses, Garden Shelters and Sheds,* and *Electronic Components Handbook.* He has written for *Family Handyman, Homeowner, Popular Science, Workbench,* and other magazines.

James Joseph has published articles on automobiles, business, the outdoors, science, and other topics in a wide variety of magazines in the U.S. and throughout the world; he also produces corporate newsletters and other publications. He is the author of *The Car-Keeper's Guide* and 21 other books.

Dave Kaiser is the author of *Outdoor Recreation Areas* and *Swimming Pools: A Design Guide.* His articles have appeared in a variety of consumer and trade periodicals, including *Fort Lauderdale Magazine, Tennis U.S.A., Miami News, Automotive News,* and *Hotel & Motel News.*

Robert Kanigel's journalism honors include ASJA's 1989 Outstanding Article Award and the 1989 Grady-Stack Award. He is the author of *Apprentice to Genius* and has written for *Hippocrates, Mosaic, The Sciences,* the *New York Times Magazine,* the *Washington Post,* and university magazines.

Wallace V. Kaufman is a book reviewer for *American Forests;* his articles have also appeared in *National Wildlife, Redbook,* the *Christian Science Monitor, Encounter,* and other leading periodicals. He is the author of *Finding Hidden Values in Your Home* and *The Beaches Are Moving.*

Evelyn Kaye, a past (1984–85) president of ASJA, was a co-founder and first president of Action for Children's Television. She has written for *Glamour, Travel & Leisure,* the *New York Times,* and other periodicals; her eleven books include *Lady in the Wild, College Bound,* and *The Hole in the Sheet.*

Bern Keating, who was founder of the Travel Journalists Guild, is the author of 25 books, most recently *Mississippi, The Flamboyant Mr. Colt and His Six-Shooter,* and *Famous American Cowboys.* He has published articles in *Travel & Leisure, Smithsonian, National Geographic,* and other leading magazines.

Kate Kelly's books include *Organize Yourself!, How to Set Your Fees and Get Them,* and *The Publicity Manual.* Her articles have appeared in many of the leading magazines, including *Glamour, Harper's Bazaar, Parents, Woman's Day, Executive Female, Ms., Working Woman, Bride's,* and *Redbook.*

Judith Kelman, an ASJA Board member, is the author of four suspense novels— *Hush Little Darlings, While Angels Sleep, Where Shadows Fall,* and *Prime Evil.* Her articles have appeared in *Good Housekeeping, Seventeen, Working Mother, Redbook,* the *New York Times,* and other major periodicals.

David W. Kennedy, past (1988–89) president of ASJA, has written for *Savvy Woman, Redbook,* and other magazines. He is the author of *Insurance: What Do You Need, How Much Is Enough?; Money Making Money;* and *The Condominium and Cooperative Apartment Buyers & Sellers Guide.*

Marty Klein, a marriage counselor and therapist, is the author of *Your Sexual Secrets: When to Keep Them, When & How to Tell.* His articles and advice columns have appeared in *MGF, Forum, McCall's, New Age Journal, Modern Bride, Parents, The New Physician,* and the *Los Angeles Times.*

Katy Koontz, a former travel editor of *McCall's,* is *Ski* magazine's fitness columnist and writes articles and essays for a variety of other periodicals, including *New Woman, Travel & Leisure, Health, Ladies' Home Journal, Savvy Woman, Playboy, Travel Life, Seventeen, Woman,* and the *New York Times.*

April Koral has written four nonfiction books for young people on a variety of topical subjects, including war refugees and the greenhouse effect. Her articles have appeared in the *New York Times, Reader's Digest, Parade, Seventeen, Newsday,* and many other magazines and newspapers.

Andrew Kreig was the recipient of a 1985–86 research grant from the Fund for Investigative Journalism and is the author of a controversial exposé, *Spiked: How Chain Management Corrupted America's Oldest Newspaper.* His articles have appeared in *Boston, Connecticut, Yankee,* and other magazines.

Judi K-Turkel and Franklynn Peterson write two syndicated columns on the subject of computers and software and are contributors to many magazines. They have published more than 20 books, including *The Author's Handbook, The Magazine Writer's Handbook,* and *Grammar Crammer.*

Kathryn Lance is the author of 20-plus books of fiction and nonfiction for adults and children, including *Sportslite, Pandora's Genes,* and *Running for Health and Beauty;* she has also ghostwritten several top-selling diet guides. Her articles have appeared in *Ladies' Home Journal* and other major magazines.

Cassandra L. Langer's books on art, present and past, include *A Bibliography of Feminist Art Criticism* and *Impressionism and Post-Impressionism: Transformations in the Modern American Mode 1885–1945.* Her articles have appeared in *American Artist, Ms., Art Journal,* and other periodicals.

Thomas A. Lankard is national affairs editor of *AutoWeek* and writes a biweekly column, "Street Smarts," for the *Sacramento Union,* as well as a monthly automotive column for *Comstock's,* a California business magazine. He also writes for *Endless Vacation* and other magazines.

George Laycock's most recent book, his 50th, is *The Mountain Men;* his earlier works include *The Wild Bears, Eye On Nature, How the Settlers Lived, The Bird Watcher's Bible, Tornadoes, America's Endangered Wildlife,* and *The Alien Animals.* He is a field editor of, and frequent contributor to, *Audubon.*

Muriel Lederer's articles on business and careers have appeared in *American Legion, McCall's, Woman's Day, Across the Board, Seventeen,* the *Christian Science Monitor,* and other leading periodicals. She is the author of *Blue-Collar Jobs for Women, Guide to Career Education,* and other books.

George deLucenay Leon has written on science and technology for such varied magazines as *Avionics, Computer Decisions, Family Computing, Dun's Monthly,* and *Radio Electronics.* His books for young people include *The Story of Electricity* and *Explorers of the Americas Before Columbus.*

Richard C. Levy is the creator of the social-interactive board game *Adverteasing.* His books include *Inside Santa's Workshop, Wife Beating: The Silent Crisis, Inventing and Patenting Sourcebook, Inventor's Desktop Companion, Plane Talk: The Consumer's Air Travel Guide,* and four others.

Robert L Liebman is the author of *Taking Off* and *Traveling Right: The Quick-Reference Guide to Efficient, Safe and Healthy Travel.* His articles on travel and other topics have appeared in *GQ,* the *New York Times,* the *New York Daily News, Newsday,* and other periodicals in the U.S. and Great Britain.

Leslie Linsley writes on crafts and decorating for *Family Circle, McCall's, Redbook, House Beautiful,* the *Chicago Sun-Times,* and other magazines and newspapers. Her more than 35 books include *The Weekend Quilt, Nantucket Style, Scrimshaw,* and *The Night Before Christmas Craft Book.*

Laurlie Lisle is the author of *Louise Nevelson: A Passionate Life* and *Portrait of an Artist: A Biography of Georgia O'Keeffe.* Her articles on art, travel, and publishing have appeared in *Working Woman,* the *Village Voice,* the *East Hampton Star,* and other magazines and newspapers.

Suzanne Loebl writes on medicine, health, and nutrition for a wide range of magazines. Her books include *The Complete Handbook of Nutrition, The Nurse's Drug Handbook, Why Can't We Have a Baby?,* and *Conception, Contraception.* She has also written medical films and professional literature.

Peter Loewer's books include *The Indoor Window Garden, A Year of Flowers, American Gardens, The Annual Garden, Gardens By Design,* and others; his articles have appeared in *American Horticulturist, Home, Horticulture, Organic Gardening,* and *Mountain Gardener.* He is also a botanical illustrator.

Bill London writes on travel, the environment, business, lifestyles, and historical subjects; his articles have appeared in *Western Outdoors, Trailer Life, Ranger Rick, Family Motor Coaching,* and *Western Boatman,* as well as newspapers and trade journals. He is co-author of *Menu Management.*

Patricia Mandell's articles on travel, the arts, nature, and other topics have appeared in *Caribbean Travel & Life, PC/Computing, New England Monthly, Americana, Walking, Savvy Woman, PC Week, Outside,* the *Christian Science Monitor,* and other magazines and newspapers.

Ana Marcelo writes on travel, food, historical subjects, the arts, the Orient, and metaphysics for a variety of national and regional magazines and newspapers. She is a contributing editor of *Sacramento* magazine.

Jane Marks is a contributing editor of *Parents;* her articles have also appeared in *Family Circle, New York, Seventeen, Glamour, Working Woman, Town & Country, Mademoiselle, Ladies' Home Journal,* and other leading magazines. She is the author of *Help! My Parents Are Driving Me Crazy.*

Jean McCann writes on all aspects of medicine, reporting news in the field for both lay and professional audiences here and abroad. Her articles have appeared in *American Health, Science News, Health, Good Housekeeping,* many newspapers, and a variety of medical and technical publications.

Michele McCormick is a contributing editor of *Army, Navy and Air Force Times;* her articles have also appeared in *People, Mature Outlook, Ford Times, Writer's Digest,* the *Washington Post,* and many other periodicals. She is the author of *Designer Drug Abuse* and *Polishing Up the Brass.*

John W. McDermott focuses on writing about travel, food, and recreational sports. He is the author of the *How to Get Lost and Found In . . .* guides covering London, Japan, New Zealand, the Cook Islands, Hawaii, Fiji, Australia, and California, and has published articles in many newspapers.

Pat McNees, an ASJA Board member, is a former book editor for Harper & Row and Fawcett. She writes on social issues, psychology, education, and consumerism for a variety of periodicals. She is also a speechwriter and has edited several anthologies, including *Familiar Faces* and *Friday's Child.*

Judith H. McQuown's books include *Inc. Yourself, How to Profit After You Inc. Yourself, Keep One Suitcase Empty, Playing the Takeover Market, The Fashion Survival Manual,* and *Tax Shelters that Work for Everyone.* Her articles have appeared in *Boardroom Reports, PanAm Clipper,* et al.

Rosalie Minkow is a contributing editor of *Accounting Today* and writes for other financial publications. She is the author of *Tax-Free, Tax-Advantaged Investments, Sylvia Porter's Borrowing Money, Creative Tax Benefits, The Complete List of IRS Tax Deductions,* and *Money Management For Women.*

S.J. (Shannon) Moffat writes on science, technology, and medicine and is co-author of *Better Homes and Gardens Handbook of Common Medical Terms.* Her articles have appeared in *Reader's Digest,* the *New York Times Magazine, Modern Medicine, Hospital Practice,* and other periodicals.

Jefferson Morgan and his wife Jinx are the authors of a number of books, including *Two Cooks in One Kitchen, The Die Song,* and half a dozen others. Their articles have appeared in many of the leading magazines, including *Reader's Digest, Self, Travel & Leisure, Bon Appétit,* and *Woman's Day.*

Stephen Morrill writes on topics ranging from architecture and historic preservation to outdoor recreation. His articles have appeared in national and regional periodicals, including *Robb Report, Horizon, Guest Informant, Vista, Southern Homes, Tampa Bay,* and a variety of business publications.

Hal Morris, former business news editor for Times-Mirror publications, has written for both consumer and trade periodicals, including *Family Circle, Nation's Business, USA Today, American Way, TWA Ambassador, Pacific Banker, Independent Banker, Computers in Banking,* and *Travel Life.*

Bruce W. Most, a past president of the Colorado Authors' League, writes on money, business, science, and social issues. His articles have appeared in the *New York Times, Parade, Modern Maturity, TV Guide, Popular Science, American Way, Amtrak Express, Travel & Leisure,* and other periodicals.

Wendy B. Murphy is the author of *Joy Through the World, Sight and Hearing, Coping with Headaches, Farming for the Future, The Common Cold, Japanese Gardens,* and *The American Presidents.* Her articles have appeared in *Bon Appétit, American Heritage, McCall's, Cosmopolitan,* et al.

Ed Nelson is former auto editor for the *Popular Mechanics Encyclopedia Yearbook* and supervisor of road safety information for the National Safety Council. His articles have appeared in *Popular Science, Car and Motor, Physician's Management, Science Digest,* and other periodicals.

Beverly Anderson Nemiro writes on food, travel, self-help, fashion, investments, and mature living for a number of periodicals. She is the author of *The New High Altitude Cookbook, Single After 50, Busy People's Cookbook, Colorado à la Carte,* and *Book of High Altitude Baking.*

Barbara Nielsen's articles on travel, adventure, nature, the environment, and other subjects have appeared in *American Way, Exploring, Modern Maturity, Southern Travel, Travel Holiday, Quest, USAir, Boys' Life, Amtrak Express, Vista/USA, Ford Times, Walking,* and many other magazines.

Karen O'Connor is the author of *Garbage: A Universal Threat; Let's Take a Walk On the Beach; Sharing the Kingdom; Contributions of Women: Literature; Sally Ride and the New Astronauts; Try These on for Size, Melody!; Maybe You Belong in a Zoo!;* and other books for young people.

Sally Wendkos Olds, a past (1981–82) president of ASJA, has written for most major magazines; she received the Society's 1983 Outstanding Article Award. Her books include *The Working Parents' Survival Guide, The Complete Book of Breastfeeding, The Eternal Garden,* and others.

Vance Packard, a past president of ASJA, has written for most of the leading magazines and is the author of *The Hidden Persuaders, The Status Seekers, The Waste Makers, The Naked Society, A Nation of Strangers, The Pyramid Climbers, Animal IQ,* and other books; his most recent is *The Ultra Rich.*

Janice Papolos writes on medicine and psychiatry as well as on music; she is author of *The Performing Artist's Handbook* and co-author of *Overcoming Depression.* Her articles have appeared in *McCall's, Newsweek, Self, High Fidelity, Chamber Music Magazine,* and a number of other periodicals.

Mary Jean Parson's books include *How to Be a Partner, Managing the One Person Business, The Single Solution, An Executive's Coaching Handbook,* and *Back to Basics: Planning.* Her articles have appeared in *New Woman, Savvy Woman, Working Woman,* and many other magazines.

Peggy Payne's articles have appeared in *Cosmopolitan, McCall's, Ms., Family Circle, Travel & Leisure, Food & Wine,* the *Washington Post,* the *New York Times,* and other periodicals. A recipient of a National Endowment for the Humanities fellowship, she is the author of a recent first novel, *Revelation.*

Robin Perry's books include *Videography, Creative Professional Photography, Welcome for a Hero, The Woods Rider,* and others on photography and cycling. His articles have appeared in *Camera 35, Flying, Popular Photography, Writer's Digest,* the *New York Times,* and other publications.

Luanne Pfeifer is the author of *The Malibu Story* and *Ski California,* as well as a contributor to *Skier's Guide to the West*. Her articles have appeared in *Snow Country, California Living, Ski Business, Westways, California Today, Intro*, the *Los Angeles Times*, and other magazines and newspapers.

Ruth Pittman, an ASJA Board member, writes on personalities, popular history, travel, health, and other subjects. Her articles have appeared in *American Legion, American Way, Ford Times, Dynamic Years, The Elks Magazine, State of the Union, Family Weekly, Amtrak Express*, and elsewhere.

Vernon Pizer is the author of *The Irrepressible Automobile, Eat the Grapes Downward, Take My Word for It, Shortchanged By History, You Don't Say, Ink, Ark. and All That*, and other books. His articles have appeared in *Esquire, American Legion, Reader's Digest, Nation's Business*, et al.

M. Lawrence Podolsky is a contributing editor of *California Traveler, Sportsmedicine Digest*, and *Cardiology World*. His articles have also appeared in *American Way, Consumers Digest, Sailing, Cruising World, Sail, Medical Economics*, and other consumer and professional publications.

John M. Ravage is the editor of *Energy: Global Prospects 1985–2000*. His articles on time management, energy, sports, business, and the outdoors have appeared in *Boston Magazine, Family Circle, Vermont Life, Yankee, Nation's Business*, the *Harvard Business Review*, and other periodicals.

Alvin H. Reiss is the editor of *Arts Management* and a columnist for *Fund Raising Management* and *Management Review;* his articles have also appeared in *Esquire, ARTnews, American Way, Playbill*, et al. His books include *Cash In!, The Arts Management Reader*, and *Culture & Company*.

Bonnie Remsberg's honors include the ASJA 1984 Outstanding Article Award and several Emmy awards. She has written for *Good Housekeeping, Family Circle, Reader's Digest, Consumer Reports, Redbook*, and other magazines, and she is the author of *The Stress-Proof Child: A Loving Parent's Guide*.

Maxine Rock is the author of *The Marriage Map, Fiction Writer's Help Book*, and *Gut Reactions*. A 1988 *Reader's Digest* feature by her became a 1989 CBS-TV special; her articles have also appeared in *New Woman, McCall's, Atlanta, Smithsonian, Woman*, the *New York Times*, and other periodicals.

Mary Augusta Rodgers writes on subjects ranging from food to travel, leisure, and recreation. Her articles have appeared in many national and regional periodicals, including *Family Circle, McCall's, Woman's Day, Reader's Digest*, the *New York Times*, and Detroit newspapers and magazines.

Roberta Roesch is the author of *Smart Talk, You Can Make It Without a College Degree, There's a Right Job for Every Woman*, and other books, and co-author of *How to Be Organized in Spite of Yourself*. She writes a syndicated newspaper column, "The Rest of Your Life," as well as magazine articles.

Elyse M. Rogers is the author of *Cross Cultural Textbook, Staying Healthy in Japan*, and *Health in the Home*. Her articles have appeared in a wide variety of magazines and newspapers in the U.S. and Japan, and she is currently a columnist for both *Tokyo Weekender* and the *Japan Times*.

Marilyn Ross's books include *The National Survey of Newspaper Op-Ed Pages, Big Marketing Ideas for Small Service Businesses*, and *The Complete Guide to Self-Publishing;* she has also produced a cassette album, *Book Promotion & Marketing*. She has written for *Executive Female, Essence*, et al.

June Roth, a past (1982–83) president of ASJA, is author or co-author of 34 books, including *Reversing Health Risks, The Executive Success Diet, The Pasta-Lover's Diet Book, The Allergic Gourmet,* and *Aerobic Nutrition.* Her column, "Special Diets/Nutrition Hotline," appears in major newspapers.

Charles A. Salter, a faculty member of the department of nutrition at the Harvard University Extension School, writes on food, nutrition, health, and psychology and is the author of *Getting It Off, Keeping It Off, Knight's Food Service Dictionary,* and *Guide to Kitchen Management.*

Norman Schreiber is a contributing editor of *Amtrak Express;* his articles have also appeared in *Cue, Soundwaves, 50 Plus, Smithsonian, Travel & Leisure, Popular Photography,* and other magazines. He is the author of *The Scouting Party Index of Independent Record Labels* and *Your Home Office.*

Dodi Schultz, a past (1985–87) president of ASJA, is a *Parents* contributing editor and columnist; her articles and puzzles have also appeared in many other magazines. She has edited several books and is author or co-author of 17 others, including *The First Five Years* and *Lupus: The Body Against Itself.*

Barbara Schwartz writes on subjects from computers and other technology to sports and business; she is also a consultant on office systems. Her articles have appeared in *Creative Computing, Discovery, Hoop, Datamation, Popular Computing, Science Digest, Output,* and other magazines.

Joan M. Scobey is author or co-author of a number of books, including *Short Rations, Survival Kit for Wives, I'm a Stranger Here Myself,* and *Cooking with Michael Field.* Her articles have appeared in *Family Circle, Reader's Digest, New Woman, McCall's, Woman's Day,* and other major magazines.

Celia G. Scully is author of *How to Make Money Writing About Fitness & Health* and co-author of *Playing God: The New World of Medical Choices.* Her articles have appeared in *Travel & Leisure,* the *Christian Science Monitor, The Travel Agent, Friends,* and other magazines and newspapers.

Anthony Serafini is the author of *Linus Pauling: A Man and His Science, Weight Training for Cats,* and *The Muscle Book* and is the editor of the college text *Ethics and Social Concern.* His articles have appeared in *Omni, Sports Afield, The Quill, Amtrak Express, Boston,* and other magazines.

Jacqueline Shannon's articles have appeared in *Seventeen, Parenting Adviser, Special Reports, Working Woman, 'Teen, San Diego Woman, Woman's Health Adviser,* and other magazines. She is the author of *Faking It, Big Guy/Little Women, Upstaged, Class Crush,* and *Too Much T.J.*

Cecile Shapiro has published articles and reviews in *ARTnews, House & Garden Guides, American Artist, Publishers Weekly,* and other periodicals. Her books include *Abstract Expressionism: A Critical Record, Fine Prints: Collecting, Buying, and Selling,* and *Better Kitchens.*

Denise Shekerjian is the author of *Uncommon Genius: How Great Ideas Are Born* and *Competent Counsel: Working with Lawyers.* Her articles on the law, food, travel, self-help, real estate, and the arts have appeared in *New Jersey Home & Garden, Travel & Leisure, Skylines,* and other magazines.

Elaine Fantle Shimberg's books include *Relief from IBS: Irritable Bowel Syndrome, Coping with Kids & Vacation, Two for the Money: A Woman's Guide to Double Career Marriage,* and *How to Be a Successful Housewife/Writer.* She has written for *Glamour, Writer's Digest,* and other magazines.

Dorothy Siegel's articles have appeared in many magazines, including *Good*

Housekeeping, McCall's, Reader's Digest, Parents, Redbook, Family Circle, American Education, New Jersey Monthly, and *Woman's Day.* Her books include *The Glory Road, Winners: Eight Special Young People,* and others.

Mary-Ellen Siegel is author or co-author of *What Every Man Should Know About His Prostate, The Nanny Connection, The Cancer Patient's Handbook, Reversing Hair Loss, More than a Friend: Dogs with a Purpose,* and other books. She is also a senior teaching associate at Mt. Sinai School of Medicine.

Isobel Silden heads ASJA's Southern California regional chapter. Her articles have appeared in *Ford Times, Modern Maturity, Woman's World,* the *Los Angeles Times, Emmy, Travel Holiday,* and other magazines and newspapers and have been distributed by the New York Times Syndicate.

Linda-Marie Singer writes on the entertainment world, broadcasting, and travel and has also produced television and radio programs. Her articles have appeared in *Reader's Digest, Woman's World, Wine Times, World Tennis,* and other magazines and have been distributed by King Features Syndicate.

Charlene Marmer Solomon is the author of *Frommer's Family Vacation Guide to California, Home Alone,* and *Help! It's Three O'Clock.* Her articles have appeared in *Los Angeles, American Baby, The Rangefinder,* the *Los Angeles Times,* the *San Francisco Examiner,* and other publications.

Shirley Camper Soman's articles have appeared in *Reader's Digest, Ms., Good Housekeeping, Home Office Computing,* the *Washington Post,* the *Christian Science Monitor,* and other periodicals. She is the author of *Preparing for Your New Baby, Let's Stop Destroying Our Children,* and *You and Your Baby.*

Elyse Sommer's books include *The Kids' World Almanac Thesaurus of Colorful Phrases, The Similes Dictionary, The Crocheter's Quilt Book,* and *On-Line Writing Effectiveness Modules.* She specializes in developing books from idea through manuscript and design to camera-ready materials.

Shari Steiner is the author of *The Female Factor: A Report on Women in Western Europe.* Her articles have appeared in *Ladies' Home Journal, Reader's Digest, Glamour, Cosmopolitan, Saturday Review, Endless Vacation, The Silver Pages,* and a variety of other periodicals both in the U.S. and abroad.

Abby Stitt is former behavioral science editor of *Mother's Manual* and nursing editor of *Emergency Medicine.* Her articles on children, family and marriage, sexuality, and behavior have also appeared in *Playgirl, Self,* and other magazines. She is the author of *The Sexually Healthy Woman.*

Helen Studley is the author of *The Chicken for Every Occasion Cookbook.* Her articles on food, fitness, travel, and lifestyles have appeared in *Ladies' Home Journal, Woman's Day, Gourmet,* the *New York Daily News, Country Style, The Travel Agent, Wine & Spirits, Hamptons,* and other periodicals.

Janice Hopkins Tanne, an ASJA Board member, is a contributing editor of *New York.* Her articles have also appeared in *Reader's Digest, American Health, Redbook, Woman's Day,* the *New York Times,* the *Times* of London, *Medical World News,* and many other periodicals in the U.S. and U.K.

Florence Temko is the author of nearly 30 crafts books, including *Paper Jewelry, Paper Tricks, Paper Pandas and Jumping Frogs, New Knitting, Elementary Art Games and Puzzles,* and *Chinese Papercuts.* Her articles have appeared in *American Crafts,* the *New York Times,* and other publications.

Carol Tonsing is co-author of *How to Buy a Fur that Makes You Look Like a Million* and *Men's Hair*, as well as the ghostwriter of the *Sydney Omarr Astrology Guides, Always Beautiful*, and *Lovescopes*. She is also a public relations and advertising copywriter.

Elise Vons Ulrich was formerly associate beauty editor of *Good Housekeeping*. Her articles have appeared in *McCall's, Playboy, Redbook, USA Today, Mature Outlook, Frequent Flyer, Health, L'Officiel, Rotarian International, Bestways, Business Week's Careers, Company*, and other periodicals.

Henry and Elizabeth Urrows are the authors of *An Academic Merger, Television in Urban Education*, and *The Incandescent Light*. Their articles have appeared in *PC Week, Computerworld, College Board Review, ChemMatters, Think, Venture, Infosystems, Electronic Business*, and other publications.

Antonia van der Meer is co-author of *The Midwife's Pregnancy and Childbirth Book, Parenting Your Premature Baby, BRIDE'S New Ways to Wed, The Private Adoption Handbook*, and other books. Her articles have appeared in *McCall's, Redbook, Cosmopolitan, Good Housekeeping*, et al.

Marta A. Vogel, past chairperson of ASJA's Washington DC regional chapter, is co-author of *The Baby Makers*. Her articles on medicine, psychology, and other topics have appeared in *Parents, Savvy Woman, Women's Sports and Fitness, National Wildlife*, the *Washington Post*, and other periodicals.

Gladys H. Walker, a former writing teacher at the University of Bridgeport, is the author of *I Don't Do Portholes!* Her articles have appeared in *Interior Design, Architectural Record, Biz*, the *New York Times*, the *Los Angeles Times*, and a variety of other magazines and newspapers.

James S. Wamsley's articles have appeared in *Reader's Digest, Architectural Digest, National Geographic Traveler, Travel & Leisure, Modern Maturity*, and other magazines. His books include *The Crafts of Williamsburg, American Ingenuity*, and *Idols, Victims, Pioneers: Virginia's Women from 1607*.

Andrea Warren's articles have appeared in many of the leading national magazines, including *Reader's Digest, Good Housekeeping, McCall's, Midwest Living, Better Homes and Gardens, American Education*, and *Writer's Digest*. She also writes advertising copy, video scripts, and young-adult fiction.

Pat Watson's articles and photographs have appeared in *Americana, Modern Bride, Prime Times, Woman's Day Needlework and Crafts, Arts Indiana, Country Gentleman, Jobs & Youth, The Freeman, Frets, Indianapolis Magazine*, the *Indianapolis Star*, and other national and regional periodicals.

Steve Weinberg is executive director of Investigative Reporters & Editors and executive editor of *The IRE Journal*. He is the author of *Armand Hammer: The Untold Story, Trade Secrets of Washington Journalists*, and *Terrace Hill;* his book reviews appear regularly in a number of periodicals.

Grace W. Weinstein, a past (1979–81) president of ASJA, has been published in most of the leading magazines. Her books include *The Bottom Line: Inside Accounting Today, Men, Women, & Money: New Roles, New Rules, Children & Money: A Parents' Guide*, and *The Lifetime Book of Money Management*.

Carol Weston is the author of *Girltalk, Girltalk About Guys*, and *How to Honeymoon*. Her articles on teen, family, and lifestyle topics have appeared in *Cosmopolitan, Bride's, Modern Bride, McCall's, Glamour, New Woman, YM, Seventeen, HG, Woman's Day, Redbook*, and other magazines.

Peter T. White is presently an editor at *National Geographic;* his articles have also appeared in a number of other leading periodicals, including *Reader's Digest* and the *New York Times Magazine.*

Nancy Whitelaw is an elementary-school teacher and a contributing editor of *Early Years;* her articles have also appeared in *McCall's, Working Mother, Cobblestone, Learning, Christian Science Monitor,* and other periodicals. She is the author of *Vocabulary Building* and is also a textbook reviewer.

Donald Wigal's books include *Smidget, The New York Times Encyclopedia of Film Vol. 13, Fascinating Facts About Animals, General Knowledge,* and *Movie Trivia Quiz.* He is also an independent researcher, fact-checker, abstractor, and developer of bibliographic materials.

Ruth Winter, a past (1977–78) president of ASJA, is author of *Eat Right: Be Bright, Build Your Brain Power, Lean Line's One Month Lighter, Thin Kids Diet Program, Consumer's Dictionary of Food Additives,* and other books. Her articles have appeared in *Parade, Reader's Digest, Omni,* et al.

Ruth K. Witkin is a columnist for *inCider* and also writes for other computer periodicals. Her books include *The Best Book of Microsoft Works for the PC, Personal Money Management with AppleWorks, Personal Money Management with Multiplan,* and *Managing Your Business with Multiplan.*

Marvin J. Wolf specializes in writing about business, science, technology, and crime. He is the author of *Platinum Crime, Fallen Angels,* and *The Japanese Conspiracy.* His articles have appeared in the *Los Angeles Times Magazine, Los Angeles, America West, California,* and other periodicals.

Helen Worth is the author of the culinary classics *Cooking Without Recipes, Down-On-the-Farm Cookbook, Hostess Without Help,* and *Damnyankee in a Southern Kitchen* and many articles. Her poetry slideshow, "Small Secrets: A Creature Garden of Verses," has been presented at leading museums.

Jan Yager's articles have appeared in *Family Circle, Harper's, Glamour,* the *New York Times, Seventeen, Modern Bride,* and other periodicals. She is the author of *Making Your Office Work for You, How to Write Like a Professional, Creative Time Management, Single in America, The Help Book,* et al.

Morton Yarmon is director of public relations for the American Jewish Committee. His articles have appeared in *Parade, 50 Plus,* and other major magazines. He is the author of *Work Smartly, Invest Smartly, The Art of Writing Made Simple, Put Your Money to Work for You,* and other books.

Louise Purwin Zobel is the author of *The Travel Writer's Handbook* and teaches many classes and seminars in travel writing. Her articles have appeared in *Better Homes and Gardens, Réalités, Modern Maturity, Parents, Westways, House Beautiful,* many other magazines, and major newspapers.

ABOUT THE SOCIETY

.

The American Society of Journalists and Authors (ASJA) is the nation-wide organization of independent nonfiction writers. Founded in 1948 as the Society of Magazine Writers (the name was changed in 1975), the Society at this writing includes approximately 800 free-lance writers of magazine articles, books, and other nonfiction who have met the ASJA's standards of professional achievement. (While many ASJA members have also written novels, plays, poetry, and short stories, the Society's membership requirements encompass only independently produced nonfiction work.)

As a nonprofit literary and educational organization, the ASJA is concerned with encouraging high standards in nonfiction writing. It furthers this goal by the exchange of information among working writers, by seminars and educational workshops, by the recognition of outstanding accomplishments in the field, and by a continuing examination of events and trends affecting the production and dissemination of information to the reading public.

The Society has led in establishing professional and ethical standards, exemplified by its Code of Ethics and Fair Practices, guidelines defining the mutual rights and responsibilities of editors and writers. The ASJA has also taken strong stands against practices likely to diminish the quality or quantity of information available to the public, and it is vigilant against encroachments upon the independent writer's rights and freedoms by government, industry, or individuals.

With its anti-censorship campaign, inaugurated in 1981, the Society has been a leader in alerting the American public to significant threats to First Amendment freedoms and mobilizing resistance to such threats. The ASJA is a participating organization—along with other leading professional, religious, and educational groups—in the National

Coalition Against Censorship and is also a co-sponsor of the annual Banned Books Week observance.

ASJA programs are presented in New York City monthly from September through June; featured speakers include writers, editors, and others associated with the world of publishing, and these meetings are open to all interested persons. Similar programs are presented from time to time by the ASJA regional chapters (currently located in the Berkshire Hills, the Midwest, Northern California, the Rocky Mountains, Southern California, and Washington DC).

The ASJA Annual Writers' Conference is held each spring in New York and has, since its inception in 1972, become a major event in the literary world. It brings together America's leading writers, editors, agents, and others who explore, in panel discussions and workshops, current markets and trends in books, magazines, and other media. The Conference is open to working and aspiring writers alike. Similar events are occasionally held by some of the ASJA regional chapters.

Several awards are given by the Society. The annual ASJA Excellence Awards recognize outstanding authors, magazine articles, and periodicals. The ASJA Conscience-in-Media Medal honors those who have demonstrated singular commitment to the highest principles of journalism at notable personal cost or sacrifice. The ASJA Open Book Awards pay tribute to the courage of individuals who, in fighting for the freedom to read, protect our society's most valued traditions of openness and choice.

ASJA membership is open to writers who can present sufficient nonfiction credits, produced on a free-lance basis, to provide evidence of professional status. Members need not be full-time free-lance writers.

For further information about the Society and its activities, programs, and publications, write the American Society of Journalists and Authors, Inc., 1501 Broadway, Suite 1907, New York NY 10036; call (212) 997-0947; or fax your request to (212) 768-7414.

SUBJECT INDEX

.

AUTHOR INDEX

.